S0-BAS-224

THE STRATEGIC EVALUATION AND MANAGEMENT OF CAPITAL EXPENDITURES

Oct. 1987

To Sam:

I hope you enjoy & benefit from the reading of this book. Best of luck in all your endeavors!

Tom Hindelang

ROBERT E. PRITCHARD and
THOMAS J. HINDELANG, CPA

The Strategic Evaluation and Management of Capital Expenditures

A DIVISION OF
AMERICAN MANAGEMENT ASSOCIATIONS

Appendix A reprinted from *Business and Financial Tables Desk Book* with permission of the publisher, Institute for Business Planning, Inc., IBP Plaza, Englewood Cliffs, NJ 07632.

Appendix B reprinted from *The Thorndike Encyclopedia of Banking and Finance Tables* with permission of the publisher, Warren, Gorham & Lamont Inc., 201 South Street, Boston, MA 02111.

Appendix C reprinted from David I. Fisher, *The Corporate Economist,* New York: The Conference Board, 1975, with permission.

Appendix E reprinted from Bruce M. Bradbury and Robert E. Pritchard, *Business and Financial Planning and Control for Small Businesses,* with permission from Glassboro State College, The Management Institute, 1979.

Library of Congress Cataloging in Publication Data

Pritchard, Robert E., 1941–
The strategic evaluation and management of capital expenditures.

Bibliography: p.
Includes index.
1. Capital investments. 2. Capital investments—Evaluation. I. Hindelang, Thomas J. II. Title.
HG4028.C4P75 658.1'54 80-69702
ISBN 0-8144-5656-1 AACR 2

First Printing

For Carol Ann and Chris

PREFACE

This book presents an integrated view of the *capital budgeting* process and the management systems of *strategic planning*. It is intended as a management tool for business owners and managers at every level who are involved with the acquisition of assets. There has long been a need for a comprehensive guide to capital budgeting in the uncertain environment which all managers face. In this book, we assume no prior knowledge of the subject and lead the reader from basic decisions to state-of-the-art criteria for the evaluation of acquisitions through purchasing and leasing.

The initial chapters provide a complete description of the capital budgeting process and of the basic tools for evaluating capital projects. The important points to consider when purchasing assets are described in detail, keeping in mind the goals of maximizing profits and reducing risk and cash outlays in an uncertain atmosphere. The book is a practical guide, with material organized to lead the reader through each step in the capital budgeting process.

With an ever changing economic environment—witness the continuing high inflation rates, changes in interest rates, and increases in petroleum prices—the *analysis of risk* is becoming increasingly important. Thus risk is discussed and integrated into the strategic planning process using the tool of *sensitivity analysis*. Sensitivity analysis indicates how "sensitive" cash flows and profits are to errors in cost and revenue estimates. Specific plans for dealing with inflation are also included.

Since the *tax environment*, through accelerated depreciation and investment tax and other credits, directly affects acquisition decisions, tax issues are described using many specific examples. Again, prior knowledge of taxes is *not* assumed.

The methods used to evaluate capital investments are based on the widely accepted *discounted cash flow* procedures. The discounted cash flow method is the cornerstone for evaluation by both financial and line managers at every level in organizations throughout the world. The procedures for using discounted cash flow are described step by step, and their application to the acquisition decision is discussed in detail.

Special chapters deal with strategic planning and sensitivity analysis, project financing, and control and abandonment of projects. We express our special appreciation to Peter K. Nevitt, President of BankAmeriLease Group Companies, for preparing the chapter on project financing.

We would like to thank several individuals who have provided input and support for this publication. Paul E. Dascher, Dean of the College of Business and Administration, Drexel University, and Leo C. Beebe, Dean of the Administrative Studies Division, Glassboro State College, were a constant source of support and encouragement throughout the writing of the book. Our students at Drexel University and Glassboro State College, along with numerous industrial specialists, provided valuable feedback in critiquing our materials. Also, we express our thanks to Robert E. Finley, Editor-in-Chief, AMACOM for the many hours spent working with the manuscript, to Peter Reimold for preparation of the copy-edited manuscript, and to Marie E. Hunt, Janice Lathrop, and Irene M. Woods, who cheerfully typed and retyped the several revisions of the manuscript.

Comments from readers are welcomed and encouraged.

Robert E. Pritchard
Thomas J. Hindelang, CPA

CONTENTS

Introduction

Judicious selection of capital equipment is of paramount importance to all managers. This is due to the fact that most businesses derive their profits directly from the use of capital equipment in producing their products or services. Generally, the decisions with respect to acquisition, depreciation, and abandonment of capital assets set the direction for the firm. Decisions made now will affect the company for many years to come. Consequently, managers at every level need to make acquisition decisions (both purchase and lease) that are consistent with the company's goals, forecasts, and risk posture. Thus there is a compelling need to integrate strategic planning processes with those of capital acquisition.

Over the past 30 years, increasingly more sophisticated analytical techniques for forecasting capital needs and evaluating the profitability of proposed capital expenditures have been developed. Quantitative tools are readily available through the use of large and minicomputers and even programmable calculators. All these tools, however, depend on sound forecasts for the future, appropriate use of those forecasts by analysts, and correct interpretation of the forecasts by management.

Unfortunately, although we have the most powerful and sophisticated forecasting tools ever available, in many instances the forecasts are just not borne out. As a result, the decisions based on these forecasts often turn out to be less than optimum.

The reasons for the mistakes in forecasting are not hard to find. Some of the underlying assumptions may have been wrong, and certain variables which at the time of forecasting were thought to be irrelevant may since have become important. Thus the inputs to the decision process may have been bad.

In view of such past errors, can we expect significant improvements in the foreseeable future? The answer is an unequivocal no. In fact, international events and the volatility of the money and capital markets make forecasting a most formidable task. But, at the same time, the very fact that we recognize that completely unknown and unpredictable external events will affect our business makes forecasting ever more important and necessitates the development of management policies to deal with the unknown.

Further, we recognize that we are in a period of rapid social, political, technological, economic, and international change. In addition, every business faces restrictions and constraints that vary with the economic and political environment. Detailed planning and, in many cases, approval of government agencies are required before major projects can be undertaken. The increased lead time for projects reduces the reliability of initial forecasts. Also, the reliability may be affected profoundly by changes in consumer preferences, which are influenced by the same social, political, technological, economic, and international changes that affect the business itself. It is no longer possible to extrapolate trends into the future. But the business must go on—management must take a position on how it will deal with the uncertainties of the future.

We propose a strategic plan for purchasing/leasing and abandoning capital investments. Our plan has six steps and is easy to apply.

1. Develop forecasts for volume, prices, and costs on the basis of historical data, industrial trends, and the like in a manner consistent with the industry.

2. On the basis of those forecasts, establish a listing of potential capital acquisitions.

3. Estimate the after-tax cost of acquiring each asset and the cash inflows that can be expected from the use of the asset during its productive life.

4. Evaluate the possible acquisitions on the basis of after-tax cash flows, using a discounted cash flow technique (described in detail later).

5. Perform a detailed *sensitivity analysis* for steps 1 through 4. The sensitivity analysis should take into account such critical inputs as the expected productive life of the project, variability in demand and costs, and the tax environment, as well as how changes in each of the factors and unforeseen events may affect the final decision.

6. On the basis of the results of the sensitivity analysis, formulate your decision in such a way as to balance risk and return. This will likely necessitate adding management controls at each stage during the acquisition process to update demand and cost estimates and thus assure continued viability of the decision. Such decisions may range widely from rebuilding existing facilities, to lease (short- or long-term), to sale and lease-back, to purchase, to purchase through project financing, to ultimate abandonment. Disposing of a segment of the business may also be a viable option.

Our strategic planning position for the 1980s is as follows: at the outset, base your acquisition/abandonment decision process on the "normal" sequence of events (that is, normal cash flows, average useful asset life, moderate inflation, and so on), but make all final decisions on the basis of a *defensive risk posture,* assuming that your normal plans *will not* meet the test of time. In other words, *plan for the long run but stake your dollars on the short run.*

In this book, we will demonstrate clearly how to go about making capital expenditure decisions. We will examine logical alternatives and lead you step by step through the decision process. The techniques which are developed are equally applicable to all decisions involving risk.

Our mission is to describe how to effectively make and implement capital acquisition/abandonment decisions. We have divided the book into 12 chapters, each of which examines a particular aspect of the total capital investment decision process. Chapter 1 provides a detailed overview of the entire capital asset management process. Chapters 2 and 3 deal with the topics of depreciation and taxation—factors that must be taken into account in computing expected after-tax cash flows. Throughout the book we will be examining the after-tax cash flows using *discounted cash flow* techniques. Discounted cash flow (DCF) is a powerful tool that permits the integration of current and expected money costs (covered in Chapter 4) with the time span over which the assets will be used and thus leads to useful answers to capital expenditure questions. DCF techniques are introduced in Chapter 6 and illustrated in their all-important application to capital investment analysis in Chapter 7.

Over the past 15 years, leasing has become an increasingly important source of capital equipment. Thus, we devote two chapters to this important topic. The first (Chapter 5) discusses the pros and cons of leasing, while the second (Chapter 9) provides an analytical framework for evaluating one lease proposal against another and against the possibility of purchase.

Because of the importance of considering the impact of unforeseen external events and changes, we present techniques for evaluating "risky" conditions in Chapter 8. In Chapter 10 we detail the strategic planning process in capital budgeting and illustrate the sensitivity of project selection to changes in conditions. In that chapter we also present our strategies for hedging against inflation within the context of fixed-asset management.

Chapter 11, "Project Financing," prepared by Peter K. Nevitt, President of BankAmeriLease Group Companies, examines alternative modes of financing that have proved valuable in periods of tight money and high interest rates. The premise underlying the discussion is that in some instances financing may be available if the economic unit in question is used as the base for loan collateral and as the source of repayment. The result may be imaginative self-supporting acquisitions that are not dependent on the parent company's credit.

Finally, in Chapter 12, we present an approach helpful in the review and control of ongoing capital projects, as well as a recommended analysis which pinpoints projects that should be abandoned. This is a continuation of the discussion of the ongoing strategic planning process.

Each topic is developed so as to lead the reader through the necessary steps to make the best capital acquisition decisions on the basis of current data and possible unforeseen events. So, join us now as we enter the capital budgeting arena.

CHAPTER 1

Strategic Planning and Capital Asset Management

This book deals with management—specifically, the management of capital expenditures in the context of strategic planning. While capital budgeting is frequently singled out for study as a topic in and of itself, the decisions regarding purchases of assets and the like cannot be isolated from the other phases of management. Capital acquisition decisions must be integrated with the company's strategic planning process. For example, capital acquisition directly affects the extent of intensification of labor versus capital in individual plants and industries and hence also affects the requirements for labor of varying degrees of skill, for supervision, for support services, and so on. It is directly involved with the frequent conflict between meeting short-term profit objectives and long-term corporate goals.

Throughout this book we closely examine the basic inputs necessary to making profitable acquisition decisions and then analyze those inputs within a logical, systematic management framework. This chapter is devoted to an overview of the management of a capital expenditure program in the context of the firm's general management system and goals. It includes a detailed management plan to help managers deal with the hard questions of resource commitments. As will be seen, resource commitments to long-range projects may adversely affect near-term profits. Further, because of forecasting errors, economic and environmental changes, and so on, some long-term decisions will prove to be wrong. Thus we need both systems to alert us to potential risks and methods to change direction, if needed.

The subject of capital budgeting generally deals with decisions for the acquisition of assets with a life of two or more years. These long-term investments include such things as land, buildings, or equipment, plus the additional working capital associated with the use of such assets. Thus capital budgeting forms a major and integral part of strategic planning. As indicated in the Introduction, the importance of capital acquisition for *most firms* is that the bulk of the profit is derived from the productive use of capital assets. However, this is not the case for all firms; retail establishments, for example, may find that investment in inventories on average produces higher returns than investment in fixed assets. Fortunately, the decision methodology presented in this book is applicable to the evaluation of the purchase of machinery or vehicles as well as to evaluation of investments in inventory or in advertising. Given the necessary cost inputs and predicted benefits, we can evaluate each proposal and ascertain its relative worth to the firm from the viewpoint of both purchase and (if feasible) leasing. On the basis of their relative worths, we can then select that group of projects, within budget and other relevant constraints, that will contribute most to increasing the owners' wealth over the long run.

Establishing Management Goals

We have selected as our management goal the maximization of owner wealth over the long run. This goal is *generally* consistent with maximizing profits, but not at the expense of forgoing preventive maintenance and the like. Again, we must deal with short-term versus long-term trade-offs. Since the future of most firms depends to a great extent on the development and implementation of a purposeful plan for capital investments, such a plan must be consistent with general management goals. This consistency may be achieved by following the guides for asset selection detailed in the following chapters.

Before moving into a discussion of the importance of capital budgeting, we need to develop a picture of the firm, which will serve as a guide in evaluating alternative investments. Just as an individual investor views his securities in terms of a total portfolio of investments that differ in current and future return, degree of risk, and so on, we view the firm as a portfolio of investments—commonly termed a portfolio of projects. Some projects represent the "bread and butter" items. These have relatively low risk and deliver a "fair" return on investment. Other projects—for example, research and development—are speculative in nature. That is, they are characterized by high risk with *potential* high return. Some projects are nondiscretionary and mandated by law and result in increased costs rather than enhanced profits. Consequently, the profitable projects must be sufficiently profitable to support those which drain funds.

To meet investor demands, as well as the demands of labor, consumers, special-interest groups, and government regulations, the firm is placed in a *satisficing position.* We must satisfy the needs and demands of each group that affects the business, such as customers, suppliers, management, and labor, while meeting regulations and other external constraints. The goal of wealth maximization must be viewed in the context of all the other requirements. This makes the task of capital acquisition more complex. Another complicating factor is that new projects must fit into the current asset portfolio. We view the firm as it presently exists as a portfolio made up of past investments. When making new investments, we must ask how each will interact with those which are already a part of the firm, and how the new portfolio as a whole will meet the needs of the various groups mentioned.

In order to reduce risk and expedite needed decisions, we recommend a simplification of management for the 1980s. Specifically, we suggest the following:

1. Establish clear and simple corporate goals and make sure that the goals are communicated throughout the organization. This necessitates a business plan. A business plan outline is provided in Appendix E.

2. Restructure the organization into small entrepreneurial units and provide broad management decision-making autonomy within those units.

3. Establish a top-level management control system, without impinging on division and middle-management decision-making authority, to assure that corporate goals are met.

4. Provide management compensation plans directly correlated to corporate goals.

5. Insist that managers at every level maintain close contact with customers on a regular basis to get first-hand information on customer

needs and to obtain ideas for product improvement and the like from customers.

6. Seek gains in productivity through capital intensification and by motivating and stimulating employees. Employees at every level must be made to understand that there is a direct correlation between their individual productivity and their standard of living.

7. Stick to areas of business that management fully understands. Do what you know how to do best.

The Importance of Capital Expenditures

Capital expenditures have a profound impact on both the individual firm and the economy as a whole. In aggregate, the total capital expenditure programs of all firms greatly influence the direction of the economy, inflation, employment and unemployment rates, productivity, interest rates, and so on. This macroeconomic aspect of capital acquisition is discussed next. After that, the microeconomic view—the importance of the capital acquisition program to the individual company—will be considered.

A MACROECONOMIC PERSPECTIVE ON CAPITAL INVESTMENTS

From the viewpoint of the economy as a whole, a primary goal of capital expenditures is to maintain, and preferably increase, productivity as measured in output per man-hour. Such increases add directly to the total product output—the total of all goods and services produced—and thereby tend to improve the overall standard of living. All other things equal, increased productivity results in lower, or relatively lower, prices (hand calculators, computer calculations, and food are prime examples) and increased employment and decreased unemployment.

From a macro perspective, capital expenditures can be divided into two primary categories: those needed to replace existing assets as the latter wear out or become obsolete, and those used to expand output in terms of either quantity or quality of production. (The latter include nondiscretionary expenditures such as those required by EPA, OSHA, and so forth.)

Economists and government planners carefully watch the projections for capital expenditures, as they are a key barometer of economic activity. Each year economists report capital expenditure plans. In recent years these have not increased significantly from year to year, after discounting for inflation. Given the fact that a major portion of investment goes to nonprofit projects (that is, those mandated by law), industry as a whole is actually becoming less capital-intensive. The aging of American industry, especially in the Northeast, is a cause for national concern. It can be argued that while certain types of projects such as pollution abatement neither are profitable to the firm nor increase output of goods or services, funds allocated to pollution abatement should have a positive impact in terms of quality of life. But this does not alter the fact that American industry is slowly deteriorating.

Productivity is directly related to capital expenditures. The rate of increase in productivity in recent years has become alarmingly low, especially compared to foreign rivals. Productivity—output per man-hour—increased about 1.5 percent per year during the 1970s, but by the end of the decade, gains in productivity had vanished. In 1979, productivity actually decreased by 1 percent. Compare this to increases of more than 5 percent a year in Germany and Japan. Although there are several factors that have held back productivity, *the primary cause is inadequate capital investment.*

Government regulation, which directly affects capital investments, acts as a deterrent to increased productivity. In nearly every area of industry new regulatory requirements by government are cutting into productivity by diverting capital expenditures to nonproductive uses. Further, research and development have been inhibited as government forced R&D toward meeting numerous government edicts and prohibited use of efficient production processes.

For the last generation, the chemical industry led other industries in productivity growth. This resulted from the invention of new processes and construction of large-scale electronically equipped plants. By 1978, however, *nearly one-quarter* of the industry's capital investment had been diverted to the purchase of pollution abatement and other unproductive assets. Other industries have been similiarly affected and have been forced into defensive positions as they had to deal with meeting regulations at minimum cost.

A MICROECONOMIC PERSPECTIVE ON CAPITAL INVESTMENTS

For the individual firm, whether it be large or small, the acquisition of capital equipment is a key factor in preserving competitive position and profitability. With shortages of capital plaguing nearly all firms, rationing of funds among those projects mandated by government and those which are discretionary is a major task. The crucial importance of controlling capital expenditures was noted by Norman E. Pflomm in an early Conference Board report:

> Ill-advised or excessive capital spending can raise operating costs and unnecessarily tie up a company's funds, thus reducing profits. In fact, misdirected capital investments, such as those that create excess capacity, may be detrimental not only to the company making them but to the entire industry as well.
>
> On the other hand, failure to make timely replacements of inefficient plant and equipment can impair the quantity and quality of a company's output and injure its competitive position. A company can also lose ground by failing to expand to meet growing market demands.
>
> It is not surprising, then, that many companies have established policies to govern their capital investments. They have also set up systems of control to make sure that their policies are carried out. These companies believe that an established policy provides a sound basis for gearing expenditures to long-range company needs. It helps to end hit-or-miss replacements or expansion, and to ensure that expenditures are made when they will do the company the most good instead of when they can best be afforded.
>
> Furthermore, these companies find that the use of a formal system of capital-expenditures review and approval eliminates "a lot of hazy thinking and off-the-cuff decisions" that lead to bad investments. The systematic presentation and review of supporting facts on each capital expenditure sharpens executive judgment and makes it easier to arrive at sound decisions.[1]

While we emphasize the importance of capital expenditures, the decision-making process takes time—and time costs money. Sophisticated analytical techniques may be cost-justified for some projects but not for others. Similarly, major decisions—that is, decisions involving large dollar expenditures, radical changes in products, and so on—require top-management approval, while smaller replacement decisions need not absorb the time of top management. This leads to the need to develop a capital expenditure authorization policy to provide guidelines for authorizing expenditures. (A budget is *not* authorization for expenditure.)

Financial Management and Risk

The financial control system, of which capital expenditure analysis and authorization is a major part, requires the establishment of the company's plans, including specific performance objectives for key members of the management team and timely measurement of performance against objectives. Basically, this is *management by objectives* (MBO) applied to the firm's financial operations. Since financial planning must be integrated into the management of the business, the participation of all the members of the management team is required to ensure success.

The financial management program is not equivalent to financial accounting, tax accounting, or examination of financial statements to evaluate past performance. Rather, it consists in looking forward, forecasting needs, and then developing the cash, profit, and capital expenditure plans. These constituent plans are inseparable, with each affecting the other two.

Financial control is indispensable for capital budgeting; but control does not mean control of the company by the finance people. Rather, it means involving line managers by providing each with specific performance objectives relating directly to cash, profit, and capital expenditures. Once the objectives against which performance can be measured are established, management action can be taken promptly to see that the objectives are met or to change objectives while minimizing the impact to the total system. This type of financial management gives the *line* managers operational control, along with the tools to meet their objectives. The finance people coordinate the efforts of line managers to assure that corporate objectives will be met, and they provide technical assistance while allowing line managers flexibility in decision making and in operating their segment of the business.

The financial control system has two primary inputs: the forecast and the profit budget. Profits relate directly to wealth maximization, and over time, profits generally lead to increase in the equity value of the firm. While profits stem primarily from purchasing goods at one price, adding value to them in some way, and then selling them for a price greater than the cost plus value added, profits are also affected by the firm's financial structure. Companies can be more efficient *both* operationally and financially.

OPERATING LEVERAGE

Operational efficiency comes about through the judicious use of *assets in relation to labor*. This is measured in terms of *operating leverage*, which results from the mix of fixed and variable costs in the operation and management of the firm. In general, the degree of operating leverage increases with the increased utilization of fixed assets—those assets with inherently fixed costs of ownership and operation. As the use of fixed assets is increased (and fixed costs increase relative to variable costs), the degree of business risk increases. Business risk encompasses all the risks inherent in the actual operation of the business, such as those arising from changes in consumer preferences, in costs, and in availability of supplies.

Use of fixed assets is, of course, necessary and desirable to every business. However, an important point needs to be made: as capital equipment is substituted for labor (that is, as fixed costs are substituted for variable costs), profits will likely increase, but the business risk also increases. Thus, to a large degree, a decision to increase capital expenditures directly increases business risk. Put another way, the profitability of capital-intensive companies will be affected to a *much larger extent* by changes in output than will the profitability of less capital-intensive companies. There is a definite trade-off involved between risk and return; the more capital-intensive the firm, the higher the potential profit and the higher the risk or variability of profit.

The sensitivity of changes in earnings before interest and taxes (EBIT) to changes in output is measured simply by the *degree of operating leverage* (DOL). While it is not necessary for readers who are unfamiliar with quantitative methods to examine the following equations and examples in detail, the effort is worth the time, since they provide prime examples of the application of sensitivity analysis while introducing the basic elements of business risk and financial risk.

The degree of operating leverage at an output Q is measured using Equation (1):

$$DOL = \frac{Q(p - vc)}{Q(p - vc) - FC} = \frac{\text{percentage change in } EBIT}{\text{percentage change in output and sales}} \quad (1)$$

where Q = level of output
p = unit selling price
vc = variable cost per unit
FC = total fixed costs
$EBIT$ = earnings before interest and taxes

The degree of operating leverage shows the responsiveness of earnings before interest and taxes to a given percentage change in output and sales: the greater the degree of operating leverage, the more rapidly earnings before interest and taxes will change relative to changes in output.

EXAMPLE 1

Degree of Operating Leverage

A firm has product price and various costs as noted. Unit sale price is \$10; fixed costs (excluding interest) are \$50,000; variable cost per unit is \$6. The output is currently 40,000 units, resulting in EBIT of \$110,000 [\$10 (40,000) − \$6 (40,000) − \$50,000]. Determine how sensitive EBIT is to a change in output at the current level. Specifically, how much will EBIT change if output changes 5 percent?

SOLUTION

Determine the degree of operating leverage at 40,000 units of output, using Equation (1).

$$DOL = \frac{40{,}000\,(\$10 - \$6)}{40{,}000\,(\$10 - \$6) - \$50{,}000}$$
$$= \frac{\$160{,}000}{\$110{,}000}$$
$$= 1.45$$

For each *1 percent* change in output, EBIT will change by 1.45 percent. Thus, if output changes 5 percent, EBIT will change 5(1.45 percent) = 7.25 percent. □

Continuing with Example 1, suppose a capital investment is available that would result in the substitution of machinery for labor so that fixed costs (excluding interest) would rise to \$110,000 while variable costs per unit would drop to \$4.25. The new EBIT at 40,000 units would be \$120,000 [\$10 (40,000) − \$4.25 (40,000) − \$110,000]. This represents an increase of \$10,000. While profits have improved, business risk as measured by the degree of operating leverage (variability in EBIT with output) has also increased. The change in risk is illustrated in Example 2.

EXAMPLE 2

Degree of Operating Leverage

Determine the degree of operating leverage, given the new costs, and comment on the change in risk.

SOLUTION

Using Equation (1), the degree of operating leverage is found as shown below:

$$DOL = \frac{40{,}000\,(\$10 - \$4.25)}{40{,}000\,(\$10 - \$4.25) - \$110{,}000}$$

$$= \frac{\$230{,}000}{\$280{,}000 - \$110{,}000}$$

$$= 1.92$$

For each *1 percent* change in output, EBIT will change 1.92 percent. Thus, if output changes 5 percent, EBIT will change 5(1.92 percent) = 9.6 percent. Note that the increased DOL will increase EBIT more rapidly as output increases (compared with Example 1), but that EBIT decreases more rapidly as output decreases. As noted earlier, whenever fixed costs are substituted for variable costs, the degree of business risk as measured by the variability in EBIT with output increases. □

The reader should note at this juncture that there exists a *risk–return trade-off* for all investments. In general, as the return on investment increases, the degree of risk for the investment also increases, but at a higher rate. Thus, in most instances higher-yield investments are accompanied by much higher risk than lower-yield investments. The reader should also note that we have just completed a *sensitivity analysis*. We have determined how sensitive the risk posture of a business (as measured, in these examples, by the degree of operating leverage) is to a substitution of machinery for labor. We will employ the concept of sensitivity analysis in many other applications throughout the rest of this book.

FINANCIAL LEVERAGE

While risk is examined in detail in Chapter 8, we want to introduce *financial risk* now in order to provide added background. Financial risk is the risk that comes about when a company uses *debt* as a part of its financial structure. Thus, by definition, if a firm were financed solely by equity, it would have no financial risk but only business risk. Financial risk is the risk of not being able to pay interest and principal on time.

The financial structure of a company usually consists of both equity and debt. A firm is said to be "financially leveraged" when it employs debt as a part of the financial structure. While some authorities disagree, most practitioners believe that debt can be used to supply funds at a lower cost than equity. This is especially important because the cost of debt—that is, interest—is tax-deductible. Obviously, there are limits to how much debt may be utilized, so an "optimum" financial structure (ratio of debt to equity) needs to be achieved. If management can achieve an optimum structure and thereby lower costs of financing, the firm may be financially more efficient than its competitors. However, it must be kept in mind that increased use of debt increases financial risk.

The use of debt is measured by the *degree of financial leverage* (DFL). The degree of financial leverage, as defined by Equation (2), provides an indication of how much earnings after taxes (EAT) or earnings per share (EPS) will change as EBIT changes.

$$DFL = \frac{EBIT}{EBIT - I} = \frac{\text{percent change in } EPS \text{ or } EAT}{\text{percent change in } EBIT} \tag{2}$$

where I = interest
EPS = earnings per share
EAT = earnings after taxes

In order to demonstrate the impact of debt financing on risk or variability of earnings, consider the situation described in Example 1 and assume that the firm did not have any debt in its capital structure. That is, assume that only business risk exists and that the degree of financial leverage is 1. This means that earnings per share and earnings after taxes change in a *one-to-one proportion* with earnings before interest and taxes.

Now assume that the capital investment requires an outlay of \$150,000,[2] of which \$120,000 is financed by debt at 14 percent interest, resulting in an annual interest payment of \$16,800. The degree of financial leverage is found in Example 3.

EXAMPLE 3
Degree of Financial Leverage

Assuming an EBIT of \$120,000 and interest payments of \$16,800, determine the degree of financial leverage.

SOLUTION

The degree of financial leverage is determined using Equation (2).

$$DFL = \frac{\$120{,}000}{\$120{,}000 - \$16{,}800}$$
$$= 1.16$$

If EBIT changes by *1 percent,* EPS and EAT will vary by 1.16 percent. The use of debt has increased the variability of earnings. □

Before we leave this introductory section on risk, note that the effects of operating and financial leverage are multiplicative in nature. That is, *the total variability in EAT and EPS related to changes in output is the product of the degrees of operating and financial leverage.* In the initial solution of Example 1, operating leverage was 1.45, and financial leverage was 1. Thus, if output changed 5 percent, EAT and EPS would change 7.25 percent. With the purchase of the new capital equipment in Example 2 and its financing described in Example 3, the variability in EAT and EPS has increased to 1.92 × 1.16 = 2.23. Thus, if output changes 5 percent, then EAT and EPS will change 5 (2.23 percent) = 11.15 percent.

As companies use greater degrees of operating and financial leverage, the variability of profit with output increases. One cost of increasing potential profits is increased risks. Airlines are a prime example. Larger planes have the potential for greatly enhancing profits, but the increased fixed costs also increase risk.

In order to develop a systematic procedure for establishing a capital budget and authorizing expenditures, it is necessary to have a framework, or a set of ground rules, in which to operate. In the next section we discuss this framework in terms of a set of basic assumptions about the firm, its owners, and their goals.

Basic Assumptions Underlying the Development of a Capital Budget

ASSUMPTION 1: *The function of management is to increase the value of the business.* The traditional theory of the firm assumes that the primary function of management is to maintain or increase the value of the business as expressed in terms of the market price of the common stock. This rests on the further assumption that the firm is operated for the benefit of the common shareholders. But, as noted earlier, others would disagree. Galbraith, for example, argues that the objective is not to maximize but rather to satisfice. This means obtaining a "satisfactory" level of profits while meeting the needs of competing interest groups.

The problems inherent in both satisficing and maximizing are well handled through mathematical programming[3] and specifically goal programming. Goal programming permits the establishment of acceptable levels of attainment for various goals and the priority structure for the various goals. Management can then decide whether it wants to merely achieve the minimum acceptable level for various goals or whether it wants to maximize or minimize performance with regard to specific goals. The use of goal programming permits management to specify a hierarchy of goals and thereby develop a capital expenditure program consistent with those goals and their associated trade-offs.

ASSUMPTION 2: *Owners have a preference for current as opposed to future income.* Since owners want to maximize their wealth over the long run, they are willing in *some* instances to invest funds in capital equipment with the expectation of realizing "sufficient" returns on those investments. But they must be compensated for postponing the recovery of their investment and the return on their investment. That is, money has a *time value:* it is worth more today than tomorrow.

Shareholders divide their funds into two parts: investment and consumption. The time value of money results from shareholders giving up current consumption with the expectation of receiving greater returns in the future. But in an uncertain world the investor must also be rewarded for assuming risk. Discounting cash flows to their present value therefore is a logical approach to the acquisition decision, since it incorporates time and risk into the decision process. In short, *timing lies at the heart of the capital acquisition decision.*

ASSUMPTION 3: *Shareholders are risk averters, and management will reflect the risk preferences of the shareholders.* (This is a corollary to Assumption 2.) The "sufficiency of return" is a function of individual owner requirements, the available returns on other investments in the marketplace, and the subjective owner-management attitude toward taking risk. Risk is very subjective. Not only do different people have different attitudes toward risk, but each person's preferences may vary over time. In simple terms, risk avoidance means that shareholders require the rate of return on an investment to increase more rapidly than the rate of increase in the risk associated with that investment. The basis for this assumption is the decreasing marginal utility of money—that is, the fact that the value of each additional dollar returned to the shareholder is lower than the value of a dollar lost.

ASSUMPTION 4: *In selecting projects, it is necessary to evaluate the incremental cash flows attributable directly to the project, as opposed to historical or sunk costs.* Historical book values and sunk costs are of no consequence except insofar as they affect tax calculations (such as the calculations of capital gains and losses, recapture of depreciation, and investment tax credits).

For purposes of financial reporting, however, historical costs must be considered. We are conscious of the need to reconcile cash flow analysis with conventional accounting statements. Further, both the expected costs and the benefits attributable to a given project must be measured in *qualitative* as well as quantitative terms. The reason for this is that the price mechanism does not capture all the costs and benefits; for example, environmental factors are typically not reflected.

ASSUMPTION 5: *Since the capital acquisition represents long-term commitments, forecasting is essential to the process.* Forecasting is based on current costs and estimates of future cash flows and hence will always err. Usually the degree of error correlates with time; short-term forecasts are generally more accurate than long-term. Hence, the degree of risk inherent in an investment usually increases with the expected life of the investment. Consequently, many investors require higher expected returns from investments with longer lives.

While we do not deal specifically with forecasting in this book, an important appendix is included from The Conference Board: Appendix C, "Sources of Economic and Financial Information." The reader will find this to be useful in forecasting.

ASSUMPTION 6: *The current trend in asset acquisition exhibits management's risk posture* (that is, the current attitude of management toward risk). Assets are acquired for long periods, and there is a degree of risk attached to each asset. The firm's business risk complexion is the composite risk of all of the firm's assets. As the attitude toward risk changes over time, management will acquire new assets and dispose of existing assets to attain the desired risk posture.

ASSUMPTION 7: *Owners and managers have a liquidity preference.* Liquidity preference refers to the individual preference for a particular combination of assets that can easily be converted to cash and of fixed assets that cannot be easily converted to cash in the short run. Liquidity has two dimensions: time and amount. Time refers to the period necessary to convert an asset into cash. Amount refers to the amount which will be realized when the conversion takes place. In general, less liquid assets (fixed assets as opposed to cash, for example) produce higher returns, but they carry an inherently greater risk, and maintaining an insufficient liquidity base may result in insolvency. The risk of insolvency (or, to a lesser degree, the inability to take discounts for prompt payments) must be carefully weighed against the benefit of greater returns. This weighing process establishes management's *liquidity preference.* Liquidity preference is also a rationale for charging interest, since interest is a reward for giving up liquidity and undertaking investment.

ASSUMPTION 8: *Fixed assets require added working capital (inventories, receivables, and so on) in order to be operated.* This is a corollary to Assumption 7. Since management's liquidity preference directly affects the level of working capital, liquidity preference becomes an important input in determining the total cash outflow necessary for the acquisition of an asset. Not only must the cost of the asset be considered, but additions to working capital needed to support the use of the asset must be included as a part of the cash outflow necessary for acquisition.

ASSUMPTION 9: *Capital budgeting always involves allocating scarce resources among competing investment opportunities.* Resources (including capital, management, labor, and technology) are limited, both in total amount and from period to period. It may be possible to increase the body of capital equipment available in this period beyond the amount that can be financed through normal growth, but there is a price: the return required for additional equity sold, for interest on added debt, and for increased financial risk possibly resulting from the use of more debt and/or more operating leverage.

Furthermore, the functions of capital acquisition and financing (raising funds) must be integrated. The timing of acquisitions must correspond to the availability of financing. Also, as the costs of money change, projects may become more or less desirable. Postponement may be mandated, or taking advantage of the current market situation may be the order of the day.

Developing the Capital Budget

Managing the capital acquisition program is an ongoing process; the firm acquires assets after the completion of an evaluation process, continually reexamines the productive value of the assets to the firm, and ultimately replaces or disposes of them—and the process continues. Fifteen distinct steps can be identified in the process.

1. *Determine the owners' investment objectives and their collective attitude toward taking risks.* For a small firm the process might be quite simple if the owners have established (or thought through) their objectives. Smaller organizations may permit direct owner–management communications to facilitate determination of owner expectations.

For a large firm with many shareholders, owner expectations are reflected in their actions in the money and capital markets. Investors present their collective judgment of a firm in terms of purchases and sales of the firm's stock. At the limit, it may be necessary to closely watch investor responses to management's actions in order to fully understand investors' feelings about risk.

2. *Establish the basic financial goals for the business.* If the goal is to maximize owner wealth, then this is synonymous with maximizing the market value of the business in the long run. Since the market value of the firm is the present (current) value of the firm (which is usually a function of its current and potential profitability), we can develop a decision rule for evaluating proposed investments: *maximize the net present value of the business.* This is accomplished by selecting investments which *collectively* will maximize the value of the business. Keep in mind that any business is nothing more than the composite of its assets. The business is a portfolio of assets. Thus, selecting that group of assets which have the maximum net present value without altering the business's risk complexion will maximize the value of the business.

The goal of maximizing shareholder wealth has not received universal acceptance in industry, however. The consequences of using other goals will probably be nonoptimum allocation of resources, a problem of which the authors are acutely aware. A study of 136 firms conducted by The Conference Board noted that 80 firms indicated multiple financial goals.[4] Two or more of the following aims were included:

Maximization of return on investment.
Maximization of earnings.
Maximization of sales.
Minimization of costs.
Paced earnings growth.
Maintenance of market share.

One statement, from the vice president of finance of a steel company, was representative of the majority of responses:

> The financial objectives of [the company's] capital expenditure policy are to provide adequate funds to maintain facilities for our lines of business and to seek out opportunities for the investment of funds which may improve sales, reduce costs, and, therefore, improve earnings. To improve corporate return on investment is the basic objective of our capital expenditure policy.

As noted earlier, it is necessary for businesses to satisfy the needs of several groups, such as customers, suppliers, the community, and government, all of which have a direct impact on the firm's long-term viability. However, every company's *primary* goal should be to meet the needs of the owners. Ultimately this group must be satisfied, or it will withdraw its investment from the company. Since the degree of owner satisfaction is reflected in the owners' collective actions in the security markets, management should act so as to maximize the value of the common stock. Maximizing this value is achieved by managing capital assets so as to maximize the net present value of the business. This may not be synonymous with objectives such as maximizing sales or minimizing costs. Therefore, if investments are made to meet an objective such as maximizing sales, the investments will probably not be optimum with respect to meeting shareholder needs.

Although we may develop a whole array of goals, in the final analysis we must return to basics. And, we must keep in mind that management works for the owners and that the owners are expecting the company to product profits—stable and increasing profits—while maintaining a constant risk posture. Profit is a very positive word. It is the engine that drives industry in a free enterprise economy. Profit should be a key goal in every strategic plan for the 1980s.

3. *Establish the basic nonfinancial goals of the firm.* Nonfinancial goals arising from a variety of sources must be integrated into the total goal structure of the firm. Several nonfinancial goals relate to community, customer, and employee relations, and to meeting legal, health, and safety requirements. One result of the growing need to meet nonfinancial requirements is the necessity to acquire assets that make little or no contribution to the present value of the firm, or that may actually decrease it. Installation of pollution abatement controls is a prime example. Acquisition of such assets places increasingly heavier burdens on those assets which do produce profits, and if the latter cannot meet the ultimate test (valuation of the firm by its owners), the firm may find itself in the position of being unprofitable and unable to secure funds from external sources, and thus forced to close. Small paper mills are a classic example of this. Nonetheless, nonfinancial goals are relevant to the firm's activities and must be incorporated into a comprehensive approach to capital investment analysis.

4. *Evaluate the firm's position within the marketplace so that long- and short-run business plans may be developed.*[5] The plans are designed to meet owner expectations and provide the basis for formulation of capital investment policies. Frequently such plans are developed for five years and updated at least annually to reflect changing conditions. In developing long-range plans, several major areas of input must be considered:

- The market size, both in terms of existing and proposed product lines and facilities and as a function of market share.
- The size, locations, and condition of existing plant and facilities, viewed in terms of accessibility to the marketplaces, availability of the inputs to production (labor, raw materials, fuels, utilities, and so on), desirability of location to attract new managerial and technological skills, and the like.
- Potential new markets for similar and related products and for both horizontal and vertical integration. Horizontal integration involves growth into areas closely related to the firm's product line. For example, an automobile sales company might purchase a car rental agency. Horizontal expansion also includes the acqui-

sition of distributors or manufacturers of similar or closely related products. Vertical integration relates to the acquisition of suppliers, distributors, or retailers of raw materials or purchased parts. It involves the integration of two or more stages of the business process, from securing raw materials to sales, in order to increase efficiency.

- Changes in economic factors, political environment, government regulations, tax laws, and, especially, expected inflation.
- Changes to the firm's business and financial risk associated with replacement of existing plant, facilities, and production lines and with expansion into new areas.

Long-range planning is not usually undertaken with the explicit purpose of establishing the exact plans for execution of expenditures. Rather, it sets the direction and guidelines for future growth. For example, a firm may have as a long-range plan the refurbishing or replacement of an existing plant. Ultimately, execution of the plan will require very specific detailed analyses to determine the possible options. Engineers will evaluate available capital equipment and facilities, the plant design will be formulated, and so on. However, as the precise cost estimates are developed and fed back to top management, along with updated demand forecasts, it may become necessary to revise the original plans. And if the actual costs differ significantly from the original estimates or if demand expectations have changed, the plans may have to be postponed or scrapped in favor of more profitable investments. Long-range plans must also be continually updated to reflect changing market and economic conditions.

Management must be flexible and modify long-range plans to meet short-run operating conditions and also must take into account the relative urgency of proposed capital investments. When formulating plans, management must assign priorities on the basis of how long various projects may be postponed. Some projects that may become critical may have been overlooked in long-range planning. In the short run, management must be able to adapt to rapidly changing market conditions, equipment failures, raw materials shortages, fluctuations in interest rates, and the like. All these factors affect capital expenditure policies.

5. *Develop management policies for the collection of information, in all areas of the firm, on capital investments that are needed or* *desirable.* Concurrently develop policies for possible expansion through merger or acquisition. In the process of collecting information, it is necessary to distinguish between projects that are independent, dependent on others, mutually exclusive, prerequisite to others, and contingent on availability of resources within the firm.

The demand for funds to be used for capital expenditures comes from many areas within the firm. Internal investments—those needed to maintain a progressive and competitive position within the industry—generally comprise the largest portion of funding requirements.

In order to obtain suggestions for capital expenditures, top management should distribute information on the general ground rules: the direction the firm is taking, the approximate amounts of funds available to each division, department, and so on, and the minimum rate of return required for a project to be given serious consideration.

6. *Develop management policies for assessing the worth of proposed projects.* This is a key area of capital acquisition and requires much thought and development. The following chapters deal with this in depth.

It is important to explore all possible alternatives. Any project can look good when compared to a sufficiently poor alternative. And, of course, one alternative is not to take any action or postpone action.

Many firms use two or several evaluation procedures. The particular choice of procedures to be used depends on the goals of the firm—and these may change over time. This means that management must be knowledgeable of the procedures available and be prepared to use different ones as conditions dictate. *However, it is always necessary to be able to estimate the return expected from proposed expenditures*—and in most instances it is possible to make such estimates. For example, the purchase of a new machine to replace one already in use may result in increased output and concurrently lower expenses through reduced utilization of labor, reduced downtime for maintenance, and so on. The increase in output and the decrease in costs may be estimated in terms of increased cash inflows and decreased cash outflows. These estimates in turn can be used to estimate the project's return and the potential value of the investment to the firm.

The greatest portion of all internally generated capital expenditures undertaken by business is for the replacement of worn-out or obsolete buildings, facilities, and equipment (capital goods). The analyses required for replacement investments are simplified if accurate records on past performance are available. Management, having had experience with the existing equipment, is aware of wage rates, materials costs, market demand for the product, and so on. The availability of this information permits management to formulate decisions in a relatively risk-free atmosphere. The decision process usually has two stages. First, management must decide if the equipment should be replaced or refurbished or just abandoned. If the decision is to replace or refurbish, then the question of the type of replacement to be acquired or the extent of overhaul becomes paramount. Usually such decisions are made using inputs from production, industrial, or manufacturing engineers, in collaboration with the management of the particular area involved.

When making replacement investment decisions, six factors warrant particular attention:

- The operating costs of the existing plant and equipment and of alternative replacements.
- The cost-effectiveness of rebuilding or overhauling versus replacement (including tax ramifications).
- The potential alternative uses and the marketability of replacement plant and equipment should demand for the output decrease. The product life cycle must be considered.
- The probability of short-run obsolescence of replacement plant or equipment resulting from technical changes or development of more efficient equipment.
- The availability of in-house expertise to fabricate new facilities and equipment. This may either reduce costs or provide technological or productive superiority over commercially available units.
- The cost-effectiveness of leasing versus purchasing or project financing.

While it would appear that the six factors listed apply primarily to questions regarding replacement of individual machines or facilities, this is not the case. Industrial engineers view the productive process as the primary factor in plant design and redesign. The buildings, equipment, and facilities are viewed as a part of the process rather than as individual entities. Hence, when replacement decisions are being made, they must be viewed in the context of the overall productive process. For example, when a plant is aging, the primary question is not whether to replace individual machines but rather whether improved manufacturing processes and technological improvement warrant redesigning the plant. In other words, replacement must be considered within the context of the total system.

Another major category of expenditures is for expansion and investment in new products. Such investments usually can be divided into four general categories:

Expansion of current production to meet increasing product demand. Depending on the expected duration of the increased demand, expansion could be achieved by greater utilization of existing facilities (such as operating two shifts instead of one), expanding the size of the existing plant, constructing or leasing a new plant, subcontracting a portion of the work, or purchasing existing facilities of a similar nature (horizontal integration) and modifying them to suit anticipated needs.

Expansion into closely related product lines, either through internal growth or through horizontal or vertical integration.

Expansion into areas not currently associated with the firm's operations. This could come about through internal expansion, but more likely through the acquisition of an existing business.

Research and development for new product lines. When a firm expands its operations, the degree of risk is greater than that involved in replacement. This results from three factors. First, costs are not known with the degree of accuracy available for ongoing operations. Second, management expertise in new or expanded areas is not as great as in existing product lines. While expansion of an existing product line involves little increased risk, undertaking research and development is likely to be very risky. Third, much more information is required for decisions regarding expansion than for replacement.

Two categories of capital investment proposals that may have no explicit return to the firm must also be considered. For example, community members may apply pressure on a firm to participate in and underwrite the costs of a neighborhood rehabilitation program. The implied return is improved community relations and employee environment. However, while such returns may be impossible to quantify and perhaps will never be realized, if the firm wants to stay in the area, participation in the program and the associated expenditures may be essential. The second category includes those nonproductive projects required by law or required for the firm to continue its operations without interruption.

Given that some projects may have explicit returns while others may be expected to produce no return whatsoever (or a negative return), it is necessary not only to evaluate individual projects but also to combine projects into budgets and then evaluate alternative budgets.

7. *Determine the cost of funds (usually termed cost of capital) for the business.* The cost of capital is the weighted average of the costs of all the components of funding used by the firm; for smaller firms it is the composite cost of debt and equity. For every business there is an optimum capital structure (that is, ratio of debt to equity), which may change over time, depending on such factors as the availability of money and interest rates.

The cost of capital represents the average after-tax-cost of funds—and this cost forms the base line or benchmark for evaluating proposed projects. It is incorrect to evaluate a project on the basis of the amount that can be borrowed to support *that* particular project. The reason is clear: the overall debt-to-equity ratio for the business will change, and ultimately the firm will run short of debt capacity and may not be able to borrow without first adding to the equity base.[6] Thus, regardless of the amount which may be borrowed to purchase a particular asset, the correct cost of funds to use as a benchmark for evaluation is the average cost of the new debt and equity, using the proportions consistent with the ongoing debt-to-equity ratio. This procedure assures the equitable and uniform evaluation of all projects.

8. *Where needed, use different evaluation criteria for projects whose inherent risk differs from that of the business overall.* This is a corollary to step 7. It may be desirable to accept some projects with expected returns lower than the cost of capital if they will reduce the business's risk complexion. Similarly, higher returns will be demanded from investments that increase overall risk.

9. *Develop a cash budget for the planning period.* The cash budget should reflect expected cash flows based on short- and long-range business plans and should include plans for acquisition of funds from external sources, payment of obligations, and so on. Development of a cash budget is necessary because the timing of the actual capital expenditures must be correlated to correspond with the cash availability within the firm.

10. *Evaluate the firm's historical spending pattern for capital investments that were not originally included in the yearly capital budget program.* Unforeseen expenditures typically result from unusual equipment failures or from unexpected investment opportunities. In developing the capital budget program, funds should be allocated for such expenditures.

11. *Undertake an evaluation of the proposed capital investment projects and develop the capital budget.* This process involves evaluating the projects collected in step 5, using the evaluation criteria of step 6, within the constraints of steps 9 and 10. The result will be a *capital budget*—that is, a preliminary ranking of acceptable projects. The budget should note possible candidates for postponement and leasing or special project financing and include information on which projects are dependent on others, which are independent, and so on. The capital budget does not represent authorization for expenditure but rather constitutes the capital expenditure planning program.

12. *Develop management policies for authorizing expenditures.* Typically, firms provide for expenditure authorization at varying management levels, depending on the cost of the asset. Seldom can land be purchased without owner approval, since this usually represents a commitment to long-term development. The Appendix to this chapter deals with authorization of capital expenditures.

13. *Implement those projects which best meet the business's needs within the budget constraints.* The capital budget and all the management policies now begin to come alive as acquisitions of property, plant, and equipment are made.

14. *Maintain a strict cost control system to measure actual costs versus estimates.* This process may include frequent reevaluations for large projects at critical times. Pre-established "go–no go" decision points will be helpful here. A decision tree or critical-path monitoring method may also be useful in this process.

15. *Periodically reassess the value of the projects in use.* This process requires estimating the amount of cash the asset would yield if sold and comparing its return to alternatives. Mathews notes a number of advantages in making such a review a part of the administrative process.

Management can profit in the future by avoiding a repetition of past mistakes. In more positive terms, experience can highlight areas in which better plans, policies, and forecasting techniques can improve capital expenditure activity.

A follow-up on performance can spotlight weaknesses in order that current projects may be revised.

Performance review can focus attention upon those individuals or organizations responsible for major or continuing errors. Of equal importance, it can reflect good performance and provide an incentive for better performance.

If top managements are correct in believing that junior officials are too frequently overoptimistic in predictions for pet proposals, the knowledge that results are to be scrutinized can breed a healthy caution at the time of initial justification. (Admittedly, however, there is a fine line to be drawn here between overconservatism and the discouragement of ideas.)

Performance review can become a useful area for training younger executives whose span of knowledge and contacts top management wishes to broaden. Inquiry into reasons for project failure or success cannot be conducted on a note basis, and the executive charged with responsibility for review necessarily finds himself involved in and developing skills in many areas, such as pricing, production, market analysis, and human relations.[7]

The 15 steps outlined here form the basis for the entire capital expenditure program. We will refer to this guideline throughout the rest of the book as we continue to address the problems inherent in capital investment analysis.

The preparation of a capital budget does not normally constitute authorization for the expenditure of funds. The actual authorization process, referred to in step 12, has been studied by The Conference Board. The results of that study are presented in the Appendix to this chapter.

NOTES

1. *Managing Capital Expenditures,* The Conference Board, Business Policy Study No. 107, 1963.
2. The authors recognize that one would not normally spend $150,000 to increase EBIT by $10,000, since with added interest burden the earnings after taxes will be adversely affected. The numbers were selected to make a point. However, the situation could well come about as a result of financing government-mandated pollution abatement devices. Further, in making the decision to use debt as opposed to equity in this example, management has explicitly altered its risk posture. As will be discussed later, the actual evaluation of capital investments should be carried out using the company's cost of capital as the primary benchmark. In general, considering specific loan

terms on an investment-by-investment basis would alter the financial structure over time and thereby alter the risk complexion.

3. For a detailed discussion of mathematical programming applied to capital budgeting, see John J. Clark, Thomas J. Hindelang, and Robert E. Pritchard, *Capital Budgeting: Planning and Control of Capital Expenditures,* Englewood Cliffs, N.J.: Prentice-Hall, 1979, Chapters 12, 13, and 14.
4. Patrick J. Davey, *Capital Investments: Appraisals and Limits,* The Conference Board, 1974.
5. For specific advice on how to develop business plans, see Appendix E and Bruce M. Bradway and Robert E. Pritchard, *Developing the Business Plan for a Small Business,* New York: AMACOM, 1980.
6. There are certain exceptions, such as government-guaranteed loans or loans for environmental projects funded through government agencies using municipal bonds. Also, certain classes of project financing (see Chapter 11) and leasing (see Chapter 5) may not affect the firm's debt-to-equity ratio negatively.
7. John B. Mathews, Jr., "How to Administer Capital Spending," *Harvard Business Review,* March–April 1959.

APPENDIX

Capital Expenditure Authorizations

While intertwined, the preparation of capital budgets and the authorization of capital expenditures are often distinct functions. As indicated earlier, capital budgets are typically made up of a selection of proposals chosen from among all those submitted by the underlying units of a company. Although the approval of a capital budget sometimes automatically includes the right to proceed with the projects included in it, this is not usually the case. Most companies insist that detailed appropriation requests relative to proposals contained in approved budgets be routed to various levels of management for final approval prior to the actual commitment of resources.

Companies that consider capital budgets as spending guides rather than buying mandates insist on close second looks—often far more detailed than those extended during the budget-preparation process—at capital investments, before expenditures are authorized. Such reconsiderations are occasionally carried out by a company's board of directors, particularly if the project being reviewed is a very substantial one. More frequently, however, final approval authority is put in the hands of review committees, or is delegated—subject to dollar limits—to hierarchical levels of management. This chapter considers the roles played by various committees in the authorization of capital expendi-

Reprinted from Patrick J. Davey, *Capital Investments: Appraisals and Limits,* The Conference Board, 1974, Chapter 4.

tures, and discusses the ways in which companies use dollar limits to control their capital investments.

Committee Participation

Eighty-eight of the companies contributing their experiences to this survey rely on committees to review or authorize certain of their capital expenditure proposals; several of these firms use two or more committees for these purposes. The remaining 48 companies do not use committees to consider capital investments, preferring instead to act on the recommendations of staff analysis departments, individual executives, or boards of directors.

Table 1 lists the names of the committees that monitor capital investments, together with their frequency of occurrence, in participating companies that use such groups. Many of these committees are formed for the exclusive purpose of dealing with capital expenditure projects, but some committees—executive, finance and budget committees, for instance—fulfill a variety of roles, only one of which has to do with the review or approval of capital expenditures.* However, regardless of whether or not the committee functions solely in the capital investment area, at least one senior financial executive is almost always a member of the group.

Functions

Committees acting in their investment monitoring roles are concerned with the review and approval of capital expenditures. In some companies these committees review certain proposals and recommend their acceptance or rejection to a higher approving authority, such as the executive committee or the board of directors. In other companies the approach differs; committees enjoy the authority to sanction projects or to reject them. In still other organizations, committees play dual roles: they recommend acceptance or rejection of projects of certain kinds or sizes, and authorize the undertaking of projects of other kinds and sizes. But whether empowered solely to recommend, solely to authorize, or to both counsel and commit funds, monitoring committees make an important contribution to the control of capital expenditures by rechecking proposals for appropriateness and accuracy in advance of their implementation. In addition, by passing on capital investments, these committees considerably lighten the burden on their companies' boards of directors by relieving them of the task of performing detailed reviews on numerous capital expenditure proposals.

A number of survey cooperators, whose review committees act solely in counseling capacities, provide brief descriptions of their committees' operations. An executive of one of these firms, the vice president—finance of a consumer products company, indicates that although his company's project study

* For a detailed discussion of the function of financially oriented committees, see *Financial Committees,* Studies in Business Policy, No. 105, National Industrial Conference Board, 1962.

Table 1. Capital expenditures monitoring committees in 88 participating companies.

Committee Name	*Number of Mentions*	*Committee Name*	*Number of Mentions*
Executive committee	13	Corporate management committee	1
Management committee	10	Corporate product review committee	1
No formal name	9	Corporate resources committee	1
Finance committee	7	Corporate review committee	1
Appropriations committee	3	Economic/finance committee	1
Ad hoc committee	2	Equipment committee	1
Budget committee	2	Executive management committee	1
Capital appropriations committee	2	Expenditures planning committee	1
Corporate planning committee	2	Facilities engineering committee	1
Operating committee	2	General committee	1
Operations committee	2	Headquarters administration committee	1
Real estate committee	2	Integration committee	1
Administrative committee	1	Investment committee	1
Appropriation review advisory committee	1	Management appropriations and special projects committee	1
Appropriations review committee	1	Management budget committee	1
Briefing room committee	1	Management coordinating committee	1
Budget review committee	1	Management council committee	1
Capital additions committee	1	Management policy committee	1
Capital budget committee	1	Manufacturing advisory committee	1
Capital expenditure control committee	1	Policy committee	1
Capital expenditure coordinating committee	1	Product planning committee	1
Capital expenditure request committee	1	Research and development committee	1
Capital investment committee	1	Screening committee	1
Chief executive committee	1	Venture development committee	1
Corporate approval committee	1		
Corporate capital review committee	1	Total	94

committee is strictly advisory, its recommendations are not taken lightly. He states:

"The committee reviews all facets of proposals, questions appropriate people (sales, production, engineering, etc.), and recommends approval or rejection to the appropriate officer. Recommendations of the committee are seldom overruled."

The monitoring committee of a steel company also plays an advisory role in the acceptance of capital projects. Additionally, however, it is empowered to reject or return proposals that do not fully meet approval standards. As its vice president—finance explains:

"All estimate and job requests with supporting data for capital expenditures and repairs over $3,000 are submitted to the committee for recommendation on approval. If recommended, capital expenditures are sent for approval to the chairman of the board when over $10,000 and to the board of directors when over $25,000. Projects in excess of $100,000 require more formal presentation to the board of directors, and data supporting such requests must be mailed to directors at least one week prior to the board meeting at which approval is being requested. Rejected requests may be sent to industrial engineering for further justification, to engineering for reexamination of estimated costs, or returned to the originator if not acceptable at all."

The monitoring committees of some companies enjoy fairly broad approval authority but others have limited powers of authorization. The capital appropriations committee of an office and computing machines company, for example, is empowered to review and approve all capital projects costing in excess of $25,000. On the other hand, the management committee of a steel company has full approval authority on capital projects costing between $20,000 and $100,000 but can only recommend on the acceptance of projects involving outlays in excess of $100,000.

Members of the survey panel were asked to indicate what sizes and kinds of projects their review committees studied. As Table 2 shows, a majority of

Table 2. Projects studied by review committees in 85 participating companies.

Kinds of Projects Studied	*Number of Mentions*
Projects involving expenditures of $25,000 or more	38
Major projects (dollar amounts not specified)	16
All projects	11
Projects involving expenditures of less than $25,000	10
Projects requiring approval of board of directors	3
Land and building purchases or leases	2
New product related expenditures	2
Other	3
Total	85

committees concentrate their efforts on projects that are classified as "major," or that involve outlays of $25,000 or more. Only about one review committee out of eight in responding concerns looks at all capital investment proposals.

Dollar Limits on Authority

One hundred and fifteen companies, or approximately five out of six of those surveyed, delegate authority to approve capital expenditures, within established dollar limits, to certain key executives and committees. The additional requirements for working capital growing out of capital expenditure projects are included in the dollar limits set by 40 of these participants, and excluded from such limits by the others.

For the most part, dollar limits seem to be set on an arbitrary basis, depending on such factors as company size, organization, philosophy, and on top management's confidence in the competence of individual executives or groups of executives. Ordinarily, companies that use dollar limits to control capital expenditures establish sliding scales of authority. A company's board of directors grants a maximum amount of spending authority to its review committee or chief executive officer. And, in turn, diminished levels of authority are established for lower levels of management.

The determination of particular dollar amounts of authority depends on individual company considerations. Limits considered satisfactory in one organization might be considered totally inadequate in another company of similar size and organization, operating within the same industry. Accordingly, over a period of time most companies work out—through trial and error—a set of limits that enables them to operate efficiently. Limits are pegged at levels with which the executive granting the authority is comfortable and at which the executive exercising the authority can function effectively.

In many cases, executives and committees from companies with larger capital budgets enjoy higher levels of capital expenditure authority than their counterparts from companies with smaller budgets. But because there are numerous instances where the reverse is true—or where companies sharing many common characteristics, including that of capital budget size, have sharply divergent dollar limits of authority—it is difficult to discern patterns in the establishment of authorization levels. Consequently, since companies set dollar limits in accordance with their unique requirements, a summarization of practices in this regard might prove misleading.

Delegation

Where they exist, dollar limits of authority are usually delegated in a formal way—in statements contained in capital expenditure manuals, in bylaws of boards of directors, or in grants of operating authority. When approval levels are specified in writing, authorizations of projects are facilitated. The delays and inconsistencies sometimes encountered when approval authority is transmitted orally are avoided because the need to recheck or get clarification on various points is largely eliminated. The following excerpts from the capital expenditure policy statements of two particpating companies reflect the attention to detail that is characteristic when dollar limits are conveyed in printed form:

"All group vice presidents have the authority to approve capital expenditures up to $25,000. Each has the authority to delegate to other members of his organization the right to approve expenditures of varying amounts, but not to exceed $15,000. This delegated authority must be in writing, listing the positions and the amounts, and a copy of the document delegating authority must be sent to the corporate controller. It is the responsibility of the general manager of the group to ascertain that all such expenditures conform to the procedure pertaining to the evaluation of capital expenditures and divestitures.

"All capital expenditures in excess of $25,000 must be approved by the president after review and recommendation of the capital expenditure committee.

"The board of directors will be advised of all capital expenditures approved by the capital expenditure committee.

"The board of director's approval is required on the following items:

(1) Expenditures in excess of $100,000

(2) Expenditures that involve the purchase of land

(3) Divestiture of capital assets in excess of $50,000

"The board of directors must ratify all disposals of real property.

"The president has the authority to approve proposed expenditures for equipping new temporary field jobs, domestic and foreign, even though the estimated cost exceeds $100,000. The board of directors will be advised at their next meeting."

—*A building products company*

"All requests must first be approved by the appropriate general manager, corporate department, or subsidiary company head.

"The following corporate personnel are authorized to give final approval to the acquisition of land improvements and general utilities, machinery and equipment, office furniture, fixtures and equipment, and other acquisitions as stated within the limitations specified below:

"1. General managers, corporate department and subsidiary company heads—less than $2,500.

"2. The director of transportation is authorized to give final approval to the acquisition of automobiles, trucks, trailers and other highway or railroad transportation equipment (excluding corporate aircraft and in-plant hauling equipment) costing less than $10,000.

"3. Such individuals appointed as an approving group by the president—$2,500 to $25,000.

"4. The appropriations committee is authorized to give final approval to the acquisition of any asset costing more than $25,000 (except investments in securities, corporate aircraft, and real estate) as well as proposals, regardless of amount, having to do with plant expansion, construction of new plants, new ventures, and new lines of business.

"5. The vice president and treasurer is authorized to finally approve investments of surplus funds in short-term securities, such as United States government obligations, certificates of deposit, and prime rate commercial paper.

"6. The board chairman is authorized to finally approve the acquisition of corporate aircraft.

"7. The board of directors must give final approval to the acquisition of real property and investments in securities of outside companies.

"Note: While final approvers *may* utilize pertinent company specialists for any special study or appraisal deemed necessary to properly evaluate a proposal, they *must,* prior to acting on the proposals indicated herein, obtain in writing the views and recommendations of:

"(a) The vice president—property investment, in connection with all proposals involving the acquisition of real property.

"(b) The executive vice president, the vice presidents of property, investment and personnel, and the director of transportation in connection with all proposals involving new sites for manufacturing or processing plants, warehouses, laboratories, etc.

"8. Except for the investment of surplus cash in short-term securities, no expenditure involving a gross investment of $100,000 or more may be implemented until and unless it first has been submitted to, and endorsed by, the president."

—*A manufacturer of industrial products*

Rationale

Relieving senior management of the responsibility of having to review numerous small capital appropriation requests is perhaps the principal reason why companies establish dollar limits of capital expenditure authority. Also, in cases where companies are large and geographically widespread, the existence of a dollar-limit system facilitates the timely completion of capital projects at branch locations. And, obviously, the imposition of dollar limits serves as a control on expenditures by curtailing the discretionary authority of committees and individuals.

There are other reasons, too, why companies find dollar limits on capital expenditure authority helpful. Their utilization in companies which do not have review committees, for instance, pinpoints the individuals responsible for various outlays. And knowing that they may be subject to criticism if projects do not work out according to plans, executives of such companies tend to reexamine proposals carefully before authorizing them. In addition, the assignment of dollar limits facilitates the approval of projects that were not included specifically in approved budgets.

Twenty-one participants do not establish hierarchical limits of capital expenditure authority. In these companies tight control over capital outlays at the top level is the rule, and the capital budget-approving authority—a top management official, review committee, or board of directors—also normally authorizes all capital expenditures.

Variations

Thirty-five of the 115 companies using dollar limits of authority vary their established capital expenditure limits to accommodate special situations. Seven companies delegate different dollar levels of authority for budgeted and nonbudgeted proposals; invariably, however, levels for budgeted proposals are higher. For example, a company that manufactures office and copying machines maintains two distinct levels of expenditure authority so as to cover items included and excluded from its capital budget. Its schedule of dollar limits shows:

Authorizer	*Dollar Limit When Project Included in Capital Budget*	*Dollar Limit When Project Not Included in Capital Budget*
Vice president concerned	$10,000	$ 5,000
Vice president-general manager (international operations)	25,000	10,000
Vice president-general manager (information products operations)	25,000	10,000
Vice president-general manager (copying products operations)	50,000	25,000
President	*	50,000

* If an authorization for capital expenditure does not exceed the amount specifically provided in the capital expenditure budget in the capital program previously approved by the board of directors, no further action by the board is required. The approval of the president will be secured in such cases. It is understood, however, that the president will inform the chairman concerning capital expenditures of unusual amount or significance. The chairman will secure the approval of the board of directors where required.

Seven other companies require top management or board approval to purchase land or buildings, regardless of the amounts involved. And five companies set special limits to cover emergency situations. Five vary limits to reflect the type of asset being purchased. Three companies vary the expenditure authority limits delegated to individual executives in accordance with risk categories established for different projects. The remaining companies that vary their dollar limits do so if expenditures have policy implications, economic conditions change, or management reorganizations occur.

Reviews and Revisions

As indicated in Table 3, annual reviews of existing levels of dollar limits on capital expenditures are favored by most respondents who schedule such examinations at fixed intervals. However 53 respondents, or exactly half of those providing information on review schedules, do not follow set schedules; they prefer to take fresh looks at existing authority limits whenever it seems appropriate to do so.

Table 3. Dollar-limit review schedules in 106 participating companies

Review Intervals	*Number of Mentions*
As needed	46
Annually	35
Infrequently	7
Biennially	6
Every 2–3 years	6
Every 5 years	2
Quarterly	1
Biannually	1
Every 18 months	1
Every 10 years	1
Total	106

Reviews enable organizations to determine if their limits are in step with the times. When examinations reveal that because of developments—mergers, divestitures or inflationary outbreaks, for instance—change is necessary, organizations update existing levels of capital expenditure authority to meet current requirements. In this regard, 71 cooperators have revised their capital expenditure limits since 1972; 37 others have changed these guidelines within the past decade; and the remaining 7 participants employing a system of limits are uncertain as to when their capital expenditure limits were last changed.

CHAPTER 2

Importance of Depreciation and Corporate Income Taxes to Capital Budgeting

In Chapter 1 we discussed the importance of capital budgeting and outlined a systematic approach for acquiring capital assets. The method described depends on obtaining accurate estimates of the cash outflows needed to acquire an asset and the inflows that are expected to result from its use. In all instances, we are concerned only with the after-tax cash flows. Consequently, it is necessary to understand those sections of the tax law which deal with the acquisition and disposition of assets, including investment tax credits, depreciation, and taxation of the ordinary income generated by the use of the assets. These are the topics of this chapter.

The reader is cautioned to follow changes in the law, including new IRS rulings, court decisions, and changes in the statutes. The material contained in this chapter is current to 1980 tax law but must be updated to reflect the ongoing stream of changes.

Depreciation[1]

Depreciation directly affects the after-tax cash flows, since it represents an accounting expense and is deductible for purposes of computing federal income taxes. Unlike most other expenses, however, depreciation does not necessitate any cash expenditure. Rather, *it is a systematic recognition of the cost of an asset so as to match expenses with revenues over the period of the asset's life.* Assets wear out, become obsolete, and so on. Depreciation recognizes this fact by applying an expense against revenues. While the depreciation expense is shown on the firm's income statement, the expense is also reflected on the balance sheet by charges to accumulated depreciation. The cost of the asset less accumulated depreciation gives the book value. Although the book value usually has little to do with the fair market value of the asset (or the productive value of the asset to the firm), it is important in asset disposition, since any differences between sale price and book value can lead to capital gains or losses and/or recapture of depreciation.

Computing depreciation for an asset requires three pieces of information: the asset's depreciable value, the asset's depreciable life, and the method of depreciation to be used. Each of these is discussed below.

The asset's depreciable value. The depreciable value represents the difference between the total cost to acquire the asset and its expected salvage value. The cost of the asset includes the purchase price and any other expenditures, such as shipping and installation, that are incurred. The salvage value is the amount expected to be realized upon disposal of the asset. Net salvage value rather than salvage value may be used. Net salvage value takes into consideration any costs of removal. Salvage value is based on an estimate, given the expected life, working conditions, maintenance policy, and the like.

The asset's depreciable life. An asset's depreciable life is the period of years during which the asset will be depreciated to its expected salvage value. There may be two different depreciable lives. The first is the depreciable life used for tax purposes. Generally, this is the shortest period permitted by law for the depreciation of the asset in question. The second is the depreciable life used to compute depreciation for the purpose of reporting earnings to shareholders. For the latter, the asset's *useful* (productive) *life* is generally used.[2] This is the period of time that the asset can reasonably be expected to operate in the manner and at the level of efficiency intended.

For computing tax liability, the depreciable life may be based on the owner's experience or on the Class Life Asset Depreciation Range (ADR) system provided by the IRS. This system permits the taxpayer to select a useful life within a designated range of years. It was designed to reduce conflict between taxpayers and the IRS over the concept of useful life of an asset. The ADR covers a very wide range of assets, and tables providing life ranges are available from the IRS.

Thus far in our discussion, we have described the selection of asset life only as it relates to federal income tax purposes. In general, *for tax purposes it is most beneficial to maximize depreciation in the early years of the asset's life*. This may be accomplished by selecting an accelerated depreciation method, as described below, and by choosing a depreciable life that is as short as allowable by the IRS. The rationale for using a short depreciable life and accelerated depreciation is to postpone payment of tax. This has the effect of increasing cash inflows in the earlier years of the asset's life and thus permits recovery of the cost of the asset as soon as possible. Early recovery of costs reduces risk and permits reinvestment of funds in other profitable projects.

For purposes of financial reporting, electing an accelerated method of depreciation and/or short asset life may not be desirable. *For financial reporting purposes it is important to reflect the costs inherent in the use and ownership of an asset as accurately as possible.* Suppose, for example, that an asset may be depreciated over four years for tax purposes but, given the maintenance program established by the firm, will probably last for seven years. For reporting to shareholders, creditors, and other interest parties, the seven-year life should be used. In addition to providing a more realistic picture, using the longer life and straight-line rather than accelerated depreciation will tend to result in smoother earnings patterns. A consistent earnings pattern is favored by shareholders and creditors. The two methods of depreciation accounting are reconciled on the firm's balance sheet and in the corporate income tax return.

One other factor needs to be considered in the selection of a depreciable life for tax purposes: *the amount of investment tax credit which may be taken on eligible assets is a function of the depreciable life selected for tax purposes*. The details of investment tax credit are discussed later in this chapter; for the present discussion it suffices to note that the amount of credit decreases as the depreciable life is reduced. Consequently, there is a trade-off between the postponement of taxes facilitated by using a short depreciable life and the potential for lost investment tax credits when a short depreciable life is used. Selecting the optimum depreciable life requires an analysis of the potential benefits of tax postponement versus the benefits of investment tax credits. The analysis will be discussed in the next chapter, where we examine cash flows.

The method of depreciation applicable to the asset. There are three primary methods of depreciation: straight-line, declining-balance, and sum-of-the-years'-digits. The latter two are termed accelerated methods. Another, less frequently used method is based on units of production. Tax law permits the use of straight-line for all types of depreciable assets but limits the use of accelerated depreciation. Twice-declining-balance (or double-declining-balance) may be used for new residential real estate and property other than real estate acquired *new* and having a life of three or more years. One-and-one-half-declining-balance may be applied to new real estate other than residential and property (other than real estate) acquired *used* and having a life of three or more years. One-and-one-quarter-declining-balance may be applied to used residential real estate with a life of 20 or more years. Sum-of-the-years'-digits is applicable to the same assets as double-declining-balance. The different methods are described and contrasted in the following section.

Methods of Depreciation: A Comparison

The simplest method of depreciation, *straight-line,* involves dividing the depreciable value by the number of years in the asset's depreciable life. The resulting depreciation is an amount that is constant over the asset's depreciable life. While this method is easy to use, it does not result in any tax advantages. However, it tends to smooth earnings, provided that expenses and revenues remain relatively constant during the period the asset is being depreciated.

Declining-balance depreciation is the most commonly used method of accelerated depreciation. It involves multiplying a constant decimal by a reducing base. The original base is the total cost of the asset (not the depreciable value). The original base is reduced each year by the cumulative depreciation taken to date. The decimals are obtained by multiplying the straight-line rate by 2, $1\frac{1}{2}$, or $1\frac{1}{4}$, depending on whether double-, one-and-one-half-, or one-and-one-quarter-declining-balance is being used. The depreciation process stops when the salvage value is reached. This may result in depreciating an asset *fully* in fewer years than the asset's depreciable life.

If an asset *does not* have a salvage value, it is necessary to switch from the declining-balance method being used to straight-line or sum-of-the-years'-digits. For double-declining-balance the switch is generally made about two-thirds of the way through the asset's life. The remaining amount to be depreciated (the book value) is divided by the number of years remaining in the asset's life to obtain the straight-line depreciation per year of remaining life. IRS permission is not required to make the change. If the class life system is used, the change may be made to either straight-line or sum-of-the-years'-digits from declining-balance, or to straight-line from sum-of-the-years'-digits. The method is demonstrated in the following example, using depreciation factors from Appendix A, "Comparative Depreciation Tables."

EXAMPLE 1

Declining-Balance Depreciation

An asset that cost $10,000 has no expected salvage value and an eight-year life. Compute the depreciation on the basis of double-declining-balance for each year, using Appendix A depreciation factors.

SOLUTION

The computations are facilitated by using a tabular format (see Table 2-1). As can be seen from that table, the switch to straight-line was

Table 2-1. Depreciation using the double-declining-balance method.

Year	*Percent Depreciation**	*Basis*	*Depreciation*	*Cumulative Depreciation*
1	.2500	$10,000	$2,500	$ 2,500
2	.1875	10,000	1,875	4,375
3	.1406	10,000	1,406	5,781
4	.1055	10,000	1,055	6,836
5	.0791	10,000	791	7,627
6	.0593 (NA)	10,000	791	8,418
7	.0445 (NA)	10,000	791	9,209
8	.0334 (NA)	10,000	791	10,000

* The percentages are obtained from Appendix A, as noted. The depreciation may also be obtained by multiplying a constant rate (.2500) by a decreasing base. The rate of .2500 is twice the straight-line rate for an eight-year life. The basis for year 1 is $10,000. For year 2 it would be $10,000 − $2,500 = $7,500. Multiplying .2500 by $7,500 will yield the same product as obtained by multiplying .1875 by $10,000.

made at the end of year 4. The cumulative depreciation at that time was \$6,836, leaving a total of \$3,164 to be depreciated, or \$791 per year to be depreciated each of the last four years. □

Sum-of-the-years'-digits (*SYD*) *depreciation* does not give as rapid an acceleration as double-declining-balance. The percentage depreciation factors comparable to those used in Example 1 are shown in Table 2-2. In addition, SYD depreciates *against the depreciable value,* whereas the declining-balance methods depreciate against the total cost of the asset.

Sum-of-the-years'-digits depreciation applies a changing rate to the depreciable value. Each year a fraction is multiplied by the depreciable value to obtain that year's depreciation. The numerator, which changes from year to year, represents the number of years remaining in the asset's useful life. The denominator is the sum of the digits representing the useful life. The denominator may be found using Equation (3).

$$S = N\left(\frac{N + 1}{2}\right) \qquad (3)$$

where S = sum-of-the-years'-digits
N = number of years in useful life

Thus, if an asset had a depreciable life of five years, the denominator of

Table 2-2. Comparison of double-declining-balance and sum-of-the-years'-digits depreciation.

	Percentage Depreciation Factors	
Year	*Double-Declining*	*SYD*
1	25.00%	22.22%
2	18.75	19.44
3	14.06	16.67
4	10.55	13.89
5	7.91	11.11
6	7.91	8.33
7	7.91	5.56
8	7.91	2.78
	100.00%	100.00%

the fraction would be $\frac{5(5+1)}{2} = 15$. The depreciation for each year would be as tabulated below.

Year	*SYD Depreciation*
1	5/15
2	4/15
3	3/15
4	2/15
5	1/15

These fractions correspond to the decimal equivalents provided in Appendix A.

Units-of-production depreciation is useful when the wearing of an asset is primarily a function of output as opposed to age. The total output of the asset in some measurable unit is first estimated. Then depreciation is taken each year on the basis of the fraction of the total output produced in that year. The method has the advantage of accurately reflecting costs against output, which should correspond to revenue.

Taxation

In this section we briefly review the basic corporate tax laws, with special emphasis on those laws which affect the acquistion and disposal of capital assets.[3]

ORDINARY INCOME[4]

The corporate taxable income is taxed at a five-tier rate structure as follows:

First $25,000 taxed at 17%
Next $25,000 taxed at 20%
Next $25,000 taxed at 30%
Next $25,000 taxed at 40%
Over $100,000 taxed at 46%

If the corporation has an operating loss, the loss may be carried back three years and forward seven, *or* carried forward seven years.[5] Thus, if a firm has had profits in the three-year period prior to the loss and if these profits are still available to apply losses against, then the firm may enjoy a tax refund that will at least partially make up for the loss. If the loss is carried forward, taxes will be reduced in future years.

Suppose, for example, that a company has made profits in each of the three years prior to 1980 and suffered a loss in 1980. The loss would be carried back and applied first against income in 1977. The tax liability for 1977 would be recomputed after subtracting the 1980 loss, and a refund would be claimed. Depending on the size of the 1980 loss compared to the 1977 income, all or part of the tax paid in 1977 would be refunded. Any loss in 1980 in excess of the 1977 income would be carried into 1978, and so on.

CAPITAL GAINS AND LOSSES

When a firm purchases and sells assets or securities that are not ordinarily bought and sold as a part of the firm's normal business, capital gains and losses may be incurred. The gain or loss on the sale of a capital asset[6] may be short- or long-term, depending on how long the asset was owned: short-term is less than a year, long-term a year or more. When considering the acquisition or disposal of plant and equipment, we are interested primarily in long-term gains and losses. Long-term capital gains are taxed at the rate applied to ordinary income or at 28 percent, *whichever is lower,*[7] whereas short-term gains are always taxed as a part of ordinary income. Land and depreciable property used in a business are not capital assets, but if they are sold or exchanged, they are in most instances treated as capital assets with respect to capital gains and losses and recapture of depreciation.

The process of taxation on capital gains is demonstrated in Example 2.

EXAMPLE 2
Tax on Capital Gains

A corporation with taxable income of $30,000 had a long-term capital gain of $40,000. Determine the corporation's tax liability.

SOLUTION

The ordinary income is taxed as follows:

$$
\begin{aligned}
\$25{,}000 \times .17 &= \$4{,}250 \\
\$\ 5{,}000 \times .20 &= \underline{\$1{,}000} \\
&\ \underline{\underline{\$5{,}250}}
\end{aligned}
$$

The first $20,000 of the long-term capital gain would be taxed at 20 percent (since that rate for ordinary income is less than 28 percent), while the next $20,000 would be taxed at 28 percent, since 28 percent is less than the 30 percent rate for ordinary income in excess of $50,000.

The capital-gains tax would therefore be as shown:

$$\begin{aligned} \$20{,}000 \times .20 &= \$4{,}000 \\ 20{,}000 \times .28 &= \underline{5{,}600} \\ & \underline{\underline{\$9{,}600}} \end{aligned}$$

The total tax is $5,250 + $9,600 = $14,850. □

RECAPTURE OF DEPRECIATION

When an asset is sold at a gain or at a price above its book value, recapture of depreciation is involved. When Section 1245 property (personal property) is sold above book value, the recapture of depreciation is taxed as ordinary income. The tax on real property (covered by Section 1250) depends on method of depreciation used, date of acquisition, and other variables. The reader is referred to a tax service, such as Prentice-Hall or Commerce Clearing House, for specific details.

EXAMPLE 3

Recapture of Depreciation and Capital Gain

Six years ago, a company acquired machinery for $200,000. The expected life and the salvage value were ten years and $20,000. The property is now six years old, having been depreciated using the sum-of-the-years'-digits method. Assuming the machinery can be sold for $220,000 and the corporation has a 46 percent marginal tax rate, determine the additional tax it will have to pay if the machinery is sold. Ignore any recapture of investment tax credit.

SOLUTION

The depreciation for the first six years (using Appendix A) is $147,276, giving a book value of $52,724. The recapture is the difference between purchase price and book value, or $147,276. (In this problem all the depreciation is recaptured, since the sale price exceeds the purchase price.) The capital gain is the sale price minus the purchase price, or $20,000. The recapture is taxed at 46 percent (the firm's marginal tax rate), while the long-term capital gain is taxed at 28 percent.

$147,276 × .46 =	$67,747
20,000 × .28 =	5,600
Total additional tax	$73,347

If the company sold the machine, the additional tax would be $73,347. □

CAPITAL LOSSES

For purposes of computing capital losses, assets are divided into two categories. The first category to be considered consists of Section 1231 assets. Section 1231 assets include the following primary types:

1. Real property used in the taxpayer's business and held for more than one year, but not regularly sold to customers as a part of the firm's usual business.
2. Depreciable property used in the taxpayer's business and held for more than one year, but not regularly sold to customers as a part of the firm's usual business.

When dealing with losses incurred on the sale of Section 1231 assets, all long-term capital gains and losses are first netted to determine the net gain or loss. If there was a net loss, it may be deducted directly from the firm's ordinary income.

Section 1231 is especially important to the timing of asset acquisition and disposal. Consider a situation where a firm could dispose of two assets. Disposing of the first will result in a $10,000 Section 1231 loss, while disposal of the second will produce a $10,000 long-term capital gain. If the two are sold in the same year, the gain and loss will just equal, so there will not be any tax effects. If, however, they are sold in different years, then—assuming no other similar transactions and a 46 percent marginal tax rate—taxes will be saved. The loss on the Section 1231 disposal will result in a .46 × $10,000 = $4,600 tax saving, while the sale of the second asset will result in a tax liability of .28 × $10,000 = $2,800. Thus, by timing the sale in two different years, net savings of $1,800 are realized.

Losses other than those covered by Section 1231 must be carried back or carried forward. These capital losses may not be deducted from ordinary income but rather must be applied against capital gains enjoyed in prior years or expected in the future. Such capital losses may be carried back three years and forward five years, in a manner similar to that used for losses on ordinary income.

INVESTMENT TAX CREDIT

When certain types of assets are acquired, the tax law permits deduction of up to 10 percent of their cost directly from the firm's tax liability. In general, the property must meet the following qualifications to permit the tax credit.

1. It must be depreciable.
2. It must have a life of three or more years.
3. It must be tangible personal property or other tangible property (except buildings and structural components) used in manufacturing, production, or extraction.
4. It must be placed in use for the production of income during the year in which the credit is taken. Property is considered to be placed in service either in the year depreciation is started or in the year the asset is available for service, whichever is earlier. The types of assets that are of primary interest for purposes of securing investment tax credit include machinery, equipment, vehicles, and property accessories, such as automobiles, air conditioners, grocery counters, and so on.

Here are some further facts:

Included in the Revenue Act of 1978 is provision extending the 10 percent investment tax credit (ITC) to expenditures incurred to rehabilitate existing nonresidential structures. These provisions are designed to give taxpayers an incentive to make use of existing buildings rather than undertake new construction. Eligible for the credit are depreciable rehabilitation costs incurred on qualifying structures, which include factories, warehouses, hotels, and retail and wholesale stores. Some important considerations:

- The building must be at least 20 years old, although it may have been purchased by the taxpayer immediately prior to renovation, for that express purpose. (Note that a building can be rehabilitated only once every 20 years under this provision).
- The use of the building *after* rehabilitation determines its eligibility for the credit (e.g., a house rehabilitated for use in a trade or business would be nonresidential and therefore would qualify for the credit).
- The expenditures which qualify for the credit include the cost of *both* removal *and* replacement for items such as plumbing, wiring, heating,

flooring, and interior partitions. (Note that routine repairs and maintenance, such as painting, would not qualify, since such expenditures are not capitalized).

- The costs attributable to expanding an existing building are not eligible for the credit, and no part of the cost of a restoration is eligible if the taxpayer does not retain at least 75 percent of the structure's exterior walls as exterior walls.
- The costs of acquiring a building or any interest therein do not qualify for the credit. However, it would appear that qualifying improvements to a leased building would be eligible for the credit.
- The expenditure must have a useful life of at least five years (rather than three years) to qualify for any credit.
- The cost of rehabilitating a certified historic structure will qualify only if it is an approved restoration, as described in the Internal Revenue Code.

Expenditures incurred after October 31, 1978, may be eligible for the credit, but determining eligibility may require a careful review of the Congressional Committee Reports and/or the Internal Revenue Service Regulations.[8]

The amount of credit which may be taken depends on the life of the asset selected for tax accounting purposes, as delineated below:

1. Property with a depreciable life of less than three years does not qualify.
2. Property with a depreciable life of three but less than five years qualifies for one-third of the credit.
3. Property with a depreciable life of five but less than seven years qualifies for two-thirds of the credit.
4. Property with a depreciable life of more than seven years qualifies for the total allowable credit.

If property is disposed of before the end of its depreciable life, the investment tax credit must be recomputed on the basis of the actual life (rather than the original estimate) and the excess credit recaptured.

For computing investment tax credits, the *total price minus any allowance for trade-in* is used. However, for used property, no more than $100,000 of the cost of the qualifying property may be considered. Further, the amount of investment tax credit taken in any one year is limited to the firm's tax liability, or $25,000 plus a percentage of the firm's total tax liability (as tabulated below), whichever is less.

Year	*ITC is limited to the firm's tax liability OR*
1978	\$25,000 + 60% of the firm's tax liability, whichever is less
1979	\$25,000 + 70% of the firm's tax liability, whichever is less
1980	\$25,000 + 80% of the firm's tax liability, whichever is less
1981	\$25,000 + 90% of the firm's tax liability, whichever is less

Unused credits may be carried back three years and forward seven years. The two restrictions (trade-in and dollar limit) are very important to both the purchase and the leasing decision.

Since the investment tax credit is applied to purchases net of trade-in value, the question of trading in an asset versus selling it outright deserves some consideration. However, there are other tax implications of the two options, beyond the question of the amount of investment tax credit received. When an asset is sold, if the sale price differs from book value, then a capital gain and/or recapture of depreciation or a capital loss may be involved, as described earlier in this section. When an asset is traded in, gains and losses are not recognized for tax purposes. Rather, the book value of the old asset (as computed for tax purposes) is added to the payment for the new asset (termed boot). The sum of these is the book value for the new asset and is the basis for depreciation for tax purposes.

EXAMPLE 4

Sale versus Trade-in, and Their Tax Ramifications

A corporation owns a machine that has a book value of \$25,000 and was originally purchased for \$100,000. The company is considering acquisition of a replacement, which will cost \$150,000 if purchased without trade-in and will have a ten-year life. A \$40,000 trade-in for the old machine would be granted by the vendor. Management believes that it could sell the existing machine for \$35,000. The company has an expected tax liability of \$80,000. Determine the tax effects if the old machine is sold outright and if it is traded in.

SOLUTION

Consider the trade-in first: The investment tax credit is based on \$110,000 at 10 percent, or \$11,000. Since a \$110,000 boot is paid and the book value of the old asset is \$25,000, the depreciable value for the new machine is \$135,000 minus any expected salvage value.

Consider the outright sale next: The investment tax credit is based on the entire \$150,000 at 10 percent, or \$15,000. A \$10,000 recapture of depreciation would result from the sale of the old machine. The firm's \$80,000 tax liability indicates a 46 percent marginal tax rate, so the tax on the recapture would be \$10,000 × .46 = \$4,600. The net effect would be a tax reduction of \$15,000 − \$4,600 = \$10,400. The basis for depreciation of the new machine would be \$150,000 minus any expected salvage value.

Comparison: In terms of immediate tax benefit, the trade-in is preferable by \$600 (\$11,000 − \$10,400). However, the \$600 incremental benefit must be weighed against the additional \$15,000 in depreciable value if the old machine is sold. Over the useful life of the new machine, the \$15,000 added depreciation will result in tax savings of \$6,900 (\$15,000 × .46). In almost all instances, the present value of the \$6,900 to be received over the ten-year life would exceed \$600. Therefore, the sale is preferable. □

Earlier in this chapter we indicated that investment tax credit is a function of the depreciable life selected for tax purposes. While a short depreciable life speeds the recovery of an asset's cost, investment tax credit may be reduced. A trade-off is involved. The outcome is demonstrated in Example 5.

EXAMPLE 5

Depreciable Life and Investment Tax Credit

A company plans to purchase an asset that costs \$10,000. It may be depreciated over a minimum five-year period for tax purposes, but management also wants to consider a seven-year depreciable life so as to enjoy the full investment tax credit benefits. Compare the two alternatives, assuming the corporation has a 46 percent marginal tax rate.

SOLUTION

If a five-year life is chosen, only two-thirds of the investment tax credit, or \$667, will be received. Selecting a seven-year life provides an additional \$333 credit. In either event the total tax benefit resulting from depreciation will be \$4,600 (\$10,000 × .46). The difference is that the \$4,600 will be recovered over five years in the first case and over seven years in the second. The relative advantage of receiving the \$4,600 tax benefit more rapidly depends on the cost of money to the company and the method of depreciation used. We do not have the tools of discounted cash flow at this time to resolve the question, but will address it later after the method of discounted cash flow has been introduced. □

In addition to the investment tax credit, tax credits are also available for certain classes of energy-related investments. Normally, these are in addition to investment tax credit. Since these credits, like other special classes of tax credits such as targeted-jobs credits, do not affect all businesses, we do not describe them here. Nonetheless, they may affect acquisition decisions and warrant consulting a tax guide or discussing the matter with a tax attorney or CPA.

The reader should note that Examples 3, 4, and 5 are applications of sensitivity analysis. In Example 3 we determined the sensitivity of tax liability to the timing of disposal of a Section 1231 asset; in Example 4 we determined the sensitivity of tax liability to a sale versus a trade-in; and in Example 5 we determined the sensitivity of tax liability to the choice of time for depreciation of an asset.

NOTES

1. At the time of writing, several major revisions to the depreciation laws had been approved by the Senate Finance Committee. The most important changes relate to depreciation of most assets other than real property. Such assets would be depreciated over two, four, seven, or ten years, depending on the category into which they fall. The net result would be depreciation about 40 percent faster than under the current Asset Depreciation Range (ADR) system.
2. The determination of an asset's useful or productive life is examined again in Chapter 12 under the heading of capital abandonment. Basically, the productive life is the period during which the present value of the cash inflows expected to be derived from the asset's use (that is, its productive value) exceeds the asset's abandonment value. Obviously, when an asset is acquired, its productive value exceeds its abandonment value, or it would not be acquired. However, during the life of the asset, its productive value may change appreciably due to changes in costs and/or revenues attributable to its use. Thus an asset may be abandoned or may be kept for a longer period than originally estimated.
3. The reader should consult a current tax guide such as Prentice-Hall or Commerce Clearing House for any recent changes in the tax laws.
4. As a part of proposed tax changes, corporate tax rates may be modified as follows for 1981:

First $25,000 taxed at 15%
Next $25,000 taxed at 20%
Next $50,000 taxed at 30%
Next $50,000 taxed at 40%
Over $150,000 taxed at 45%

For 1982 and later the rates could be further changed:

First $25,000 taxed at 15%
Next $25,000 taxed at 20%
Next $25,000 taxed at 25%
Next $25,000 taxed at 30%
Next $50,000 taxed at 35%
Next $50,000 taxed at 40%
Over $200,000 taxed at 44%

5. An election not to carry losses back may be made for tax years ending after 1975. This would be advantageous if the taxpayer had investment credit carry-overs that would be lost as a result of carrying back the operating loss and if he had good prospects of income in future years against which the loss could be offset.
6. For purposes of federal taxation, the IRS has defined capital assets as being any property except the following: (1) inventories; (2) property held primarily for sale to customers in the ordinary course of business; (3) depreciable property used in a trade or business; (4) real property used in a trade or business; (5) short-term non-interest-bearing government obligations issued at a discount basis; (b) copyrights, literary, musical, or artistic compositions, letters, or similar property; and (7) accounts and notes receivable received in the ordinary course of business for services rendered or from the sale of property.
7. Proposed corporate capital gain rates would be reduced for exchanges after August 20, 1980, from 28 percent to 20 percent or the rate applied to ordinary income, whichever is lower.
8. From *The Week in Review,* February 23, 1979, Deloitte, Haskins and Sells.

CHAPTER 3

Computing Cash Flows to Evaluate Capital Investment Decisions

The decision criterion for investment which we have recommended will maximize the net present value of the business as reflected by the market value of the common stock. This is synonymous with maximizing the net present value of the portfolio of assets which comprise the firm. In order to proceed with this task it is necessary to compare the net *after-tax* cash outflows resulting from the acquisition of an asset with the *after-tax* cash inflows resulting from its use and ultimate disposal. The materials in Chapter 2 dealing with depreciation and taxation will be applied in this chapter to convert cost and revenue estimates into after-tax cash flows.

As noted in Chapter 1, it is necessary to develop management policies for the collection of information within the firm on capital investments that are needed or desirable in various areas of the firm. In most firms, the ideas for major projects and expansion come from top management, whereas equipment replacement decisions and the like are generated at lower levels. In many instances the originators may not have access to all the cost figures or be able to estimate accurately the *incremental revenues* that are likely to result over the project's life. Hence it is necessary to employ industrial and manufacturing engineers, in conjunction with financial analysts, to develop accurate cash flow estimates. Further, since estimates are almost never completely accurate, it is important to have some probability distribution included with the estimate. At a minimum, "most likely," "worst case," and "best case" estimates should be made to provide management with a measure of the risk associated with the proposal. We will examine procedures useful in analyzing risk in Chapter 8.

The methods for analyzing risk discussed in Chapter 8 provide a framework for comparing projects that have inherently different levels of risk. In essence, the methods described permit the use of common denominators so that projects of varying risk can all be reduced to the same base line for comparison. Use of the procedures depends, of course, on having both the best available estimates for cash flows and the best estimates of the degree of risk or error associated with those cash flows. Even the most sophisticated of mathematical evaluation techniques applied to poor estimates will yield poor-quality results. Accurate estimates of cash flows are essential to a quality capital investment program.

Capital budgeting is a process that results in expenditures of time and money. Since both resources are limited in any organization, their judicious allocation is important. If an economic trade-off is necessary, we recommend spending *more* time and money on obtaining high-quality estimates and *less* on evaluating the estimates. In most instances the basic procedures outlined in Chapter 7 will suffice. Naturally, the larger the projects, the more important it is to obtain the best possible cash flow estimates and to use the best available analytical techniques.

Normally, cash flows can be divided into two parts: the outflows needed to acquire the asset and the inflows resulting from its operation. In this chapter we examine how cost and revenue estimates are converted into cash flows. Later in the book we will examine these cash flows in conjunction with the cost of funds to the firm to determine the desirability of making an investment.

Cash Outflows

When an asset is being evaluated for acquisition, it is necessary to consider all the costs, as well as any related benefits such as tax credits and funds realized from disposal of assets if the new item is a replacement. The various costs and possible benefits are described below.

First we must consider the cost of acquisition. For most assets, the cost consists of two parts: the purchase price and any associated costs of acquiring the asset, such as costs for transportation, installation, and the like. While some of these costs are not always capitalized, *for purposes of financial analysis* they are always included. The cost of *net* additional working capital must also be added, since additions to working-capital accounts (such as inventory and receivables) require the use of funds. It should be noted that working capital is *not* capitalized and will be recovered at the termination of the use of the asset. Further, if a new asset represents a replacement, the sale of the existing asset may result in payment of tax. If this is the case, we must add this tax to obtain the total cash outflow.

In some instances projects are acquired over a period of time and interest payments and/or property taxes may be incurred. These costs are also included in computing the total acquisition cost.

Next we consider any funds that may be realized at the time an asset is acquired. These may come from several sources, such as the sale of existing assets, investment tax credits, tax reductions if an existing asset is sold below book value, and the tax reduction resulting from interest and/or property taxes paid during construction. We will now proceed with a series of examples to demonstrate how the cash outflows are determined.

EXAMPLE 1
Cost of Acquisition

A corporation owns a machine that orginally cost $25,000 and has been depreciated to a book value of $8,000. A replacement machine costs $40,000 and has an expected ten-year life. If the new machine is purchased, the old machine would be *sold* for $11,000. The new machine requires less labor than the old machine and operates more rapidly. This will result in the following changes to working-capital accounts:

Cash	No change
Receivables	Increase $3,000
Inventories	Increase $6,000
Payables	Increase $2,000
Accrued wages	Decrease $500

The corporation has a 46 percent marginal tax rate. Determine the after-tax cash outflow necessary to acquire the new machine.

SOLUTION

The old machine will be sold for $11,000, resulting in $3,000 recapture of depreciation, since the selling price exceeds the asset's book value of $8,000 by $3,000. This is subject to tax as ordinary income at a 46 percent rate ($3,000 × .46 = $1,380 tax). Thus the old machine will net $11,000 − $1,380 = $9,620.

Working capital = current assets − current liabilities. Current assets will increase by $9,000 while current liabilities will increase by only $1,500. The net increase in working capital will be $7,500.

The full investment tax credit of 10 percent will be enjoyed on the new asset, since it has a life longer than seven years and the old machine is being sold. The costs and inflows are tabulated below.

Cost of new machine	$40,000
Increase in working capital	+7,500
Sale of old machine	−9,620
Investment tax credit	−4,000
Net after-tax cash outflow	$33,880

It will cost the corporation $33,880 to acquire the new machine and put it into service. □

As noted in Chapter 2, trade-ins are treated differently for tax purposes than outright sales of existing assets. With a trade-in, recapture of depreciation and capital gains and losses are not recognized at the time the new asset is acquired. Further, investment tax credit is allowed only on the net cost of the asset (purchase price less trade-in). If an asset is traded in, the depreciable value of the new asset for tax purposes is the sum of the cash paid (called boot) plus the book value of the asset traded in.

EXAMPLE 2

Acquisition with Trade-in

Consider Example 1, but assume that the existing machine is traded in for $11,000.

SOLUTION

The trade-in allowance is subtracted directly from the cost: $40,000 − $11,000 = $29,000. Investment tax credit is computed using the

$29,000 figure, which yields $2,900. Recapture of depreciation is not realized. Working capital is the same as in Example 1. The costs and inflows are tabulated below.

Cost of new machine	$40,000
Increase in working capital	+7,500
Trade-in allowance	−11,000
Investment tax credit	−2,900
Net after-tax cash outflow	$33,600

The difference in the results between Examples 1 and 2 is very small, but other factors need to be considered. □

In most instances the trade-in allowance is significantly higher than the amount that a firm could realize on the sale of a machine. The reason is that the vendor has ready access to customers interested in buying used or rebuilt machinery. However, the depreciation will be lower for the new machine if the old machine is traded in for an amount in excess of its book value. The basis for depreciating the new machine is the book value of the old machine *plus* the boot, minus the expected salvage value of the new machine. Example 3 demonstrates both of the factors just discussed, using the same method as outlined in Chapter 2.

EXAMPLE 3
Acquisition with Trade-in

Consider Example 1 with a trade-in of $15,000. Determine the cash outflow necessary for the acquisition of the new machine and the depreciation of the new machine, using straight-line depreciation with a ten-year life and $10,000 expected salvage value.

SOLUTION

The cash outflows are determined as shown in Example 2. The cost is $40,000 − $15,000 = $25,000. Investment tax credit is $2,500. The costs and inflows are tabulated below.

Cost of new machine	$40,000
Increase in working capital	+7,500
Trade-in allowance	−15,000
Investment tax credit	−2,500
Net after-tax cash outflow	$30,000

The depreciation on the new machine, based on the *sale* (not trade-in) of the old machine, would be determined as follows: \$40,000 (cost) − \$10,000 (salvage value of new machine) = \$30,000 (depreciable value of new machine). Annual depreciation therefore is \$30,000 ÷ 10 = \$3,000.

The depreciation on the new machine, based on the *trade-in* of \$15,000, would be determined as follows: \$25,000 (boot) + \$8,000 (book value of old machine) − \$10,000 (salvage value of new machine) = \$23,000 (depreciable value). Annual depreciation is \$23,000 ÷ 10 = \$2,300.

The IRS allows only \$2,300 in annual depreciation in the trade-in case since the firm had a "gain" on the trade-in of the old machine of \$7,000 (\$15,000 trade-in value minus \$8,000 book value). This \$7,000 gain is "taxed" over the ten-year life of the new asset, since the annual depreciation on the trade-in is \$700 (\$3,000 − \$2,300) less than the annual depreciation if the old machine were sold. □

EXAMPLE 4

Disposition of an Asset with Recapture and Capital Gain

A corporation is considering disposing of an airplane. It was originally acquired for \$400,000, now has a book value of \$100,000, and can be sold for \$600,000. Determine the amount of funds the corporation will realize if it disposes of the airplane. Assume a 46 percent marginal tax rate with 28 percent for capital gains.

SOLUTION

There will be a \$300,000 recapture of depreciation and a \$200,000 long-term capital gain. They are taxed as follows:

\$300,000 × .46 =	\$138,000
200,000 × .28 =	56,000
Total tax	\$194,000

The net amount that will be realized on the sale is \$600,000 − \$194,000 = \$406,000. □

In many instances the timing of the cash flows will differ by months or even years. In the case of construction of reactor-heated electricity-generating facilities, the process may extend from eight to twelve years. Construction of large manufacturing plants may also take three to five years or more from inception and engineering studies to start-up of production. The timing of each cash flow, as well as the tax ramifications of each, is important. The next example demonstrates an interesting aspect of timing with respect to disposal of Section 1231 assets.

EXAMPLE 5

Disposal of Section 1231 Assets

A corporation in the 46 percent marginal tax bracket is considering the purchase of a new machine priced at $50,000. It has a ten-year life and zero expected salvage value. Because of changes in the domestic market, the old machine being replaced has a market value of only $6,000, although it has a book value of $20,000. The old machine could be traded in for $12,000 credit against the new machine. Determine the out-of-pocket cost to acquire the machine using a trade-in and an outright sale of the old machine. For each case also determine the annual depreciation on the new machine. Assume that the corporation does not have any other capital gains or losses and working capital will not be affected, and that straight-line depreciation will be used.

SOLUTION

Consider the outright sale first. A Section 1231 capital loss of $14,000 will be incurred, providing tax savings of $14,000 × .46 = $6,440. The cost of the new machine is determined below:

Price of new machine	$50,000
Investment tax credit	−5,000
Sale of old machine	−6,000
Tax savings on sale of old machine	−6,440
Net after-tax cash outflow	$32,560

The depreciation for the new machine will be $50,000 ÷ 10 = $5,000 per year.

Next consider the trade-in. A capital loss is not recognized, and the investment tax credit is reduced to $3,800.

Price of new machine	$50,000
Trade-in on old machine	−12,000
Investment tax credit	−3,800
Net after-tax cash outflow	$34,200

The depreciation is based on the sum of the book value of the old machine ($20,000) plus the boot ($38,000), or $58,000. Annual depreciation is $58,000 ÷ 10 = $5,800. □

In this section we have examined the cash outflows needed to acquire assets. The following section deals with the determination of the cash flows expected to be realized over the useful life of the asset. We will note how accelerated depreciation affects the timing of the cash flows and why it may be useful to employ accelerated depreciation for tax purposes.

Cash Inflows

In order to evaluate the value of a proposed acquisition it is necessary to compare cash outflows and inflows. In this section we determine the change in cash inflows resulting from asset operation. We also note the impact on the firm's income statement.

EXAMPLE 6

Cash Flow from Asset Operation

A corporation in the 46 percent marginal tax bracket is considering the purchase of a machine that costs $50,000 and has a ten-year life and a salvage value of $10,000. The machine will permit production of a new product with anticipated annual sales of $15,000. Concurrently, operating expenses will increase by $7,000. Determine the impact of the machine on the firm's income statement, using straight-line depreciation, and the cash flows over the asset's life.

SOLUTION

As shown in Table 3-1, the cash flow will be $6,160 for years 1 through 9, with an additional $10,000 salvage in year 10, for a total of $71,600. The total earnings after taxes are $21,600. □

EXAMPLE 7

Cash Inflows from Asset Operation

Consider Example 6, but use double-declining-balance depreciation.

Table 3-1. Changes to income statement and cash flows.

	Change to Income Statement	*Change to Cash Flows*
Revenues	$15,000	$15,000
Operating expenses	− 7,000	− 7,000
Depreciation	− 4,000	
Earnings before taxes	$ 4,000	
Tax	− 1,840	− 1,840
Earnings after taxes	$ 2,160	
Increased cash flow		$ 6,160

SOLUTION

First determine the depreciation for each year. Employ the depreciation factors from Appendix A. (Note that the depreciation is terminated when the salvage value of $10,000 is reached.) The result is shown in Table 3-2.

With the depreciation calculated, we proceed to determine the earnings after taxes and the cash flows in tabular form (see Table 3-3). The totals for earnings after taxes and cash flow over the asset's life are the same as when straight-line depreciation was used. However, note the significant increase in the cash inflow over years 1 through 4 of the asset's life. □

Table 3-2. Depreciation using double-declining balance.

Year	*Basis*	*Depreciation Factor**	*Depreciation*	*Cumulative Depreciation*
1	$50,000	.2000	$10,000	$10,000
2	50,000	.1600	8,000	18,000
3	50,000	.1280	6,400	24,400
4	50,000	.1024	5,120	29,520
5	50,000	.0819	4,095	33,615
6	50,000	.0656	3,280	36,895
7	50,000	.0524	2,620	39,515
8	50,000	.0419	485	40,000
9	50,000	.0336	0	40,000
10	50,000	.0268	0	40,000

* From Appendix A.

Table 3-3. Annual earnings and cash flows using double-declining-balance depreciation.

Year	Revenues	Costs	Depre-ciation	EBT	Tax	EAT	Cash Flow
1	$15,000	$7,000	$10,000	($2,000)	($ 920.00)	($ 1,080.00)	$ 8,920.00
2	15,000	7,000	8,000	0	0	0	8,000.00
3	15,000	7,000	6,400	1,600	736.00	864.00	7,264.00
4	15,000	7,000	5,120	2,880	1,324.80	1,555.20	6,675.20
5	15,000	7,000	4,095	3,905	1,796.30	2,108.70	6,203.70
6	15,000	7,000	3,280	4,720	2,171.20	2,548.80	5,828.80
7	15,000	7,000	2,620	5,380	2,474.80	2,905.20	5,525.20
8	15,000	7,000	485	7,515	3,456.90	4,058.10	4,543.10
9	15,000	7,000	0	8,000	3,680.00	4,320.00	4,320.00
10	15,000	7,000	0	8,000	3,680.00	4,320.00	4,320.00
		Totals:	$40,000			$21,600.00	$61,600.00

EXAMPLE 8

Cash Flow from Asset Operation

Consider the trade-in described in Example 3. Compute the change to earnings after taxes and cash flows if the machine in Example 3 will generate revenues of $15,000 with concurrent operating costs of $8,000.

SOLUTION

Consider first the situation with a sale rather than a trade-in. The annual depreciation is $3,000. Table 3-4 summarizes the effects on the firm's earnings and cash flow. Next consider the trade-in. Annual de-

Table 3-4. Changes to income statement and cash flows with sale.

	Change to Income Statement	*Change to Cash Flow*
Revenue	$15,000	$15,000
Operating expense	− 8,000	− 8,000
Depreciation	− 3,000	
Earnings before taxes	4,000	
Tax	− 1,840	− 1,840
Earnings after taxes	$ 2,160	
Increased cash flow		$ 5,160

preciation in this case was $2,300. The changes to earnings and cash flow are shown in Table 3-5. The cash flow under the trade-in is reduced by $5,160 − $4,838 = $322 for each year of the ten-year life, in favor of the outright sale of the old machine. However, comparison of Examples 2 and 3 indicates that there is a saving at the time of acquisition of $33,880 − $30,000 = $3,880 when the old machine is traded in rather than sold. The $3,880 saving at the present time is greater than the increase in cash flow of $3,220 over ten years for the outright sale. If we considered the time value of money, the immediate benefit of the trade-in is even more attractive than the prospect of having to wait ten years to gain the increased cash flows if the asset were sold. The trade-in obviously is more attractive than the sale. □

While the situation in Example 8 favored the trade-in, this may not always be the case. Recall that in Example 4 from Chapter 2 the trade-in resulted in an immediate tax benefit of $600, while an additional $15,000 in depreciable value would result from the sale of the old machine. The $15,000 equated to a $6,900 tax saving, since the firm was in the 46 percent marginal tax bracket. Thus, unless the cost of money was prohibitively high, the sale would be favored. The relative cash flows are shown in Example 9.

EXAMPLE 9

Trade-in Versus Sale of Old Asset

On the basis of the information provided in Chapter 2, Example 4, determine the relative cash flows attributable to trade-in versus sale of

Table 3-5. Changes to income statement and cash flows with trade-in.

	Change to Income Statement	*Change to Cash Flow*
Revenue	$15,000	$15,000
Operating expense	− 8,000	− 8,000
Depreciation	− 2,300	
Earnings before taxes	4,700	
Tax	− 2,162	− 2,162
Earnings after taxes	$ 2,538	
Increased cash flow		$ 4,838

the existing asset, using straight-line and double-declining-balance depreciation.

SOLUTION

Consider straight-line first. Since the asset life is ten years, the tax benefit will be spread equally over ten years, or $690 per year. The relative cash flows are shown below.

Time	*Trade-in*	*Sale*
Present	+ $600	—
Years 1–10	—	+ $690

Next consider double-declining-balance. The tax benefits will be spread over the ten-year life. Using the factors from Appendix A and a switch to straight-line after the fifth year, we have the cash flow sequence shown in Table 3-6.

A comparison of the different options shows that using the accelerated depreciation distributes the tax benefits into the early years of the asset's life. Thus, in terms of cash flow, it is much more favorable than straight-line and also makes the sale a more viable alternative. □

In Chapter 2 we discussed the potential merits of selecting a short depreciable life for tax purposes and noted that such a selection might reduce investment tax credits. In Example 10 we compare the cash flow sequences developed in Chapter 2, Example 5, wherein an asset that costs $10,000 is being considered for depreciation over five- and seven-year lives. We note that depreciation over a five-year life will result in the loss of $333 of investment tax credits.

Table 3-6. Relative cash flows, using double-declining-balance depreciation.

Time	*Trade-in*	*Sale*
Present	+$600	—
Year 1	—	$1,380.00
Year 2	—	1,104.00
Year 3	—	883.20
Year 4	—	706.56
Year 5	—	565.11
Years 6–10	—	452.23

Table 3-7. Relative tax benefits of five- versus seven-year life, using straight-line depreciation.

Time	*Five-Year Life*	*Seven-Year Life*	*Difference (column 2 − column 3)*
Present	—	$333	−$333
Year 1	$920	657	+ 263
2	920	657	+ 263
3	920	657	+ 263
4	920	657	+ 263
5	920	657	+ 263
6	0	657	− 657
7	0	657	− 657

EXAMPLE 10

Alternative Depreciable Lives

An asset that costs $10,000 and is subject to investment tax credit may be depreciated over a five- or seven-year life for tax purposes. Assuming a 46 percent marginal tax rate, determine the relative tax benefits of each life for straight-line and double-declining-balance depreciation.

SOLUTION

Consider straight-line first. The relative tax benefits are shown in Table 3-7. Next consider double-declining-balance. The relative tax benefits are summarized in Table 3-8.

Table 3-8. Relative tax benefits of five- versus seven-year life, using double-declining-balance depreciation.

Time	*Five-Year Life*	*Seven-Year Life*	*Difference (column 2 − column 3)*
Present	—	$ 333	−$333
Year 1	$1,840	1,314	526
2	$1,104	939	165
3	662	671	− 9
4	497	479	18
5	497	399	98
6	0	399	− 399
7	0	399	− 399

As can be seen from the tables, the cash flow sequence using double-declining-balance is much more favorable to the five-year life than when straight-line is used. The question of which life is preferable still necessitates a discounted cash flow analysis, the topic of Chapter 6. In Chapter 6 we will revisit this problem and show that the choice of depreciable life depends on the firm's cost of capital—the topic of the next chapter. □

Once the cash flows for asset acquisition and use have been obtained, we can analyze them in order to determine the acceptability of proposals and then to rank those proposals. We need a basic benchmark for acceptance, which is the company's cost of capital. In the next chapter we will discuss the various sources of financing and indicate how to determine the cost of each source as well as the composite cost of capital. This composite cost, termed the firm's cost of capital, will be applied throughout subsequent chapters of the book.

CHAPTER 4

Sources of Financing and the Cost of Capital

The decisions to acquire assets and to secure financing are not independent; funds must be available to pay for the acquisitions, or financing arrangements must be established. In this chapter we examine the sources of funding, the question of optimum use of financial leverage, the timing of expenditures to correlate with the availability of funds, and the firm's cost of capital. The goal will be to determine the firm's cost of capital, which will be used as a benchmark for the acceptance of proposed projects.

Market Value Versus Book Value

For the ongoing business, the primary sources of funding are the earnings retained from profits and the funds generated through depreciation. Various types of debt are also used. For most firms, issues of new common stock are infrequent and the use of preferred stock is practically nonexistent except for regulated utilities.

In order to discuss the sources of financing we need to first examine the balance sheet as it reflects, in a historical setting, the current financial mix of the firm. We will then contrast balance sheet values with market values.

The right-hand side of the balance sheet is a presentation of the firm's debt and equity portfolios in a historical sense. The book value of equity seldom is related directly to the market value, and the same holds true for *some* types of debt. This being the situation, one might ask why we examine the balance sheet at all. The answer is that the balance sheet does reflect accurately *some* debt obligations, and using other information from it, we may determine the market values of the remaining components of debt and of the equity.

Consider the section of the balance sheet shown in Figure 4-1. The current-liabilities section accurately indicates the amounts owed. Further, while current liabilities do turn over, they often form a *permanent* part of the firm's financing package. When one is paid, another is generated. Also, as the firm expands, it is usual for the current liabilities to expand proportionately.

The amounts shown for long-term debt indicate the dollar amount of the obligation at the time of maturity. The notes payable listed probably have a market value close to the $3 million shown *because* their maturity is near at hand. However, the bonds mature in some 20 years. If current interest rates are significantly different from the 7 percent listed, the market price of the bonds will differ from the book value. For example, if the current interest rate for newly issued comparable

Figure 4-1. Sample balance sheet.

	(in thousands)	*(in percent)*
Accounts payable	$ 4,000	9.88
Accrued taxes	1,000	2.47
Accrued wages	500	1.23
Current liabilities	$ 5,500	13.58
Notes payable (2 years)	$ 3,000	7.41
Bonds (7% due 2000)	8,000	19.75
Long-term debt	$11,000	27.16
Total liabilities	$16,500	40.74
Common stock ($1 par 2,000,000 shares outstanding)	$ 2,000	
Paid-in capital	8,000	
Retained earnings	14,000	
Owners' Equity	$24,000	59.26
Total liabilities and owners' equity	$40,500	100.00

quality bonds is 10 percent, the outstanding bonds might be selling for $800. This means that the actual outstanding bond debt is only 80 percent of that shown on the books, or $6,400,000.[1]

The values shown in the common-stock and paid-in-capital accounts indicate how much the firm realized when the stock was originally sold. Retained earnings tells us how much the firm has retained out of all its after-tax profits since its start.[2] *The true value of the equity is the market price, which represents the collective judgment of all the participants in the marketplace.* The book value of the common stock has little bearing on the market value, which reflects primarily current and expected earnings and dividends. The book value in this example is $12 per share ($24 million ÷ 2 million shares outstanding). Suppose the market value of the common stock is $20. Then the *market-valued* liability and owners' equity would be as shown in Figure 4-2. The market value of the common stock captures *all* the owners' equity accounts.

Note how the total amount of financing has changed. The book value was $40,500,000, whereas the market value is $54,900,000. The market value indicates the true value of the business. Note also how the debt-to-equity ratios have changed. Based on book values, the ratio is $16,500,000:$24,000,000, or .69:1. That is, for every dollar of equity, the *balance sheet* showed 69¢ of debt. The situation is dramatically

Figure 4-2. Balance sheet adjusted to reflect market values.

	(in thousands)	*(in percent)*
Accounts payable	$ 4,000	7.29
Accrued taxes	1,000	1.82
Accrued wages	500	.91
Current liabilities	$ 5,500	10.02
Notes payable (2 years)	$ 3,000	5.46
Bonds	6,400	11.66
Long-term debt	$ 9,400	17.12
Total liabilities	$14,900	27.14
Common stock (2,000,000 shares at $20/share)	$40,000	72.86
Total liabilities and owners' equity	$54,900	100.00

altered when market values are used: $14,900,000:$40,000,000, or .37:1. The *market* indicates only 37¢ of debt for each dollar of equity.

Thus far in this chapter we have established that the true financing picture of the firm is shown by the *market values,* and that the debt-to-equity ratios are provided by *market* and *not* by book values. One further observation needs to be made. The market has valued this firm's assets as being worth $54,900,000, not the $40,500,000 which would be shown on the balance sheet. The market says that the productive value of the assets is some $14,400,000 greater than the book value. This implies that the book values shown for *some* of the assets on the balance sheet are not consistent with their market valuations.

Internally and Externally Generated Funds

The financing of a company from *external* sources such as the issuance of new debt and equity tends to be lumpy in nature. Due to the prohibitively high costs of issuing securities, it is necessary to either issue stock or borrow—but almost never both at the same time. When stock is sold, enough is issued to support another increment of debt at a later date. As a consequence, the firm's debt-to-equity ratio will vary over time. Funds generated *internally* tend to flow in relatively constantly throughout the year, with exceptions, of course, for seasonal fluctuations in business and periodic issuance of cash dividends. The funds generated through after-tax profits and depreciation cash throwoffs and retained in the firm may be invested judiciously. If this takes place and is manifested by increases in earnings and perhaps dividends at a rate greater than that anticipated by the market, then the market price of the stock is likely to increase. The increase in market price means that the equity base has increased and may permit further borrowing without adversely changing the financial risk posture of the firm. As a consequence, for many firms the financing program includes little use of new equity but rather reinvestment of internally generated funds to increase the equity base and then increase borrowing consistent with the preplanned debt-to-equity ratio.

The selection of debt instruments depends to a great extent on the availability of money and the relative terms of the different types. In periods of high interest, short-term or intermediate-term notes may be preferable to lower-interest-rate long-term bonds. Or a higher-interest-rate callable bond may be useful because it has the dual advantages of providing for a long-term commitment if interest rates should increase and being callable at a stated price if interest rates should decrease. With the rapid changes in the structure of the money and capital markets, pat answers to the question of the best type of debt instrument to use do not exist. Each case must be evaluated individually, using the counsel of commercial and investment bankers.

Optimum Financial Structure: The Leverage Question

The use of debt incurs financial risk. As a consequence, the cost of debt may be divided into two parts: the *explicit* cost, which is the interest, and the *implicit* cost, which represents the additional return that equity investors (common shareholders) will require when debt is used and the risk posture of the firm is changed toward a more risky position. The implicit cost is expressed in the marketplace by a bidding downward of the price of the common stock. This comes about by an excess of supply over demand for the stock in the marketplace. When the market price of the stock declines, two significant events take place: *the total equity base decreases* (and with it, the ratio of debt to equity increases), and the *cost of equity* (that is, the return required by shareholders) *increases*. As will be noted later in this chapter, these two simultaneous events tend to *increase* the overall cost of the equity component of the financial package. Within limits, however, the use of debt may have the net result of reducing the firm's overall cost of funds.

The *explicit cost of debt* tends to be lower than that of equity for two reasons. First, since debt provides a fixed interest and since creditors are higher on the list for payoff in the event of bankruptcy, the nominal cost of debt is usually less than that of equity. Second, since the explicit cost of debt—that is, interest—is tax-deductible, the after-tax cost of debt is in many instances reduced significantly (by up to 46 percent under current tax law).

Table 4-1 demonstrates the concept of optimum financial structure. Note that $100 of financing is needed and that various proportions of equity and debt may be used. As more debt is used, both the implicit and explicit costs start to increase. The goal is to adopt that particular combination which will result in the lowest total cost.

Table 4-1. Developing an optimum financial structure.

Total Financing	*Equity Portion*	*Equity Rate*	*Dollar Cost*	*Debt Portion*	*Rate**	*Dollar Cost*	*Total Cost*
$100	$100	14%	$14.00	0	—	0	$14.00
100	90	14	12.60	$10	6%	$0.60	13.20
100	80	14½	11.60	20	6¼	1.25	12.85
100	70	15	10.50	30	6½	1.95	12.45
100	60	16	9.60	40	7	2.80	(12.40)
100	50	18	9.00	50	7½	3.75	12.75
100	40	20	8.00	60	8	4.80	12.80

* This refers to the after-tax cost of debt. This will be discussed in greater detail later in this chapter.

The optimum financial structure is the one which results in the lowest total cost of funds. In the example demonstrated in Table 4-1, the best mix is 60 percent equity and 40 percent debt, with a total cost of $12.40. In general, the *implicit cost of debt,* which is reflected by increases in the cost of equity, goes up only slightly at first. However, since most investors are risk averters, the cost tends to increase at an increasing rate as greater amounts of debt are used.

The selection of the financial structure that results in the lowest cost of financing should result in the highest earnings per share and thereby maximize the market value of the common stock. The next logical question is how to determine the optimum financial structure (that is, ratio of debt to equity) for a given firm. In theory one could experiment using different amounts of debt and note the results, but this is obviously not feasible, at least over a broad range of values. The more useful approach is to study the industry ratios and those of major firms within the industry and then seek the advice of competent investment bankers.

Timing of Expenditures

The capital budget is just that: a budget. As such it does not authorize expenditures. The ordering or purchasing must be timed so that the acquisitions can be phased into operation to meet the firm's needs and so that funds are available for payment. The first part of the process requires the joint efforts of manufacturing and/or industrial engineers and finance and purchasing personnel. The exact specifications must be known, along with the dates when the items are needed. Next, ordering lead time and terms for payment must be determined. If any of the capital projects being undertaken are dependent on other acquisitions, the problem is further complicated. And, of course, contingency plans must be prepared to deal with delays in shipments and the like.

These problems require detailed analysis, but they are certainly not without resolution. We recommend that a PERT or critical path method (CPM) be employed, with all the projects plotted on a time scale over the planning horizon. Once this is done, dollar cash flows can be added and summarized for each week or month. Then the time-sequenced capital appropriations can be integrated with the cash budget for the same period. The first attempt to perform this integration may show problem areas—in particular, time periods when sufficient funds are not expected to be available. The next step is either to change the timing of expenditures to meet the availability of funds and/or to provide for additional funds when needed. This is a part of the firm's forward financial planning, and each step should be evaluated in terms of its potential effect on the bottom line, financial ratios for the reporting period, and so on.

The Cost of Capital

The firm's *cost of capital* is the average return expected by those who contribute funds to the firm, namely, the owners and the creditors. The average is weighted consistent with the relative amounts of equity and debt which the firm *desires* to use as it moves forward in financing its acquisitions. The implication here is that the firm's existing debt-to-equity ratio may *not* be the ratio which is planned for the future. Further, existing costs of financing are not necessarily valid predictors of costs that will be incurred to fund new projects. Hence we are interested in expected costs.[3]

Before we enter into a discussion of the calculation of the cost of capital, several aspects of this topic warrant examination. We have discussed briefly the basic elements of risk and noted how risk is incorporated into the cost of the firm's funds. Earlier in this chapter we indicated that risk affects both the explicit and the implicit costs of debt. This leads to the conclusion that *the cost of capital takes into consider-*

ation both the firm's existing business and financial risk. Since the cost of funds, or cost of capital, captures the existing risk posture of the firm, the cost may be thought of as consisting of two parts. The first is a rate of *return for risk-free securities,* and the second is a *premium to cover the total risk* for the particular firm. This premium for risk varies among both industries and firms within an industry, depending on the *market perception* of the risk. Thus different firms have different costs of capital.

Since the cost of capital is based on the desired debt-to-equity ratio *and* the anticipated costs of new funds, the cost of capital really is the average of the rates at which *additional* financing can be secured. It is the marginal cost of each component in the financing mix, averaged in accordance to the ratio of various types of financing to be employed. As such, *the cost of capital is the minimum return required to maintain the price of common stock and debt obligations at their present levels.* This, of course, must be taken within the context of the overall movement of the securities markets.

In order to calculate the cost of capital it is necessary to first compute the after-tax cost of each individual component. We will examine common-stock equity, preferred stock, various types of debt, retained earnings, and depreciation. All these represent sources of funds to the firm. Then we will average them to obtain the firm's cost of capital.

COMMON STOCK

There are at least three ways to obtain the cost of the firm's common stock. The first is based on a combination of the risk-free interest rate and premiums for business and financial risk. The second is the *dividend valuation model.* The third relies on *the capital asset pricing model* (CAPM). We will discuss the first two in this section. The third has not, as yet, received wide acceptance, because it is difficult to apply in many situations, and therefore is not discussed.

The cost of common-stock equity capital does not depend per se on the dividend (or lack thereof). One might think that if a firm does not pay a dividend, then the cost of the common stock is zero—the funds are free. This is, of course, absurd. The return on common stock is either a dividend *and/or* capital appreciation. Investors expect one or the other, or both. The rate or return is a function of the return available on risk-free securities such as treasury notes, plus increments to compensate for business and financial risk. The return is noted in Equation (4).

$$K_e = i + B + \Phi \tag{4}$$

where K_e = the firm's cost of common-stock equity
i = risk-free interest rate
B = premium for business risk
Φ = premium for financial risk (zero if the firm does not employ debt or preferred stock)

Equation (4) assumes that the minimum return required is the risk-free rate and adds on from there. Thus, if the risk-free rate were 9 percent, an investor might require 10 percent or 14 percent or 20 percent or 30 percent or whatever return *he* requires, given *his* perceptions of the combined business and financial risk for the firm. If an investor perceives a firm as providing a return equal to or greater than the return he requires for that firm, then he is likely to purchase stock or, if he is already an owner, not to sell. If the return is lower than the investor requires, then a purchase will not be forthcoming, and if the investor is already a shareholder, he is likely to sell the stock already owned.

The model provided in Equation (4) is especially useful for smaller firms, which may not declare dividends. It may be applied equally well by the investor or the financial manager attempting to determine the return required on the common stock.

The second model, the dividend valuation model, is based on the current dividend and the anticipated dividend growth rate, as shown in Equation (5).

$$K_e = \frac{D_1}{P_0} + g \tag{5}$$

where K_e = the firm's cost of common-stock equity
D_1 = expected dividend in the next period
P_0 = current market price
g = expected annual growth rate of the dividend

Using Equation (5), the cost disaggregates into two parts: the current dividend and the *additional* return needed to sustain the anticipated dividend growth rate. Equation (5) is applicable to the firm's outstanding common stock, since it is based on the *current* dividend, price, and dividend growth rates. It must be modified for stock being issued to take into consideration flotation costs. Equation (6) is applicable for new issues.

$$nK_e = \frac{D_1}{P_0(1 - F)} + g \tag{6}$$

where nK_e = firm's cost of new common-stock equity
F = flotation cost as a percentage of market price

Since the securities markets do not distinguish between new and already issued common stock, earnings must be sufficient to cover the flotation costs of the new shares.

RETAINED EARNINGS

The earnings retained from after-tax profits are a major source of funds for most firms. However, the market price of the common stock *includes* all the equity components in the firm's financial structure. (This was demonstrated earlier in this chapter when we discussed financial structure.) As a consequence, the return that must be earned on those funds retained from profits is included as a part of the return on the common stock.

PREFERRED STOCK

Since preferred shareholders, like creditors, have preference over common shareholders in the event of liquidation, but preferred-stock dividends are *not* tax-deductible, few firms issue preferred stock. The cost of outstanding preferred stock is given in Equation (7).

$$K_p = \frac{D_p}{P_p} \tag{7}$$

where K_p = firm's cost of existing preferred stock
D_p = dividend on existing preferred stock
P_p = market price of existing preferred stock

For new preferred stock, Equation (7) is modified to Equation (8).

$$nK_p = \frac{nD_p}{nP_p(1 - F)} \tag{8}$$

where nK_p = the firm's cost of new preferred stock
nD_p = dividend on the new stock

nP_p = sale price of the new preferred stock
F = flotation cost as a percentage of the sale price

DEBT

Since most firms have short- and long-term debt and various types of each, it is necessary to average the costs of these to find the average cost of debt. However, this can rarely be done using historical data. The question is the incremental costs and the types and proportions of *additional* debt to be used. We need to determine how much and what types of debt will be added to the already existing portfolio of debt.

Since interest is tax-deductible, the after-tax cost of debt is found using Equation (9).

$$K_i = K(1 - t) \tag{9}$$

where K_i = after-tax cost of debt
K = pretax cost of debt (coupon rate on the debt)
t = firm's marginal tax rate on operating income

For new issues of debt, when flotation costs are involved, Equation (9) is modified to Equation (10).

$$K_i = \frac{I(1 - t)}{P(1 - F)} \tag{10}$$

where I = dollar amount of interest
P = sale price of debt
F = flotation cost as a percentage of the sale price

Equations (9) and (10) are demonstrated in Example 1.

EXAMPLE 1
Cost of Debt

A firm with a 46 percent marginal tax rate needs $1 million, of which $500,000 is to be funded using debt with the following characteristics:

Debt	*Amount*	*Pretax Cost*	*Flotation Cost*
Current liabilities	$200,000	5%	0
Long-term	300,000	12%	½%

Determine the after-tax cost of debt.

SOLUTION

Equation (9) applies to the current liabilities, since a flotation cost is not involved.

$$K_i = .05\,(1 - .46)$$
$$= .027 = 2.7\%$$

Equation (10) applies to the long-term portion.

$$K_i = \frac{\$36{,}000\,(1 - .46)}{\$300{,}000\,(1 - .005)}$$
$$= \frac{\$19{,}440}{\$298{,}500}$$
$$= .065 = 6.5\%$$

Last, the two costs are averaged in proportion to their amounts, as shown below.

Debt	*Amount*	*Proportion*	*Cost*	*Weighted Cost*
Current liabilities	$200,000	.4	0.027	0.0108
Long-term	300,000	.6	0.065	0.0390
	$500,000	1.0		.0498 = 4.98%

The after-tax cost of debt is just under 5 percent. □

DEPRECIATION

The funds resulting from depreciation write-offs are frequently used for reinvestment. These funds are the return *of* investment. Since this is the case and the investments were made using funds composed of equity, debt, and so on, funds resulting from depreciation have the same cost as the cost of capital. Consequently, it is not necessary to consider them when computing the firm's cost of capital.

Computing the Firm's Marginal Cost of Capital

With the costs of each of the various components known, it is possible to compute the cost of capital by taking a simple weighted average of each. This is demonstrated in Example 2.

EXAMPLE 2

Weighted Average Cost of Capital

Refer to Example 1 and assume the $500,000 will be raised using a new flotation of common-stock equity. The common stock will sell for $25 per share, the dividend is $1.25, the dividend growth rate is 6 percent, and the flotation cost is 8 percent.

SOLUTION

First determine the cost of the new common stock, using Equation (6).

$$nK_e = \frac{\$1.25}{\$25.00\,(1 - .08)} + .06$$
$$= \frac{\$1.25}{\$23} + .06$$
$$= 11.43\%$$

Now take a weighted average of the equity and debt, using the tabular format shown below.

Funding	*Amount*	*Proportion*	*Cost*	*Weighted Cost*
Common Stock	$ 500,000	.5	0.1143	0.05715
Debt	500,000	.5	0.0498	0.02490
	$1,000,000	1.0		.08205 = 8.2%

The weighted average after-tax cost of capital for this firm is about 8.2 percent. □

In many cases the alternative of leasing may be preferable to raising funds internally or through debt or equity. Since capital asset acquisition is so closely linked to the process of funding investments, we next move to a discussion of leasing. Chapter 5 describes the various positive and negative aspects of leasing. In Chapter 6 we discuss the method of discounted cash flow. Using the tools of discounted cash flow, we will revisit the question of leasing in Chapter 9. In Chapter 9 we describe how to evaluate various lease terms, how to decide among leases, and how to determine whether it is preferable to lease or to purchase.

NOTES

1. This explains why when interest rates are very high, some companies actually repurchase their own debt on the open market. This method, while using cash, reduces debt at a discount.
2. Unless there have been stock dividends, in which case the common-stock and paid-in-capital accounts would have been increased at the expense of retained earnings.
3. The key question is the costs of equity and debt to be obtained at the time the project is financed, using the ratio of debt to equity which is felt to be optimum over the long run at that time (that is, the planned debt-to-equity ratio).

CHAPTER 5

Leasing as an Alternative to Purchasing

In Chapter 4 we examined sources of financing capital acquisitions and the development of an optimum capital structure. Unfortunately, in some instances businesses, especially small businesses, have difficulty in raising needed funds or find them to be prohibitively expensive. Leasing may prove to be a viable alternative source of funding. In this chapter we discuss leasing as a source of financing, reviewing the various advantages and disadvantages of using it.[1] Later in the book we will look again at leasing to see how it can be integrated directly into the capital expenditure decision process.

We first look at the advantages and disadvantages of leasing. Next we discuss briefly the structure of the leasing industry. Last, we outline some of the important aspects of the different types of leasing available.

Why Lease?

The particular combination of reasons which a firm uses as the basis for making the decision to lease or purchase has grounding in basic economics. For some, the reason is a dearth of money—there is no other choice; it is either lease or do without. Unfortunately, this is often the situation for the smaller firms, and the decision then is to find the best leasing arrangement, tailored (if possible) to the specific needs of the lessee. The larger firm should weigh the quantifiable economic parameters as well as those which are not so easy to label with a dollar value (the possibility of technical or market obsolescence, for example). Within the quantifiable area, we will later introduce the discounted cash flow methodology, which is easily applied to the evaluation of lease and lease-versus-purchase decisions. Several of the primary advantages of leasing are listed in the following paragraphs.

1. *Leasing may be less expensive than purchase.* The lower cost may come about from two distinct and not mutually exclusive causes. First, a firm may not be able to take full advantage of the tax benefits resulting from accelerated depreciation and investment tax credits. To take advantage of the former, a firm must have sufficient earnings before taxes; to enjoy the latter, the firm must be paying taxes sufficient to equal the allowable tax credit.[2] Many small firms, and also some larger firms, such as airlines and, in particular, bankrupt railroads, cannot take advantage of the tax benefits even when they can raise the funds required for purchase. The lease company can take full advantage of such benefits and pass them along to the lessee as a part of the rental agreement.

Second, due to the lower overall risk posture of a lessor, the cost of funds (both equity and debt) may be somewhat less than to an operating firm. This situation is not uncommon. Only the most credit-worthy firms have access to the issuing side of the commercial-paper markets, for example. Thus, to almost all firms, this relatively low-cost short-term financing is unavailable. Further, many leasing companies are subsidiaries of banks and, as a consequence, have access to funds at lower costs than are available even to prime bank customers.

2. *Leasing provides an alternative source of capital.* For firms that have limited funds for capital investment, leasing may provide a viable alternative to increasing the firm's capitalization. At the limit, when the firm's capitalization may no longer be increased, leasing may be the only means for expansion and replacement.

3. *Leasing provides constant-cost financing.* Unlike some forms of debt financing which may vary in cost as a function of the prime interest rate, lease payments are almost always uniform over the length of the lease (except when specifically tailored otherwise). One common exception is space in shopping malls. Leases for shops usually tie rental to gross sales receipts, but not to the prime interest rate.

4. *Leasing extends the length of financing.* In contrast with typical equipment loans, which are generally available only for a period of time significantly less than the economic life of an asset, leases may be obtained for nearly the total length of the asset's life. The result is reduced cash outflow during the initial period of the asset's life, with the cost spread over a longer time period. The benefit is twofold. First, costs tend to be more nearly correlated with revenues over the entire life of the asset. Second, a discounted cash flow analysis will usually indicate a higher return on investment when cash payments are spread out over the entire asset life. This will be demonstrated later in the book.

5. *Leasing extends the length of financing* (a corollary of the preceding item). Another aspect of extended-length lease financing as opposed to short- or intermediate-term loan financing warrants strong consideration. Recall that many intermediate-term loans have balloon repayment features whereby the bulk of the principal is due at the end of the loan and, if the firm maintains its credit rating, forms the basis for a new loan. Such refinancing exposes the firm to additional financial risk if interest rates and/or the availability of capital change. The uncertainty of the availability of refinancing necessitates a more conservative liquidity position. Possible changes (and fluctuations in interest rates if interest is tied to the prime rate) make cash budgeting more difficult and, again, negatively affect the firm's financial risk posture.

6. *Leasing conserves existing credit.* The use of leasing generally conserves existing sources of credit for other uses and, in most instances, does not restrict a firm's borrowing capacity. Many loan indentures do restrict additional borrowing and may also limit manager/owner compensation and dividend payout.

7. *Leasing provides total financing.* Unlike debt financing, which requires some equity investment, leasing affords 100 percent financing. However, in many instances, a security deposit is required, and the return on this escrow deposit may be quite low (frequently, current passbook interest rate or lower). Also, lease payments must usually be paid at the start of each period, with the first payment due at the start of the lease. Loan repayments are usually made at the end of each period, with the first payment due at the end of the month (or some other period) after purchase. These factors affect the cash flow budget and the timing of cash flows.

8. *Leasing may include all costs of acquisition* (a corollary of the preceding item). The total acquisition cost, including all sales taxes and delivery and installation charges, may be included as a part of the total lease package. These front-end costs may be substantial and, thereby, may result in heavy initial cash outflows if assets are purchased.

9. *Leasing provides a hedge against inflation.* Leasing may provide a hedge against inflation, since the lease payments will be made with "cheaper" dollars. The same line of reasoning may apply to loan principal and interest repayments, if the latter are constant. If, however, interest rates are tied to the prime rate, then the interest rate will tend to move with the rate of inflation and, hence, the loan will not be as good a hedge against inflation as the fixed lease payment.

Although leasing may act as a hedge against inflation, inflation also provides the basis for strong arguments supporting ownership. Many firms anticipate purchasing or re-leasing leased assets at the end of the initial lease. With inflation, the actual fair market price may well exceed the price anticipated when the lease was negotiated. Airlines, in particular, have suffered from this, since the Federal Aviation Administration requires airplanes to be maintained with regular overhauls in order to remain in use. In many instances, the fair market value of fuel-efficient planes at the lease termination has been greater than the expected amount. Leasing companies benefit greatly from this inflation. In fact, in competitive areas, the primary profit derived by leasing companies results from the sale of the asset at the termination of the lease.

10. *Leasing provides fast, flexible financing.* Leasing tends to be faster and more flexible than borrowing funds. Not only do leases not contain the typical restrictive covenants found in loan agreements, but lease payments may be tailored to the specific need of the lessee. For example, lease payments may be arranged to meet the seasonal cash flows of the lessee. Again, budgeting is facilitated.

11. *Leasing simplifies bookkeeping.* For tax accounting purposes, leasing avoids the need to establish depreciation schedules and account for depreciation and interest.

12. *Leasing provides for tax write-off of land.* Land may not be depreciated. Thus, if it is owned, the only tax benefits realized are through property taxes and interest paid on financing. With leasing, the entire lease payment on land is tax-deductible. While this tax benefit is valuable, it must be considered within the context of generally appreciating land values and the absence of lessee ownership at the end of the lease.

13. *Leasing reduces risk of obsolescence.* Many lease agreements place the risk of obsolescence on the owner. Computer leasing is a case in point. Introduction of the IBM 370 immediately outdated its predecessor. This is a most important consideration in areas of rapid technological change.

14. *Leasing provides trial use periods.* In some instances, management is considering the acquisition of the new equipment and may not have sufficient confidence in the estimates of projected cash flows to warrant purchase of long-term leasing. In such instances, it may be possible to lease the equipment for a limited period on a trial basis and then either extend the lease or purchase.

Each of the preceding points warrants close consideration both from the viewpoint of economic analysis and the practical constraints imposed upon the firm. Those factors which come to bear heavily today may prove to be of lesser consequences in years to come; the analysis must be ongoing. Beyond the practical constraints, however, lies the very important factor of ownership: the use of the asset for extended time periods or enjoyment of residual value. In periods of long-term inflation, it is necessary to estimate as precisely as possible what the fair market value of the asset will be at the end of the lease period.[3] Thought should not be given to salvage value in terms of depreciation, since depreciation usually does not even closely approximate asset value change. Depreciation is an accounting tool not appropriate to market value estimation.

Structure of the Leasing Industry

If one were to characterize the leasing industry, it would probably be as heterogeneous and fragmented. There are literally thousands of leasing companies, varying in size from thousands of dollars of assets to hundreds of millions. Many automobile dealerships hold captive leasing companies. There are independent lessors, manufacturer and distributor captive leasing, and bank-held leasing companies. Insurance companies and financial-service conglomerates are also involved. The industry is complex, with lessors offering widely differing services.

The structure of the industry has changed almost as dramatically as the rate at which the industry has grown. Initially, the industry was composed primarily of *third-party leasing companies,* which purchased assets for lease, raising needed funds through equity and debt financing. The banking community became involved by providing loans and soon realized that it could enjoy the profits of leasing companies. This precipitated the rapid growth of bank leasing companies.

Vendor lessors offer greater service than their competitors. They may be able to provide repair service, maintenance, temporary replacement during breakdowns, and so on. Automobile dealers and machinery vendors are examples. In some instances, the lease contract will be with the vendor lessor; in others, the vendor may have a close working relationship with a bank leasing company, which becomes the lessor.

It should be noted that the vendor-related lessor is interested not only in providing financing but also in customer service. Further, by being in the business, the vendor may be able to offer a high degree of flexibility in meeting lessee needs—a degree of flexibility which might not be available through a financing lessor. But service has its price, and terms must therefore be critically analyzed to obtain the best deal in terms of the lessee's needs.

Third-party lessors, unlike vendor lessors, have no specific interest in the assets leased but rather act as a financial intermediary. They do not, in general, ever expect to recover the asset but at lease termination will either release or sell it. The number of independent third-party lessors has diminished by half since 1972. They have been replaced by lessors representing financial institutions, such as commercial banks and investment bankers.[4] Thus a major shift has taken place within the industry, and, as a consequence of the high level of competition, probably only the strongest third-party lessors will survive.

Many larger banks are involved in leasing. While some banks still participate in the leasing industry by lending funds to third-party lessors, their primary (and most profitable) interest is in acting as lessor directly or through a subsidiary leasing company. Banks may also put together leveraged leases, which require only a small investment but may result in a large fee. In this area commercial banks are overlapping with investment bankers.

Since the primary profit of many insurance companies is derived from their investment portfolio, their interest in leasing is not surprising. Initially, insurance companies acted as lenders for large leveraged leases. However, within the limitations of their individual charters, we now see some insurance companies moving directly into leasing, and this trend is likely to continue.

Investment bankers' function in the leasing industry is primarily (if not exclusively) as a financial intermediary and lease packager. As in their other investment banking functions, they are very aware of the current availability of capital and its sources. Many have departments to locate sources of capital and structure leases.

From this brief description of the structure of the leasing industry, the reader should note its continued growth as a financial, as opposed to service, industry. This trend is likely to continue, and we expect the industry to become dominated by financial institutions—commercial banks for small leases and investment bankers and insurance companies for larger leases.

Types of Leases

One of the primary incentives to leasing lies in the tax benefits: the total cost of the lease payment is deductible as an expense for computing federal income tax liability. In order to enjoy this benefit, the lease must be "true," as opposed to a conditional sales contract as defined by the Internal Revenue Service. In general, a conditional sales contract exists if the lessee has acquired, or will acquire, title of or an equity interest in the asset being leased. In a true lease the lessee does not acquire ownership or title.

Revenue Ruling 55-540 established the framework for differentiating between a lease and conditional sales agreement. In general, an agreement will be construed to be a conditional sale if one or more of the following conditions are present:

1. Portions of the periodic payment are specifically applicable to the acquisition of an equity interest in the asset.

2. Title will be acquired upon payment of a stated amount required to be made under the contract.

3. The total payment required for a relatively short period of use constitutes an excessively large portion of the total sum required to be paid to secure transfer of title.

4. The agreed payments materially exceed the current fair lease payment value.

5. The property may be obtained under a purchase option at a price that is nominal in relation to the value of the property at the time the option is exercised.

6. Some portion of the periodic payment is specifically designated as interest or is otherwise readily recognizable as the equivalent of interest.

7. Title will be acquired upon payment of an aggregate amount (total of payments plus option price, if any) that approximates the price, plus interest and carrying charges, at which the asset could have been purchased upon entering into the agreement.

Assuming the agreement represents a "true" lease, we proceed to discuss the more important types of leases, noting some of the particular benefits and shortcomings of each.

Within the leasing industry there are various titles or names by which leases are known. There are several names distinguishing lease arrangements and lease types. Certain lease title designations are based on the duration and monetary value of the lease; others derive from the financial and marketing arrangements. The accounting profession has reinterpreted existing lease classifications and introduced new ones in order to help resolve the problems in accounting for leases. Further, some leases are known by reference to restrictive covenants contained within the lease agreement. As a consequence, there is a great deal of overlap, and the same type of lease may be known to lessee, lessor, and financial analyst by different names.

In this section, we will provide some of the basic distinctions among types of leases, with two primary goals. First, we want to make the reader aware of the differences in lease types as they pertain to financial reporting and, specifically, to the requirements of FASB-13.[5] Second, through definition and classification, we want to further explore the types of leasing agreements available so as to provide the reader with a sense of the industry and the jargon and, hopefully, place him in a more favorable bargaining position.

CAPITAL LEASES

For financial reporting purposes of a lessee, FASB-13 distinguishes between two types of leases: capital and operating. For a lease to be considered a capital lease, it must meet one or more of the following four criteria; otherwise, it is by definition an operating lease.[6]

1. The lease transfers ownership of the property to the lessee by the end of the lease term. This term is defined as the fixed, noncancelable term of the lease plus any options specified in the contract.

2. The lease contains a bargain option or a provision which allows the lessee at his option to purchase the leased property for a price lower than the expected fair market value of the property.

3. The lease term is equal to 75 percent or more of the estimated economic life of the leased property. If, however, the beginning of the lease falls within the last 25 percent of the total economic useful life of the leased property, including earlier years of use, this criterion is not used for classifying the lease.

4. The present value of the lease at the beginning of the lease term of the minimum lease payments, excluding *executory costs* such as insurance, maintenance, and taxes to be paid by the lessor, but including any profit on the lease, equals or exceeds 90 percent of the excess fair market value of the leased property to the lessor at the inception of the lease over any related investment tax credit retained by the lessor and expected to be realized by him. This criterion is not used if the lease term falls within the last 25 percent of the total estimated economic life of the leased property. The lessor computes the present value using the *implicit interest rate,* while the lessee uses his incremental *borrowing rate,* unless he can use the lessor's implicit interest rate. The lessor's implicit interest rate must be used if this rate is lower than the incremental borrowing rate.

OPERATING LEASES

The term operating lease (or, alternatively, service or maintenance lease) is used by FASB, the IRS, and the leasing community, but not always in the same context. FASB-13 defines an operating lease both in terms of the lessee and lessor as follows:

- For the lessee it includes all leases that are not capital leases.

- For the lessor it includes all other leases (that is, those which are not direct-financing leases, leveraged leases, and so on).

The leasing community views an operating lease as one having the following characteristics:

1. The lease does not involve an extension of credit or a long-term fixed commitment.
2. The lessor may provide special services, such as maintenance.
3. The lease is of short length, compared to the economic life of the asset.
4. The lease is cancelable within reasonable restrictions.

McGugan and Caves[7] note that a lease may also be classified as an operating lease if the asset is available only on a lease basis or if the price to purchase is set unrealistically high so as to preclude purchase.

In most instances, an operating lease, as defined in this section, will be construed by the IRS to be a "true" lease. The distinguishing characteristic of an operating lease within this context is the continued ownership of the asset by the lessor, with all the benefits and risks of ownership residing with the lessor.

Operating leases offer several special advantages to the lessee who is confronted with the lease-versus-purchase decision. First, *the lessee may lease a piece of equipment for a short period of time,* which provides an opportunity to try it out.

Second, *operating leases reduce the risk of obsolescence.* Since operating leases are non-full-payment and cancelable upon due notice from the lessee, the risk of obsolescence is borne by the lessor.

Third, *the lessee is not exposed to the risk of ownership* under an operating lease. Obsolescence is only part of the risk of ownership; another part is the burden of selling a second-hand piece of equipment, regardless of the reason underlying the sale. If the lessee had purchased the equipment and later attempted to sell it, he would be at a disadvantage, since his primary business is not selling his used equipment.

Fourth, since the lessor is a specialist in dealing with the equipment and operates on large volume, he can provide two important services himself. The first is equipment service and maintenance. *The lessor can care for and maintain the equipment efficiently by utilizing trained service technicians, special service equipment, and a full stock of spare parts.* Second, the lessor can bring in replacement equipment at short notice if the leased equipment should suffer a major breakdown or require extensive service or maintenance.

Last, *the operating lease may provide middle-management flexibility*. Normally, major capital expenditures require top-management approval, whereas in many firms decisions relating to operating leases may be made at middle-management levels. This provides flexibility at the branch management level that would otherwise be unavailable.

FINANCIAL LEASES

A financial lease, as the word financial connotes, is a method of asset financing whereby the lessor extends credit to the lessee and transfers to the lessee all the responsibilities of ownership, including maintenance, insurance, taxes, and so on, for a period of time close to the economic life of the asset. In most instances, at the termination of the lease, the lessee may either purchase the asset at a price not less than its fair market value or return the asset to the lessor. The option to purchase generally states the method to be used to determine fair market values (frequently by appraisals by both lessor and lessee). Financial leases are differentiated from conditional sales agreements in that the lease period ends while there is still some economic life remaining.

Most financial leases are *full-payout*. In a full-payout lease, the cash is returned to the lessor to cover the asset costs, cost of financing, lessor's overhead, and a rate of return acceptable to the lessor. The full-payout lease is contrasted to the *non-full-payout* lease, in which the lessor must depend upon the salvage value to cover the purchase cost and achieve an acceptable return on investment. Operating leases are usually non-full-payout.

DIRECT LEASES

The direct lease is essentially a hybrid of operating and finance leases. Direct leases are usually full-payout and provide for renewal or purchase options, but do not include lessor service such as maintenance.

The FASB includes direct leasing as a type of lease applicable only to lessors. As defined by FASB, a direct lease is one which does not include provision in the lease payment for lessor profit, meets one or more of the criteria used to define a capital lease, and has a reasonably high predictability of collection of lease payments.

MIDDLE-MARKET LEASES

Middle-market lease is a term applied to a lease that has characteristics of both the direct and the leveraged lease, as follows:

1. The lease term generally ranges from five to fifteen years.

2. The assets leased have value ranging from about $500,000 to several million dollars.

3. Financing may be through one or more third parties. While similar to leveraged leases, the middle-market lease is usually for a shorter duration and involves assets of lower value.

MASTER LEASES

A master lease establishes an open-ended contract with rates and terms for equipment needed both at the present time and in the future. It is usually written for a period longer in term than the life of any asset leased and places responsibility upon the lessor to provide up-to-date equipment throughout the lease period. The quantity of such equipment may vary seasonally or with the lessee's needs. Master leases are often used for truck and car fleet leasing and peripheral-equipment leasing.

The master lease is similar to a blanket purchase order and, in effect, also establishes a line of credit between lessee and lessor and eliminates the need to negotiate a new lease contract each time additional equipment is needed.

SALE-AND-LEASEBACK

Using a sale-and-leaseback arrangement, a firm may sell a portion of its assets, such as equipment or buildings, to a lessor and then lease them back. The lessee thus converts fixed assets into cash. The arrangement is beneficial to the lessee in that additional cash is available while the firm still has use of the assets, and a profit or recapture of depreciation may be realized in the sale, since market value frequently exceeds book value, especially for buildings and land.

NET AND NET-NET LEASES

The term net lease is sometimes applied to a financial lease. The lessee agrees to make lease payments and also bears the cost of maintenance, insurance, taxes, and the like and assumes the risks of ownership. The net-net lease goes one step further in adding to the lessee's risk burden by requiring the lessee to return to the lessor at lease end an asset having a pre-established value. The lessee is thus responsible for any variation in the actual resale value from the present amount.

LEVERAGED LEASES

Leveraged leases are similar to financial leases in that they are noncancelable, full-payout net leases. However, in the case of a leveraged lease there are usually five or six parties involved, while in a financial lease there are only two: the owner (lessor) and the lessee. The difference in the number of parties involved results from the fact that in leveraged leases the owner puts up only a fraction of the investment cost (usually 20 percent to 35 percent) and borrows the rest from other sources. The reason for borrowing on the part of the lessor is the fact that leveraged leases involve a lot of money. The products leased through leveraged leasing are large-ticket items and include airplanes, railroad cars, ships, off-shore drilling equipment, nuclear fuel, pipelines, and entire plants.

NOTES

1. For a detailed discussion of leasing and the leasing industry see Robert E. Pritchard and Thomas J. Hindelang, *The Lease/Buy Decision,* New York: AMACOM, 1980.
2. As noted in Chapter 2, the limitations are being expanded to permit credit of up to the firm's tax liability or $25,000 plus 90 percent of the firm's tax liability, whichever is less, by 1981.
3. The authors view this consideration to be very important, since inflation is likely to continue at high levels throughout the 1980s.
4. For a detailed description of the leasing industry, and forecasts for future trends, see *The Equipment Leasing Market,* Report No. 382, Frost and Sullivan, 106 Fulton Street, New York, NY 10038.
5. "Accounting for Leases," Statement of Financial Accounting, Standards No. 13, Financial Accounting Standards Board, November 1976.
6. For further reference on leasing terminology see "Selected Leasing Terminology," *Data Management,* May 1977, p. 34.
7. Vincent J. McGugan and Richard E. Caves, "Integration and Competition in the Equipment Leasing Industry," *Journal of Business,* July 1974, pp. 382–385.

CHAPTER 6

Discounted Cash Flow Analysis for Capital Budgeting Decisions

In the preceding chapters we have examined depreciation, taxation, cash flows, and sources of financing, including leasing. We have pointed out that the benchmark for investment is the firm's marginal after-tax cost of capital and indicated how this can be calculated. Further, we introduced the elements of business and financial risk and indicated that the cost-of-capital benchmark should be modified to accommodate the evaluation of projects with above- and below-average risk. This risk adjustment is the topic of Chapter 8.

The methodology for evaluating alternative investment opportunities relies on determining the present value of cash inflows and outflows (with appropriate adjustments to compensate for differences in risk among projects). The procedures for determining present value are introduced in this chapter and will be applied to the capital-budgeting and lease-versus-purchase decisions in the following chapters.

The procedures for computing interest and their reciprocal, discounting of funds to their present value, are basic to the evaluation of proposed capital expenditures. In addition, they have numerous other applications within the field of finance. In this chapter, we examine interest, annuity, and discounted cash flow calculations and provide examples to illustrate their use. Throughout, we will demonstrate the use of the extended interest and present value tables found in Appendix B.

Simple and Compound Interest

Since the computations for simple and compound interest form the basis for discounted cash flow analysis, we examine these first. *Simple interest* is computed using Equation (11).

$$I = (P)(i)(t) \tag{11}$$

where I = dollar amount of simple interest earned
P = principal
i = rate of return (interest rate)
t = time period over which funds are invested

The accumulated fund at the end of the time period in question would simply be the amount of interest earned (I) plus the original principal (P).

When we speak of simple interest, it is assumed that the interest will be withdrawn of paid as soon as it is earned. *Compound interest,* on the other hand, is earned on the fund consisting of both the principal and previously earned interest; thus we are earning "interest on interest" to produce the compounding effect. Equation (12) shows how to determine the value of a fund at the end of a period of time over which interest has been left to compound.

$$S_n = P(1 + i)^n \tag{12}$$

where S_n = compound sum after n years
n = number of years

For computational purposes, we refer to Column 1 in Appendix B, which provides compound interest factors $(1 + i)^n$ for interest rates between 1 percent and 40 percent and time periods up to 50 years. The use of these factors is illustrated in Example 1.

EXAMPLE 1
Simple vs. Compound Interest

An investor places $20,000 in an 8 percent account. How much will he have at the end of six years?

SOLUTION

$$\begin{aligned} S_6 &= \$20{,}000\ (1.586874) \\ &= \$31{,}737.48 \end{aligned}$$

The investor will have \$31,737.48 in six years. Thus he has earned \$11,737.48 in interest, since he left the interest along with the original principal to earn additional interest. The amount of simple interest earned each year would be \$1,600, which means that \$9,600 of simple interest would have been earned over the six-year period. The extra \$2,137.48 of interest are the result of the compounding. □

In many instances, interest is compounded more frequently than annually. If this is the case, then the compound sum is found using Equation (13).

$$S_n = P\left(1 + \frac{i}{m}\right)^{m \times n} \tag{13}$$

where m = number of times interest is compounded per year

Appendix B may be helpful in solving for the compound sum, but its usefulness is limited. See Example 2.

EXAMPLE 2

Compound Interest

An investor places \$1,000 at 8 percent interest. Determine the amount that will have accrued after three years if the interest is compounded annually, semiannually, quarterly, and monthly.

SOLUTION

Consider annual compounding first: Use Column 1 from Appendix B as in Example 1.

$$S_n = \$1,000\,(1.259712) = \$1,259.71$$

Consider semiannual compounding next: First solve using Equation (13).

$$\begin{aligned} S_3 &= \$1,000\left(1 + \frac{.08}{2}\right)^{2\times 3} \\ &= \$1,000\,(1.04)^6 \\ &= \$1,000\,(1.2653189) \\ &= \$1,265.32 \end{aligned}$$

Appendix B can be used to solve this problem, which involves the equivalent of 4 percent for six years. Thus the factor for 4 percent and six years is obtained from Appendix B.

$$S_3 = \$1{,}000\,(1.265319) = \$1{,}265.32$$

Consider quarterly compounding next: First solve using Equation (13).

$$\begin{aligned} S_3 &= \$1{,}000\left(1 + \frac{.08}{4}\right)^{4\times 3} \\ &= \$1{,}000\,(1.02)^{12} \\ &= \$1{,}000\,(1.2682418) \\ &= \$1{,}268.24 \end{aligned}$$

Appendix B can also be used to solve this problem, which involves the equivalent of 2 percent for 12 years. Thus the factor for 2 percent and 12 years is obtained from Appendix B.

$$S_3 = \$1{,}000\,(1.268242) = \$1{,}268.24$$

Finally, solve for monthly compounding: First solve using Equation (13).

$$\begin{aligned} S_3 &= \$1{,}000\left(1 + \frac{.08}{12}\right)^{12\times 3} \\ &= \$1{,}000\,(1.006666)^{36} \\ &= \$1{,}000\,(1.2702321) \\ &= \$1{,}270.23 \end{aligned}$$

Appendix B cannot be used to solve this problem, since it involves the equivalent of two-thirds of 1 percent interest for 36 years and the compound interest factor for this is not included in Appendix B. □

It is interesting to note in Example 2 how more frequent compounding leads to higher effective interest yields. The initial compoundings (yearly to semiannual) result in a greater increase in effective yield than do subsequent increases (semiannual to quarterly). At the limit, interest may be compounded continuously. Compound sums may be found utilizing Equation (14) when continuous compounding is involved.

$$S_n = Pe^{in} \tag{14}$$

Values of e^x are contained in Table 6-1.

EXAMPLE 3

Continuous Compounding

A depositor placed $2,000 at 10 percent interest compounded continuously for five years. Determine the compound sum at the end of the five-year period.

Table 6-1. Values of e^x.

x	e^x	x	e^x	x	e^x
0.01	1.0101	0.08	1.0833	0.35	1.4191
0.02	1.0202	0.09	1.0942	0.40	1.4918
0.03	1.0305	0.10	1.1052	0.45	1.5683
0.04	1.0408	0.15	1.1618	0.50	1.6487
0.05	1.0513	0.20	1.2214	0.55	1.7333
0.06	1.0618	0.25	1.2840	0.60	1.8221
0.07	1.0725	0.30	1.3499	0.65	1.9155

SOLUTION

Use Equation (14) and Table 6-1.

$$\begin{aligned} S_5 &= \$2{,}000e^{(0.10)5} \\ &= \$2{,}000e^{0.50} \\ &= \$2{,}000\,(1.6487) \\ &= \$3{,}297.40 \end{aligned}$$

If interest had been just compounded annually, the compound sum would have been \$2,000 (1.610510) = \$3,221.02. The continuous compounding resulted in an additional \$76.38 of interest. □

Compound Sum (Future Value) of an Annuity

Sometimes deposits are made regularly on an annual basis into a savings or pension fund (such as an IRA). To determine the amount which will accumulate after a number of years, we use Equation (15).

$$F = A\left[\frac{(1+i)^n - 1}{i}\right] \tag{15}$$

where F = future value of an annuity payment
A = annual *year-end* annuity payment
i = rate of return (interest rate)
n = number of years

The factors corresponding to the bracketed portion of Equation (15) are found in Column 2 of Appendix B for interest rates from 1 percent to 40 percent up to 50 years. Their use is demonstrated in Example 4.

EXAMPLE 4

Future Value of an Annuity

An investor places $1,400 per year at the *end* of each year into an IRA for 25 years. Interest is compounded annually at 8 percent. Determine the amount in the account at the end of the period.

SOLUTION

$$F = \$1,400\,(73.015940)$$
$$= \$102.348.31$$

The investor will have $102,348.31 in 25 years. □

EXAMPLE 5

Future Value of an Annuity

Repeat Example 4 using 6 percent and 10 percent interest rates.

SOLUTION

At 6 percent, F = $1,400(54.864512) = $76,810.32
At 10 percent, F = $1,400(98.347059) = $137,685.88 □

The results of Examples 4 and 5 are tabulated for comparison below.

Interest Rate	*Future Value of Annuity*	*Incremental Difference*
6%	$ 76,810.32	
		$25,537.99
8	102,348.31	
		35,337.57
10	137,685.88	

The differences between the future values resulting from the three interest rates selected are very substantial. The differences become greater as the interest rate is increased. If, for example, we selected a 12 percent rate, the increase over 10 percent would be $48,981.53. The reason for the size of the differences is that the compound interest factors increase exponentially. Interest factors for 5 percent, 7 percent, and 9 percent are plotted in Figure 6-1 over a 20-year time horizon to demonstrate the importance of the exponential increase.

Sometimes annuities are paid at the beginning of the year rather than at the end. If this is the case, the future value will be substantially greater. Finding the future value of an annuity paid at the start of the

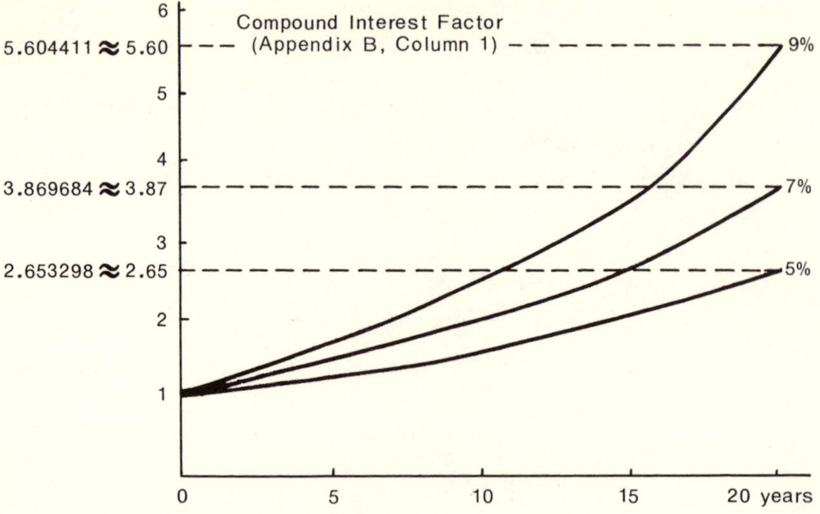

Figure 6-1. Compound interest factors for three interest rates.

year involves the use of both the compound interest (column 1) and future value of an annuity (column 2) tables. The procedure is demonstrated in Example 6.

EXAMPLE 6

Future Value of an Annuity Paid at the Start of the Year

An investor pays $1,400 per year into an IRA for 25 years. Interest is compounded annually at 8 percent. Determine the amount in the account in 25 years.

SOLUTION

Since future-value tables are computed for *end-of-year payments,* it is necessary to use the compound interest table for the initial payment and then the future-value tables for 25 years, subtracting 1, corresponding to the final year-end payment which is not made (since payments are made at the start of each year).

$$F = \$1{,}400\,(6.848475 + 73.105940 - 1)$$
$$= \$1{,}400\,(78.954415) = \$110{,}536.18$$

The difference between the year-end payment annuity found in Example 4 and the start-of-the-year payment annuity determined above is \$8,187.87. □

Sinking Funds

A special type of compound annuity is the sinking fund. The creation of a sinking fund involves determining the amount which needs to be invested each year at a given rate of return in order to pay off a debt or other obligations at the end of the stated time period. Sinking-fund factors are provided in column 3 of appendix B.

EXAMPLE 7
Sinking Fund

A corporation needs \$20 million in 20 years to pay off a bond issue. Assuming it places payments into an 8 percent fund at the end of each year, determine the yearly year-end sinking-fund payment necessary to retire the \$20 million.

SOLUTION

The annual year-end sinking-fund payment is

$$\$20{,}000{,}000\,(0.02185221) = \$437{,}044.00. \qquad \square$$

Present Value

The goal of present-value calculations is to determine the amount of money which a firm or investor would accept at present in place of a given amount at some future date. The computation is just the reverse of the compound interest and compound-sum-of-an-annuity calculations demonstrated earlier. The present value of a sum to be received in the future is found using Equation (16), which is simply a rearrangement of Equation (12).

$$PV = \frac{S}{(1+i)^n} = S\left[\frac{1}{1+i}\right]^n \qquad (16)$$

Appendix B, column 4, provides the present-value factors (PVF) corresponding to the bracketed portion of Equation (16).

EXAMPLE 8
Present Value

A corporation will receive \$20,000 in three years as a payment from a customer. The current rate of interest is 10 percent. Determine the present value of the \$20,000.

SOLUTION

Using Column 4 from Appendix B, we have

$$PV = \$20{,}000\,(.751315) = \$15{,}026.30$$

At 10 percent, the \$20,000 has a present value of \$15,026.30. □

Present Value of an Annuity

Frequently, funds are received uniformly from year to year as a result of investment in equipment or pension funds and the like. The present value of an annuity is found using Equation (17).

$$PV = S\left[\frac{(1+i)^n - 1}{i(1+i)^n}\right] \tag{17}$$

Values corresponding to the bracketed portion of Equation (17) may be found in Appendix B, Column 5.

EXAMPLE 9
Present Value of an Annuity

A firm will receive \$2,000 each year at the *start of each year* for eight years. Using an 8 percent discount rate, determine the present value of the cash inflows.

SOLUTION

The cash flows consist of an initial \$2,000 payment plus *seven* annual year-end payments. The present value is determined as follows:

$$\begin{aligned} PV &= \$2{,}000 + \$2{,}000\,(5.206370) \\ &= \$2{,}000 + \$10{,}412.74 \\ &= \$12{,}412.74 \end{aligned}$$

The cash inflows have a present value of $12,412.74 when discounted. Notice that the factor (5.206370) is taken from the 7-year row for 8 percent in column 5, Appendix B, since the cash flows in question will have an initial payment and then one at *the end of each of the next seven years.* □

EXAMPLE 10
Present Value

Assuming the cash flows tabulated below are discounted at 10 percent, determine their present value.

Years	*Amount*
1–5	$1,000
6–10	1,200
11–20	900

SOLUTION

The answer may be determined using the factors in Appendix B, column 5, adjusted as follows.

1. The factor for years 1–5 is obtained directly from the tables: 3.790987.

2. The factor for years 6–10 is obtained by subtracting the factor for years 1–5 from the factor for years 1–10: 6.144567 − 3.790787 = 2.353780.

3. The factor for years 11–20 is obtained by subtracting the factor for years 1–10 from the factor for years 1–20: 8.513564 − 6.144567 = 2.368997.

Amount	*Present-Value Factor*	*Present Value*
$1,000	3.790787	$3,790.79
1,200	2.353780	2,824.54
900	2.368997	2,132.10
		$8,747.43

The present value of the stream of cash inflows shown in this example is $8,747.43. □

EXAMPLE 11

Present Value of Alternative Depreciable Lives

In Chapter 3 we developed the cash flow tax benefits of using a five-year versus a seven-year depreciable life for an asset costing $10,000 and subject to investment tax credit. The relative tax benefits as developed in Chapter 3, using straight-line depreciation, are summarized in Table 6-2 as they were shown in Chapter 3.

Determine the present value of the difference, using 10, 15, and 20 percent discount rates.

SOLUTION

Year	*Difference*	*PVF 10%*	*PV 10%*	*PVF 15%*	*PV 15%*	*PVF 20%*	*PV 20%*
Present	−$333	1	−$333	1	−$333	1	−$333
1–5	+ 263	3.790787	+ 997	3.352155	+ 882	2.990612	+ 786
6–7	− 657	1.077632	− 708	0.808265	− 531	0.61398	− 403
			−$ 44		+$ 18		+$ 50

At 10 percent, the tax benefits of using the seven-year life exceed those of the five-year life. That is, it would be preferable to get the additional $333 investment tax credit at the expense of spreading the depreciation over seven rather than five years. However, at 15 percent the situation has changed, and it is preferable to select the five-year life. The present value of the difference in tax benefits resulting from taking depreciation in five versus seven years more than offsets the loss in investment tax credits. However, if the discount rate is increased still further, ulti-

Table 6-2. Relative tax benefits of five- versus seven-year life, using straight-line depreciation.

Year	*Five-Year Life*	*Seven-Year Life*	*Difference (column 2 − column 3)*
Present	—	$333	−$333
1	$920	657	+ 263
2	920	657	+ 263
3	920	657	+ 263
4	920	657	+ 263
5	920	657	+ 263
6	—	657	− 657
7	—	657	− 657

mately the seven-year life will prevail once again, since the investment tax credit will become the dominant factor. □

The concepts of present and future value can be combined to perform useful functions such as determining the payments which must be made to a pension fund in order to be able to draw a given amount upon retirement (a defined benefit plan). This is demonstrated in Example 12.

EXAMPLE 12
Present and Future Value

Smith wants to retire in 25 years with an annual pension of $30,000, for a period of 20 years. Assuming Smith can obtain 9 percent return, determine the amount he must place in his pension each year at year-end.

SOLUTION

First, determine how much Smith must have in 25 years to be able to draw $30,000 per year for 20 years at 9 percent return; that is, determine the present value of the $30,000 for 20 years.

$$PV = \$30{,}000 \times 9.128546 = \$273{,}856.38$$

The payments over 25 years required to yield the needed $273,856.38 are determined using the future-value tables, column 2.

$$\begin{aligned} FV &= \$273{,}856.38 \\ \text{Payment} \times FV \text{ factor} &= \$273{,}856.38 \\ \text{Payment} \times 84.700896 &= \$273{,}856.38 \\ \text{Payment} &= \frac{\$273{,}856.38}{84.700896} \\ &= \$3{,}233.22 \end{aligned}$$

Smith must contribute $3,233.22 for 25 years in order to be able to draw $30,000 for 20 years from his defined benefit pension plan. □

The pension of $30,000 in Example 12 may seem rather high. However, if inflation were 7 percent a year for the 25-year period, the purchasing power of the $30,000 in terms of today's dollars would be only 0.184249 ($30,000) = $5,527.47. The discount factor corresponds to the present value at 7 percent for 25 years. If inflation were to average 10 percent for the 25-year period, the $30,000 payment would be worth only 0.092296 ($30,000) = $2,768.88. Further, note that the present values for the pension fund payments are for the *first year* of payment only. If inflation continued, subsequent years' payments would have even less purchasing power.

EXAMPLE 13
Defined Contribution Pension Plan

An executive aged 40 plans for retirement at age 65. His current earnings are $40,000 per year. He estimates that his earnings will average as tabulated below.

Age	*Average Earnings*
41–45	$47,000
46–50	55,000
51–55	63,000
56–60	70,000
61–65	78,000

Assuming he places 10 percent of his salary into a defined contribution plan at the end of each year, determine how much will have accrued at 9 percent return. Then determine how much he will be able to draw each year for the next 20 years.

SOLUTION

Use Appendix B, column 2. Since the average salary is given for five-year periods, the annuity factors may be added for each five-year increment. The first (for years 41–45) corresponds to years 21 to 25 in column 2. Table 6-3 shows the resulting figures.

At age 65 the executive would have $477,933.85 in his pension fund. The amount that he will be able to draw for the next 20 years is computed below.

$$\text{Payment} = \frac{\$477{,}933.85}{PV \text{ factor}}$$

$$\text{Payment} = \frac{\$477{,}933.85}{9.128546}$$

$$= \$52{,}355.97$$

The annual pension would be $52,355.97 □

Table 6-3. Funding of defined contribution pension plan.

Age	Years to Retirement	Average Contribution	Compound Interest Factor	Value at Age 65
41–45	25–21	$4,700	33.540776*	$157,641.64
46–50	20–16	5,500	21.799204	119,895.62
51–55	15–11	6,300	14.167986	89,258.31
56–60	10–6	7,000	9.208219	64,457.53
61–65	5–1	7,800	5.984711	46,680.75
				$477,933.85

* 33.540776 = 84.700896 − 51.160120 (year 25 less year 20 from Appendix B, column 2).

In this chapter, the tools of discounted cash flow analysis have been developed. Our next task is to apply them to various problems in the field of capital budgeting. We will commence with this task in Chapter 7, under conditions of "certainty." In this context "certainty" means normal risk. In Chapter 8 we explain how to deal with the evaluation of projects that are expected to have risk outside of the normal bounds for a company. In Chapter 9, the methods of discounted cash flow are applied to the evaluation of leases.

CHAPTER 7

How to Evaluate Capital Investment Projects

In the first six chapters, we described how to go about making capital acquisition decisions. A 15-step plan for developing a capital budget was presented in Chapter 1. On the basis of this plan, we systematically described how to obtain the requisite cash flow estimates based on marketing, financial, and manufacturing forecasts while considering the important tax implications of acquisition decisions. This was the subject of Chapters 2 and 3.

We next noted that acquisition plans cannot be made without considering how the acquisitions are to be financed. This led us to consider the firm's financial structure and to compute the cost of capital. The cost of capital, which represents the composite of the costs of funds that will be used to acquire the assets, provides a key benchmark for project evaluation: projects with expected returns greater than the benchmark cost will be considered as candidates for acceptance, whereas other projects will not. Obviously, such a criterion for selection has exceptions. Some essential projects may not meet the test. Nearly all government-mandated projects will not. But such projects will be accepted nonetheless. Further, some projects that do meet the test may be undesirable because they will change the business risk complexion or be undesirable for various other reasons. Consequently, these will not be undertaken. While there are exceptions, the *cost of capital in most instances provides a very useful basis for project evaluation.*

Since asset acquisition through purchase may be either undesirable or not feasible, the alternative of asset acquisition through leasing must be examined. In Chapter 5 we discussed the merits and drawbacks of using leasing as opposed to purchasing. We will revisit the question of leasing in Chapter 9. At that time we will explain how to evaluate alternative leases and how to decide between purchasing and leasing.

In Chapter 6 we presented the basics of discounted cash flow analysis, which form the keystone to the most useful methods for analyzing the worth of projects to a business. The discounted cash flow method is fundamental to project evaluation. We will be using it throughout the rest of the book.

At this juncture we are prepared to commence with the analysis of proposed capital investment projects. Throughout this and the following chapters we will be discussing decisions using as primary inputs the expected after-tax cash inflows resulting from the operation. In most instances, the benchmark for acceptance will be the company's cost of capital or the cost of capital adjusted to compensate for risk.

In our initial discussion of project evaluation we will assume that the acceptance of projects under consideration will not alter the business risk. This very important assumption will not hold for all investments available to a company. However, the bulk of capital expenditures is for the replacement of aging and/or wearing plant facilities, vehicles, and the like. In general, the acquisition of replacements or even new plant and equipment for expansion within the bounds of the company's current business will not alter the risk complexion. Thus the value of most projects can be accurately assessed using the criteria described in this chapter.

In the following chapter we will describe processes that permit the evaluation of projects which, if accepted, would change the company's risk position.

In all phases of the process of evaluating capital investments, it is essential to use accurate cash flow estimates. If the estimates are not accurate, the results of the evaluation process will be erroneous. The most sophisticated of analytical techniques applied to poor inputs will still produce inaccurate results. Thus, if you are unsure about the cost and cash flow estimates for any project, we suggest making a thorough review of the project and, at the minimum, developing three sets of estimates: most likely, best case, and worst case. The figures corresponding to each set of estimates can then be used as inputs and the expected results obtained for each. Depending on the results and the likelihood of each, a decision for acceptance or rejection can be made.

An Overview of Project Evaluation Techniques

To provide a point of departure, we cite three factors that Norman E. Pflomm[1] has noted as basic to the capital project evaluation process:

1. The computed measures of project attractiveness should be *consistently* applied to all projects.
2. The quantitative measure(s) should be used as a guide rather than as the sole basis for approval or rejection of capital projects.
3. Management should completely understand the assumptions made in the analysis, how the computations were carried out, and what the final results really mean.

Each of these points is sound advice to management. Consistency in evaluation is very important—the same measure(s) should be applied to each proposed project. The results of the analysis should be used as guides for management; but in the final rounds of decision making, it is the all-important management judgment that must carry the day. The results of the quantitative analysis are important inputs, but they are only *inputs*. Expert judgment based on experience will have the final say. Finally, it is very important for management to understand fully just how the quantitative results were obtained. Without this understanding, misinterpretation and misapplication of the results will occur.

Many different methods for evaluating proposed projects have been developed. Each has particular strengths that make it especially useful depending upon the particular circumstances. Most companies therefore use more than one method; some companies use several. Naturally, for larger-size projects the desirability of using more than one evaluation criterion increases.

Glen H. Petry[2] has studied the reasons for managements' choice of techniques and for employing multiple methods. The reasons cited for selecting a particular evaluation method are summarized in Table 7-1, while the reasons for using multiple techniques are summarized in Table 7-2.

Table 7-1. Reasons for using the various capital budgeting techniques.

Reasons Cited	*Number of Corporations Citing Reasons*	*Percentage of Total*
Recognizes time value of money	37	17
Required for regulated business	27	12
Easy to use	26	12
Familiar to management	22	10
Accepted in our industry	20	9
Capital-intensive industry	18	8
Ease of comparison	15	7
Long-lived investments	15	7
Appropriate	9	4
Other	9	4
High rate of equipment or merchandise obsolescence	8	4
High risks	5	2
Labor-intensive industry	4	2
High cash flow in early years	3	1
Volatile product prices or demand	3	1
Total	221	100

The tables indicate that managers differ with respect to how proposed capital investments should be evaluated. There *should* be differences, because companies are different. Thus it becomes very important to understand how and why each method is used. With this knowledge, the most appropriate evaluation technique can be selected.

Table 7-2. Reasons for using multiple techniques.

Reason	*Number of Responses*	*Percentage of Total*
Multiple criteria	46	21
Different types of projects	43	20
Different types of products	32	15
Different project lives	25	12
Different divisions	19	9
Different sizes of projects	12	6
Different cash flow patterns	8	4
Different approval levels	8	4
Different project locations	7	3
Different personal preferences	6	3
Other	7	3
Total	213	100

With this in mind, we will introduce six commonly used techniques, indicating the importance and shortcomings of each. They fall into two groupings: those which are *not* based on the discounted cash flow (DCF) methodology and those which are. We will initially examine the two methods which fall into the first category: *payback* and *return on investment*.

Payback and Return on Investment

Payback, especially, is a widely used criterion for evaluating projects. Its popularity stems in large part from the fact that it is simple to use and the results are easy to understand. Little explanation is required. Payback just measures the period of time required to recover the investment in the project. It is the period during which the cumulative net cash inflows generated by the project just equal the net cash outflows necessary for the project.

Since payback measures only the time period necessary to recover the investment, it is really not a measure of profitability but rather of the *particular project's expected liquidity*. The degree of project liquidity is viewed as important by many managers, but since payback does *not* measure profitability, it is almost always used in conjunction with another evaluation criterion. Using the payback method to determine the payback period is illustrated in Examples 1 and 2.

EXAMPLE 1

Payback with Equal Annual Cash Inflows

A corporation is evaluating a project that requires a \$60,000 cash outlay and is expected to generate annual net cash inflows of \$8,000 over its 15-year useful life. Determine the payback period for the project.

SOLUTION

The payback period is equal to the net cash outlay divided by the annual net cash inflow:

$$\text{Payback period} = \frac{\text{net cash outlay}}{\text{annual net cash inflow}} = \frac{\$60{,}000}{\$8{,}000} = 7.5 \text{ years}$$

The result indicates that after seven and one-half years the firm's \$60,000 cash outlay will be recovered. □

When net cash inflows are not equal from year to year, the payback period is found as shown in Example 2.

EXAMPLE 2

Payback with Unequal Annual Cash Inflows

ABC Company is evaluating a capital project that requires a $38,000 net cash outlay and will generate net cash inflows of $10,000 for each of the first two years, $8,000 each for years 3 and 4, and $6,000 for each of years 5 through 10. Determine the payback period.

SOLUTION

Table 7-3 is helpful in determining the payback period. As can be seen, the cumulative net cash inflows become equal to $38,000 sometime during year 5. If the cash inflows occur equally throughout the year, this point would be one-third of the way into the year ($2,000 ÷ $6,000). Thus the payback period for this project is 4⅓ years. □

Once the payback period is determined, projects are accepted or rejected depending on the length of the period required to recover their investments. For example, management may feel that it wants to recover investments in discretionary projects within three years. If this benchmark were established then projects having a payback period in excess of three years would be rejected. It is also possible to rank projects using the payback period wherein the ordering is from shorter

Table 7-3. Annual and cumulative expected cash inflows.

Year	*Net Cash Inflow*	*Cumulative Cash Inflows*
1	$10,000	$10,000
2	10,000	20,000
3	8,000	28,000
4	8,000	36,000
5	6,000	42,000
6	6,000	48,000
7	6,000	54,000
8	6,000	60,000
9	6,000	66,000
10	6,000	72,000

to longer payback period. In practice, however, we find that *the payback criterion is more frequently used as a method for identifying potentially undesirable projects than for ranking projects.*

As with other evaluation methods, the use of payback requires a benchmark for acceptability. The benchmark is the maximum number of years permitted for recovery of the project's cost. Establishing this constraint is frequently somewhat arbitrary but should not be. If payback is used, it should be used as a device to identify the projects which management feels will require a long period for cost recovery. These projects may be of above-average importance to the company, since they will tie up capital for an extended period of time. Thus the payback method is useful to alert management to a long-term commitment of capital.

If payback is to be used as a constraint to eliminate some proposed projects, the acceptable payback period should be established consistent with the life cycle of the product being produced, potential for obsolescence due to changes in technology or consumer preference, and the like. Thus the same cutoff should *not* be applied to all projects. Rather, the cutoff should be consistent with the project's expected and intended use and useful life.

Before employing payback, the user should be aware of its drawbacks and limitations:

1. As indicated earlier, payback does not measure profitability. It does provide a measure of the degree of project liquidity. It simply indicates how long it will take to recover the investment and consequently has been called the "fish bait" test.

2. If payback is used as a cutoff constraint to eliminate projects, the user must be aware that *all cash inflows beyond the payback period will be ignored.* Consequently, use of payback in this manner may result in the rejection of some projects that are potentially very profitable.

3. Payback ignores the cost of funds to support the project—even during the payback period. As a consequence, and especially in periods of high cost of money, one very important cost is *not* considered.

Since payback suffers from important limitations, we recommend its use only in conjunction with another evaluation procedure. Specifically, we recommend that payback be used as a supplemental measure to *net present value,* which will be discussed later in this chapter.

Return on Investment (ROI) is a term that has many meanings. Consequently, it is very important that the user define precisely what is meant by return on investment. At least four forms of ROI are in common use. These are summarized in Figure 7-1.

Figure 7-1. Return on investment computed by four different methods.

Proposal—Bench Lathe

Investment	$1,000.00
Estimated useful life	5 years
Income: Year 1	300.00
" 2	300.00
" 3	300.00
" 4	300.00
" 5	300.00
Total	$1,500.00

Method 1: Annual Return on Investment:

$$\frac{\text{annual income}}{\text{original investment}} \times 100 = \frac{300}{1{,}000} \times 100 = 30\%$$

Method 2: Annual Return on Average Investment:

$$\frac{\text{annual income}}{\dfrac{\text{original investment}}{2}} \times 100 = \frac{300}{500} \times 100 = 60\%$$

Method 3: Average Return on Average Investment:

$$\frac{\text{total income} - \text{original investment}}{\dfrac{\text{original investment}}{2} \times \text{years}} \times 100 = \frac{500}{\dfrac{1{,}000}{2} \times 5 \text{ years}} \times 100 = 20\%$$

Method 4: Average Book Return on Investment:

$$\frac{\text{total income} - \text{original investment}}{\text{weighted average investment}^{a}}$$

$$= \frac{500}{\dfrac{1{,}000 + 800 + 600 + 400 + 200}{5} \times 5 \text{ years}} \times 100 = 16\tfrac{2}{3}\%$$

[a] Sum of book values of asset each year, straight-line depreciation over life of project.
Source: Norman E. Pflomm, *Managing Capital Expenditures,* New York: The Conference Board, 1963, p. 43.

Not only are there several differences in definition, but each method may be computed either on a pre- or after-tax basis, which further confuses the situation. Example 3 illustrates four possible ROI calculations.

EXAMPLE 3

Return on Investment Calculations

A firm is evaluating a project which has an original investment of \$24,000 and a project salvage value of \$4,000 at the end of its six-year life. The net income before taxes generated by the project each year is:

Year	*Net Income Before Tax*
1	\$2,000
2	3,500
3	4,000
4	2,400
5	2,000
6	1,000

The firm's marginal tax rate is 40 percent. Determine:

(a) ROI before tax on original investment.
(b) ROI before tax on average investment.
(c) ROI after tax on original investment.
(d) ROI after tax on average investment.

SOLUTION

For parts (a) and (b), we start by determining the average annual net income (NI) before taxes:

$$\text{Average NI before tax} = \frac{\$2{,}000 + 3{,}500 + 4{,}000 + 2{,}400 + 2{,}000 + 1{,}000}{6}$$

$$= \$2{,}483.33$$

$$\text{(a)}\quad \begin{matrix}\text{ROI before tax on}\\ \text{original investment}\end{matrix} = \frac{\$2{,}483.33}{\$24{,}000} = 10.35 \text{ percent}$$

$$\text{(b)}\quad \begin{matrix}\text{ROI before tax on}\\ \text{average investment}\end{matrix} = \frac{\$2{,}483.33}{(\$24{,}000 + \$4{,}000)/2} = \frac{\$2{,}483.33}{\$14{,}000}$$

$$= 17.74 \text{ percent}$$

For parts (c) and (d), we must determine average annual net income after taxes. If the firm's marginal tax rate is assumed to remain constant at 40 percent over the six-year life of the project, then the average annual net income after tax will merely equal the average annual before-tax figure multiplied by 1 minus the 40 percent tax rate:

$$\begin{aligned}\text{Average NI after tax} &= (\text{average NI before tax})(1 - \text{tax rate})\\ &= (\$2{,}483.33)(1 - .4)\\ &= \$1{,}490.\end{aligned}$$

(c) ROI after tax on original investment $= \dfrac{\$1{,}490}{\$24{,}000} = 6.21$ percent

(d) ROI after tax on average investment $= \dfrac{\$1{,}490}{(\$24{,}000 + \$4{,}000)/2} = \dfrac{\$1{,}490}{\$14{,}000}$

$= 10.64$ percent □

There is nothing too challenging about computing the return on investment. However, as pointed out at the beginning of this chapter, management should understand how the ROI benchmark figures have been calculated so that a relevant comparison can be made for the project under evaluation.

There are three major shortcomings of the ROI criterion:

1. The timing of the inflows from the asset's operation is ignored. That is, the time value of money is not considered. Thus an asset with high cash inflows late in its life would have the same average return as an asset with high inflows early in its life. Obviously, the two assets are not of equal value to a company.

2. The meaning of the resulting ROI value is not entirely clear, since balance sheet book values are used in the calculations. These book values have no particular relationship to the market value or the productive value of the asset under evaluation.

3. There is no benchmark for project acceptance (as there is for payback and the discounted cash flow criteria). The cost of capital is based on the after-tax cost of funds used for financing. Comparing pretax ROI with the cost of capital is therefore erroneous. Further, even if ROI is computed on an after-tax basis, the fact that the time value of money is ignored renders the cost of capital invalid as a benchmark.

Given the shortcomings described and the fact that ROI has almost as many definitions as users, we strongly discourage its use.

We now turn to the consideration of the discounted cash flow methods, which provide accurate and meaningful representations of the profitability and attractiveness of the projects under evaluation.

Discounted Cash Flow Evaluation Criteria

There are four important discounted cash flow evaluation procedures which we will examine in this chapter: *net present value, profitability index, internal rate of return,* and *equivalent annual charge*. As we will see, the net present value is superior in nearly all applications; if consistently used, it will lead to achieving the goal of maximizing the value of the business. Further, we will note that the equivalent-annual-charge method is valuable for special applications such as establishing rate structures and for internal billing purposes when it is appropriate to allocate acquisition costs over the asset's life. We now start with net present value, once again limiting the discussion to the evaluation of projects that will not affect the company's risk posture.

NET PRESENT VALUE

Net present value involves discounting the expected after-tax cash inflows (and outflows, if they take place over a period of time) relating to a project back to their present value. The discounting process is the one described in Chapter 6. After the discounting process has been completed, the present value of the inflows is compared with the present value of the outflows. If the present value of the inflows exceeds the present value of the outflows, it follows that the productive value of the asset to the firm is greater than the cost, at the discount rate being used. The project would therefore be a viable candidate for acceptance, and its use should increase the value of the business. The appropriate discount rate to use is the firm's cost of capital, since this has been established as the benchmark for acceptance.

The net present value method for project evaluation involves algebraically summing the present values of the expected inflows and outflows from the operations of a project. The difference is the net present value (NPV), found using Equation (18).

$$NPV = \sum_{t=0}^{n} \frac{S_t}{(1 + k)^t} - A_0 \tag{18}$$

where A_0 = present value of the after-tax cost of the project
S_t = cash inflow to be received in period t
k = the appropriate discount rate, usually the firm's cost of capital
t = time period

A_0 represents the present value of the cash outflows. If an asset is purchased, the outflow is likely to take place at one point in time, whereas if the asset is leased, the outflow will be over several periods, as shown in Equation (19).

$$A_0 = \sum_{t=0}^{n} \frac{A_t}{(1 + k)^t} \tag{19}$$

where A_t = cash outflow in period t

When NPV is used as the criterion for project or lease selection, the goal is to accept those projects (or leases) that have the highest net present value at the appropriate discount rate. We now illustrate the use of the net present value method in Example 4.

EXAMPLE 4

Net Present Value Calculations

Apex Company, in its ongoing quest to achieve new heights, is evaluating a project with the following expected cash flows:

Year	*After-Tax Cash Flow*
Present	−$40,000
1	+ 15,000
2	+ 18,000
3	+ 20,000
4	+ 6,000
4 (salvage value)	+ 5,000

Apex has a weighted average after-tax cost of capital of 16 percent. Because Apex is uncertain about the appropriate discount rate to use, it wants to determine the project's NPV for 16 percent and 20 percent.

SOLUTION

The NPV for this project can be computed using Equation (18) or with the aid of Tables 7-4 and 7-5, which reflect the appropriate discount

Table 7-4. Computation of discounted cash flows at 16 percent discount rate.

Time	*After-Tax Cash Flow*	*Discount Factors @ 16 Percent*	*Discounted Cash Flows*
Present	−$40,000	1.000000	−$40,000.00
1	+ 15,000	.862069	+ 12,931.04
2	+ 18,000	.743163	+ 13,376.93
3	+ 20,000	.640658	+ 12,813.16
4	+ 6,000	.552291	+ 3,313.75
4	+ 5,000	.552291	+ 2,761.46
		NPV =	+$ 5,196.34

factors from column 4 in Appendix B. Table 7-4 summarizes the results for a discount rate of 16 percent. Since the NPV for this project is positive, it is a quantitatively attractive candidate for acceptance if 16 percent is the appropriate discount rate.

For a discount rate of 20 percent, see Table 7-5. Again, since the NPV is positive, the project is a viable candidate for acceptance at a 20 percent required rate of return. □

Net present value is based on the time value of money, does measure profitability, and provides a firm basis for project acceptance or rejection when used in conjunction with the firm's cost of capital. We strongly recommend its use.

When net present value is used, the goal is to first identify those projects with positive net present values. Then, subject to the con-

Table 7-5. Computation of discounted cash flows at 20 percent discount rate.

Time	*After-Tax Cash Flows*	*Discount Factors @ 20 Percent*	*Discounted Cash Flows*
Present	−$40,000	1.000000	−$40,000.00
1	+ 15,000	.833333	+ 12,500.00
2	+ 18,000	.694444	+ 12,500.00
3	+ 20,000	.578704	+ 11,574.08
4	+ 6,000	.482253	+ 2,893.52
4	+ 5,000	.482253	+ 2,411.27
		NPV =	+$ 1,878.87

straints of urgency and the like, the group of projects with the greatest net present value (within the limits of funding available for capital acquisition) is acquired. Further, some projects may be candidates for leasing or project financing. Leasing and project financing may provide a way to expand the limits of a capital budget and permit acquisition of more assets than could be purchased. A note of caution is in order here. Some projects that are not acceptable as purchases *may be* acceptable if leased. Also, some proposed projects that are acceptable if purchased *may not be* acceptable if leased. These differences result from differences in some of the discount rates used in evaluating leases (the subject of Chapter 9).

PROFITABILITY INDEX

The profitability index (PI) is closely related to the NPV criterion and merely determines the ratio of the discounted cash inflows to the discounted cash outflows, as shown in Equation (20).

$$PI = \frac{\text{discounted cash inflows}}{\text{discounted cash outflows}} \tag{20}$$

The use of Equation (20) is demonstrated in Example 5.

EXAMPLE 5

Profitability Index Calculations

Calculate the PI for the project shown in Example 4, first using a 16 percent discount rate and then using a 20 percent discount rate.

SOLUTION

$$PI_{16\%} = \frac{\$45{,}196.34}{\$40{,}000.00} = 1.13$$

$$PI_{20\%} = \frac{\$41{,}878.87}{\$40{,}000.00} = 1.05$$

As you might expect, the PI approaches 1.0 as NPV approaches 0. □

The results of the preceding discussion lead to the following summary of the decision benchmarks for the NPV and PI techniques:

Case	*NPV Criterion*	*PI Criterion*	*Result*
1	NPV $\geq$ 0	PI $\geq$ 1.0	Project is attractive from a quantitative standpoint.
2	NPV < 0	PI < 1.0	Project is not attractive from a quantitative standpoint.

The profitability index is useful in that it provides a measure of the profitability per dollar of investment. The higher the index, the greater the profit per dollar of investment. The index may be used as a ranking device. Projects that have expected high profitability per dollar of investment are ranked highest. But caution must be observed, since the profitability index could lead to ranking a typewriter above a production facility. Again, we stress that to achieve the goal of maximizing the firm's wealth, selection of projects should be based on obtaining the greatest net present value for the *entire group selected.*

INTERNAL RATE OF RETURN

When we calculated the net present value, we used a given discount rate (normally the company's cost of capital). The result was a net present value. If the net present value was positive, we concluded that the productive value of the asset to the business was *greater* than the cost and therefore that the asset warranted consideration for acquisition. In a like manner, if the net present value was negative, we concluded that the productive value of the asset to the business was *lower* than the cost and therefore that the asset should not be considered for acquisition. While the net present value criterion is the most highly recommended discounted cash flow technique, it does not provide the rate of return which the asset is expected to yield over its life.

The *internal rate of return* (IRR) is the rate of return which the asset is expected to yield over its entire life. The internal rate of return is also that discount rate which equates exactly the present value of the cash inflows with the present value of the cash outflows. It is the discount rate which yields a net present value of zero. It may be found using Equation (21).

$$\sum_{t=0}^{n} \frac{S_t}{(1 + r)^t} = \sum_{t=0}^{n} \frac{A_t}{(1 + r)^t} \tag{21}$$

where r = internal rate of return

The internal rate of return is generally found by trial and error (or by using a computer or programmable calculator), since there is no algebraic method to solve Equation (21) for r.

Under the (ideal) conditions that a project generates equal annual cash inflows throughout its life and has a zero salvage value, the IRR is found in a straightforward manner. First, the payback period is calculated as illustrated in Example 1. Second, we look for the factor in column 5 of Appendix B in the row for the useful life of the asset that comes closest to the payback period. Finally, the IRR is the interest rate for which the factor described in the second step comes closest to the payback period. This method is illustrated in Example 6.

EXAMPLE 6

The IRR for Equal Annual Cash Inflows

XYZ Corporation wants to compute the IRR for the project described in Example 1.

SOLUTION

Following the three-step framework, we would find:

1. The payback period for this project as computed in Example 1 is 7.5 years.
2. We now look for the factor 7.5 in column 5 of Appendix B in the 15-year row (since this asset had a 15-year useful life).
3. Looking in row 15 and column 5 on the page for 10 percent, we find that the factor is 7.60608; the corresponding factor on the 11 percent page is 7.19087. The IRR for the project is therefore between 10 percent and 11 percent (since 7.5 is between 7.19087 and 7.60608) and closer to 10 percent. Finding the approximate rate for the IRR, as we have done here, is usually sufficiently accurate. □

In the evaluation of capital investment projects, we often find that projects have varying cash inflows over their lives and that they have significant salvage values at the end of their useful lives. Under such circumstances, we have to resort to the trial-and-error approach alluded

Table 7-6. Cash flows discounted by the internal rate of return.

Time	*After-Tax Cash Flows*	*Discount Factors @ IRR Percent*	*Discounted Cash Flows*
Present	−$40,000	1.0000	−$40,000.00
1	+ 15,000	unknown	unknown
2	+ 18,000	unknown	unknown
3	+ 20,000	unknown	unknown
4	+ 6,000	unknown	unknown
4	+ 5,000	unknown	unknown
		NPV =	$0

to earlier. It is often helpful to use a tabular approach as illustrated in Example 4. The main difference is that, since we are solving for the IRR, we do not know in advance what discount factors should be used in column 3 of the table. Consider now Example 7.

EXAMPLE 7

The IRR for a Complex Cash Flow Series

Determine the IRR for the project under evaluation by Apex Company in Example 4.

SOLUTION

The IRR is the discount rate whose discount factors, when multiplied by the project's cash flows, will exactly equate the discounted cash inflows to the discounted cash outflows (that is, result in NPV = 0). Therefore, Table 7-6 is helpful in posing the problem.

We found in Example 4 that the NPV of the project in question was $5,196.34 for a 16 percent discount rate and $1,878.87 for a 20 percent discount rate. Therefore, the IRR must exceed 20 percent, since the NPV will decrease toward zero as we move to a higher discount rate. As our next trial for IRR, let's use 22 percent. Table 7-7 shows the results.

We see that NPV is still positive but is close to zero. If we repeated the above process for 23 percent, we would find the NPV to be −$353.66. Therefore, the IRR is between 22 percent and 23 percent and is very close to 22.5 percent, since the positive NPV at 22 percent was approximately the same numerical value as the negative NPV at 23

Table 7-7. Computation of discounted cash flows at 22 percent discount rate.

Time	*After-Tax Cash Flows*	*Discount Factors @ 22 Percent*	*Discounted Cash Flows*
Present	−$40,000	1.000000	−$40,000.00
1	+ 15,000	.819672	+ 12,295.08
2	+ 18,000	.671862	+ 12,093.52
3	+ 20,000	.550707	+ 11,014.14
4	+ 6,000	.451399	+ 2,708.39
4	+ 5,000	.451399	+ 2,257.00
		NPV =	+$ 368.13

percent. Again, for our purposes, knowing that the IRR is between 22 and 23 percent is accurate enough. Of course, many business calculators today have an "IRR function" that calculates the IRR correct to several decimal places. □

The IRR shows us the discounted rate of return on the project. A project's attractiveness is determined by comparing the IRR with the firm's cost of capital. Thus the summary matrix presented at the end of the previous section can be expanded to include the IRR criterion, as shown here.

Case	*NPV Criterion*	*PI Criterion*	*IRR Criterion*	*Result*
1	NPV $\geq$ 0	PI $\geq$ 1.0	IRR $\geq$ cost of capital	Project is attractive from a quantitative standpoint.
2	NPV $<$ 0	PI $<$ 1.0	IRR $<$ cost of capital	Project is not attractive from a quantitative standpoint.

We now turn to the final DCF technique, the equivalent-annual-charge approach.

EQUIVALENT ANNUAL CHARGE

The equivalent-annual-charge (EAC) approach determines the annual benefits and costs related to a given project, considering all cash flows over the project's life. The widest use of the EAC method is among utilities, where the annual charge to its customers must be determined in order to cover capital costs, operating costs, and a desired rate of return on a given power-generating plant. The EAC is found using a series of four steps:

1. Find the present value of the salvage value of the project.
2. Subtract the amount found in step 1 from the original cost of the project and multiply the result by the capital recovery factor (that is, the reciprocal of the present value of an annuity factor and the factor shown directly in column 6 of Appendix B) for the required rate of return and the useful life of the project.
3. If the annual operating costs of the project are uniform over the life of the asset, then the equivalent annual charge will be the sum of the value found in step 2 and the annual operating costs; otherwise, go to step 4.
4. When the annual operating costs are unequal, we first must find the present value of the operating costs over the project's life. Next, we multiply this present value by the capital recovery factor for the required rate of return and the useful life of the project. Finally, we add this amount to the amount found in step 2.

The computations involved in this procedure can be summarized as shown in Equation (22).

$$EAC = \begin{array}{l}\text{equivalent annual}\\\text{cost associated with}\\\text{the capital invested}\\\text{in the project}\end{array} + \begin{array}{l}\text{equivalent annual cost}\\\text{associated with operating}\\\text{the project over its life}\end{array} \qquad (22)$$

Steps 1 and 2 are required to compute the first term on the right side of the equation, and either step 3 or step 4 is required to compute the second term.

The determination of the EAC is illustrated in Example 8.

EXAMPLE 8

Computation of Equivalent Annual Charge

An electric utility wants to determine the equivalent annual charge associated with a project that has an original cost of $1,800,000, a salvage value of $200,000 at the end of its ten-year useful life, and operating costs of $150,000 per year in years 1–4, $225,000 in years 5–8, and $250,000 in years 9 and 10. The firm's required rate of return is 14 percent. Determine the EAC of this project.

SOLUTION

The solution will follow the steps outlined for Equation (22).

Step 1: The present value of the salvage value is

($200,000)(.269744) = $53,949

Step 2: The "capital recovery factor" for 14 percent and ten years is .19171354, which is found directly in column 6 of Appendix B and is the reciprocal of the present value of an annuity factor 5.216116 found in column 5 of Appendix B. The capital recovery factor is multiplied by the difference between the original cost and the value found in step 1:

($1,800,000 − $53,949) × (.19171354) = $334,742

Since the operating costs are not equal each year, we proceed to step 4.

Step 4: The present value of the operating costs over the life of the project is found in Table 7-8.

Next we find the equivalent annual operating cost by multiplying this present value by the capital recovery factor:

($969,529)(.19171354) = $185,872

Finally, we find the EAC by adding this amount to the value found in step 2:

EAC = $334,742 + $185,872 = $520,614

Thus this project has uniform annual costs of $520,614, which will cover annual operating costs, annual recovery of the investment in the project, and a rate of return of 14 percent. □

Table 7-8. Computation of present value of operating costs.

Year	*Operating Cost*	*PV Factor @ 14%*	*PV of Operating Cost*
1	$150,000	.877193	$131,579
2	150,000	.769468	115,420
3	150,000	.674972	101,246
4	150,000	.592080	88,812
5	225,000	.519369	116,858
6	225,000	.455587	102,507
7	225,000	.399637	89,918
8	225,000	.350559	78,876
9	250,000	.307508	76,877
10	250,000	.269744	67,436
		PV of Operating Costs =	$969.529

The EAC method is a valuable managerial tool, since it takes into account all the cash flows over the life of the project, the time value of money, and the firm's cost of capital or required rate of return. We recommend its use not only by regulated firms but by firms in the *evaluation of significant nondiscretionary capital expenditures that do not generate profits*. For example, many firms must meet clean-air and/or clean-water standards imposed by state, local, and federal regulatory bodies. The EAC method is ideal for comparing alternative types of pollution control equipment that have varying patterns of expenditures over their lives.

This concludes our survey of the discounted cash flow (DCF) techniques for evaluating proposed capital projects. The next section discusses the assumptions underlying each of these four approaches.

A Closer Look at the Four DCF Methods

As the four DCF methods for evaluating capital projects were discussed and illustrated in the preceding sections, several questions will have arisen in the minds of our readers. To anticipate some of these questions and to provide guidance concerning the final decision on any proposed capital project, we now discuss a number of the characteristics of the approaches. Because of the restricted area of application of the EAC approach, we limit our comments here to the first three DCF methods, NPV, PI, and IRR.

Initially, we should stress that all three DCF methods—NPV, PI, and IRR—will provide consistent recommendations to either accept or reject a *single proposed capital investment project*. This was evident as the reader studied the summary table presented at the end of the section discussing the internal rate of return.

The three methods differ in the following two significant ways. First, the NPV method provides an *absolute measure of attractiveness* for the project(s) under evaluation; this absolute measure is the dollar amount of the excess of discounted cash inflows over discounted cash outflows. On the other hand, both the PI and IRR methods provide *relative measures of attractiveness* for the project(s) under evaluation; the PI shows the number of dollars of discounted cash inflow per dollar of discounted cash outflow, and the IRR shows the percentage rate of return per dollar of investment in the project.

This means that the NPV method will tend to prefer projects that require larger cash outlays, because such projects would also tend to have a greater absolute excess of discounted cash inflows (DCI) over discounted cash outflows (DCO). Conversely, PI and IRR would tend to prefer projects that require smaller cash outlays, because these projects tend to have a larger ratio of DCI to DCO and a higher percentage return per dollar of investment.

The second difference among the three methods is the implicit assumption which is made concerning the return earned on the *reinvestment of the project's intermediate cash flows* (cash inflows which occur throughout the life of the project). This is referred to as the "reinvestment assumption." The NPV and PI methods assume that a project's intermediate cash flows can be reinvested at the firm's cost of capital or the required rate of return on the project; on the other hand, the IRR approach assumes that intermediate cash flows can be reinvested at the calculated IRR for the project under evaluation.

The respective models have the stated reinvestment assumptions because the rate of return on intermediate cash flows is assumed to be equal to the interest rate used to discount all the cash flows. NPV and PI discount cash flows at the firm's cost of capital or required rate of return. Hence this is the rate at which these methods implicitly assume intermediate cash flows can be reinvested. The IRR method discounts cash flows at the IRR for the project under consideration; hence this is its assumed reinvestment rate.

We would argue that the reinvestment assumption made by the NPV and PI methods is more realistic and more conservative than the assumption made by the IRR method. The firm would always be able to reinvest intermediate cash flows at its cost of capital, because this is the minimum attractive rate of return used in the evaluation of proposed projects. Of course, the same statement could not be made about reinvesting cash flows at the particular IRR earned on an especially attractive project. For example, consider a firm that has a 15 percent cost of capital and is evaluating a project that has an IRR of 25 percent; the IRR method would tend to overstate the attractiveness of this project unless the intermediate cash flows could be reinvested at 25 percent, which would be unlikely, since this firm would tend to have the opportunity to invest in new projects that have a return approximating its cost of capital. The NPV and PI methods would not similarly overestimate this project's attractiveness because of their more conservative reinvestment assumption.

To conclude this section, we again state our preference for the NPV model. There are two major reasons for this. First, it measures the absolute increase in the firm's value that will result if the project is accepted. We have stated earlier that the global goal of financial managers should be to maximize the value of the firm. The NPV approach provides the firm with the most relevant information concerning its global goal. Second, the NPV approach carries with it a more appropriate reinvestment assumption.

Possible Conflicts in Project Ranking

We mentioned earlier that when the firm is evaluating a single project (or a project that is independent of all other projects), the NPV, PI, and IRR approaches will provide consistent accept or reject signals. However, when the firm is evaluating multiple projects from which only a subset can be accepted, conflicts in project ranking can occur among the NPV, PI, and IRR models.

There are two common situations in which only a subset of the projects under evaluation can be undertaken by the firm. First, the firm may be evaluating mutually exclusive projects (that is, a set of two or more projects that perform the same function, so that only a single project can be accepted). Second, the firm may operate under "capital rationing"—that is, it may not have sufficient capital available to accept all projects which it feels are attractive.

Either of these conditions, plus one or more of the following three characteristics of the projects, could lead to conflicts in project ranking:

1. The projects require different net cash outlays.
2. The projects exhibit differing timing of cash inflows.
3. The projects have unequal useful lives.

The resolution of conflicts in project ranking which may occur in these circumstances is quite involved. Our recommendations would be:

1. In general, follow the NPV criterion because of its superiority.
2. Consider qualitative factors that differentiate the mutually exclusive projects and determine whether those factors are sufficiently strong to swing the decision to a different "preferred project."
3. Perform a "sensitivity analysis" on the projects under evalua-

tion in order to ascertain how much conditions over the project's life would have to change before there would be a different "preferred project." This complex but very important dimension of capital project evaluation is explored in the next chapter and in Chapter 10.

4. Given the preceding steps and the trade-offs discovered among the projects, select the project or portfolio of projects that best meets the firm's hierarchy of goals.

Summary of Recommendations for the Evaluation of Capital Expenditures

At this point we should summarize our recommendations for the evaluation of proposed capital projects. First, the use of more than a single evaluation technique (including non-DCF approaches) is often helpful in gaining insight into various relevant aspects of the projects under evaluation. Second, the NPV technique should be viewed as superior to all others, because it greatly assists firms in their achievement of the global goal of shareholder wealth maximization and because it is based on realistic assumptions concerning reinvestment of project cash inflows. Third, performing sensitivity analysis and risk analysis provides management with valuable insights into the impact of changing conditions on project selection.

Maximization of net present value generally leads to maximization of shareholders' wealth over the long run. However, the maximization of NPV must be tempered by the evaluation of the impact the investment decision will have on the firm's other significant goals. Ranking projects using a discounted cash flow technique does not consider ramifications on the firm's other goals.

It is possible, in fact, for a DCF analysis to favor projects that, while attractive in the long run, may produce erratic year-to-year earnings. Since management and investors place heavy emphasis on both stability of earnings and regular growth from year to year, we must consider maximization of NPV within the constraints of earnings stability as well as other goals. In addition to a qualitative evaluation of the impact of projects on the firm's relevant goals, sophisticated mathematical programming approaches have been recommended.

Lerner and Rappaport[3] have developed a linear-programming solution to the problem of asset selection within the budget constraints as well as the constraint of maintaining earnings stability. Their approach to the problem and its solution are discussed in detail by Clark, Hindelang, and Pritchard.[4] The assumptions underlying the Lerner and Rappaport model are realistic, the solution methodology is straightforward, and the results are consistent with the requirements for regular, steady earnings growth. In addition, other models (for example, goal programming) have been recommended to simultaneously consider a firm's entire hierarchy of goals. But, as with any other evaluative procedure, there is added cost for the increase in information—which brings us to the next area for management consideration.

The process of evaluating capital expenditures is expensive in manpower, time, and facilities. Generally, the larger the firm, the more sophisticated the process. Also, more expensive projects warrant closer scrutiny. Hence management may find it desirable to establish cutoff points with respect to project cost and limit the amount of evaluation to be consistent with the importance of the decision at hand. Establishing a cost-efficient procedure which considers the relevant dimensions of capital expenditure evaluation is the primary goal. In some instances, the degree of examination is pragmatically limited by several constraints on the firm.

While most of the decision process is centered on asset acquisition, management should follow up with periodic revisits to the assets. Several questions deserve close attention. Are the cash flows consistent with the forecasts, and, if not, why not? Is the project producing the promised profits and internal cash flows? Should the project be abandoned? The selection process should be updated at regular intervals, using current information on actual performance. If mistakes were made, as indicated by large inconsistencies with the forecasts that formed the basis for acquisition, the reasons need be understood and incorporated into the evaluation procedure for future projects. In Chapter 11, we examine in detail the procedure for reviewing, auditing, and controlling capital expenditures.

This concludes our examination of the evaluation of proposed capital projects that are assumed to leave the firm's risk posture unchanged. The next chapter explores the question of project evaluation under a change in risk posture.

NOTES

1. *Managing Capital Expenditures,* New York: The Conference Board, 1963.
2. "Effective Use of Capital Budgeting Tools," *Business Horizons,* October 1975; and Patrick J. Davey, *Capital Investments: Appraisals and Hints,* New York: The Conference Board, 1974.
3. Eugene M. Lerner and Alfred Rappaport, "Limit DCF Capital Budgeting," *Harvard Business Review,* September–October 1968, pp. 133–138.
4. John J. Clark, Thomas J. Hindelang, and Robert E. Pritchard, *Capital Budgeting: Planning and Control of Capital Expenditures,* Englewood Cliffs, N.J.: Prentice-Hall, 1979, Chapters 7, 12, 13, and 14.

CHAPTER 8

Risk and Capital Budgeting

An essential element in the management of capital expenditures is an evaluation of the degree of risk associated with proposed capital projects. This evaluation considers how much variability exists in the possible cash flows that may accrue over the project's life. In addition, the evaluation takes into account the firm's risk preferences, its current risk posture, and the interaction of the projects under consideration with the existing operations of the firm.

To a large degree risk and forecasting[1] are directly intertwined. As the quality of forecasts is improved, the degree or risk surrounding an acquisition will decrease. But in an era of very rapid changes it is not possible to know how accurate forecasts will be. Past track records of good forecasting performance may not be maintained in this decade. Accordingly, your position is to base your acquisition/abandonment decision on the "normal" sequence of events (that is, normal cash flows, average useful asset life, moderate inflation, and so on) but make all final decisions on the basis of a *defensive risk posture,* assuming that your normal plans *will not* meet the test of time. In other words, *plan for the long run but stake your dollars on the short run.*

Adopting this "defensive" posture requires modifications of the evaluation procedures described in Chapter 7. One simple way to achieve this defensive goal—a method being used by many companies—is to revert to the payback criterion. If the project is not expected to recover its investment within a relatively short period (perhaps three years), the project is rejected regardless of its net present value or internal rate of return. Such a management decision has the several drawbacks described in Chapter 7. Nonetheless, payback is being used—and we still do not recommend it.

In order to develop a rational method of dealing with risk, it is necessary to come to grips with the basic limitations of forecasting in a period of rapid change. Even given the most sophisticated analytical techniques, we view forecasting today as suffering from two primary limitations:

1. The degree of error in the forecasts is directly correlated to the horizon of the forecast. When we look beyond a very short horizon (perhaps as little as a year), the chance for error increases so rapidly as to put the accuracy of the forecast in serious question.

2. Because of rapidly changing economic factors which *differently* affect each input used to estimate cash flows, it is necessary to forecast and reforecast each input. The aggregate errors may cancel one another (a hoped-for possibility), but the errors may also be cumulative and result in a highly inaccurate forecast.

An example of the second problem is the fact that inflation, although commonly measured by a single index, actually affects each expense item differently. Thus, in forecasting it is necessary to estimate how inflation will affect each income-statement expense item that will be changed as a result of a project's acquisition. Further, it is necessary to estimate the cross-elasticity of demand (how demand for one product or service will be affected as the prices of others are changed). The primary forecasting problem is inflation—inflation that affects every expense item to a different degree and inflation that in aggregate may change over a range of 10 percent in a single year.

In this chapter, we examine procedures for measuring the degree of risk present in a capital project under evaluation. Further, we present alternative approaches for evaluating the trade-offs between risk and return in capital projects. Namely, we introduce two widely accepted techniques for handling risk in capital expenditures analysis: tree diagrams and the risk-adjusted discount method. As will be seen, the risk-adjusted discount approach is a modification of the net present value approach, which was introduced in Chapter 7.

We begin our discussion with a series of definitions that will facilitate our development of the two new approaches.

Conditions of Certainty Versus Risk

In evaluating capital investment projects, the firm may be faced with conditions of "certainty" or "risk." Conditions of certainty are said to exist if the manager knows precisely what the future holds. Of course, seldom, if ever, does the firm face "certain" conditions. Conditions of risk exist if the manager feels that he must resort to an assessment of the probability of various outcomes.

Most managers and analysts are familiar with the technique of specifying "optimistic," "pessimistic," and "most likely" outcomes. In this chapter we will call upon this technique to help represent the uncertain conditions that the firm usually faces relative to future events. For example, consider Figure 8-1, which shows a bar chart representing "optimistic," "pessimistic," and "most likely" estimates for the original cost and the annual net cash inflows over the life of the project. Notice that the height of the bars shows the likelihood or probability that each of the values will occur. Notice further that the sum of the probabilities must equal 1.

Analysts within the firm would arrive at the estimates and their associated probabilities in Figure 8-1 by drawing upon the judgments provided by informed individuals within the firm and by referring to these values for similar projects implemented by the firm. Without question, forecasting future cash flows and their probabilities is no easy task. However, the process becomes more familiar and more accurate as analysts gain experience with repeated use and achieve

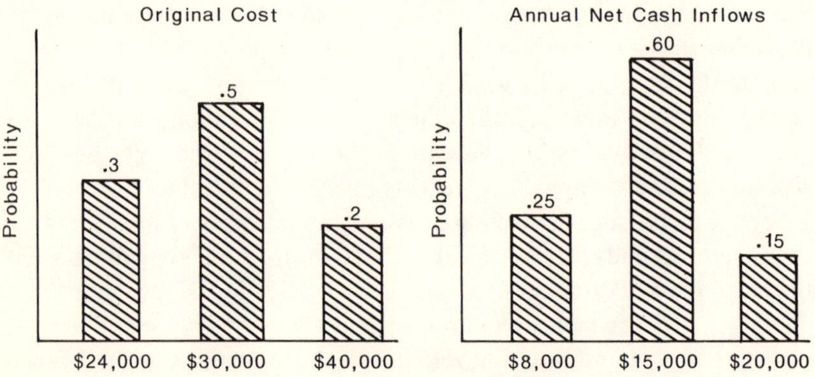

Figure 8-1. Bar charts representing optimistic, pessimistic, and most likely estimates for capital project A2.

greater insight as feedback is obtained by comparing actual values with original estimates.

Upon arriving at estimates such as those shown in Figure 8-1, the analyst often finds it necessary to summarize the values for the original cost and the net cash inflows. This summarization is the next topic.

Expected Values and Variability Measures for Probability Distributions

When the firm faces conditions or "risk" as defined in the previous section, it is helpful to determine both the expected value (or the mean) and the variability in the estimates. There are several measures of variability in the probability distributions shown in Figure 8-1 that could be determined, such as the range (the difference between the lowest and highest values), the variance, and the standard deviation (these latter two measures will be defined presently). However, the most frequently used measure is the standard deviation.

The *expected value* of a probability distribution is just a weighted average of the estimates where the weights used are the probabilities assigned to the "optimistic," "pessimistic," and "most likely" values. The expected value of the estimates for the original cost of the project shown in Figure 8-1 would merely be the amount the firm would expect to pay on the average if projects with similar estimates were purchased a large (say 15 to 20) number of times.

The standard deviation measures collective differences between the weighted average of each item and the expected value, where the item's "weight" in the calculation is the probability that it will occur. Thus *the standard deviation measures the average variability of each item around the expected value;* the greater the standard deviation, the greater the risk or variability in the distribution and the less representative the expected value of the outcomes that could occur.

The expected value of a probability distribution is computed using Equation (23).

$$\overline{R} = \sum_{i=1}^{M} R_i P_i \tag{23}$$

where $\overline{R}$ = the expected value

R_i = the return associated with the ith outcome of the probability distribution

P_i = the probability of occurrence of the ith outcome

M = number of possible outcomes

The standard deviation is computed by Equation (24).

$$\sigma = \sqrt{\sum_{i=1}^{M} P_i(R_i - \overline{R})^2} \qquad (24)$$

where σ = the standard deviation, and all other symbols are as defined above

Equations (23) and (24) are illustrated in Example 1.

EXAMPLE 1

Computing the Expected Value and the Standard Deviation

For the capital project shown in Figure 8-1, determine the expected value and the standard deviation for both the original cost and the annual net cash inflows.

SOLUTION

For the original cost, the expected value is

$$\begin{aligned}\overline{R}_{\text{cost}} &= (.3)(\$24{,}000) + (.5)(\$30{,}000) + (.2)(\$40{,}000)\\ &= \$7{,}200 + \$15{,}000 + \$8{,}000 = \$30{,}200\end{aligned}$$

The standard deviation for the original cost (σ_{cost})

$$\begin{aligned}&= \sqrt{(.3)(24{,}000 - 30{,}200)^2 + (.5)(30{,}000 - 30{,}200)^2 + (.2)(40{,}000 - 30{,}200)^2}\\ &= \sqrt{11{,}532{,}00 + 20{,}000 + 19{,}208{,}000} = \$5{,}546\end{aligned}$$

Thus the cost of the project would be $30,200 on the average with an average variability around the expected value of $5,546.

For the annual net cash inflows, the expected value is

$$\begin{aligned}\overline{R}_{\text{cash inflow}} &= (.25)(\$8{,}000) + (.6)(\$15{,}000) + (.15)(\$20{,}000)\\ &= \$2{,}000 + \$9{,}000 + \$3{,}000 = \$14{,}000\end{aligned}$$

The standard deviation for the annual net cash inflows ($\sigma_{\substack{\text{cash}\\ \text{inflow}}}$)

$$\begin{aligned}&= \sqrt{(.25)(8{,}000 - 14{,}000)^2 + (.6)(15{,}000 - 14{,}000)^2 + (.15)(20{,}000 - 14{,}000)^2}\\ &= \sqrt{9{,}000{,}000 + 600{,}000 + 5{,}400{,}000} = \$3{,}873\end{aligned}$$

Therefore, the project has expected net cash inflows each year of its life of $14,000; in addition, the average variation of the cash inflows around the mean is $3,873. □

It would probably be helpful to provide additional coverage of the importance of the standard deviation. Figure 8-2 shows the normal distribution, which is one of the most widely used distributions under conditions of risk.

The following characteristics of the normal distribution deserve mention. Normal distributions are bell-shaped, symmetric distributions. The *mean* (or expected value), *median* (the middle value), and the *mode* (the most frequent or most probable value), are all the same and equal to $\overline{R}$. The total area under the curve, or the total probability, is equal to 1.0. Since the distribution is symmetic (that is, the distribution on one side of $\overline{R}$ is a mirror image of the distribution on the other side), the area on each side of $\overline{R}$ equals .5. The standard deviation is used to make probability statements as follows:

1. The probability that any value falls in the range $\overline{R} \pm 1\sigma$ is about 68 percent.
2. The probability that any value falls in the range $\overline{R} \pm 2\sigma$ is about 95 percent.
3. The probability that any value falls in the range $\overline{R} \pm 3\sigma$ is about 99 percent.

Thus the standard deviation is an important value for determining probabilities for the normal distribution. The probabilities summarized here are based on Appendix D.

Finally, consider the two normal distributions shown in Figure 8-3. Notice that the two distributions *A* and *B* have the same expected values ($\overline{R}_A = \overline{R}_B$), but distribution *A*'s standard deviation is significantly smaller than distribution *B*'s standard deviation. We would say that distribution *A* has significantly less risk or variability around its mean or expected value compared with distribution *B*. Distribution *A*'s expected value is more representative of the values in the entire distribution because of its smaller standard deviation compared to distribution *B*, in which the credibility of the expected value is challenged by

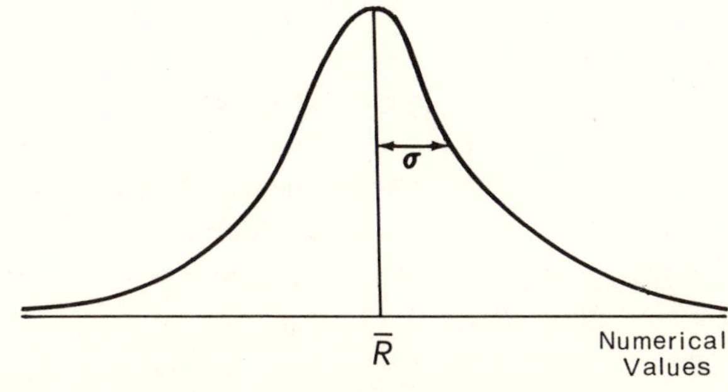

Figure 8-2. The normal distribution.

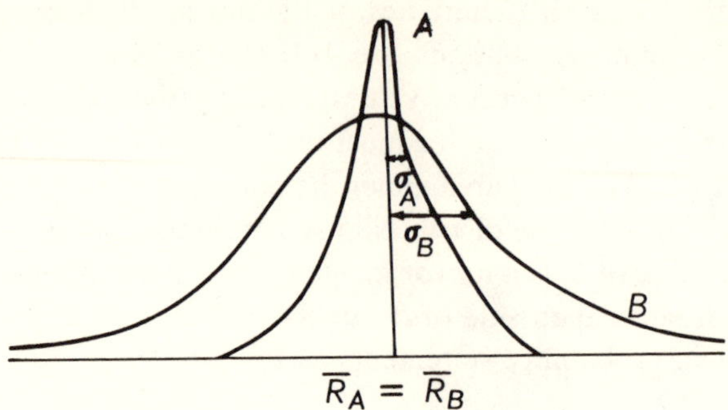

Figure 8-3. Two normal distributions.

the very large standard deviation (which shows the great amount of variability of the values around the mean).

We now turn to a discussion of the most widely used method of evaluating capital investment projects under conditions of risk: *the risk-adjusted discount rate* (RADR) *technique*. As we will see, this model makes use of the expected value and the standard deviation of the returns on the project throughout its useful life.

The Risk-Adjusted Discount Rate Technique

The risk-adjusted discount rate (RADR) technique is a modification of the NPV model discussed in Chapter 7 wherein the discount rate k is adjusted either upward or downward, depending on whether the project under evaluation has greater or smaller risk than those normally undertaken by the firm. The rationale for adjusting the discount rate is that *projects should achieve hurdle rates that reflect their degree of risk; more risky projects should offer greater expected returns in order to be acceptable to management.*

Advocates of the RADR approach suggest that cash inflows generated by projects should be discounted for both the time value of money (using the risk-free rate)[2] and the degree of risk associated with the project (using a risk premium that is added to the risk-free rate).

Equation (25) shows how the expected net present value is determined using a risk-adjusted discount rate.

$$\overline{RAR} = \sum_{t=0}^{n} \frac{\overline{R}_t}{(1 + r')^t} \qquad (25)$$

where $\overline{RAR}$ = expected value of the probability distribution of discounted cash flows over the life of the project

$\overline{R}_t$ = expected value of the distribution of cash flows in period t

r' = risk-adjusted discount rate based on the perceived riskiness of the project

n = number of years in the project's life

It should be noted that since the cash flows (both original cost in year 0 and cash inflows in years 1 through n) for each period are known only by a probability distribution, the risk-adjusted discounted cash flows over the project's life will also be a probability distribution, which has $\overline{RAR}$ as its expected value. This latter distribution also has a standard deviation, which will be discussed presently. Furthermore, if the cash flow distributions are all normal, then the risk-adjusted return distribution will also be normal. In practice, the cash flow distributions often depart from a normal distribution. However, the error involved in assuming a normal distribution is usually not significant.

The way for management to implement the RADR technique is to categorize projects according to their riskiness and then use the discount rate that is felt appropriate for projects in that risk class. The extent of the risk premium assigned to the various risk classes of projects can differ significantly from firm to firm. Management generally uses the following factors to determine the risk premium:

Its perception of the risk associated with the project per se.
Its view of risk–return trade-offs.
The firm's initial wealth position.
The project's impact on the firm's other goals.

Table 8-1 presents one possible approach for classifying projects and the risk premiums that one firm's management felt appropriate after its evaluation of the four factors just enumerated. Example 2 illustrates the use of Equation (25) and Table 8-1.

EXAMPLE 2

Computation of the Expected RAR Value

Acme Company is evaluating the project shown in Figure 8-1. This project has a three-year useful life, and the management of the firm has classified it into new-investment category II (that is, management feels that the appropriate risk-adjusted discount rate for this project is the

Table 8-1. Return requirements for different investment groups.

Investment Grouping	*Required Return*
Replacement investments—category I (new machines or equipment, vehicles, etc., which will perform essentially the same function as older equipment which is to be replaced)	Risk-free rate plus 6%
Replacement investments—category II (new machines or equipment which replace older equipment but are more technologically advanced, require different operator skills, require different manufacturing approaches, or the like; examples would include implementation of electronic data processing equipment to replace manual accounting and payroll systems)	Risk-free rate plus 9%
Replacement investments—category III (new facilities such as buildings and warehouses which will replace older facilities; the new plants may be in the same or a different location)	Risk-free rate plus 12%
New investment—category I (new facilities and associated equipment which will produce or sell the same products as already being produced)	Risk-free rate plus 7%
New investment—category II (new facilities or machinery to produce or sell a product line closely related to the existing product line)	Risk-free rate plus 10%
New investment—category III (new facilities or machinery or acquisition of another firm to produce or sell a product line unrelated to the company's primary business)	Risk-free rate plus 18%
Research and development—category I (research and development which is directed toward specific goals such as developing new computer circuitry with which the firm's engineers are already very familiar)	Risk-free rate plus 15%
Research and development—category II (research in basic areas where goals have not been precisely defined and the outcome may be unknown)	Risk-free rate plus 25%

From John J. Clark, Thomas J. Hindelang, and Robert E. Pritchard, *Capital Budgeting: Planning and Control of Capital Expenditures,* Englewood Cliffs, N.J.: Prentice-Hall, 1979, pp. 128 and 132. Reprinted by permission of the publisher.

risk-free rate plus 10 percent). Forecasts have been made for the risk-free rate over the next three years, with 6 percent per year being the best estimate. Determine $\overline{RAR}$, using Equation (25).

SOLUTION

In Example 1, we found that the expected cost of the project was \$30,200 and the expected net cash inflow each year over the asset's three-year life was \$14,000. When we use these values in Equation (25), cash outflows will become negative values and cash inflows will be positive values. As determined from Table 8-1, the appropriate risk-adjusted discount rate is 16 percent (the estimated risk-free rate of 6 percent plus the risk adjustment of 10 percent), since this project has been placed into new-investment category II by management. The computation of $\overline{RAR}$ is as follows:

$$\begin{aligned}\overline{RAR} &= \sum_{t=0}^{n} \frac{\overline{R}_t}{(1 + tr')^t} \\ &= -\$30{,}200 + \frac{\$14{,}000}{(1.16)} + \frac{\$14{,}000}{(1.16)^2} + \frac{\$14{,}000}{(1.16)^3} \\ &= -\$30{,}200 + \$31{,}442.46 \\ &= \$1{,}242.46\end{aligned}$$

The same results are obtained using the discount factors from Appendix B (see column 5, row 3, for a 16 percent discount rate):

$$\begin{aligned}\overline{RAR} &= -\$30{,}200 + \$14{,}000(2.245890) \\ &= -\$30{,}200 + \$31{,}442.46 \\ &= \$1{,}242.46\end{aligned}$$

Since this project has a positive $\overline{RAR}$, it is a candidate for acceptance, but we must consider the amount of variability in the distribution of the RAR values over the project's life. □

The next section explores the method we use to determine the standard deviation of the RAR distribution.

VARIABILITY IN THE RISK-ADJUSTED NPV DISTRIBUTION

In Chapter 7 we saw that the NPV model assessed project attractiveness on the basis of whether or not the computed NPV was positive. Further, projects were ranked according to the magnitudes of their NPVs, since this value shows the increase in shareholders' wealth position as a result of accepting the project. Such a criterion is appropriate where the project's cash flows are assumed to be known precisely. However, under conditions of risk, we must consider both the expected value of the risk-adjusted NPV distribution ($\overline{RAR}$) *and* the amount of variability present in this distribution. *Under conditions of risk, many firms utilizing the risk-adjusted NPV model have an acceptance criterion which sets a minimum probability that the project will achieve a positive risk-adjusted NPV over its useful life.* That is, the firm, using a discount rate appropriate for the risk class of the project under evaluation, may state that the probability must be at least .8 that the project will achieve a positive risk-adjusted NPV.

In order to make such a probability statement, we must determine the standard deviation of the risk-adjusted NPV distribution. Given this standard deviation and the expected value of the distribution, found above, *plus the assumption that the cash flow distribution for each year of the project's life is approximately normal,* we can determine the probability of achieving a positive RAR value in a straightforward manner. This is accomplished through the use of the table of normal distribution (see Appendix D) and the widely used Z formula shown in Equation (26).

$$Z = \frac{DV - \overline{RAR}}{\sigma_{RAR}} \tag{26}$$

where Z = standardized Z value that will be used to determine probabilities from the normal table

DV = desired value for the risk-adjusted NPV to exceed for the project under evaluation

$\overline{RAR}$ = expected value of the risk-adjusted NPV distribution for the project under evaluation

σ_{RAR} = standard deviation of the risk-adjusted NPV distribution

Note that Equation (26) will determine the standarized Z value associated with any desired risk-adjusted net present value. If the manager were interested in determining the standardized Z value associated with, say, $10,000, this amount would be substituted for DV in Equation (26). Using this standardized Z value, a probability statement could be made about the likelihood that the risk-adjusted NPV for the project under evaluation would exceed $10,000. Of course, *an important value to consider for DV is zero, because the firm is interested in determining how likely it is that the project will increase shareholders' wealth, given the riskiness of the project.* Other positive values, such as \$5,000, \$10,000, or \$50,000, used for DV would show the desired increase in shareholders' wealth if the project were accepted and its benefits discounted at a rate consistent with its risk. Example 3 illustrates the use of Equation (26).

EXAMPLE 3
Probability Statements about RAR

For the project shown in Example 2, compute the probability that the risk-adjusted NPV will equal or exceed (a) a value of zero, (b) a value of \$2,000. For the purposes of this example, assume that σ_{RAR} equals \$1,000.

SOLUTION

For each of the desired values shown, we would just substitute it into Equation (26) for DV, along with $\overline{RAR}$ = \$1,246.46 as in Example 2 and σ_{RAR} = \$1,000 as given above. The probability that the risk-adjusted NPV will exceed zero is found using Equation (26) as follows:

$$Z = \frac{0 - \$1{,}242.46}{\$1{,}000} = -1.24$$

Looking up the value of 1.24 in Appendix D, we see that it is associated with an area under the normal curve of .3925. The diagram in Figure 8-4 is helpful in arriving at a probability statement about the likelihood that the RAR value is positive. As can be seen from the figure, the

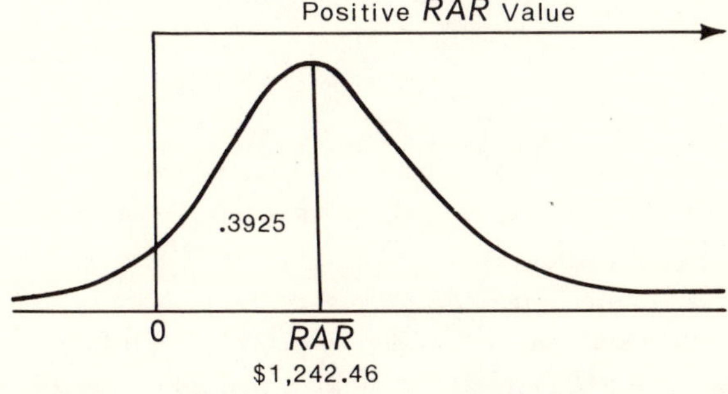

Figure 8-4. Normal distribution showing probability that *RAR* values will exceed zero.

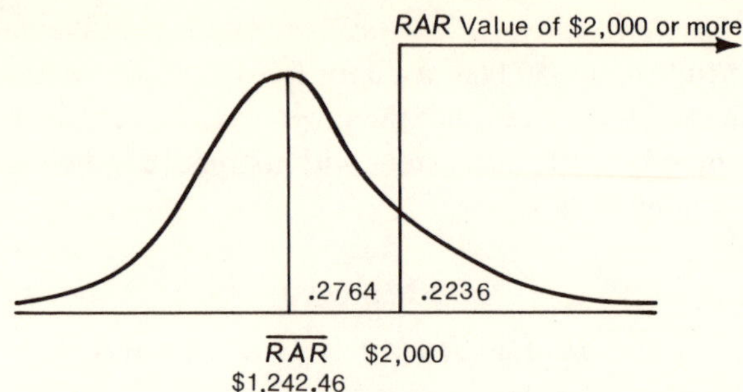

Figure 8-5. Normal distribution showing probability that *RAR* values will exceed $2,000.

probability that the risk-adjusted NPV will be positive is .8925 (.3925 + .5).

The probability that the risk-adjusted NPV will exceed $2,000 is found using Equation (26) as follows:

$$Z = \frac{\$2{,}000 - \$1{,}242.46}{\$1{,}000} = .76$$

We see that the standardized Z value is positive, and from Figure 8-5 we see that the probability that the RAR value exceeds $2,000 falls in the upper tail of the distribution. The area between the mean and $2,000 is .2764, since the Z value is +.76. Thus the probability that the project will achieve a value of $2,000 or greater is .2236 (.5 − .2764).

These probabilities would be compared to the firm's "minimum required probability for acceptance" in order to see whether the project was a candidate for acceptance. Further, these probabilities would be used to rank all projects that are candidates for acceptance. □

Tree Diagrams

In order to facilitate the determination of σ_{RAR}, we first introduce a helpful tool in the evaluation of capital investment projects under conditions of risk, namely, *tree diagrams*.

A tree diagram can be used to show the cash flows for a single project which could occur with some probability over the life of the project. *Tree diagrams are particularly helpful for projects whose cash flows in the later years of the useful life are dependent upon the cash flows in earlier years.* For example, the project shown in Figure 8-1 had a three-year useful life, but it was assumed that the optimistic, pessimistic, and most-likely estimates for the cash inflows, as well as their probabilities of occurring, would remain the same each year over the project's life. On the other hand, informed opinion within the firm might have indicated that cash inflows for this project in years 2 and 3 were dependent upon the magnitude of the cash inflow that occurred in year 1.

Analysts within the firm reached agreement that the tree diagram shown in Figure 8-6 accurately represented the best estimates of possible cash flows and their probabilities over the project's three-year life. Notice what the tree diagram conveys: given that the year-1 cash

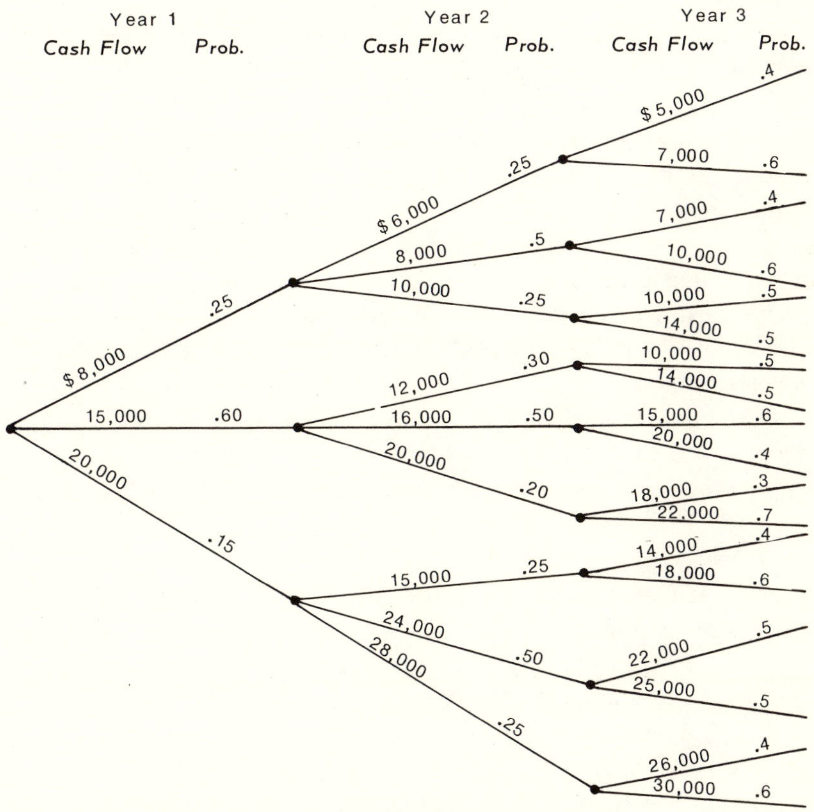

Figure 8-6. Tree diagram for project A2.

inflow was \$8,000, the year-2 cash inflows could be \$6,000, \$8,000, or \$10,000, with probabilities of .25, .5, and .25, respectively; similar interpretations can be given the other branches in the tree diagram. It should be mentioned that the probabilities in years 2 and 3 are referred to as "conditional probabilities" because they are dependent or conditional on the outcomes of earlier years. In addition, we can multiply the probabilities along any set of connected branches in years 1, 2, and 3 and the resulting probability will show how likely it is to obtain the respective cash flows in the three successive years. For example, consider the three branches \$8,000 in year 1, \$8,000 in year 2, and \$10,000 in year 3; the product of the probabilities .25, .5, and .6, or .075, shows the chances of having these three cash flows. One final detail: the cash inflows shown are flows before discounting, and we will see presently that we will have to discount these flows back to present in our analysis of this project.

For projects like that shown in the tree diagram in Figure 8-6, we will slightly modify our approach for finding $\overline{RAR}$. Namely, we recommend using the following five-step process:

1. For each branch in the final year of the project's life, find the product of the probabilities along the path leading to this terminal branch (call this probability P_s).

2. For each branch in the final year of the project's life, find the risk-adjusted present value of the cash inflows by multiplying each year's cash inflow by the appropriate discount factor and summing these values along the path leading to this terminal branch (call this discounted value A_s).

3. Find the expected value of the risk-adjusted present value of the project's cash inflows by using Equation (27).

$$\overline{RACI} = \sum_{s=1}^{S} P_s A_s \tag{27}$$

where $\overline{RACI}$ = expected value of the project's risk-adjusted cash inflows

P_s = probability of path s through the tree diagram occurring (see step 1)

A_s = risk-adjusted present value of the cash inflows along path s through the tree diagram (see step 2)

S = total number of paths through the tree diagram or total number of branches in the final year of the project's life

4. Determine the expected value of the original cost of the project, as shown in Example 1, using Equation (23) (call this value $\overline{COST}$).

5. Compute $\overline{RAR}$ using Equation (28).

$$\overline{RAR} = \overline{RACI} - \overline{COST} \tag{28}$$

We illustrate this process in Example 4.

EXAMPLE 4

Computations on a Tree Diagram

For the project shown in Figure 8-6, determine $\overline{RAR}$, using the five-step process just outlined. Recall that the estimates for the original cost of this project are shown in Example 1. In addition, recall that the firm feels that this project requires the use of a 16 percent risk-adjusted discount rate.

SOLUTION

Step 1: Table 8-2 shows the values computed in step 1. The values in the P_s column for each of the 18 branches in year 3 of Figure 8-6 are computed by multiplying the probabilities for each of the three years. Notice that the sum of all the P_s values is equal to 1.0, since that table shows all possible paths through the tree diagram.

Step 2: Table 8-3 shows how the A_s values are computed for each of the 18 branches through the tree. The discount factors are from Appendix B, column 4 on the 16 percent page.

Step 3: We now multiply the values from the final columns in Tables 8-2 and 8-3 in order to determine $\overline{RACI}$, using Equation (27). The results are shown in Table 8-4.

Step 4: The expected value of the original cost was found in Example 1 to be \$30,200 = $\overline{COST}$.

Step 5: Using Equation (28):

$$\begin{aligned}\overline{RAR} &= \overline{RACI} - \overline{COST} \\ &= \$32{,}873.80 - \$30{,}200 = \$2{,}673.80\end{aligned}$$

Thus the risk-adjusted NPV for the project, using the estimates for the cash flows shown in the tree diagram in Figure 8-6, is \$2,673.80. □

On the basis of the approach illustrated here, we are now ready to show how to compute the standard deviation for the risk-adjusted NPV

Table 8-2. Calculation of joint probabilities P_s.

	Year 1		Year 2		Year 3		
Branch s	Cash Inflow	Prob.	Cash Inflow	Prob.	Cash Inflow	Prob.	P_s
1	\$ 8,000	.25	\$ 6,000	.25	\$ 5,000	.4	.025
2	8,000	.25	6,000	.25	7,000	.6	.0375
3	8,000	.25	8,000	.50	7,000	.4	.05
4	8,000	.25	8,000	.50	10,000	.6	.075
5	8,000	.25	10,000	.25	10,000	.5	.03125
6	8,000	.25	10,000	.25	14,000	.5	.03125
7	15,000	.60	12,000	.30	10,000	.5	.09
8	15,000	.60	12,000	.30	14,000	.5	.09
9	15,000	.60	16,000	.50	15,000	.6	.18
10	15,000	.60	16,000	.50	20,000	.4	.12
11	15,000	.60	20,000	.20	18,000	.3	.036
12	15,000	.60	20,000	.20	22,000	.7	.084
13	20,000	.15	15,000	.25	14,000	.4	.015
14	20,000	.15	15,000	.25	18,000	.6	.0225
15	20,000	.15	24,000	.50	22,000	.5	.0375
16	20,000	.15	24,000	.50	25,000	.5	.0375
17	20,000	.15	28,000	.25	26,000	.4	.015
18	20,000	.15	28,000	.25	30,000	.6	.0225
							1.0000

distribution (σ_{RAR}). Of course, the approach for finding σ_{RAR} is analogous to that for finding the standard deviation, shown in Equation (24). The procedure for finding σ_{RAR} is as follows:

Step 1: Find $\overline{RACI}$ as shown in Equation (27) and as illustrated in Example 4.

Step 2: Subtract $\overline{RACI}$ from each A_s value for each branch in the tree diagram in the final year of the project's life; these differences are then squared and multiplied by the corresponding probability P_s.

Step 3: Determine the standard deviation for the project's cash inflows, using Equation (29).

$$\sigma_{CI} = \sqrt{\sum_{s=1}^{S} P_s(A_s - \overline{RACI})^2} \tag{29}$$

Step 4: Determine the standard deviation for the cost of the project (σ_{COST}), using Equation (24), as illustrated in Example 1.

Step 5: Under the assumption that the project's cash inflow distributions are independent of the project's original cost probability

Table 8-3. Calculation of A_s values.

Branch s	Year 1 Cash Inflow	Year 1 Discount Factor	Year 2 Cash Inflow	Year 2 Discount Factor	Year 3 Cash Inflow	Year 3 Discount Factor	A_s
1	\$ 8,000 ×	.862 +	\$ 6,000 ×	.743 +	\$ 5,000 ×	.641 =	\$14,561
2	8,000		6,000		7,000		15,843
3	8,000		8,000		7,000		17,327
4	8,000		8,000		10,000		19,250
5	8,000		10,000		10,000		20,736
6	8,000		10,000		14,000		23,300
7	15,000		12,000		10,000		28,256
8	15,000		12,000		14,000		30,820
9	15,000		16,000		15,000		34,433
10	15,000		16,000		20,000		37,638
11	15,000		20,000		18,000		38,788
12	15,000		20,000		22,000		41,352
13	20,000		15,000		14,000		37,359
14	20,000		15,000		18,000		39,923
15	20,000		24,000		22,000		49,174
16	20,000		24,000		25,000		51,097
17	20,000	↓	28,000	↓	26,000	↓	54,710
18	20,000	.862	28,000	.743	30,000	.641	57,274

distribution (which is virtually always the case), find σ_{RAR}, using Equation (30).

$$\sigma_{RAR} = \sigma_{CI} + \sigma_{COST} \tag{30}$$

This process is illustrated in Example 5.

EXAMPLE 5

Computation of σ_{RAR}

SOLUTION

Step 1: This step was performed in Example 4.

Step 2: Table 8-5 shows the subtraction of $\overline{RACI}$ from each A_s, the squaring of these values, and the multiplication of the squared values by P_s for each branch in the tree diagram.

Step 3: $\sigma_{CI} = \sqrt{\sum_{s=1}^{S} P_s(A_s - \overline{RACI})^2} = \sqrt{109{,}876{,}705.4}$

$= \$10{,}482.21$

Table 8-4. Calculation of $\overline{RACI}$.

Branch s	P_s	A_s	$P_s \times A_s$
1	.025	$14,561	$ 364.03
2	.0375	15,843	594.11
3	.05	17,327	866.35
4	.075	19,250	1,443.75
5	.03125	20,736	648.00
6	.03125	23,300	728.13
7	.09	28,256	2,543.04
8	.09	30,820	2,773.80
9	.18	34,433	6,197.94
10	.12	37,638	4,516.56
11	.036	38,788	1,396.37
12	.084	41,352	3,473.57
13	.015	37,359	560.39
14	.0225	39,923	898.27
15	.0375	49,174	1,844.03
16	.0375	51,097	1,916.14
17	.015	54,710	820.65
18	.0225	57,274	1,288.67
		$\overline{RACI}$ =	$32,873.80

Step 4: σ_{COST} = \$5,546, as computed in Example 1.

Step 5: $\sigma_{RAR} = \sigma_{CI} + \sigma_{COST}$

$$= \$10{,}482.21 + \$5{,}546 = \underline{\underline{\$16{,}028.21}}$$

Project A2, therefore, has an $\overline{RAR}$ = \$2,673.80, as found in Example 4, and σ_{RAR} = \$16,028.21. We could use the procedure shown in Example 3 to find the probability that the RAR value will fall in various ranges. This is done in Example 6, following the method of Example 3. □

EXAMPLE 6

Probability Statement about RAR

Since $\overline{RAR}$ = \$2,673.80, there is a 50 percent probability that RAR will equal or exceed \$2,673.80. As indicated earlier, the most important probability is that RAR will equal or exceed zero. The probability that RAR equals or exceeds zero is the probability that the project will have a yield equal to or greater than the required return of 16 percent.

Table 8-5. Determination of σ_{CI}.

Branch s	A_s	$A_s - \overline{RACI}$	$(A_s - \overline{RACI})^2$	P_s	$P_s \times (A_s - \overline{RACI})^2$
1	$14,561	−18,312.8	335,358,643.8	.025	8,383,966.1
2	15,843	−17,030.8	290,048,148.6	.0375	10,876,805.57
3	17,327	−15,546.8	241,702,990.2	.05	12,085,149.51
4	19,250	−13,623.8	185,607,926.4	.075	13,920,594.48
5	20,736	−12,137.8	147,326,188.8	.03125	4,603,943.401
6	23,300	− 9,573.8	91,657,646.44	.03125	2,864,301.451
7	28,256	− 4,617.8	21,324,076.84	.09	1,919,166.916
8	30,820	− 2,053.8	4,218,094.44	.09	379,628.50
9	34,433	1,559.2	2,431,104.64	.18	437,598.835
10	37,628	4,764.2	22,697,601.64	.12	2,723,712.197
11	38,788	5,914.2	34,977,761.64	.036	1,259,199.419
12	41,352	8,478.2	71,879,875.24	.084	6,037,909.52
13	37,359	4,485.2	20,117,019.04	.015	301,755.286
14	39,923	7,049.2	49,691,220.64	.0225	1,118,052.464
15	49,174	16,300.2	265,696,520.00	.0375	9,963,619.502
16	51,097	18,223.2	332,085,018.2	.0375	12,453,188.18
17	54,710	21,836.2	476,819,630.4	.015	7,152,294.46
18	57,274	24,400.2	595,369,760.0	.0225	13,395,819.6
				$\Sigma P_s (A_s - \overline{RACI})^2 =$	109,876,705.4

SOLUTION

Employ Equation (26).

$$Z = \frac{0 - \$2,673.80}{\$16.028.21} = -.17$$

Looking up the value of .17 in Appendix D, we see that it is associated with an area under the normal curve of .0675. Thus the probability that the risk-adjusted NPV will be positive is .5675 (that is, .0675 + .5).

□

IMPLEMENTATION OF THE RISK-ADJUSTED NPV APPROACH

Admittedly, the process of determining the amount of variability in the risk-adjusted NPV distribution is somewhat involved. But computer programs are readily available to perform the tedious arithmetic computations tabulated above. The only managerial requirement is to estimate the cash flows and assign probabilities to each. Under conditions of uncertainty concerning future cash flows, we must shift our acceptance criterion from a simple "accept if NPV ≥ 0 and reject otherwise" to one that incorporates both the risk and the return of the project. Very often this is accomplished by setting minimum acceptable probabilities that the project will achieve desired levels of risk-adjusted NPV, utilizing a discount rate appropriate for the project under evaluation. Hence it is necessary for us to determine both $\overline{RAR}$ and σ_{RAR} so that the risky project can be properly evaluated. Furthermore, it is necessary for firms and divisions to address the difficult questions of how much risk they are willing to take, what impact risky projects will have on their most important goals and objectives, what kinds of trade-offs between risk and expected return they are willing to accept, and how much risk they can afford to take, given their vulnerabilities on several fronts. The answers to these questions are needed in order to arrive at appropriate discount rates for various risk classes of projects, in order to set the minimum acceptable probabilities for desired levels of risk-adjusted NPV over the project's life, and in order to select and implement optimum diversification strategies to reduce variability in returns.

Finally, the firm should let the project stand as a candidate for acceptance if it sufficiently satisfies its preferences concerning risk taking, risk–return trade-offs, and its other relevant goals and objectives. *That is, the quantitative aspects of any risky project under evaluation (that is, $\overline{RAR}$, σ_{RAR}, $\overline{R}_t$, σ_t) must be tempered by careful evaluation and judgment and must be balanced against the qualitative aspects in the final decision.* These include management's preferences for ranking alternatives on the basis of the degree of risk it is willing to accept, the risk–return trade-offs desired, and the impact of the project on all other relevant goals and objectives of the firm.

One final caution to analysts and managers using the risk-adjusted NPV methodology: *the use of a constant risk-adjusted discount rate over the life of the project implicitly assumes (due to the compounding process) that the risk of the project is growing exponentially with time.* Thus, an increasingly greater penalty for risk is assigned to cash flows that occur progressively later in the project's life. For many projects this may be appropriate, since there could very well be greater uncertainty and greater forecasting difficulty later in the project's life. However, this is not necessarily the case for all projects. Some projects could very well have less risk associated with later cash flows once the initial uncertainty of the project is resolved. In such cases, and especially if the project has a very long life, the use of a constant risk-adjusted discount rate over its life overpenalizes the project for its risk. *Recall that the risk-adjusted-discount-rate approach discounts for the time value of money at the risk-free rate and discounts for the riskiness of the project by adding a risk premium that is appropriate for the project under evaluation.* Again, the methodology must be tempered by the judgment of the analyst and management.

Summary

This chapter provided an overview of the important conditions of risk that are characteristic of the usual decisions on capital expenditures. Conditions of risk are present when the manager feels that he must resort to a probability distribution to reflect possible future outcomes. The presence of probability distributions for cash flows necessitates the computation of the mean and the standard deviation of such distributions, which are then used in assessing project attractiveness.

The risk-adjusted NPV approach, wherein both $\overline{RAR}$ and σ_{RAR} are determined, was illustrated, since it is the most widely used technique of project evaluation under conditions of risk. Under such conditions, the focus of the project acceptance criterion shifts from one concentrating only on expected return (accept projects that have positive NPVs) to one that incorporates returns, variability in those returns, and the firm's preferences. The latter approach says, accept projects that have a sufficiently high probability of achieving desired returns. Last, we illustrated the use of decision trees in assisting the firm in coping with conditions of risk in the evaluation of capital projects.

Having introduced the methodology for dealing with risk, we now have the tools necessary to evaluate leases. This is the topic of the next chapter.

NOTES

1. Although we do not deal specifically with forecasting, Appendix C, "Sources of Economic and Financial Information from The Conference Board," is included as a valuable reference for gathering information needed in forecasting.
2. The risk-free rate is the rate normally associated with the return on treasury bills. This rate is, of course, not static but constantly changing with money and capital market conditions.

CHAPTER 9

How to Evaluate Leases

In Chapter 5 we introduced the important and comprehensive area of leasing. We discussed leasing as an alternative method of financing capital investment projects, pointed out the advantages and disadvantages of leasing, provided an overview of the leasing industry, and defined various types of leasing arrangements. Subsequently, we examined the methodology of discounted cash flow analysis, various techniques of evaluating proposed capital investment projects, and the importance of risk analysis in capital budgeting. At this juncture, the reader has the tools to revisit the leasing alternative and compare its impact on the organization with that of purchasing the asset. Thus we are now ready to see how leasing can be integrated directly into the capital expenditure decision process.

The next section provides an overview of lease/purchase analysis. Following sections illustrate a tabular approach that facilitates the evaluation of various lease alternatives and the purchase alternative.

An Overview of the Lease/Purchase Analysis

The evaluation of lease and purchase alternatives is a part of the overall capital expenditure decision process. Hence the perspective taken here parallels that presented throughout the book. At this point it would probably be well for us to review this perspective as we begin our analysis of lease/purchase alternatives.

First, as we have stressed throughout, organizations and their managements and owners have various goals and objectives with differing priorities, weightings, and trade-off preferences. This fact permeates the entire analysis and necessitates the consideration of the multiple relevant facets of the capital expenditure and lease/purchase decision setting.

Second, because of competing goals and the complexity of the problem setting, both quantitative and qualitative factors that differentiate the alternatives must be carefully evaluated in a comprehensive analysis that leads to the selection of the preferred course of action. Quantifiable aspects are subject to uncertainties about future events, and qualitative dimensions are subjective in nature. Nevertheless, both dimensions are clearly relevant and must be incorporated into the decision process.

Next, we have recommended that a "cash flow perspective" be taken in evaluating alternative capital investment projects. Further, consistent with traditional financial analysis, we have discussed the tax implications of these cash flows. In the lease/purchase setting there are several important tax considerations that must be factored into the analysis and the final decision process. A full discussion of these considerations is beyond our scope here, but we have treated them elsewhere.[1] Our after-tax cash flow perspective has also pointed to the need to consider both operating and financing cash flows; this need carries over to lease/purchase analysis.

Fourth, we have also recommended a discounted cash flow approach (namely, the net present value method) in order to reduce the after-tax cash flows (which can vary widely in their time patterns among the alternatives) to similar terms (namely, the excess of discounted cash inflows over discounted cash outflows, expressed in present dollars).

Fifth, we have recommended the use of discount rates in the net present value approach to reflect the degree of risk or uncertainty associated with the various cash flows (the lower the risk, the lower the discount rate). The end result is a net present value figure for each proposed capital expenditure which takes into account both variations in the timing of the after-tax cash flows and the amount of risk that is felt to exist in each of the cash flows.

Sixth, we have divided capital investment projects into two categories: "sustaining" or "mandatory" investments (those which must be undertaken in order to continue the normal operations of the organizations or those required by regulatory bodies—that is, those for which alternatives do not exist) and "generative" or "discretionary" investments (those which generate traceable cash inflows or cash savings compared to current operations). As we move to the lease/purchase arena, we see that sustaining projects require only an evaluation of the various financing alternatives (lease, purchase for cash, or purchase with a loan) whereas generative projects necessitate an analysis of the attractiveness of the various alternative proposals as capital investments and an analysis of how the proposal should be financed (lease or purchase).

Finally, we have stressed the importance of performing a "sensitivity analysis" before the final decision is made in order to see how much conditions would have to change before the "preferred" alternative is no longer preferred. Sensitivity analysis enables us to hedge against uncertainties about the future as well as those inherent in the assumptions that have been made in the analysis. In lease/purchase analysis, we will find it helpful to evaluate the sensitivity of changes in operating cash flows, residual values of assets, risk-adjusted discount rates, and the like.

We now turn to our recommended formal approach. Our main objective in designing the approach is to arrive at a comprehensive, systematic evaluation of all relevant dimensions of the lease and purchase alternatives.

The Recommended Lease/Purchase Approach

In evaluating the lease/purchase decision, there are three critical issues that must be addressed:

1. Is the firm concerned with a capital investment decision, a financing decision, or both?
2. What are the relevant cash flows that must be considered under each of the feasible alternatives?
3. What are the appropriate discount rates for each of the cash flows and each of the feasible alternatives, given the degree of risk present?

In order to arrive at a correct evaluation of the feasible alternatives, each of these issues must be resolved. Figure 9-1 provides an overview of our recommendation for systematically dealing with these issues. The figure stresses the fact that lease/purchase analysis is concerned with investment implications, financing implications, renegotiation opportunities, and the need for sensitivity analysis. The reader should study Figure 9-1 carefully before proceeding in order to get the flavor of the often complex analysis which is to follow. In studying Figure 9-1, note that there are two decision modules: the financing evaluation module and the investment and financing module (treated in this chapter). In addition there is the sensitivity analysis module (covered in Chapter 10).

The *financing evaluation module* would be called upon if the firm has gone through a prior decision process to evaluate the attractiveness of the project and determined that it is a viable candidate for acquisition, *or* if the project is required for a firm's continued existence (that is, if it is a sustaining investment). Under such conditions, the firm must decide upon the most favorable financing arrangement: purchase for cash, borrow and buy, or enter into one of several leasing contracts. Again, as we shall see, each of these alternatives has its own relevant cash flows and requires the use of appropriate risk-adjusted discount rates.

The *investment and financing evaluation module* simultaneously looks at the attractiveness of the project and the financing of the project. A number of approaches have recommended to the contrary that the investment must first be justified on the basis of purchase before a particular mode of financing may be considered. We see this as a fallacy and argue that such an approach would never allow a very attractive lease to reverse an original negative purchase decision. Thus *the investment and financing module simultaneously determines whether the expected benefits of the project exceed the operating and financial costs associated with the best financing alternative among those under evaluation, as well as (by necessity) the identity of the best financing alternative*.

The major difference between the financing evaluation module and the investment and financing evaluation module is that the latter must consider the benefits that will result from the investment, as well as the operating and financial costs associated with the various financing alternatives. On the other hand, the financing module considers

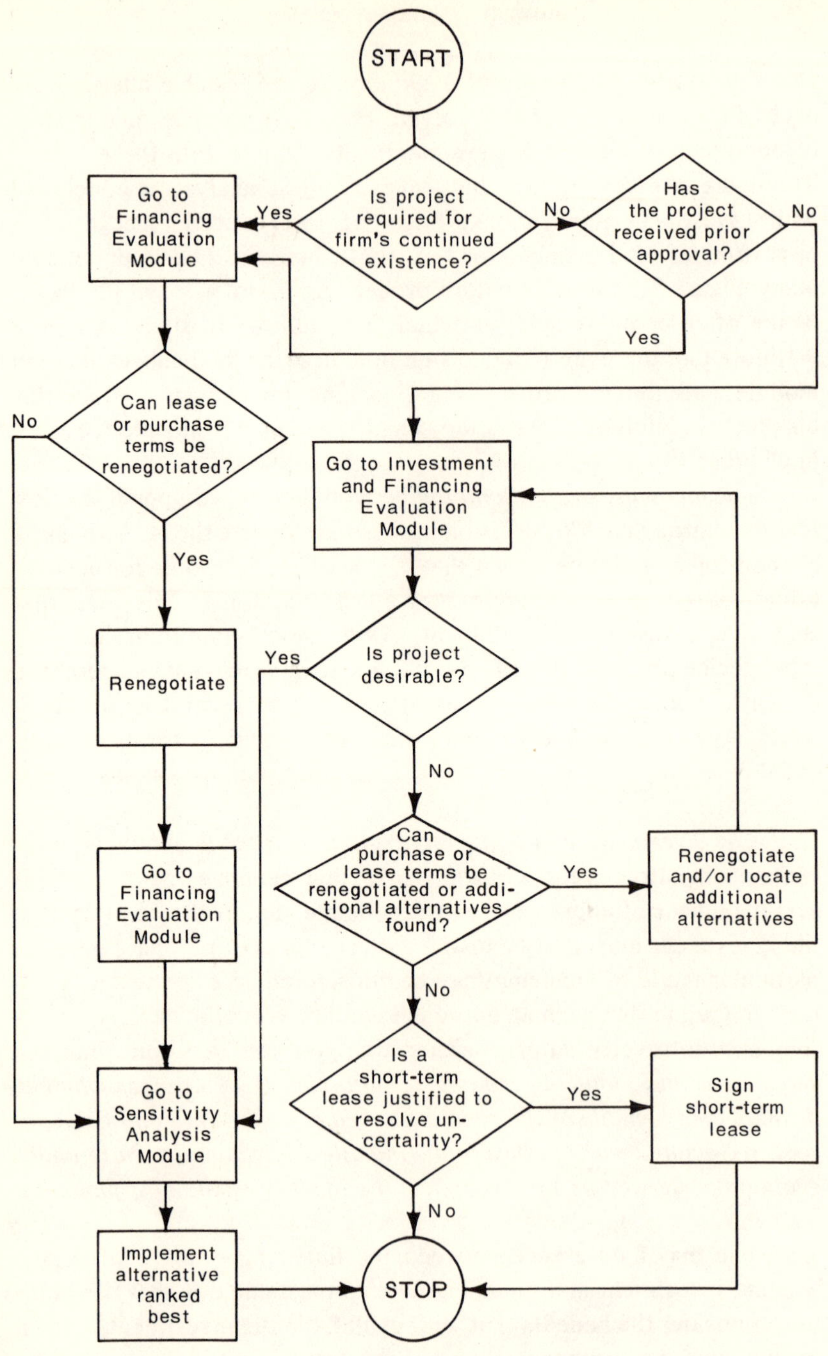

Figure 9-1. Overview of lease/purchase decision analysis.

only the relevant operating and financial cash outflows, and the related tax effects associated with the various financing alternatives. That is, the revenues or benefits generated by the investment are excluded from consideration in the financing evaluation module, since they will be the same for all the financing alternatives and since the project has already been designated attractive. Thus the decision criterion for the investment and financing evaluation module is that the project is attractive if at least one financing alternative has a positive NPV; otherwise it is not attractive. Further, the best financing alternative is the one with the largest NPV, considering all relevant cash flows and using appropriate risk-adjusted discount rates. On the other hand, the decision criterion for the financing evaluation module is to select the financing alternative with the minimum present value of the operating and financial cash outflows.

We now turn to a discussion of the relevant cash flows associated with the various financing alternatives in the lease/buy decision setting.

Recommended Analysis for the Leasing Alternative

In the lease/purchase decision setting, there are three major categories of financing alternatives: (1) lease the asset under one of several leasing arrangements, (2) buy the asset for cash from the pool of funds available for capital investment, and (3) borrow funds specifically to buy the asset. The third alternative may require a mortgage agreement.

The determination of the relevant cash flows, as well as the tax impacts and alternative depreciation methods, for the second category have already been discussed in Chapters 2 and 3. In addition, Chapters 7 and 8 cover the evaluation of such projects. Thus we will proceed with a discussion of the other two categories and only briefly expand on the prior coverage of category 2.

Under the lease alternative, the obvious cash outflows are the lease payments over the term of the contract. However, these payments can take on a wide variety of patterns: equal monthly payments at the beginning of each month, payments in arrears (at the end of the month), ballooning payments at various times over the lease to meet the needs of the lessor or the lessee, and so on. In addition, most lease contracts require a security deposit or a prepayment of some number of lease payments, which is an additional cash outflow. A recent survey of 520 financial leases with an average outlay cost to the lessor of $9,863 indicated that the average prepayment requirement was 9.5 percent of the original cost of the asset, with 65 percent of the leases requiring a prepayment between 10 percent and 15 percent of the original cost.[2]

Offsetting the security deposit and the initial lease payments is the fact that the investment tax credit (ITC) can be passed on to the lessee. The above-mentioned survey indicated that 30 percent of the lease contracts had the ITC passed on to the lessee.[3] It should be noted here that when the ITC is passed on to the lessee, it is computed on the basis of the fair market value of the leased asset.

Other cash outflows related to the lease are those for maintenance, taxes, and insurance (in the case of a net lease), and the amount required to bring the asset up to the pre-established value at the end of the lease (in the case of a net-net lease).

All these cash outflows have the tax shield associated with them. Thus the net cash outflow will be the after-tax cash outflow—that is, before-tax cash outflow times (1 − tax rate on ordinary income) equals the after-tax or net cash outflow. The timing of these cash flows is important in that each must be discounted to present value, using the appropriate discount rate. This yields the present value of the costs associated with the leasing alternative or the net present value (that is, both benefits and costs) of the project acquired through the lease. The appropriate discount rates are now discussed.

There has been considerable debate over the appropriate discount rates to use in evaluating component cash flows in the lease/purchase setting. Our purpose here is to suggest a correct decision approach and strategies of performing sensitivity analysis before the final decision is made.

FINANCING EVALUATION MODULE

The recommended approach in the financing evaluation module will be to find the present value of the after-tax cash outflows related to the lease. As will be illustrated in tabular form, this requires determining the following items:

1. The present value of the after-tax lease payments over the term of the lease; plus

2. The present value of the after-tax payments for maintenance, property taxes, and insurance required by the lease, if it is a net lease; plus

3. The present value on an after-tax basis of the single payment (if required) at the end of the lease to bring the asset up to a pre-established value; less

4. The present value of the investment tax credit if it is passed on by the lessor to the lessee.

In computing these present values, we recommend using *one risk-adjusted discount rate for all financial cash flows related to the lease* (that is, the first, third, and fourth cash flows enumerated above) and a *second risk-adjusted rate for the cash flows related to the operations of the asset* (that is, the second cash flow described above). That is to say, we recommend using the firm's after-tax borrowing rate to discount all the financial flows related to the lease, whereas for the operating cash flows we recommend the use of an after-tax risk-adjusted discount rate appropriate for any asset in the risk class of the project under evaluation.

The firm's after-tax borrowing rate is appropriate for discounting all the financial flows of the lease because it will usually closely approximate the lessee's implicit after-tax cost of leasing. The second discount rate mentioned is appropriate for the operating cash flows because, as we argued in the presentation of the risk-adjusted-discount-rate approach in Chapter 8, *cash flows should be discounted at a rate that is consistent with the uncertainty or variability that exists in their probability distributions of possible outcomes*. The firm is bound to the financial flows by contractual obligations, which necessarily means that very little uncertainty exists about the magnitude of such flows. Thus the low after-tax borrowing rate is appropriate. On the other hand, costs and benefits from the asset's operations are subject to much greater variability, which argues for the higher risk-adjusted discount rate for the appropriate risk class of assets.

To summarize our discussion to this point, we have included Figure 9-2, which provides a handy reference for the analysis to be performed.

The following example will illustrate the recommended approach of lease evaluation in the *financing evaluation module*.

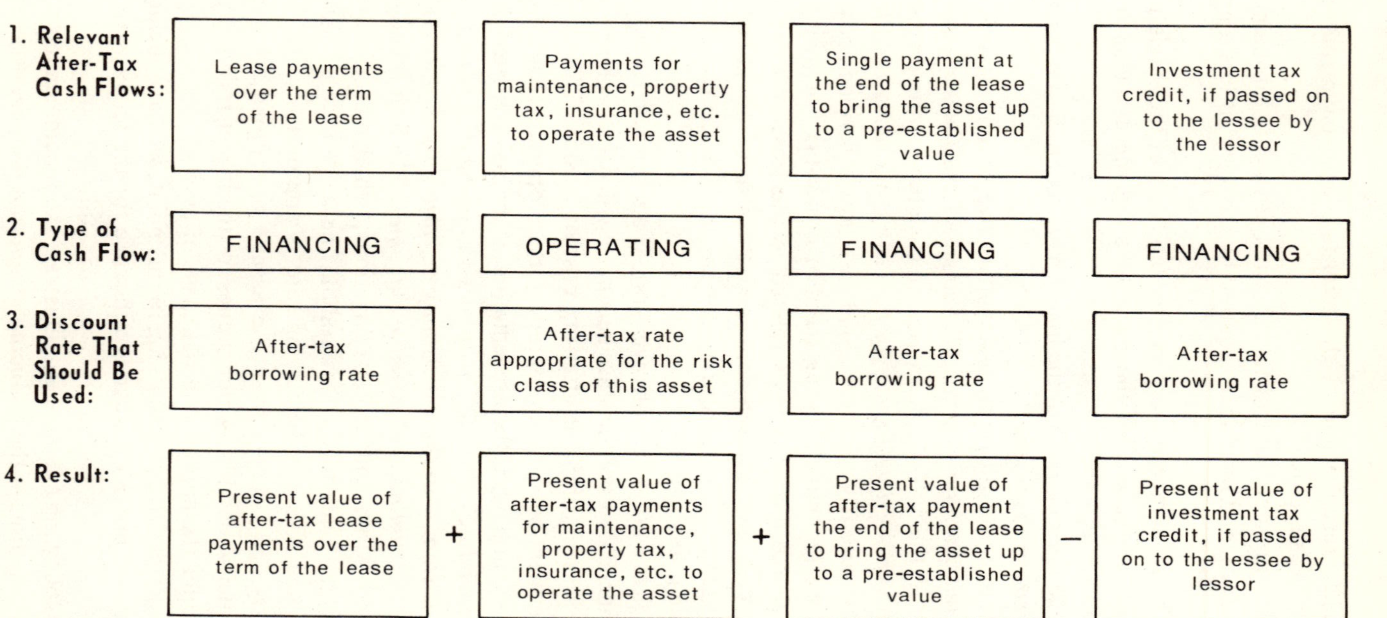

For Each Lease Alternative, Determine:
1. Relevant After-Tax Cash Flows:
Lease payments over the term of the lease
Payments for maintenance, property tax, insurance, etc. to operate the asset
Single payment at the end of the lease to bring the asset up to a pre-established value
Investment tax credit, if passed on to the lessee by the lessor
2. Type of Cash Flow:
FINANCING
OPERATING
FINANCING
FINANCING
3. Discount Rate That Should Be Used:
After-tax borrowing rate
After-tax rate appropriate for the risk class of this asset
After-tax borrowing rate
After-tax borrowing rate
4. Result:
Present value of after-tax lease payments over the term of the lease
+
Present value of after-tax payments for maintenance, property tax, insurance, etc. to operate the asset
+
Present value of after-tax payment the end of the lease to bring the asset up to a pre-established value
–
Present value of investment tax credit, if passed on to the lessee by lessor
5. Final Value:
Present Value of All Relevant After-Tax Cash Flows Associated with This Lease

Figure 9-2. Financing evaluation module.

EXAMPLE 1

Comparison of Two Leasing Options

A firm with a 40 percent marginal tax rate, a before-tax borrowing rate of 10 percent, and a required after-tax rate of return of 14 percent is evaluating various financing plans for an asset that is required for one of the firm's major product lines. The firm feels that its required rate of return is an appropriate risk-adjusted discount rate for this asset. The purchase price of the asset is $250,000, which is the current fair market value of the asset; cost to deliver and install the asset is $16,400; useful life of the asset is five years; and estimated salvage value is $20,000. The firm is considering two leasing plans:

1. A five-year net-net lease wherein *annual* lease payments paid in arrears amounting to $64,700 would be required; annual maintenance, tax, and insurance would be $4,600; the ITC would be retained by the lessor; and there would be an estimated payment at the end of the five years of $3,800 to bring the asset up to the value desired by the lessor.

2. A five-year net lease wherein *quarterly* payments in advance of $16,330 would be required; in addition, a prepayment of two payments is required; the ITC would be passed along to the lessee; and the annual maintenance, tax, and insurance payment would be $4,600.

Determine the present value of the costs associated with each lease, using the approach outlined above. It can be assumed that the lease is written to cover both the purchase price of the asset and the cost to deliver and install it. The payment for maintenance and so on is made at the end of each year, and the benefit for the ITC will be received at the end of the first year.

SOLUTION

For Lease #1, the relevant calculations, following the framework shown in Figure 9-2, are shown in Figure 9-3. It should be pointed out again that all the cash flows shown in row 1 are on an after-tax basis; these values are arrived at by multiplying the before-tax flows by 1 minus the firm's tax rate of 40 percent. Notice also that the discount factors shown in row 3 are annuity factors for the first two sets of cash flows, since each of these flows takes place annually for five years; on the other hand, the third discount factor is a single-payment factor, since the third cash flow takes place at the end of year 5. The final value

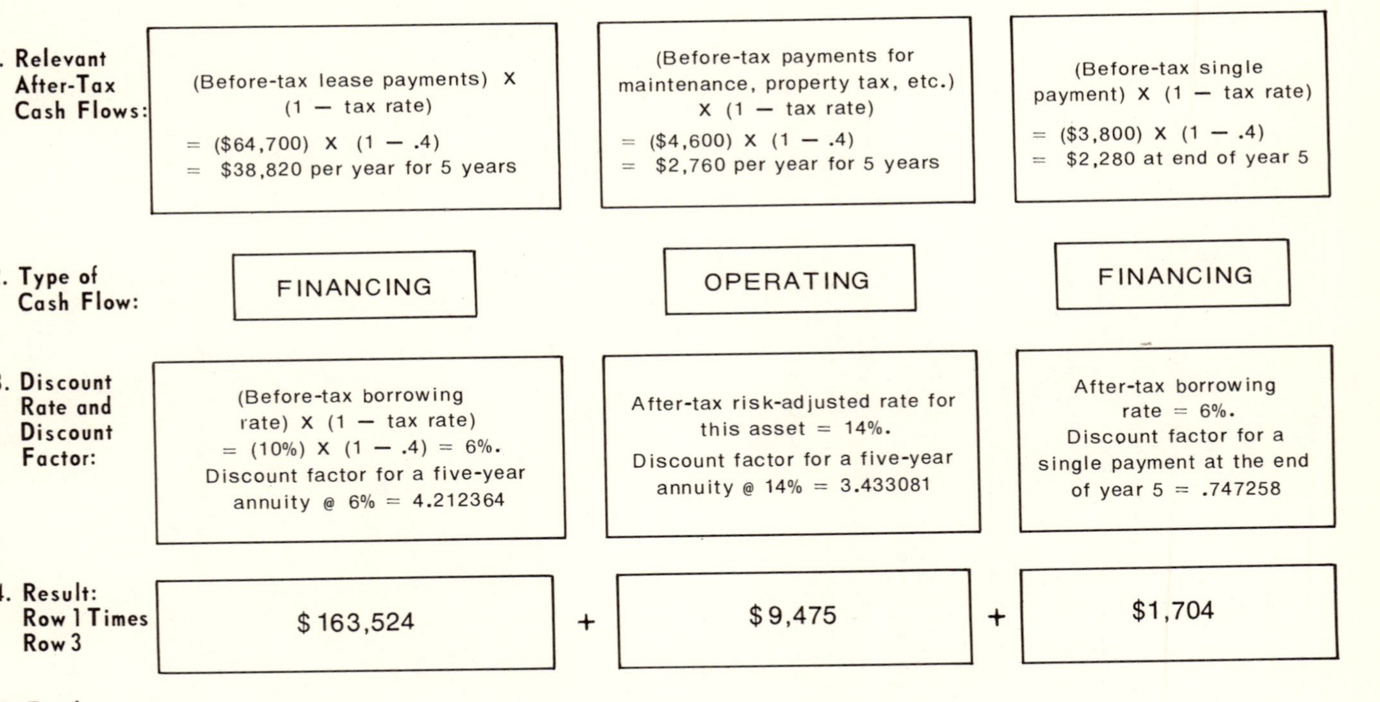
1. Relevant After-Tax Cash Flows:
(Before-tax lease payments) X (1 — tax rate)
= ($64,700) X (1 — .4)
= $38,820 per year for 5 years
(Before-tax payments for maintenance, property tax, etc.) X (1 — tax rate)
= ($4,600) X (1 — .4)
= $2,760 per year for 5 years
(Before-tax single payment) X (1 — tax rate)
= ($3,800) X (1 — .4)
= $2,280 at end of year 5
2. Type of Cash Flow:
FINANCING
OPERATING
FINANCING
3. Discount Rate and Discount Factor:
(Before-tax borrowing rate) X (1 — tax rate)
= (10%) X (1 — .4) = 6%.
Discount factor for a five-year annuity @ 6% = 4.212364
After-tax risk-adjusted rate for this asset = 14%.
Discount factor for a five-year annuity @ 14% = 3.433081
After-tax borrowing rate = 6%.
Discount factor for a single payment at the end of year 5 = .747258
4. Result: Row 1 Times Row 3
$163,524
+
$9,475
+
$1,704
5. Final Value:
Present Value of All Cash Flows Associated with Lease #1 = $174,703

Figure 9-3. Evaluation of Lease #1.

shown in row 5 ($174,703) is the present value of all relevant after-tax cash flows associated with Lease #1.

We now turn to Lease #2. The calculations for Lease #2 are shown in Figure 9-4, which again uses the framework shown in Figure 9-2. These calculations are complicated slightly by the fact that quarterly lease payments in advance as well as prepayment of two payments are required. The quarterly lease payments require that we determine the present value of an annuity factor for 1.5 percent per quarter (since the annual after-tax borrowing rate is 6 percent) and 17 quarters (since a total of 20 payments is required and three payments are made at present, which leaves one for each of the next 17 quarters). This factor is determined using Equation (17) in Chapter 6, where i = 1.5 percent and n = 17:

$$\begin{aligned}\text{PV of an annuity factor for 1.5\% quarterly interest over a 17-quarter period} &= \frac{(1+i)^n - 1}{i(1+i)^n}\\ &= \frac{(1.015)^{17} - 1}{.015(1+.015)^{17}}\\ &= \frac{1.28802 - 1}{(.015)(1.28802)}\\ &= 14.9076\end{aligned}$$

As can be seen in Figure 9-4, the present value of all cash flows for Lease #2 is $169,203 (versus $174,703 for Lease #1)—a saving of $5,500 over the term of the lease discounted to present value.

Just as important as the preceding comparison of the two lease alternatives is a more complete analysis of why Lease #2 has a lower present value of cash outflows. Such a summary is provided in Table 9-1.

Notice that the present value of Lease #2 payments exceeds that of Lease #1 payments by almost $12,000. The maintenance, insurance, and tax payments have equal present values under the two leases. Lease #1 has a disadvantage to the tune of $1,704 due to the final payment required. Finally, *the PV of the ITC which is passed on to the lessee in Lease #2 is $15,731, which is the only reason why Lease #2 has a present-value saving of $5,500 compared to Lease #1.* A table such as this should prove helpful in the lessee's attempts to locate other leasing alternatives and in renegotiating the terms of current lease options.

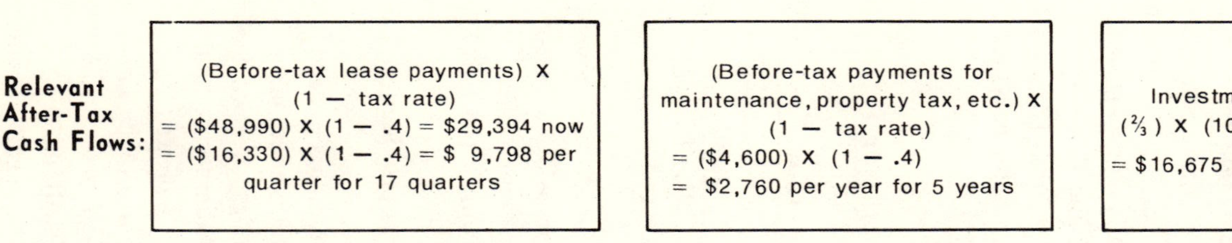

1. Relevant After-Tax Cash Flows:	(Before-tax lease payments) X (1 — tax rate) = ($48,990) X (1 — .4) = $29,394 now = ($16,330) X (1 — .4) = $ 9,798 per quarter for 17 quarters	(Before-tax payments for maintenance, property tax, etc.) X (1 — tax rate) = ($4,600) X (1 — .4) = $2,760 per year for 5 years	Investment tax credit (⅔) X (10%) X ($250,000) = $16,675 at end of year 1
2. Type of Cash Flow:	FINANCING	OPERATING	FINANCING
3. Discount Rate and Discount Factor:	(Before-tax borrowing rate) X (1 — tax rate) = (10%) X (1 — .4) = 6% annually or 1.5% quarterly. Discount factor for 1.5% and 17 quarters = 14.9076	After-tax risk-adjusted rate for this asset = 14%. Discount factor for a five-year annuity @ 14% = 3.433081	After-tax borrowing rate = 6%. Discount factor for a single payment at the end of year [1] = .943396
4. Result: Row 1 Times Row 3	$29,394 X 1.0000 = $29,394 9,798 X 14.9076 = 146,065	+ $9,475	— $15,731
5. Final Value:	Present Value of All Cash Flows Associated with Lease #2 = $169,203.		

Figure 9-4. Evaluation of Lease #2.

Table 9-1. Comparison of two leases.

	PV of Lease Payments	*PV of Payments for Maintenance, Insurance, etc.*	*PV of Payment at End of Lease*	*PV of ITC*	*Total PV*
Lease #1	$163,524	$9,475	$1,704	0	$174,703
Lease #2	175,459	9,475	0	($15,731)	169,203
Difference* (2 − 1)	$ 11,935 U	0	$1,704 F	$15,731 F	$ 5,500 F

* U = unfavorable (i.e., Lease #1 is preferred to Lease #2); F = favorable (i.e., Lease #2 is preferred to Lease #1).

In addition, firms concerned about possible cash flow problems should find Table 9-2 of assistance in determining the impact of the two lease alternatives on their cash budget.

Notice that during the first year of the lease, Lease #2 requires cash outflows before tax benefits of $49,610 in excess of those required for Lease #1, due to Lease #2's requirement for a security deposit and payments in advance rather than in arrears as for Lease #1. In fact, before Lease #1's first payment must be made, Lease #2 has required cash outflows of $81,650. The before-tax cash flows are relevant in preparing the cash budget because of the time lag involved in receiving the tax benefits. For example, for Lease #2 (and any lease requiring payments in advance), there could be a time delay of as much as 15 to 18

Table 9-2. Impact of leases on cash budgets.

	Before-Tax Security Deposit	*Cumulative Before-Tax Cash Outflow Over Year 1*	*Before-Tax Annual Lease Payments for Years 2, 3, and 4*
Lease #1	0	$64,700	$64,700
Lease #2	$32,660	81,650*	65,320
Difference (2 − 1)†	$32,660 U	$16,950 U	$ 620 F

* Exclusive of security deposit.
† U = Unfavorable (i.e., Lease #1 is preferred to Lease #2; F = Favorable (i.e., Lease #2 is preferred to Lease #1).

months in receiving the benefits from the tax shield or the ITC if the lease became effective at the beginning of the firm's fiscal year. The impact of the timing of cash flows and tax benefits could be of great importance to firms. □

INVESTING AND FINANCING MODULE

Example 1 illustrated the analysis of two competing leases as it would be carried out in the *financing evaluation module*. Closely related to that analysis is the one undertaken for the *investment and financing evaluation module*. In this module, the net present value of each lease alternative is determined. Two new input variables are required in order to compute the net present value. The first is the revenue generated by the asset in each period of the lease. The second is the operating expenses of the asset, including raw materials, direct labor, variable overhead, and fixed overhead in each period of the lease. Since both of these cash flows are operating cash flows, the net difference between the two (after-tax) is discounted at the after-tax risk-adjusted discount rate appropriate for the risk class of the asset. Thus, in order to determine the net present value of each lease alternative (as summarized in Figure 9-5), we must find:

1. The present value of the after-tax net cash inflow of the asset. This is determined for each period by subtracting the operating costs (for raw materials, direct labor, and overhead, as well as the operating expenses for maintenance, insurance, and property taxes) from the revenues generated by the asset, subtracting income tax expense, and then discounting at the asset's risk-adjusted discount rate; plus

2. The present value of the investment tax credit if it is passed on by the lessor to the lessee; minus

3. The present value of the after-tax lease payments over the term of the lease contract; minus

4. The present value on an after-tax basis of the single payment (if required) at the end of the lease to bring the asset up to a preestablished value.

It should be mentioned that each of the last three cash flows (that is, 2, 3, and 4 above) should be discounted at the firm's *after-tax borrowing rate,* since they represent financial cash flows (as opposed to the operating cash flows described in 1), which are *discounted at the appropriate risk-adjusted discount rate for this asset's risk class*. Ex-

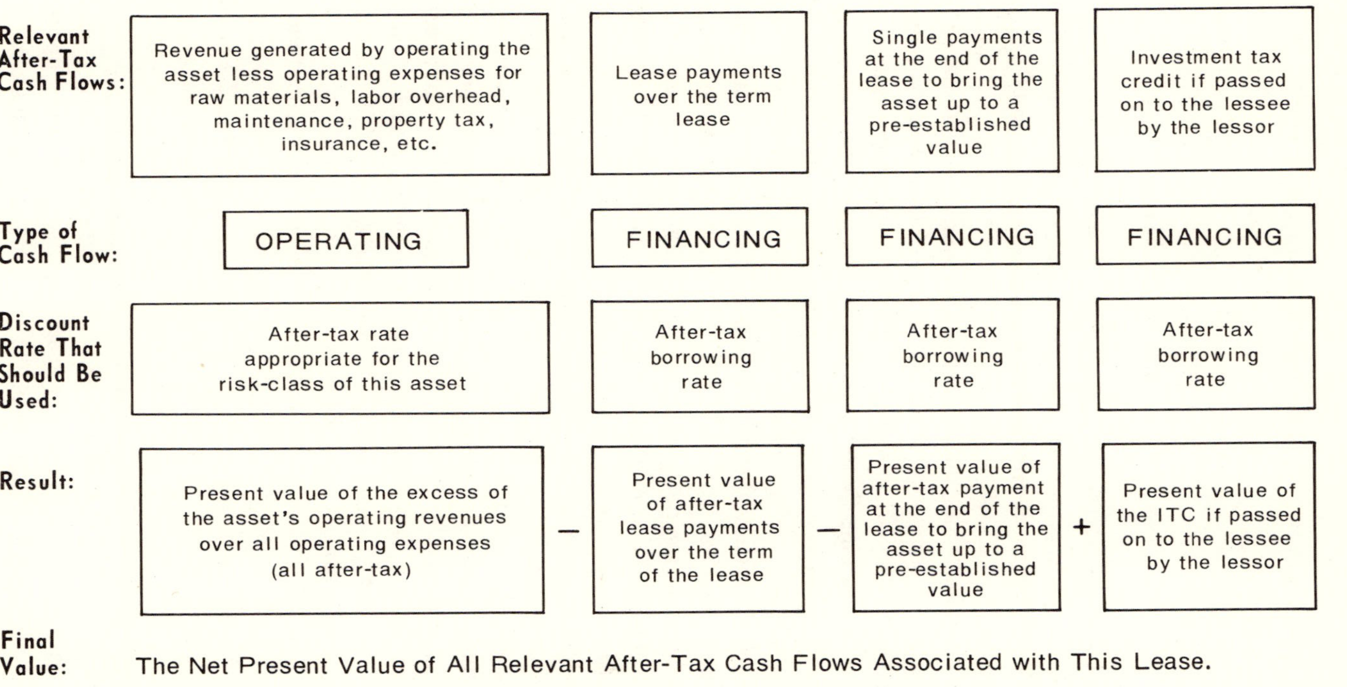
For each lease alternative, determine:
1. Relevant After-Tax Cash Flows:
Revenue generated by operating the asset less operating expenses for raw materials, labor overhead, maintenance, property tax, insurance, etc.
Lease payments over the term lease
Single payments at the end of the lease to bring the asset up to a pre-established value
Investment tax credit if passed on to the lessee by the lessor
2. Type of Cash Flow:
OPERATING
FINANCING
FINANCING
FINANCING
3. Discount Rate That Should Be Used:
After-tax rate appropriate for the risk-class of this asset
After-tax borrowing rate
After-tax borrowing rate
After-tax borrowing rate
4. Result:
Present value of the excess of the asset's operating revenues over all operating expenses (all after-tax)
–
Present value of after-tax lease payments over the term of the lease
–
Present value of after-tax payment at the end of the lease to bring the asset up to a pre-established value
+
Present value of the ITC if passed on to the lessee by the lessor
5. Final Value:
The Net Present Value of All Relevant After-Tax Cash Flows Associated with This Lease.

Figure 9-5. Investment and financing evaluation module.

ample 2 shows how to compute the net present value of any lease alternative.

EXAMPLE 2

Net Present Value Determination for Two Leasing Options

For each of the two leases described in Example 1, find the net present value, using the approach just outlined (which is also summarized in Figure 9-5). The asset will generate additional revenue of $190,000, $205,000, $325,000, $350,000, and $480,000 over its five-year life. In addition, direct material, direct labor, and variable overhead are expected to be 55 percent of revenue each year, and fixed expenses are expected to be $40,000 in year 1 and increase by 10 percent per year thereafter. Determine the NPV of each lease.

SOLUTION

In order to determine the NPV of each lease, we use the approach shown in Figure 9-5. The evaluation of Lease #1 is shown in Figure 9-6. We see that the net present value of Lease #1 is negative. This means that over the term of the lease, the present value of its financial cash *outflows* exceeds the present value of the asset's cash inflows from operations by $2,754. We now turn to an evaluation of Lease #2, which is shown in Figure 9-7.

We see that the net present value of Lease #2 is positive. This means that the present value of the asset's new cash inflows from operations exceeds the present value of the financial flows of Lease #2 by $2,746. *Thus, even though the asset was unattractive if financed through Lease #1* (*since it had a negative NPV of $2,754*), *it is attractive if financed using Lease #2* (*since the latter lease has a positive NPV of $2,746*). Notice also that Lease #2 is more attractive than Lease #1 by the same margin in present-value terms as in Example 1; namely, Lease #1 had a negative NPV here of $2,754 and Lease #2 had a positive NPV of $2,746, making Lease #2 more attractive by $5,500 ($2,754 + $2,746) in present-value terms. This agrees with the difference in favor of Lease #2 shown in Example 1.

Finally, it should be pointed out that in evaluating this asset, we have followed the convention of assuming that the asset's operating cash flows occurred at the end of the year rather than uniformly over the year. The asset becomes much more attractive in NPV terms if we

1. Relevant After-Tax Cash Flows:

Yr.	Rev. —	Var. Exp. —	Fixed Exp. —	Maint. Exp. —	Tax Exp. =	After-Tax Oper. Cash Flow
	(in thousands)					
1	$190 —	104.5 —	40. —	4.6 —	16.36 =	24.54
2	205 —	112.75 —	44. —	4.6 —	17.46 =	26.19
3	325 —	178.75 —	48.4 —	4.6 —	37.3 =	55.95
4	350 —	192.5 —	53.24 —	4.6 —	39.864 =	59.796
5	480 —	264.0 —	58.564 —	4.6 —	61.134 =	91.702

(Before-tax lease payment) X (1 — tax rate)
= ($64,700) X (1 — .4)
= $38,820 per year for 5 years

(Before-tax single payment) X (1 — tax rate)
n ($3,800) X (1 — .4)
= $2,280 at the end of year 5

2. Type of Cash Flow:

OPERATING — FINANCING — FINANCING

3. Discount Rate and Discount Factors:

After-tax risk-adjusted rate = 14% Discount Factors:

Yr.	Factor	Yr.	Factor
1	.877193	3	.674972
2	.769468	4	.592080
		5	.519369

After-tax borrowing rate = 6%. Discount factor for a five-year annunity @ 6% = 4.212364

After-tax borrowing rate = 6%. Single-payment discount factor at end of year 5 = .747258

4. Result: Row 1 Times Row 3

Yr.	After-Tax Oper. Cash Flow	x	Discount Factor	=	Result
1	$24,540		.877193		$21,526
2	26,190		.769468		20,152
3	55,950		.674972		37,765
4	59,796		.592080		35,404
5	91,702		.519369		47,627
			Total	=	$162,474

— $163,524 — $1,704

5. Final Value: Net Present Value Associated with Lease #1 = ($2,754.)

Figure 9-6. Evaluation of Lease #1.

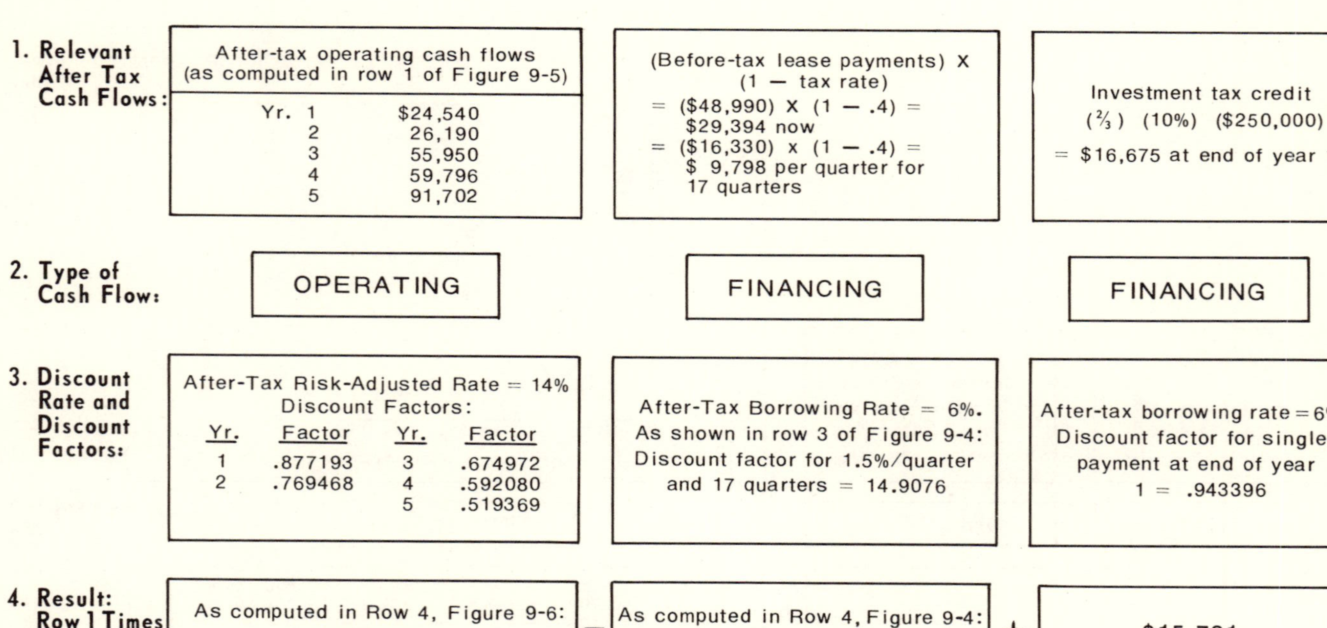

1. Relevant After Tax Cash Flows:
After-tax operating cash flows (as computed in row 1 of Figure 9-5)
Yr. 1 $24,540
2 26,190
3 55,950
4 59,796
5 91,702
(Before-tax lease payments) X (1 — tax rate)
= ($48,990) X (1 — .4) = $29,394 now
= ($16,330) x (1 — .4) = $ 9,798 per quarter for 17 quarters
Investment tax credit
(⅔) (10%) ($250,000)
= $16,675 at end of year 1
2. Type of Cash Flow:
OPERATING
FINANCING
FINANCING
3. Discount Rate and Discount Factors:
After-Tax Risk-Adjusted Rate = 14%
Discount Factors:
Yr. Factor Yr. Factor
1 .877193 3 .674972
2 .769468 4 .592080
5 .519369
After-Tax Borrowing Rate = 6%.
As shown in row 3 of Figure 9-4:
Discount factor for 1.5%/quarter and 17 quarters = 14.9076
After-tax borrowing rate = 6%.
Discount factor for single payment at end of year 1 = .943396
4. Result: Row 1 Times Row 3
As computed in Row 4, Figure 9-6:
$162,474
—
As computed in Row 4, Figure 9-4:
$175,459
+
$15,731
5. Final Value:
Net Present Value Associated with Lease #2 = $2,746

Figure 9-7. Evaluation of Lease #2.

assume that the operating cash flows occur quarterly, consistent with the lease payment.

We would find that the NPV of Lease #2 is $7,685 if quarterly cash inflows were assumed. This is almost a $5,000 increase over the NPV for Lease #2, under the assumption that operating cash flows did not occur until the end of each year.

The above analysis is more accurate if, in fact, cash flows take place on a quarterly basis rather than at the end of each year. Of course, if we assume quarterly rather than annual cash flows, Lease #1 will also become more attractive than it was originally. However, Lease #2 will continue to outperform Lease #1 by the present-value amount of $5,500 found in our previous analysis in both Examples 1 and 2. □

Recommended Analysis for the Purchase Alternative

As mentioned earlier, we want to discuss both the option where the asset is purchased using the firm's general pool of funds for capital investments and the option of borrowing funds specifically to purchase the asset under evaluation. As was also mentioned, we will expand only briefly on the previous coverage given the purchase option. Our elaboration will take on the form of the overviews shown in Figures 9-2 and 9-5 that were recommended to evaluate the leasing alternatives.

As with the lease option, most of the relevant "purchases flows" and the corresponding appropriate risk-adjusted discount rates become obvious with a careful examination of the facts. In the *financing evaluation module,* we must determine the present value of (1) all cash flows related to the financing of the asset and (2) the tax shields related to owning the asset. In this module, as was seen in the lease analysis carried out in the preceding section, it is necessary to consider the benefits related to the operation of the asset, since the asset's attractiveness or necessity has already been established.

We therefore must determine the following:

1. The present value of the cash outflow required to purchase the asset; less

2. The present value of the investment tax credit associated with the asset; less

3. The present value of the tax shield associated with the depre-

ciation deduction for tax purposes, as well as the interest deduction if the firm entered into a loan agreement specifically to purchase this asset; plus

4. The present value of the after-tax payments for maintenance, property taxes, insurance, and so on, related to ownership of the asset; less

5. The present value of the after-tax cash flow associated with the salvage value of the asset at the end of its useful life.

In computing the present values, in order to be consistent with our analysis of leasing alternatives, the cash flows related to the asset's operations (that is the depreciation tax shield in 3, as well as the flows described in 4 and 5) should be discounted at the *risk-adjusted discount rate* that is appropriate for the asset under evaluation,[4] the ITC (that is, 2 above) should be discounted at the firm's after-tax borrowing rate, the cash outflows to purchase the asset for cash should be discounted at the firm's weighted average after-tax cost of capital, and the cash outflows minus the tax shield associated with interest (when the asset is purchased through a loan) should be discounted at the firm's after-tax cost of borrowing.

These discount rates deserve further comment. The ITC for the purchase alternative should be discounted back one period at the same discount rate as was used in evaluating the lease option (hence the recommended use of the firm's after-tax borrowing rate). In a similar way, all cash flows related to the asset's operations require the use of the proper risk-adjusted discount rate to compensate for the risk present in this asset's risk class. Finally, financing cash flows and their related tax shields should be discounted at the rate corresponding to the after-tax cost of funds utilized; that is, when the asset is purchased for cash from the firm's general pool of funds for capital expenditures, the firm's weighted average after-tax cost of capital is appropriate. On the other hand, when the asset is purchased through a loan, the loan outflows minus tax shields for interest should be discounted at the firm's after-tax borrowing rate for the loan.

The recommended approach is summarized as before in Figure 9-8. Because we have treated the purchase alternative throughout the entire book and because the recommended approach for this alternative parallels that for the evaluation of lease options illustrated earlier in this chapter, it is not felt necessary to show extensive examples of the purchase alternative here. The reader who feels the need for a more in-depth coverage is referred to our treatment elsewhere.[5]

For the purchase alternative, determine:

1. Relevant After-Tax Cash Flows:	Cash outflows required to purchase the asset (net of tax effects)		Investment tax credit associated with the asset		Payments for maintenance, property tax, insurance, etc., related to owning the asset		Tax Shield associated with depreciation deduction for tax purposes		Cash Flow associated with the salvage value of the asset
2. Type of Cash Flow:	FINANCING		FINANCING		OPERATING		OPERATING		OPERATING
3. Discount Rate that Should Be Used:	After-tax borrowing rate where the asset is purchased through a loan		After-tax borrowing rate		After-tax rate appropriate for the risk class of this asset				
4. Result:	Present value of after-tax cash outflows to purchase the asset	–	Present value of ITC associated with the asset	+	Present value of after-tax payments for maintenance, property tax, insurance, etc.	–	Present value of tax shield associated with depreciation deduction	–	Present value of after-tax cash flow from salvage value

5. Final Value: Present Value of All Relevant After-Tax Cash Flows Associated with Purchasing the Asset.

Figure 9-8. Financing evaluation module continued.

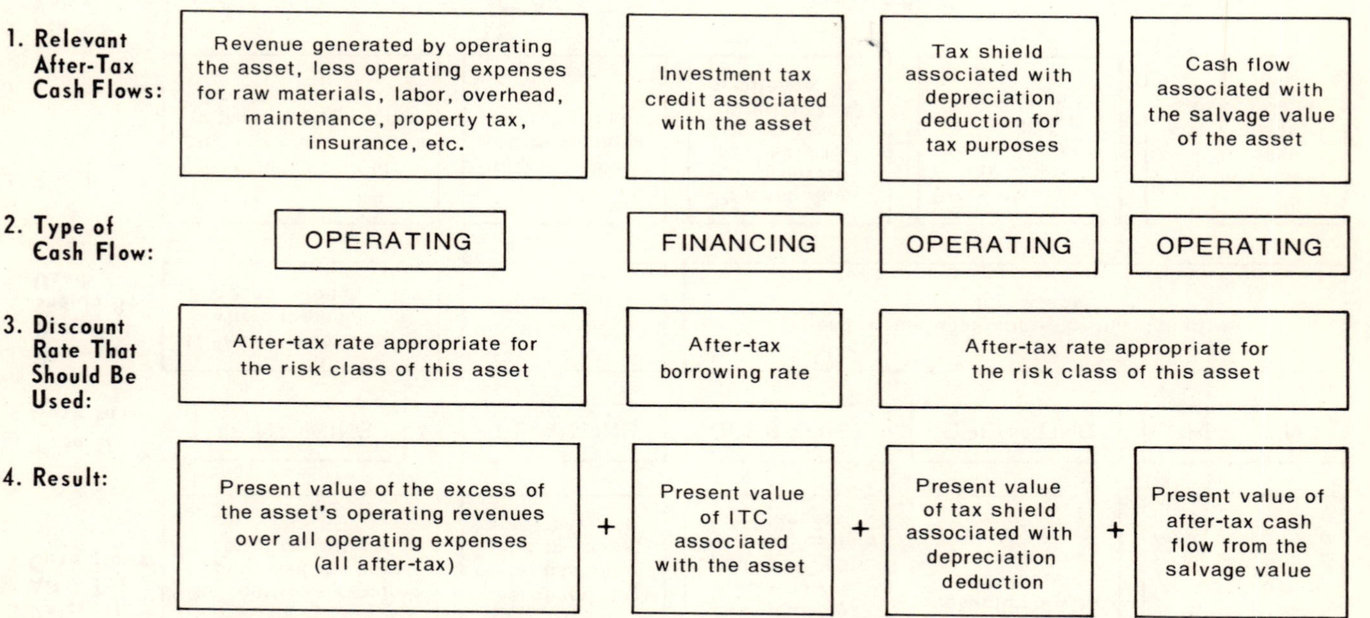

For the purchase alternative, determine:
1. Relevant After-Tax Cash Flows:
Revenue generated by operating the asset, less operating expenses for raw materials, labor, overhead, maintenance, property tax, insurance, etc.
Investment tax credit associated with the asset
Tax shield associated with depreciation deduction for tax purposes
Cash flow associated with the salvage value of the asset
2. Type of Cash Flow:
OPERATING
FINANCING
OPERATING
OPERATING
3. Discount Rate That Should Be Used:
After-tax rate appropriate for the risk class of this asset
After-tax borrowing rate
After-tax rate appropriate for the risk class of this asset
4. Result:
Present value of the excess of the asset's operating revenues over all operating expenses (all after-tax)
+
Present value of ITC associated with the asset
+
Present value of tax shield associated with depreciation deduction
+
Present value of after-tax cash flow from the salvage value
5. Final Value:
The Net Present Value of All Relevant After-Tax Cash Flows Associated with Purchasing the Asset.

Figure 9-9. Investment and financing evaluation module continued.

Next, we will illustrate the recommended procedure for evaluating the purchase alternative in the *investment and financing evaluation module*. As with the lease option, the only modification to the analysis is that both the benefits and the costs associated with ownership must be taken into account so that the net present value of the asset can be determined. The parallel approach here will again show that we merely subtract the fixed and variable operating expenses from the revenue generated by the asset in each period, reduce this amount by the tax liability, and then discount to present value, using the relevant risk-adjusted discount rate; from this amount we subtract the present value of the after-tax operating and financial cash flows determined in the financing evaluation module. As usual, if the NPV is positive, the asset is a candidate for acceptance if it is purchased. The approach is summarized in Figure 9-9.

It should be reiterated in closing this section that the end product obtained in either the financing evaluation module or the investment and financing evaluation module is a present-value or net-present-value figure for each lease and purchase alternative under consideration. However, these figures, rather than point to a clear-cut decision, provide the basis for performing sensitivity analysis and for renegotiating terms on existing financing alternatives or seeking out other financing arrangements before a final decision is made. Sensitivity analysis is the topic of the next chapter.

Summary

This rather extensive chapter has given in-depth treatment to lease/purchase analysis. We proceeded through flowchart, verbal, mathematical, and tabular approaches to the recommended evaluation techniques. A powerful yet flexible approach was illustrated for *analyzing financing alternatives* (lease versus lease, lease versus purchase for cash, and lease versus purchase with a loan) when the project has received prior approval. In addition, the methodology was provided for a *simultaneous consideration of the investment's attractiveness and the best method of financing*. We now are ready for the next vitally important step, sensitivity analysis, which should be performed before the final decision is made. This is the topic of the next chapter. We recommend performing sensitivity analysis in all capital expenditure decision settings, whether or not the lease alternative is considered.

NOTES

1. See Robert E. Pritchard and Thomas J. Hindelang, *The Lease/Buy Decision,* New York: AMACOM, 1980, Chapter 10.
2. I. W. Sorensen and R. E. Johnson, "Equipment Financial Leasing Practices and Costs: An Empirical Study," *Financial Management,* Spring 1977, pp. 33–40.
3. Ibid., p. 34
4. Some authors argue that the salvage value (that is, cash flow 5) should be discounted at an even higher risk-adjusted discount rate than that specified for the asset's risk class because of the uncertainty involved in estimating residual values. However, we reject this complication because of the already high risk penalty that is attached to the salvage value and because this problem is more efficiently and effectively handled using sensitivity analysis, which is discussed in the next chapter.
5. See Pritchard and Hindelang, op. cit., Chapter 8.

CHAPTER 10

Strategic Planning and Sensitivity Analysis

In Chapter 1 we presented a 15-step procedure for the selection, implementation, and monitoring of capital investments. Subsequently we introduced and discussed the analytical tools needed to evaluate proposed purchases and leases under conditions of both changing and unchanging risk. Throughout we noted that the environment is constantly changing and that, while the analytical procedures will produce accurate answers if the inputs are correct, the inputs are subject to change. Throughout we have implicity argued for *strategic planning* within the arena of capital asset acquisition.

The primary goal of strategic planning is to assure that the firm will achieve a high degree of success in attaining its goals within a rapidly changing environment. Strategic planning has as its output a set of strategies or policies. These strategies are extremely useful in providing the framework for planning. Within the area of capital asset acquisition, the various strategic plans are developed by undertaking sensitivity analyses of the numerous inputs used in making the acquisition decision. Thus strategic planning at the outset is long-term in nature. The strategic plans are used to make long-term commitments of funds to fixed assets. But, as the environment changes, the plans must be revisited, which leads to the process of capital abandonment—the subject of Chapter 12.

Strategic planning involves examining alternative courses of action. In capital asset acquisition, two come to mind immediately: purchasing and leasing. In Chapters 5 and 9 we discussed different types of leases, that is, leases differing with respect to the payment terms and the benefits involved. At this juncture, however, we have examined purchasing from only two perspectives: using available cash or borrowing funds. In order to broaden the imaginative horizon of acquisition, Chapter 11, which describes several unique acquisition strategies under the heading of project financing, has been included.

The formation of initial strategies depends upon the consideration of the varied situations in which the firm may be involved. Each situation will result in changes to one or more of the input variables and thus to some degree will affect the output and subsequent acquisition decision. In order to assess the magnitude of the change that will occur as input variables such as the cost of capital are changed, we undertake a *sensitivity analysis*—the topic of this, the first of three chapters incorporating strategic planning into the capital acquisition process. As a part of this chapter we also outline our strategy for dealing with inflation when planning for asset acquisition.

At this juncture, the basic ideas of sensitivity analysis should not be foreign to the reader. For example, in Chapter 2 we applied sensitivity analysis in three examples. In each instance we determined the sensitivity of a company's tax liability to possible management decisions. In the first case, the question was the timing of disposal of Section 1231 assets. The second related to an outright sale versus the trade-in of a used asset. The last example dealt with the selection of the depreciable life for an asset. The reader will also recall that sensitivity analysis was illustrated in several other chapters.

Within several of the previous chapters, we have stressed the importance of performing sensitivity analysis as part of the capital expenditure decision process. Sensitivity analysis[1] brings the following three relevant aspects into focus before the final decision is made:

1. Qualitative differences among the alternatives.
2. Quantitative differences among the alternatives that were too complex to incorporate directly into the recommended evaluation of the alternatives.
3. The extent to which surrounding conditions would have to change before the preferred alternative would be different.

Each of these aspects will be examined in turn.

Qualitative Factors in Capital Expenditure Decisions

Every decision setting is surrounded by both quantifiable and nonquantifiable attributes that require consideration and evaluation before we can arrive at a final decision. Any model or approach called upon to assist in the evaluation of alternatives necessarily must be selective in deciding which aspects of the decision setting can and should be incorporated into the analysis. In general, the strategy is to build in the most critical dimensions that can be accurately estimated or quantified. Hence many intangible or qualitative factors are not directly incorporated in the analysis. However, such factors can be of significant importance to the firm in both the short and long run. We therefore recommend that a careful, detailed analysis of the qualitative dimensions of capital expenditure decisions be performed by the firm before final action is taken.

At various points in previous chapters, we pointed to numerous considerations that could be relevant to a given firm in a given capital expenditure problem setting. Such relevant qualitative considerations are the subject matter of the careful and detailed analysis just mentioned. In addition to the factors discussed, the following aspects deserve consideration:

1. How will each alternative proposed capital project affect the other major goals of the firm? How will each proposal influence growth, competition, risk reduction, stability in earnings, product diversification, return on assets, return on equity, and the like?

2. Do the alternatives differ significantly in terms of compliance with directives of various regulatory agencies, or local and state public ordinances? Do any of the alternatives have special tax implications, or are there special funding sources for them at the federal, state, or local level?

3. What impact will the financing decision (that is, lease, purchase with debt fund, or purchase with equity funds) have on the firm's degree of financial leverage? What impact will the financing decision have on the firm's coverage of fixed interest and other financial charges? What impact would the financing alternatives have on the firm's existing restrictive covenants in its bond indenture(s)? What impact would there be on future financing decisions? Can the term of a given lease be shortened or extended? Could the loan in a borrow-and-buy arrangement be renewed or prepaid? Is the loan callable? What impact will the financing decision have on the combined degree

of operating and financial leverage? What will be the impact on balance sheet presentation? Several of these considerations are covered in Chapter 11, which discusses project financing.

4. Among the several lending institutions, lessors, or equipment manufacturers that may offer competitive terms to a given firm, which one would be selected? There are numerous considerations here which must be taken into account. A firm must evaluate these considerations before the final decision.

5. What are the relevant nonfinancial and non-tax aspects of the proposals that must be factored into the final decision? This is a broad area with several important ramifications that must be considered by the organization.

Upon addressing these issues and weighing the advantages and disadvantages that they imply for the alternatives under consideration, the evaluation committee should arrive at a summary of the qualitative dimension of the decision. This result will later be merged with that obtained in the next two phases of sensitivity analysis.

Additional Quantitative Factors in the Capital Expenditure Decision

The recommended approaches in Chapters 7, 8, and 9 were not always a straightforward or simple analysis of the alternatives under evaluation. Nevertheless, the approaches were, in fact, simplified, because a number of additional complexities were not directly incorporated into the analysis. Such additional quantitative complexities would include a complete consideration of the conditions of risk surrounding the decision; a consideration of changing tax laws; treating the impact of inflation on the analysis; consideration of changing the terms of a lease or financing during the original contract once accepted by the parties; the option to abandon the asset or cancel the lease; and the like.

In our experience, direct quantitative treatment of such factors renders the quantitative analysis of alternatives too complex. Further, the benefit in terms of accuracy and additional insight provided is limited. Therefore, we recommend that these complexities be incorporated into the analysis using the approach of the previous section in conjunction with that of the following section. This dual approach should prove more effective and efficient in obtaining greater insight into the decision setting and improved accuracy in specifying the preferred alternative.

Analysis of Changes in the Data Inputs to Project Evaluation

The major analytical phase of sensitivity analysis is that of determining the impact of changes in the data inputs on the selection of the preferred decision alternative. We are interested in determining the extent to which errors made in forecasting future financial and operating cash flows will affect the net present value of the alternatives under evaluation. Of course, some forecasting errors or changes in the decision environment will make the preferred alternative more attractive, while others could lead to selection of a different preferred alternative. In the latter case, the decision maker would want to assess the likelihood of such errors or changes. If it is felt that the probability is great enough, then the new preferred alternative should be carefully considered for implementation. In addition, qualitative factors must be weighed in making the final decision, as was discussed earlier in this chapter.

Forecasting and Sensitivity Analysis[2]

Every forecast is based on assumptions—and the development of a forecast necessitates that assumptions be made. This process is enlightening, because it requires thought as to what is likely to happen in the business. The easiest way to start is to look at the income statements over the past three to five years and identify problem areas (Table 10-1).

Each year sales as measured in dollars have increased and profits have likewise improved. For forecasting purposes, it is necessary to convert the income statements to percentage form for purposes of comparison (Table 10-2).

With the statements shown in percentages, it is immediately obvious that profit margins as measured by earnings after taxes are slipping, even though profits in dollars are increasing. Most costs are holding in line with sales, but two in particular are increasing rapidly: fuel and utilities. These represent "red flag" areas. A manager might well

Table 10-1. Income statements for ABC, Inc.

	Year 1	*Year 2*	*Year 3*
Revenue:			
Net sales	$100,000	$115,000	$134,000
Costs and expenses:			
Cost of goods	35,000	40,000	47,000
Labor	25,000	29,000	34,000
Rent	8,000	9,000	10,000
Fuel	2,000	4,000	7,000
Utilities	3,000	4,000	6,000
Depreciation	6,000	6,000	6,000
Administrative	10,000	11,000	11,500
	$ 89,000	$103,000	$121,500
Earnings before interest and taxes	$ 11,000	$ 12,000	$ 12,500
Interest	4,000	4,000	4,000
Earnings before taxes	$ 7,000	$ 8,000	$ 8,500
Taxes*	1,400	1,600	1,700
Earnings after taxes	$ 5,600	$ 6,400	$ 6,800
Unit sales volume	100	108	117

* This assumes a 20% rate.

call for a complete energy audit by a utility or professional energy auditor. Based on these findings, the manager can implement specific changes, both short and long term. The changes will, of course, impact the assumptions underlying the forecast and budget.

Next, several questions need to be answered:

1. What will be the change in unit sales volume and/or in product mix?
2. How will a change in unit sales volume and product mix affect dollar sales volume and each of the costs?
3. What will be the inflation rate? How will it impact each expense item? Can increased expenses be passed along to customers?
4. Will interest rates change and how will this affect the cost of interest?
5. What capital expenditures are necessary or desirable?
6. How will capital expenditures change revenues and costs?

Table 10-2. Income statements in percentages for ABC, Inc.

	Year 1	*Year 2*	*Year 3*
Revenue:			
Net sales	100.0	100.0	100.0
Costs and expenditures:			
Costs of goods	35.0	34.8	35.0
Labor	25.0	25.2	25.4
Rent	8.0	7.8	7.5
Fuel	2.0	3.5	5.2
Utilities	3.0	3.5	4.5
Depreciation	6.0	5.2	4.5
Administrative	10.0	9.6	8.6
Earnings before interest and taxes	11.0	10.4	9.3
Interest	4.0	3.5	3.0
Earnings before taxes	7.0	6.9	6.3
Taxes	1.4	1.4	1.3
Earnings after taxes	5.6	5.5	5.0
Unit sales volume: percent increase over previous year		8	8

7. Can any unprofitable segments of the business be eliminated or can work be subcontracted at a cost reduction?

The answers to these and other questions form the set of assumptions for the forecast. As a practical matter, it is best to discuss these questions and those relating to the impact of inflation with members of a trade association.

The following paragraphs present a sample forecast. The forecast requires a set of assumptions that correspond to the questions listed above.

1. The product mix will remain constant.
2. Sales volume will increase by 7 percent (note the 8 percent increases in the last two years). All costs will concurrently increase by 7 percent except rent, depreciation, interest, and taxes.
3. The overall rate of inflation will be 10 percent. Inflation will impact the various areas listed below:

	Percent Increase
Cost of goods	10
Labor	8
Rent	8
Fuel	30
Utilities	15
Depreciation	N/A
Administration	8

Selling prices will increase by 9 percent over the year.

4. Interest rates will go up 2 percent, from 10 percent to 12 percent (a 20 percent increase in cost).
5. Capital expenditures will be required with a resulting cost of \$10,000 and increases in depreciation of \$2,000 and interest of \$1,000. Note that the interest will increase from \$4,000 to \$6,000: (4,000 + \$1,000) × 1.20 = \$6,000. (The factor 1.20 results from the increase in interest rates as noted in assumption 4.)
6. The capital expenditures will result in negligible changes in revenues and costs.
7. The business will be operated as usual without any subcontracting.

Incorporating the assumptions requires two steps. The first deals with unit volume and capital expenditures, the second with inflation. The pro forma income statements are shown in Table 10-3.

This example produces some unpleasant predictions. Earnings after taxes decreased, and the profit margin slipped. It indicates how sensitive this particular operation is to inflation and to the proposed capital expenditures. The forecaster is now in the position to ask some very important questions: (1) What would be the effect of reducing actual consumption of fuel and utilities by 10 percent? (2) What would be the effect of postponing the capital expenditure if it would necessitate increasing labor cost by \$1,000? Obviously, capital expenditures cannot be postponed forever, but leasing might offer some advantages. The utility and fuel question will be considered first (Table 10-4).

The result of reducing fuel and utility usage by 10 percent is an increase in earnings after taxes from the first forecast of \$5,100 to \$6,500 (a 27 percent increase). This process, known as a *sensitivity analysis,* reveals that after-tax earnings are very sensitive to changes in fuel and utility use. The next step in the sensitivity analysis would be to determine the effect of postponing the capital expenditure. For the sake of

Table 10-3. Pro forma income statement for ABC, Inc., year 4.

	Changes Resulting from Increased Sales Volume	*Changes Resulting from Inflation*	*Year 4*	*Percentage Format*
Revenue:				
Net sales	$134,000 × 1.07 =	$143,000 × 1.09 =	$156,300	100.0
Costs and expenses:				
Cost of goods	47,000 × 1.07 =	50,300 × 1.10 =	55,300	35.4
Labor	34,000 × 1.07 =	36,400 × 1.08 =	39,300	25.1
Rent	10,000 × 1.07 =	10,000 × 1.08 =	10,800	6.9
Fuel	7,000 × 1.07 =	7,500 × 1.30 =	9,800	6.3
Utilities	6,000 × 1.07 =	6,400 × 1.15 =	7,400	4.7
Depreciation	6,000 + $2,000 =	8,000 × 1.00 =	8,000	5.1
Administration	11,500 × 1.07 =	12,300 × 1.08 =	13,300	8.5
	$121,500	$130,900	$143,900	92.0
Earnings before interest and taxes	$ 12,500	$ 12,500	$ 12,400	8.0
Interest	4,000	6,000 × 1.00	6,000	3.8
Earnings before taxes	$ 8,500	$ 6,500	$ 6,400	4.2
Taxes	1,700	1,300	1,300	0.8
Earnings after taxes	$ 6,800	$ 5,200	$ 5,100	3.4
Unit sales volume	117 × 1.07 =	125 × 1.00 =	125	

brevity, these calculations are omitted. This general problem is considered in greater depth in the next section.

NPV Profiles

A helpful tool in performing sensitivity analysis for capital expenditures is that of *NPV profiles*. An NPV profile is a graphic representation of the net present value (NPV) for a given project as the cost of capital, or discount rate, is allowed to take on various values. NPV profiles provide insight to the decision maker into the impact of changing conditions on a single project or a set of mutually exclusive projects. Consider the project shown in Example 1.

Table 10-4. ABC income statement with 10 percent reduction in fuel and utilities for year 4.

		Percentage Format
Revenue:		
Net sales	$156,300	100.0
Costs and expenses:		
Costs of goods	$ 55,300	35.4
Labor	39,300	25.2
Rent	10,800	6.9
Fuel	8,800	5.6
Utilities	6,700	4.3
Depreciation	8,000	5.1
Administration	13,300	8.5
	$142,200	91.0
Earnings before interest and taxes	$ 14,100	9.0
Interest	6,000	3.8
Earnings before taxes	$ 8,100	5.2
Taxes	1,600	1.0
Earnings after taxes	$ 6,500	4.2

EXAMPLE 1

Determination of the NPV Profile for Project X

A firm is evaluating Project X, which has an estimated eight-year useful life and the following cash flows:

Year	*Cash Flow*
Present	−$100,000
1–8	+$ 40,000

Determine the NPV for this project at discount rates in 5 percent increments from 0 percent to 50 percent and sketch the results, showing NPV on the vertical axis and the discount rates on the horizontal axis.

SOLUTION

Table 10-5 shows Project X's discounted cash inflows (DCI), cost, and NPV for each of the discount rates. The NPV profile would be sketched as in Figure 10-1. Notice that the NPV profile crosses the hor-

Table 10-5. Discounted cash inflows and net present values at varying discount rates.

Discount Rate	*DCI*	*Cost*	*NPV*
0%	$320,000	$100,000	$220,000
5%	258,529	$100,000	158,529
10%	213,379	$100,000	113,397
15%	179,493	$100,000	79,493
20%	153,486	$100,000	53,486
25%	133,156	$100,000	33,156
30%	116,988	$100,000	16,988
35%	103,927	$100,000	3,927
40%	93,224	$100,000	−6,776

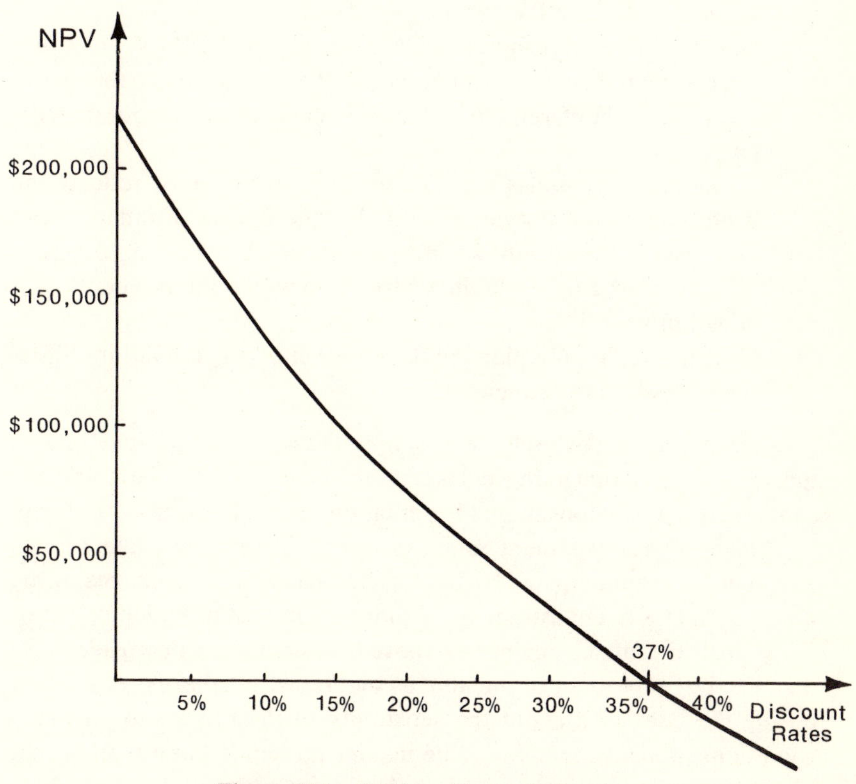

Figure 10-1. NPV profile for Project X.

izontal axis at approximately 37 percent. According to the definition of the internal rate of return (IRR) in Chapter 7, Project X has an IRR of about 37 percent, because this is the discount rate at which the NPV for Project X equals zero. □

The NPV profile derived in Example 1 provides management with a vehicle to answer "what if" questions concerning the attractiveness of Project X. For example, all the following questions (and others) can be answered by reference to the NPV profile and the analysis underlying its development:

- How much could the firm's cost of capital increase from its present level before the project would cease to be attractive on an NPV basis?
- Given that inflation often results in cost overruns, by how much could the cost of the project increase and still have the project be attractive on an NPV basis?
- Given that forecasting errors can show cash inflows which are overestimated, by how much could the annual net cash inflows decrease without rendering the project unattractive on an NPV basis?
- Given that technological change can significantly reduce the useful life of the project and/or that the effects of inflation can drive the net cash inflows in "real dollar" terms to zero before the end of its useful life, how attractive would the project be if it ended in year 5?
- How would combinations of the above changing conditions affect the project's attractiveness?

Such questions should be raised by management because, unfortunately, capital budgeting decisions are subject to the complexities and uncertainties imposed by high inflation rates, changing cost of capital, changing reinvestment rates, errors in forecasting project costs and benefits, unanticipated technological changes, and changes in the firm's competitive environment. Without the insight provided by sensitivity analysis, management is exposed to significant downside risks that are the by-product of the above conditions. Furthermore, without raising the questions about the sensitivity of the project to changing conditions, management would be making an implicit assumption that it will encounter throughout the project's life precisely the "ideal results" that were initially estimated.

Thus we strongly recommend that sensitivity analysis be performed for all major capital expenditure and leasing decisions.

Sensitivity Analysis and Inflation

Sensitivity analysis can be employed to deal with the numerous problems resulting from the impact of inflation on costs and forecasts. We illustrate the methodology of sensitivity analysis in Example 2.

EXAMPLE 2
Sensitivity Analysis on Project X

For Project X shown in Example 1, the firm evaluating it raises the following questions.

1. The firm's present cost of capital is 20 percent; how much could it increase before Project X's NPV would be zero or negative?
2. If the firm's cost of capital remained at 20 percent, by what amount could the cost of Project X increase and still leave the project's NPV positive?
3. If the firm's cost of capital remained at 20 percent, by what amount could the annual net cash inflows decrease and still leave Project X's NPV greater than zero?
4. If the firm's cost of capital remained at 20 percent, would Project X still be attractive in NPV terms if the cash inflows dropped to zero after five years?
5. How would questions 2, 3, and 4 be answered if the firm's cost of capital increased to 25 percent?

SOLUTION

Each of the five questions raised is basically a "break-even" question. Most managers and analysts deal with such questions regularly. In addition, the answers to such questions are facilitated by reference to the NPV profile introduced earlier and derived for Project X in Example 1.

1. Since the NPV profile for Project X crosses the horizontal axis at about 37 percent, the project will continue to generate a positive NPV with any cost of capital lower than 37 percent. Thus, at a 37 percent cost of capital, the firm would break even on an NPV basis with Project X. Hence the firm's cost of capital could increase by up to 17 percent and the project would still have a postive NPV.

2. At a 20 percent cost of capital, Project X's discounted cash inflows equal \$153,486, as shown in Example 1, and its NPV is \$53,486. Therefore, Project X's cost could increase by up to \$53,486 and the project would still have a positive NPV.

3. At a 20 percent cost of capital, Project X will have an NPV value that is attractive (that is, greater than zero) as long as the discounted cash inflows equal or exceed the project's \$100,000 cost. In determining the discounted cash inflows at a cost of capital of 20 percent in Example 1, we multiplied the annual net cash inflows of \$40,000 by the present value of an annuity factor for 20 percent and eight years: (\$40,000) × (3.83716) = \$153,486. Thus, to find the annual net cash inflow (χ) that would lead to a total discounted cash inflow of \$100,000, we would simply solve the following equation.

$$(\chi) \times (3.83716) = \$100{,}000$$

$$\chi = \frac{\$100{,}000}{3.83716}$$

$$\chi = \$26{,}061$$

Therefore, Project X's annual cash inflows could drop from \$40,000 to \$26,061, or by \$13,939 per year, and Project X would still be attractive in NPV terms. Similarly, Project X would still be attractive in NPV terms as long as the discounted cash inflows over the project's life (using a 20 percent discount rate) equaled or exceeded \$100,000; that is, cash inflows could vary from year to year, but as long as the present value of all future cash flows ≥ \$100,000, the project is attractive.

4. At a 20 percent cost of capital, if the project had cash inflows of only \$40,000 for five years, its NPV would be:

$$\begin{aligned} NPV_x &= (\$40{,}000) \times (\text{PV annuity factor for 5 years at 20\%}) - \$100{,}000 \\ &= (\$40{,}000) \times (2.990612) - \$100{,}000 \\ &= \$19{,}624 \end{aligned}$$

Thus, even if all cash inflows cease at the end of year 5, Project X generates benefits that exceed its cost by \$19,624 in present-value terms if the firm's cost of capital or required rate of return is 20 percent.

5. As shown in Example 1, if the firm's cost of capital increases to 25 percent, Project X's discounted cash inflows equal \$133,156 and its NPV is \$33,156. Thus, in answer to question 2: the cost of the project could increase by up to \$33,156 and the project would still have an

NPV $\geqslant$ 0. In answer to question 3, we would solve the following equation for the annual net cash inflow (χ):

$$(\chi) \times (3.328911) = \$100{,}000$$
$$\chi = \frac{\$100{,}000}{3.328911}$$
$$\chi = \$30{,}040$$

That is, the annual net cash inflows could drop from \$40,000 to \$30,040 and Project X would still have an NPV $\geqslant$ 0. In answer to question 4: if Project X had annual cash inflows of \$40,000 for five years and the required rate of return were 25 percent, the NPV would be:

$$\begin{aligned} NPV_x &= (\$40{,}000) \times (\text{PV annuity factor for 5 years at } 25\%) - \$100{,}000 \\ &= (\$40{,}000) \times (2.68920) - \$100{,}000 \\ &= \$7{,}568 \end{aligned}$$

Therefore, under these conditions Project X still increases the value of the firm by \$7,568 in present-value terms. □

Example 2 summarizes the approach taken in performing sensitivity analysis. In addition, it illustrates our recommended approach for handling the *inflationary conditions which seem very much a part of the decision environment in the 1980s.*

Inflation and the comcomitant condition of tight money will very likely lead to an increase in the cost of capital. Such an increase leads to the natural question, *how attractive are projects as the required rate of return increases to offset a similar increase in the cost of obtaining capital?* This led to the first question raised in Example 2. Next, inflationary conditions cause concern about the estimates that have been made for the cost of projects under consideration, as well as about the "real benefits" generated (these were the topics of questions 2 and 3 in Example 2). Finally, the presence of inflationary conditions makes it natural to consider limiting the planning horizon to five years to compensate for the significant decrease in the value of "real benefits" *generated by capital investment projects.*

Thus, Example 2, while illustrating our recommended approach to handling sensitivity analysis in capital project evaluation, also points to our *strategy for hedging against inflation:*

1. Determine the attractiveness of projects under the condition of significant increases in the cost of capital (and thus in the required rate of return).

2. Verify the continued viability of capital projects as their costs show prospects of major increases and as their "real future benefits" show possible downward trends and lower present values due to inability to pass cost increases on to customers.

3. Limit the planning horizon for capital projects to five years or about one-half of their estimated useful life in order to hedge against both inflationary conditions and unforeseen technological changes.

Sensitivity Analysis for Mutually Exclusive Projects

In Chapter 7, we mentioned that when the firm is evaluating two or more mutually exclusive investments, the net present value (NPV) model could yield a different ranking of the projects than the ranking arrived at using the profitability index (PI) or the internal rate of return (IRR). We pointed out that such conflicts in project ranking could occur if the mutually exclusive projects under evaluation exhibited one or more of the following characteristics: (1) different net cash outlays required, (2) different timing and magnitude of the cash inflows, and (3) unequal useful lives. Under these conditions, NPV profiles provide assistance in performing sensitivity analysis and in resolving the conflicts in project ranking. The approach is illustrated in Example 3.

EXAMPLE 3

NPV Profiles for Two Mutually Exclusive Projects

A firm whose cost of capital is 12 percent is evaluating the following two projects that exhibit a time disparity (that is, differences in the timing and amount of the annual cash inflows).

Year	*Project X*	*Project Y*
Present	−$100,000	−$100,000
1	+ 60,000	+ 35,000
2	+ 50,000	+ 40,000
3	+ 40,000	+ 50,000
4	+ 30,000	+ 50,000
5	+ 30,000	+ 60,000

Determine the NPV for each project, using discount rates between 0 percent and 40 percent in 10 percent increments, as well as 33 percent and 37 percent. Sketch the two NPV profiles on the same graph and discuss the implications of the conflicts in project ranking and how the NPV profiles can be used to resolve the conflicts and to perform sensitivity analysis.

SOLUTION

Table 10-6 exhibits the net present values of Project X and Project Y for the different discount rates. The rankings of the two projects by NPV, PI, and IRR are as follows:

	Project X	*Project Y*
$NPV_{12\%}$	\$58,000	\$64,470
Rank by NPV	2	1
$PI_{12\%}$	1.58	1.64
Rank by PI	2	1
IRR (approximate)	37.5%	33.5%
Rank by IRR	1	2

Thus we see that the ranking of the two projects by IRR conflicts with that assigned by NPV and PI. A sketch of the two NPV profiles is shown in Figure 10-2.

As can be seen from the NPV profiles and the supporting calculations, Project Y has a higher NPV value at all discount rates *below* 20 percent, but Project X has a higher IRR (37.5 percent versus 33.5 percent for Project Y). Thus there will be a conflict in ranking these two projects by NPV (or PI) and by IRR if the firm's cost of capital is 20 percent or greater. The main reason for the conflict (as discussed in *Chapter 7) is the fact that the NPV and PI models assume that a project's intermediate cash inflows can be reinvested over the remaining*

Table 10-6. NPVs of Project X and Project Y for different discount rates.

Discount Rate	*NPV of Project X*	*NPV of Project Y*
0%	\$100,000	\$135,000
10	65,000	73,815
20	34,320	34,085
30	12,510	6,985
33	7,170	550
37	740	(7,070)
40	(3,720)	(12,250)

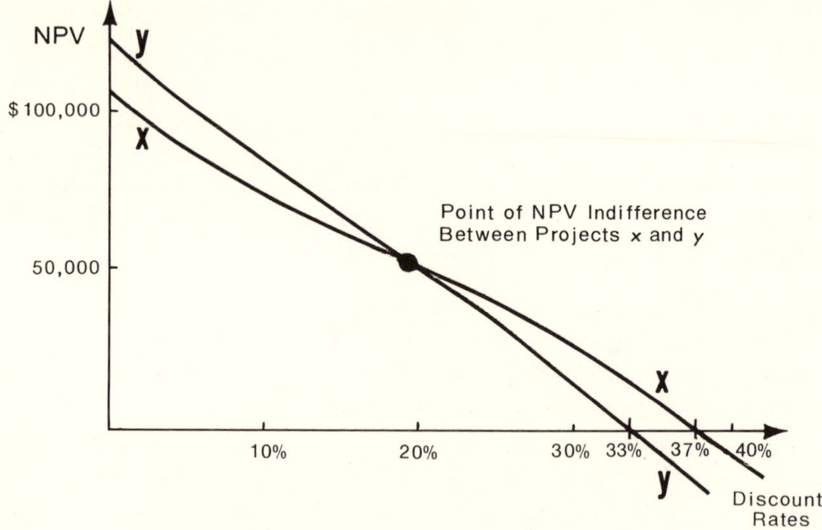

Figure 10-2. NPV profiles for Project X and Project Y.

life of the project at a return equal to the firm's cost of capital (here 12 percent) *whereas the IRR model assumes that these intermediate cash flows can be reinvested at the IRR rate* (here 37.5 percent for Project X and 33.5 percent for Project Y). In this example, there is clearly a significant difference between these two assumed reinvestment rates. □

Our recommended approach for resolving conflicts in project ranking similar to those found in Example 3 is:

1. In general, select the project with the greater NPV at the firm's cost of capital, because the *NPV model provides greater assistance to the firm in maximizing the value of the firm* and because the *NPV model has a more conservative reinvestment assumption.*

2. Consider qualitative factors that differentiate the mutually exclusive projects; these factors, plus management's judgment, are important considerations in making the final decision, as discussed earlier.

3. Using the NPV profiles, address relevant sensitivity questions about changes in conditions in the decision environment and determine whether the likelihood is sufficiently great that such changes could result in a different alternative becoming preferable under the NPV criterion.

For the two projects in Example 3, on the first pass we would see that Project Y would be preferred, because its NPV at the firm's cost of capital of 12 percent is $64,470 versus $58,000 for Project X. Next, management would have to evaluate qualitative differences between the two projects. Finally, looking at the NPV profiles, we see that Project X starts to achieve the greater NPV value at the "crossover" or "indifference" discount rate of 20 percent. The important questions that now must be addressed are:

- How likely is it that the firm's cost of capital will increase from the current 12 percent to over 20 percent over the five-year life of either project? In fact, the firm's cost of capital would have to take on an average in excess of 20 percent over the next five years in order for Project X to achieve the greater NPV value compared with Project Y.
- How likely is it that the firm will be able to reinvest the cash inflows from either project at a compounded annual rate over the next five years in excess of 20 percent? If the firm can reinvest these cash flows at such a rate, Project X is more attractive to the firm, because it will have a greater value than Project Y at these higher reinvestment rates. At all reinvestment rates below the 20 percent indifference rate, Project Y will continue to have a greater value to the firm.
- Is either project more vulnerable to downside risks due to its special characteristics? Several changes in each project can be tried out, as illustrated in Example 1, and the new resulting NPV profiles graphed for the two projects.

Sensitivity Analysis and Changes in Residual Values

Another important feature in evaluating capital projects and in lease/buy analysis is the residual or salvage value of the asset. In inflationary times, the future market value of an asset could significantly exceed the best estimate for this value at the present time. Higher salvage values make the acquisition of assets more attractive. Hence these higher values make the purchase alternative in lease/purchase decisions more attractive. In fact, our interviews with a number of major lessors have shown *residual values are one of the major determinants of whether lessors consider a lease profitable to them.* Of course, this means that had the lessee purchased the asset instead, the higher salvage value would have been his rather than the lessor's at the end of the project's life.

Errors in estimating an asset's salvage value are partially offset by tax implications and the discounting process (since such cash inflows occur several periods out in the future). However, the net effect can still be significant and can swing the decision to a different preferred alternative. Hence we recommend considering the impact of changes in the salvage value when performing sensitivity analysis for capital expenditures, as demonstrated in the following example.

EXAMPLE 4
Changes in Salvage Values

In Chapter 9, we evaluated the acquisition of an asset through two lease alternatives in both the financing evaluation module (Example 1) and the investment and financing evaluation module (Example 2). We did not carry out the analysis of the purchase alternative because it closely parallels the analysis of the two leases, which was presented in detail. However, consider the following facts for the purchase alternative: purchase price, including delivery and installation expense = $266,400; investment tax credit to owner = $16,675 one year after date of purchase; estimated salvage value = $20,000 at the end of year 5; the firm used sum-of-the-years'-digits depreciation for tax purposes, and it ignored the salvage value, as allowed by IRS, since it is less than 10 percent of the purchase price of the asset; the firm incurred $5,200 per year for maintenance, insurance, and property taxes under ownership of the asset; the firm's tax rate is 40 percent.

In the financing evaluation module, the present value of the costs associated with the purchase alternative is $175,638. In the investment and financing evaluation module (assuming the same revenues and variable and fixed expenses as were assumed for the two leases in Example 2 of Chapter 9), the NPV for the purchase alternative is ($3,688).

Consider the impact on the attractiveness of the alternative if the salvage value were: $10,000, $25,000, $30,000, $40,000, $40,576, and $50,000 rather than $20,000.

Prepare a table showing the change in the present value and the net present value of the purchase alternative under each of the new salvage values. For each new salvage compare the present values and net present values of the two leases with the revised values for the purchase alternative. Also, show the results using a graphic approach, with present value or net present value on the vertical axis and salvage values on the horizontal axis.

SOLUTION

Looking back at Examples 1 through 4 in Chapter 9, we see that:

Present value (Lease #1) = $174,703	NPV (Lease #1) = ($2,754)
Present value (Lease #2) = $169,203	NPV (Lease #2) = $2,746
Present value (Purchase) = $175,637	NPV (purchase) = ($3,688)

Thus the differences between the purchase alternative and each lease alternative are:

PV (purchase) − PV (Lease #1) = $935
PV (purchase) − PV (Lease #2) = $6,434
NPV (purchase) − NPV (Lease #1) = $935
NPV (purchase) − NPV (Lease #2) = $6,434

Notice that these differences are the same for present values as for net present values. *An increase in the salvage value will reduce the present value of the purchase and increase the NPV of the purchase by the same dollar amount.* Of course, any such increase in salvage value will reduce the difference in present values or NPVs shown above by the same dollar amount. A decrease in the salvage value will have the opposite effect.

Table 10-7 shows the change in present values or NPVs for each of the new salvage values. Notice that if the salvage value increases by less than $5,000, the purchase alternative becomes more attractive than Lease #1. Further, if the salvage value increases to more than $40,576, the present value of the cost of purchasing is less than the present value of the cost of Lease #2. The graph in Figure 10-3 illustrates the impact of changes in the salvage value on the present values of the three alternatives.

In Figure 10-3, the horizontal lines for the two leases indicates that their present values are invariant under changes in the salvage value. With all salvage values lower than $40,576, Lease #2 has a lower present value of cash flows than the purchase alternative (Lease #2 also dominates Lease #1). *With a salvage value of exactly $40,576, the firm would be indifferent, from a quantitative standpoint, between Lease #2 and purchasing.* Purchasing becomes more advantageous than Lease #2 if the salvage value exceeds $40,576. The firm would then want to address the question: how likely is it that the salvage

Table 10-7. Change in present values of salvage values.

	Salvage Value					
	$10,000	*$25,000*	*$30,000*	*$40,000*	*$40,576*	*$50,000*
Tax impact*	$ 4,000	10,000	12,000	16,000	16,231	$20,000
Net cash inflow	6,000	15,000	18,000	24,000	24,345	30,000
Old net inflow†	12,000	12,000	12,000	12,000	12,000	$12,000
Difference	($6,000)	3,000	6,000	12,000	12,345	$18,000
Discount factor‡	.519369	.519369	.519369	.519369	.519369	.519369
Change in PV§	$ 3,116	($1,558)	($3,116)	($6,232)	($6,412)	($9,349)

* Recall that the book value of this asset was zero for tax purposes, so that the salvage value would be recovery of depreciation, which is taxed at 40 percent, the ordinary tax rate.

† The old net cash inflow was the estimated $20,000 salvage value minus the tax impact of 40 percent of $20,000, or $8,000, which equals $12,000.

‡ The discount factor for the 14 percent risk-adjusted discount rate for the end of year 5 is .519369.

§ The increase (decrease) in the present value of the cost of purchasing is the product of the difference in the net cash inflows and the discount factor. If the difference is negative, there will be an increase in the present value of purchasing; if the difference is positive, the present value of the purchase option will decrease. As mentioned before, an increase (decrease) in the present value of the cost of purchasing will lead to a decrease (increase) in the NPV of the purchase alternative.

value in year 5 will exceed $40,576? The answer points to the firm's preferences for either Lease #2 or the purchase alternative.

A graph similar to Figure 10-3 but using net present values instead of present values is shown in Figure 10-4. The same points of intersection and advantage areas are found. Notice that the salvage value would have to equal $32,000 before the purchase alternative would have a positive NPV. Of course, since we want to maximize NPV, Lease #2 is advantageous compared to the purchase at all salvage values lower than $40,576. □

Sensitivity Analysis and Changes in Discount Rate

The final aspect of sensitivity analysis that will be illustrated is that of modifying the risk-adjusted discount rate or the required rate of return

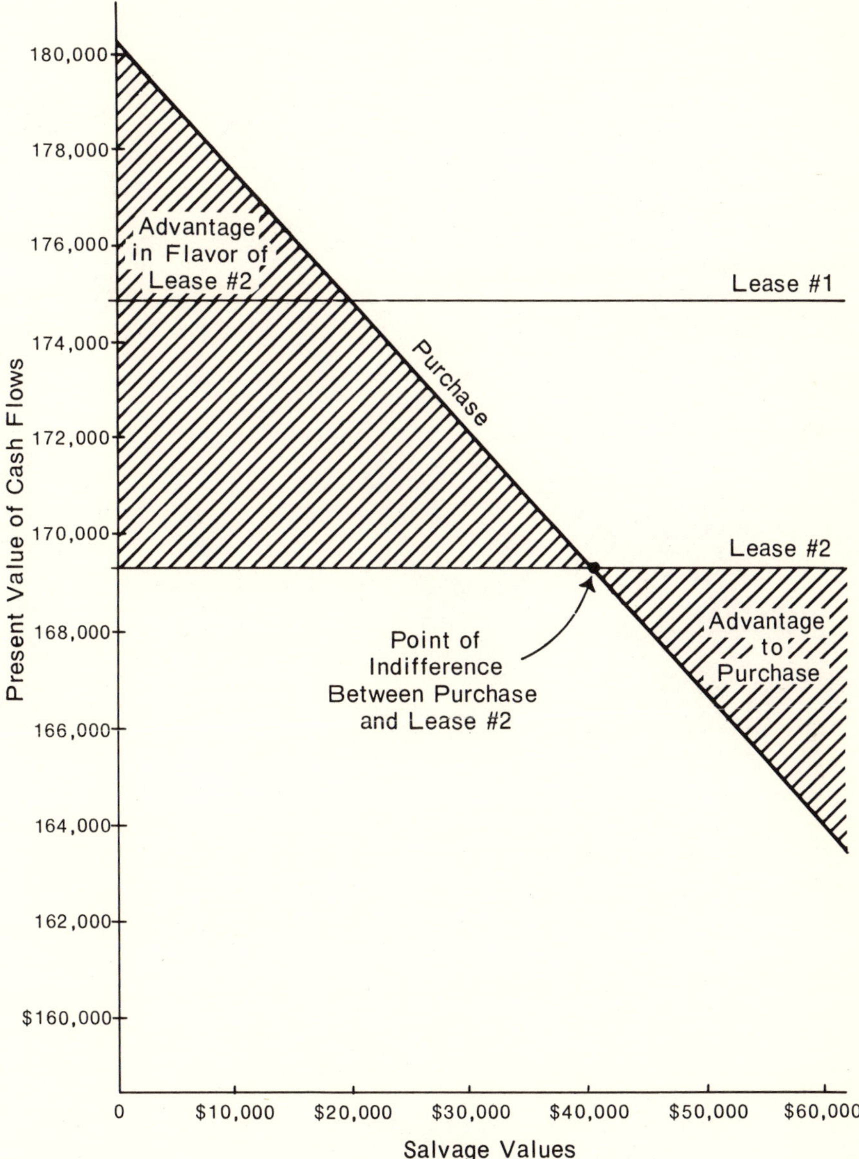

Figure 10-3. Sensitivity of present value of lease and purchase alternatives to changes in salvage value.

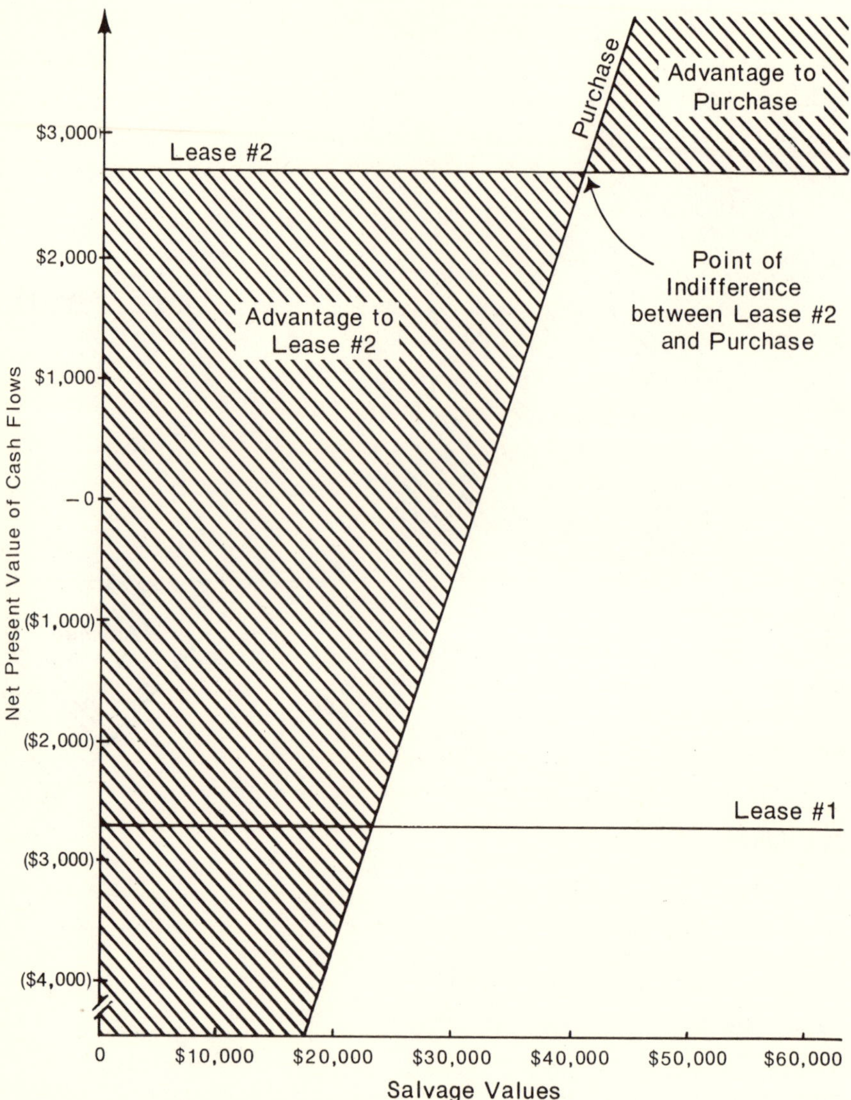

Figure 10-4. Sensitivity of NPVs of lease and purchase alternatives to changes in salvage value.

for the project under evaluation. It was assumed in our analysis of lease/purchase alternatives in Chapter 9 that the adjusted discount rate utilized was appropriate for the project under evaluation. Changes in this discount rate could lead to a different preferred alternative. Example 5 illustrates the analysis.

EXAMPLE 5

Evaluation of Changes in the Risk-Adjusted Discount Rate

For the project considered in Example 4 as well as in Chapter 9, determine the risk-adjusted NPV, using discount rates of 10 percent and 20 percent, so that comparisons can be made with the NPVs using the 14 percent rate (as shown in the solution to Example 4).

It should be noted that the present value of the financial cash flows for each alternative will be unaffected by the change in the risk-adjusted discount rate used to discount *operating cash flows* for the project. These present values of financial cash flows ($165,228 for Lease #1, $159,750 for Lease #2, and $250,669 for the purchase alternative) will be subtracted from the present values of the operating cash inflows in order to determine the NPVs.

The operating cash flows for the two leasing alternatives are $24,540, $26,190, $55,950, $59,796, and $91,702, respectively, in years 1–5. The operating cash flows plus depreciation tax shield that will be discounted at the different rates for the purchase alternative are $59,700, $54,246, $76,906, $73,644, and $110,446 in years 1–5, respectively. Besides showing results in a tabular framework, also show them graphically with NPV on the vertical axis and different risk-adjusted discount rates on the horizontal axis.

SOLUTION

Tables 10-8 and 10-9 are helpful in analyzing changes in the risk-adjusted discount rates. The results are summarized in Table 10-10.

As can be seen from the tables, if the risk-adjusted discount rate were lower than 11 percent, the purchase alternative would have the greatest NPV. At all discount rates above 11 percent, Lease #2 would have the greatest NPV. Lease #2 would cease to have a positive NPV at all risk-adjusted rates in excess of 15 percent. Once again, management would want to estimate the likelihood that the required rate of return for the project would be lower than 11 percent or higher than 15

Table 10-8. The leasing alternatives.

		10% Discount Rate		20% Discount Rate	
Year	*Operating Cash Inflows*	*Discount Factors*	*PV of Cash Inflows*	*Discount Factors*	*PV of Cash Inflows*
1	$24,540	.909091	$ 22,309	.833333	$ 20,450
2	26,190	.826446	21,645	.694444	18,187
3	55,950	.751315	42,036	.578704	32,378
4	59,796	.683013	40,841	.482253	28,837
5	91,702	.620921	56,940	.401878	36,853
PV of Net Operating Cash Inflows			$183,771		$136,705
NPV (Lease #1)			$ 18,543		($ 28,523)
NPV (Lease #2)			$ 24,021		($ 23,045)

Table 10-9. The purchase alternative.

		10% Discount Rate		20% Discount Rate	
Year	*Operating Cash Inflows Plus Depreciation Tax Shield*	*Discount Factors*	*PV of Cash Flows*	*Discount Factors*	*PV of Cash Flows*
1	$ 59,700	.909091	$ 54,273	.833333	$ 49,750
2	54,246	.826446	44,831	.694444	37,671
3	76,906	.751315	57,781	.578704	44,506
4	73,644	.683013	50,300	.482253	35,515
5	110,446	.620921	68,578	.401878	44,386
PV of Cash Flows			$275,763		$211,828
NPV (Purchase)			$ 25,094		($38,841)

Table 10-10. Comparison of lease and purchase options for different risk-adjusted discount rates.

	Risk-Adjusted Discount Rate		
Alternatives	*10%*	*14%*	*20%*
Lease #1	$18,543	($2,754)	($28,523)
Lease #2	$24,021	$2,746	($23,045)
Purchase	$25,094	($3,688)	($38,841)

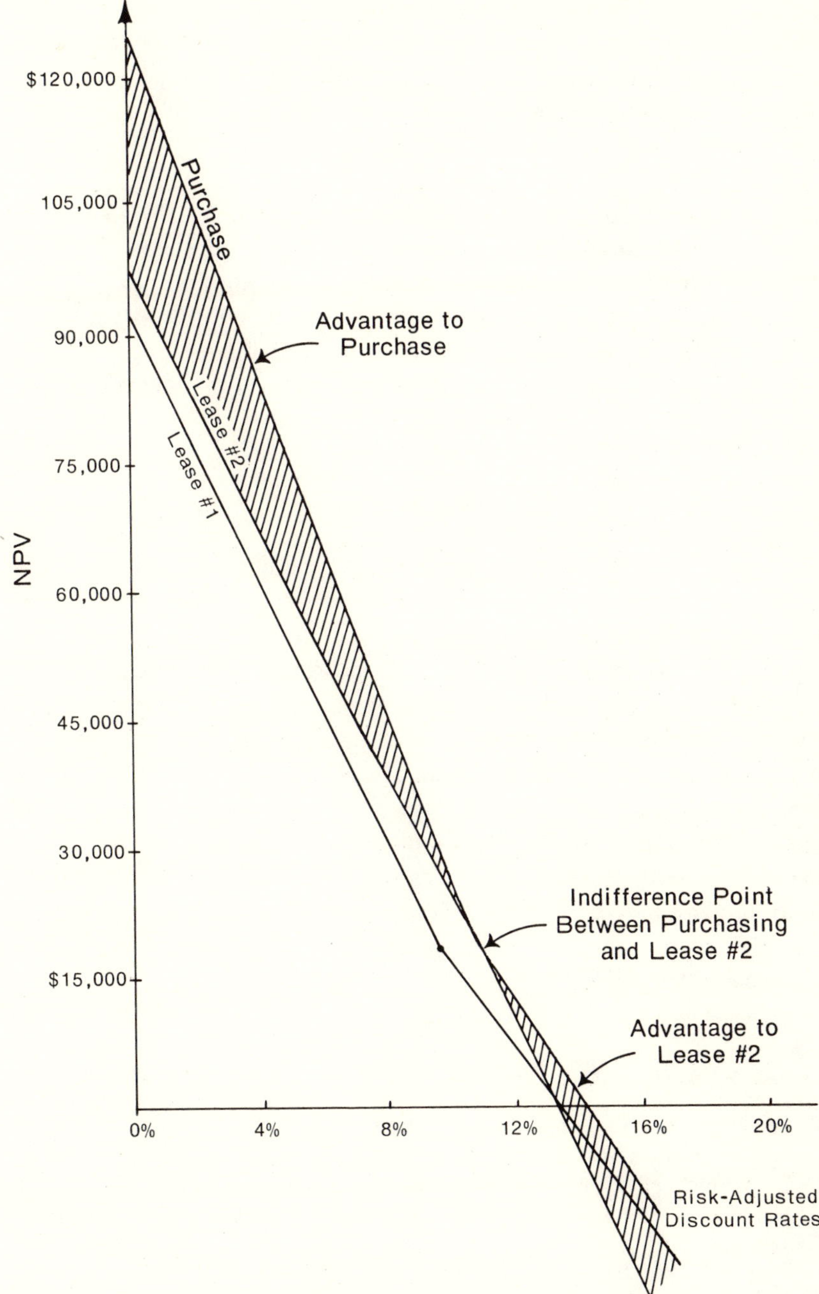

Figure 10-5. Sensitivity of NPVs of lease #1, lease #2, and purchase alternatives to changes in risk-adjusted discount rates.

percent. In the former case, the preferred alternative is no longer Lease #2 but rather the purchase alternative. In the latter case, the project is not attractive from a quantitative standpoint, because no financing alternative generates a positive NPV. Figure 10-5 also shows the results. □

This completes our treatment of sensitivity analysis. The impact of various combinations of the changes illustrated in Examples 1 through 4 could be pinpointed by merely integrating such multiple changes in a single approach. Obviously the use of a computer to answer these "what if" questions would eliminate the need for tedious computations and allow management to focus attention on the analysis of the results.

Summary

This chapter has discussed in depth the critical importance of incorporating qualitative aspects of the problem setting. In addition, we illustrated the valuable insight gained from sensitivity analysis and the importance of factoring it into the decision process before selecting the single preferred alternative. Of course, this combined analysis requires management to address complex issues, to call upon subjective estimates or probabilities, and to rank alternatives on the basis of more than just quantitative aspects. However, it is only by a careful analysis and exploration of such dimensions that management improves the decision-making process and increases the likelihood of selecting the optimum alternative.

We now turn to another important area in the management of capital expenditures, project financing.

NOTES

1. Sensitivity analysis depends on accurate, up-to-date forecasts. While we do not examine forecasting in any detail here, Appendic C, "Sources of Economic and Financial Information from The Conference Board," is included as a very valuable source of information used in forecasting.
2. The materials in this section are reprinted from Bruce M. Bradway and Robert E. Pritchard, *Developing the Business Plan for a Small Business*, New York: AMACOM, 1980, pp. 24–28.

CHAPTER 11

Project Financing–Imaginative Approaches to Strategic Planning in Asset Acquisition

Project financing is a unique and recently developed concept for business managers and planners. While the underlying concepts are simple, the creative use of project financing can lead to acceptance of projects that would ordinarily be rejected or postponed due to a lack of capital. Project financing recognizes the continual scarcity of capital and the fact that capital available through normal sources such as profits must be allocated to that combination of profitable and nondiscretionary projects that best meet the firm's goals. But what about other projects that are profitable and that will increase the firm's wealth but are beyond the budget constraint? The financing of these projects is the topic of this chapter.

As examples of the applications of project financing, consider the development of a mineral property or the construction of a processing facility that may be unattractive for a company when compared with alternative investment opportunities which offer a much higher rate of return. If, however, the amount of capital required to develop the mineral property or to construct the plant can be reduced disproportion-

The authors gratefully acknowledge the preparation of this chapter by Peter K. Nevitt, president of BankAmeriLease Group, San Francisco, California. Portions of the materials are drawn from Peter K. Nevitt, *Project Financing*, BankAmeriLease Group Companies. Used with permission.

ately when compared to the earnings that will be generated by the project, the return on investment will increase dramatically, and in many instances the project will provide a return that will exceed the alternative opportunities for use of capital. Further, in some instances it is possible for a company to raise capital for a project without adversely affecting its ability to borrow funds for other capital expenditures. Thus the project's attractiveness relative to alternative uses of funds may be substantially improved.

Basic Concepts of Project Financing

The term "project financing" is generally defined as follows:

> The financing of a particular economic unit in which a lender is satisfied to look initially to the cash flows and earnings of that economic unit as the source of funds from which its loan will be repaid.

The key word in this definition is "initially." While lenders may be satisfied to look *initially* to the project for repayment of the loans used to finance the project, lenders in a project financing will *always* expect to be repaid by someone able to assume that obligation in the event the project is unable to meet its financial commitments.

There is a popular misconception that "project financings" may be arranged on the basis of optimistic assumptions and projections with little or no capital or debt support provided by the sponsoring or interested parties. This is not the case. Banks and institutional lenders are not equity risk takers. They accept lending risks only. While they may be satisfied to look *initially* to the projections, cash flows, and earnings of a project as a source of funds from which their loans to the project will be repaid, they will *require additional credit support for the project from a financially strong guarantor* who will assume the obligations of the project with a minimum of formalities in the event of a default.

The key to a successful project financing is structuring financing of a project with as little recourse as possible to the sponsor while at the same time providing sufficient credit support through guarantees or undertakings of the sponsor or interested third parties so that lenders will be satisfied with the credit risk of lending to the project. There are two common methods of structuring project financings to achieve this objective:

1. The credit risk (guarantees of payment if the project's cash flows are insufficient) is *shifted* from the sponsor or promoter of the project to one or more interested *third parties* such as a user or supplier. This guarantor may be a private company or some interested government agency. Sometimes such a guarantee can be diminished after the critical high-risk construction and start-up phases of the project, when the successful operation of the plant and generation of cash flows are assured.

2. The sponsor *shares* or *assumes* the credit risk in a way that minimizes the risk's impact on the sponsor's financial statement. This can be accomplished through use of joint ventures and through use of *take-or-pay contracts.* A take-or-pay contract is a long-term contract to make periodic payments over the life of the contract in certain minimum amounts as payments for a service or a product. The payments are in an amount sufficient to service the debt needed to finance the facility that provides the services or the product, and to pay operating expenses of the project. The obligation to make minimum payments is unconditional—the payments must be made whether or not the service is actually furnished or the product actually delivered. These contracts look and act like a guarantee of cash flows sufficient to service debt to the lenders, but they are *not* considered to be debt or unconditional direct guarantees for financial reporting purposes.

The Financial Accounting Standards Board is in the process of enacting a rule that would extend existing disclosure rules on guarantees to include "indirect guarantees and unconditional obligations." The proposed rule would require disclosure and quantification of the nature and amount of the commitment, including a schedule for the next five years if the contract stipulates periodic payments. Many companies already provide this information, and the proposed rule would standardize such reporting. The proposed rule will still permit the use of indirect guarantees and long-term unconditional contracts to achieve many project financing objectives.

Objectives in Project Financing

While the usual objective in project financing is to generate profits from a project with as little investment as possible by the sponsor and as little impact upon the ability of the sponsor to use or raise capital for other projects, project financing is used for many purposes. Reasons for project financing include the following:

Accounting considerations—"off-balance sheet financing." Project financing is sometimes referred to as off-balance-sheet financing.* The potential accounting benefits of some project financings have a great appeal to sponsors seeking any of the following accounting objectives with regard to the reporting of project debt:

- Avoid showing debt on the face of the balance sheet.
- Avoid showing debt on the balance sheet, so as not to affect financial ratios.
- Avoid showing a direct unconditional guarantee of debt.
- Avoid showing debt in a particular footnote.

The fact that the sponsor may remain *indirectly liable* for project debt may not be material to the sponsor if its accounting objectives can be achieved.

Shifting debt responsibility. Shifting the burden of the debt repayment to the project itself and to some third party (an interested user, supplier, or government agency) while retaining earnings disproportionate to the capital risk may prove to be very advantageous.

Existing credit agreement limitations. Project financing may be used to avoid an obligation that will be within the scope of restrictive covenants. (This might relate to the accounting classification of the project debt on the financial statement of the sponsor.) Further, it may be possible to avoid a "debt" definition by using a lease, for example, or to avoid an open-end mortgage.

Limited timeframe. A project may be feasible for a sponsor if its credit exposure is limited to only a *fraction* of the total life of the project. This might, for example, be during the critical construction and start-up phase of a project, after which the credit risk can be shifted to a take-or-pay obligor, or the project may eventually be self-supporting. In other words, a project that would not be feasible in a capital expenditure budget if a 20-year or 25-year guarantor obligation is involved may be feasible if the guarantor obligation is limited to four or five years during construction and start-up.

* Off-balance-sheet financing is not to be confused with hiding a liability from lenders or investors. The objective of the accounting treatment is to segregate the financial statement of the sponsor from the financial statement of the project so that each may be judged on its own merits.

Limited liability. A project may be feasible if the liability exposure of the sponsor is limited to a certain amount, such as a first loss deficiency guarantee, or to a narrowly defined liability, such as an overrun risk. Acceptance of this level of risk by the sponsor, coupled with acceptance by other interested parties, may be sufficient to support the financing of the total project. Yet, in the final analysis, the risk/reward factors for the sponsor will still remain at acceptable levels.

Credit sources. Credit sources not available to the sponsor may be available to projects. In some projects, the sponsor may be quite willing to leverage itself to any extent necessary to get a project built. However, lenders may regard the sponsor as a poor credit risk and be unwilling to finance an otherwise credit-worthy project for that reason. By segregating the project from the credit of the sponsor, the project may be readily financed.

Guarantees available. Guarantees may, likewise, be available to a project for the same reason credit sources not available to a sponsor may be available to a project. If a project is segregated so that its cash flows cannot be diverted to an owner or sponsor (particularly a weak owner or sponsor), guarantors will feel more comfortable in providing support. In some instances where government guarantees are sought, isolation of the project from the parent may be required.

Lower interest rates. For the same reason that credit sources or guarantees may be available to a project and not to a sponsor, better credit terms and interest rates may be available to a project in situations in which a sponsor's credit is weak.

Avoidance of regulatory problems. If the sponsor of a project belongs to a regulated industry, regulatory problems associated with that industry may sometimes be avoided by assigning the project to a separate company. Likewise, lenders may feel more comfortable lending to a project in which the cash flows will not be subject to the whims of a consumer-oriented regulatory commission.

Cost of recovery for a utility. From the standpoint of a regulated sponsor, segregating the costs of a supply in a project financing may be advantageous in that it assists in recovering the true costs of such supply.

Construction work in process. Interest on construction debt can be more readily capitalized through use of a project company to avoid a negative affect on current earnings of the sponsor during construction.

Risk sharing. Some projects are of such size that a single company may not wish to assume the risk involved. A joint venture, with a number of companies assuming risk in a project company, may provide a solution.

Economies of size. Economies of size often motivate groups of companies to join together in project financings.

Labor contracts. A sponsor will sometimes wish to segregate a project from its operations in order to avoid onerous labor contracts that would imperil the productivity and profitability of the project.

Efficient use of tax shelter. Where the sponsor cannot currently use tax benefits, project financing can often be structured so that the project can receive such benefits indirectly through the use of tax shelters by an interested third party or lessor.

Characteristics of Viable Project Financing

Project financing, like most proposed capital expenditures, must be considered on a case-by-case basis. The degree of credit support and risk/reward factors vary a great deal with the facts and circumstances of a particular transaction. Since the objective is to make the project as self-supporting from a credit standpoint as possible and thus to finance the project with as little outside credit support as possible, a review of the characteristics of an ideal project financing is appropriate.

As discussed earlier, the project must be backed by strong credit. This credit backing may be provided by the sponsor or by a third party. The credit backing may be limited to the critical construction and start-up period. It may take the form of direct or indirect guarantees or take-or-pay contracts.

The project should involve a credit risk rather than an equity risk or a venture capital risk. As noted previously, lenders are not in the business of taking equity risks.

The financial viability of the project must be shown. Conservative projections of assured internally generated cash flows must be prepared and verified by appropriate independent feasibility and engineering studies. The cash flow projections obviously must be sufficient to service any debt contemplated, provide for cash needs, pay operating expenses, and still provide an adequate cushion for contingencies.

Supply contracts for products and energy required by the project must be assured at a cost consistent with the financial projections.

A market for the projects, products, or services must be assured at a price consistent with the financial projections. Appropriate marketing studies should be made. If take-or-pay contracts are being relied upon for credit support, they must be as unconditional as possible.

Transportation for materials required by the project and for the products produced by the project must be assured at a cost consistent with the financial projections.

The expertise of the contractor who is to construct the project facility must be well established. The contractor must be financially strong and have the resources to overcome problems if they arise.

The financial capability and the technical expertise must be available to cover cost overruns and complete the project so that it will operate in accordance with cost and production specifications.

The project should not involve a new technology. The reliability of the process and the equipment to be used must be well established. The technical reliability and commercial viability of the project must be clear. If a new technology is involved, more than a lending risk is involved.

The sponsor or the beneficiary of the sponsorship should have available the expertise to operate such a facility. The need to go to the outside to hire the expertise to operate the new facilities sometimes raises serious questions.

In addition to operating expertise, management personnel must be available to manage the project. If the sponsor is already short on management personnel, the project is suspect.

The properties and facilities being financed ideally should have value to parties other than those involved in the project. Although not essential, this is helpful to arranging financing.

The political environment for the location of the project and the type of project must be reasonably friendly and stable. Stability of the government and the possibility of restrictive government requirements, for example, must be closely examined.

The sponsor must make an equity contribution consistent with its capability, interest in the project, and risk of the project. Lenders want to see an investment that is large enough to prevent the sponsor from abandoning the project.

An adequate insurance program must be available at a reasonable expense.

One other caution needs to be observed. *Exchange risk* must be carefully considered if the company contemplates loans that must be repaid in currencies different from the currencies that will be generated from sale of the product of the project.

Obviously, not all of these requirements are required in every project financing. A government guarantee, for example, might eliminate the need for a substantial sponsor investment. Each project financing is different and must be reviewed on its own merits.

Use of Guarantees in Project Financing

Guarantees are especially useful in project financing, since they permit *shifting of certain specific risks* inherent in a project financing transaction to interested parties that have no desire to become directly involved in the operation of the project or to directly provide the capital for the project. By assuming the commercial risks of a transaction through a guarantee rather than a loan or contribution to capital, a third-party guarantor sponsor keeps the guaranteed liability off balance sheet as a direct liability while achieving the objective of getting the project built. In discussing guarantees, however, it is well to keep in mind that the term "guarantee" may be as broad or as limited as the needs of the transaction dictate.

The usual guarantor of a project financing transaction is the owner of the project. Typically, an undercapitalized subsidiary is set up to own and operate a project that has insufficient capital or operating history to support borrowings on the merits of its own credit standing. Therefore, lenders must be provided with a guarantee from a satisfactory credit. As a practical matter, this means the parent must provide the guarantee unless the circumstances of the project make it possible for the parent to substitute a satisactory third-party guarantor. When a parent company guarantees debt of a controlled subsidiary, the debt will appear on its consolidated balance sheet.

Third-party guarantees are attractive to owners or sponsors who are not guarantors because they permit the sponsor or owner of the project in many instances to keep a liability off balance sheet and outside loan restrictions. Third-party guarantors nearly always receive benefits from a transaction in order to make their undertaking attractive. Third-party guarantors generally may be divided into four groups: suppliers, sellers, users, and interested government agencies.

A *supplier* may see the project as satisfying a need for its product, particularly if the project provides further processing on the supplier's product. Therefore, a supplier may be motivated to provide a guarantee, if necessary, to a third-party owner and/or operator of the project in order to get a processing plant constructed and operating. In other cases, the supplier may see the market for its product disappearing because a major user of its product is unable to compete without drastic modification or remodeling of its processing facilities. Again, the supplier might be motivated to provide a guarantee in order to bring these changes about and to preserve its market.

A *seller* may have a surplus of plant or equipment with little prospect of selling the plant or equipment except to an undercapitalized company which the seller feels has good prospects. In such a situation a guarantee by the seller may be necessary to enable the purchaser to obtain financing. The seller realizes cash. The purchaser achieves project financing.

The *user* of a product of a potential project may be motivated to financially aid or guarantee debt required to finance the project in order to get the project built and ensure a needed supply. Similarly, a user may be motivated to provide credit support for transportation of a product in or out of its facilities.

Government guarantees are often necessary in order to build needed projects. The nature of the economic and political risks may be such that guarantees are simply not available from other sources. This is particularly true in the case of projects located outside the United States.

Typical third-party guarantors include the following:

- U.S. and foreign manufacturers of products to be used in the project.
- Users of products or services to be produced or provided by the project.
- Agencies of the U.S. government interested in getting a project built, such as the U.S. Maritime Administration or the U.S. Department of Energy.
- Government agencies responsible for promoting exports.

- International agencies, such as the World Bank or Area Developmentment Banks.

Guarantees cover several general types of risk. The most important is the *commercial* (financial) *risk*—the risk involved in repayment and performance of the loan agreement. Other areas of guarantees include political, casualty, and war risks and acts of God. There are generally two types of guarantees: *direct* and *limited*.

In discussing guarantees, the emphasis is usually on direct, unconditional guarantees by a guarantor, under which the guarantor assumes the responsibility to perform all the obligations of the guaranteed party. In many cases, this is the only kind of guarantee that will suffice to support the transaction.

In many other cases, however, the guarantee need not be all-encompassing in order to provide sufficient support to the transaction to enable it to be financed. Guarantees may be limited as to amount and as to time; they may be indirect, contingent, or implied. In a given situation, something less than a full unconditional guarantee of all obligations of the guaranteed party may be sufficient to support the transaction from the standpoint of the guarantor. This may be very important for the guarantor, since the impact on its credit standing and financial statements may be considerably lessened by a guarantee that is tailored to provide needed support for a transaction but that does not constitute an unconditional obligation to pay or perform under any circumstances.

Examples of Project Financing

In order to provide some ideas for project financing, several examples are included in the following pages (see Figures 11-1 through 11-11). The types of project financing illustrated in these figures represent alternative ways to approach the financing of many larger projects. However, project financing is a creative financing tool, and the models shown are by no means exhaustive; many others have been devised.

We now move to Chapter 12, which deals with the control and abandonment of projects. This is a critical area in the capital acquisition process, since in a rapidly changing economic and technical environment there is a continued need to revisit prior decisions and update them.

Figure 11-1. Project financing supported by a third-party guarantee.

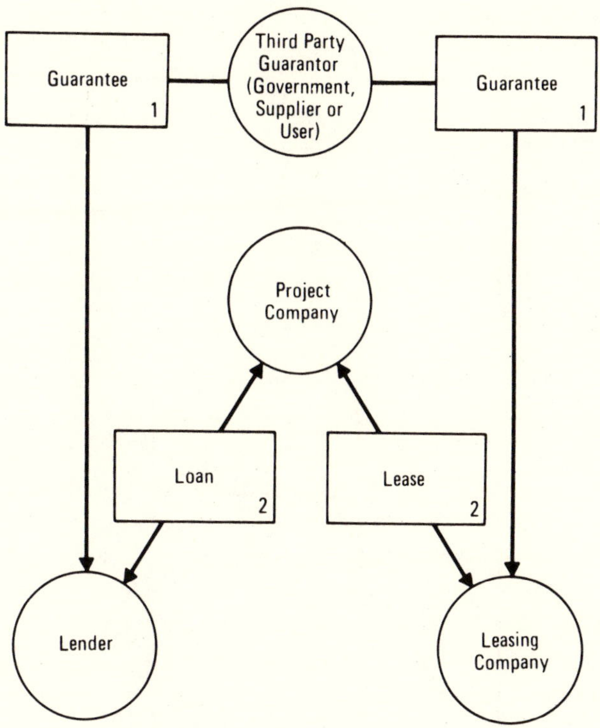

1. A third-party guarantor which does not own or control the project company enters into a guarantee agreement whereby it guarantees loan obligations and/or lease obligations of the project company.
2. On the basis of the guarantee, a lender and/or a leasing company enter into a loan or lease, respectively, with the project company.

Figure 11-2. Project company supported by user-sponsor's guarantee.

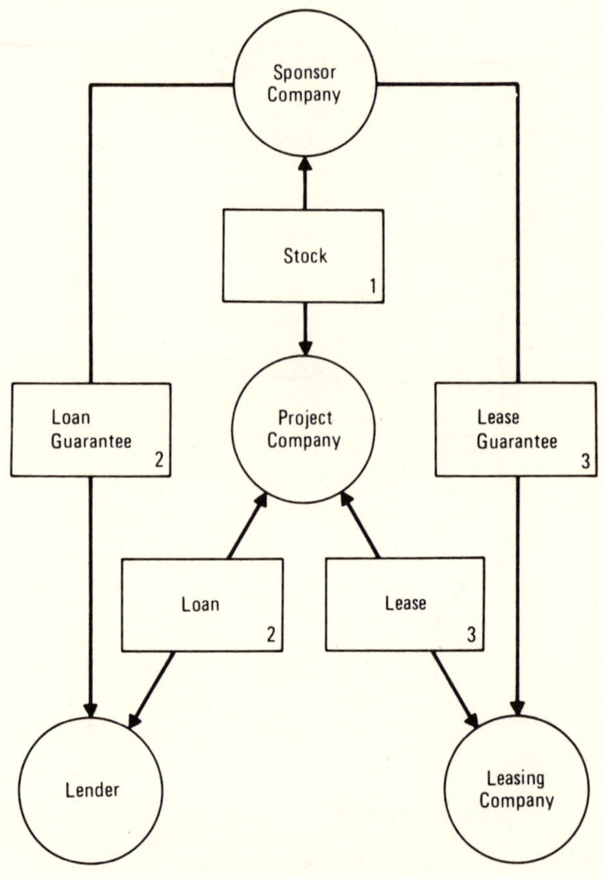

1. The sponsor company establishes a wholly owned subsidiary to own and operate a project.
2. The project company arranges a loan from a lender backed by a guarantee from the sponsor.
3. The project company arranges a lease from a leasing company backed by a guarantee from the sponsor.

Figure 11-3. Jointly owned company capitalized to independently borrow to finance project.

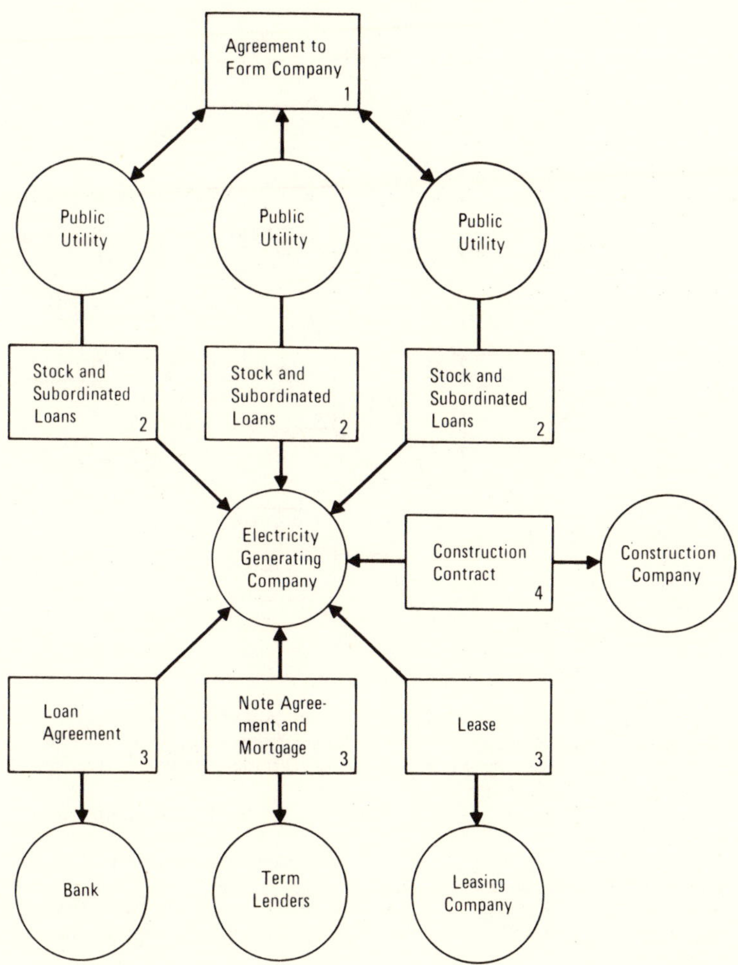

1. Three utilities enter into an agreement to form a corporation to build and operate an electricity-generating plant.
2. Each of the utilities purchases stock and makes subordinated loans to the electricity-generating company in accordance with their agreement.
3. On the basis of the capital contributions and prospects for the jointly formed company, construction loans and long-term debt to take out the construction loans or a lease to take out the construction loans are arranged.
4. The generating company arranges for the construction of the facility; thereafter, the generating company operates as an independent company arranging its own financing as needed.

Figure 11-4. Guarantee by sponsor company, using a security trustee.

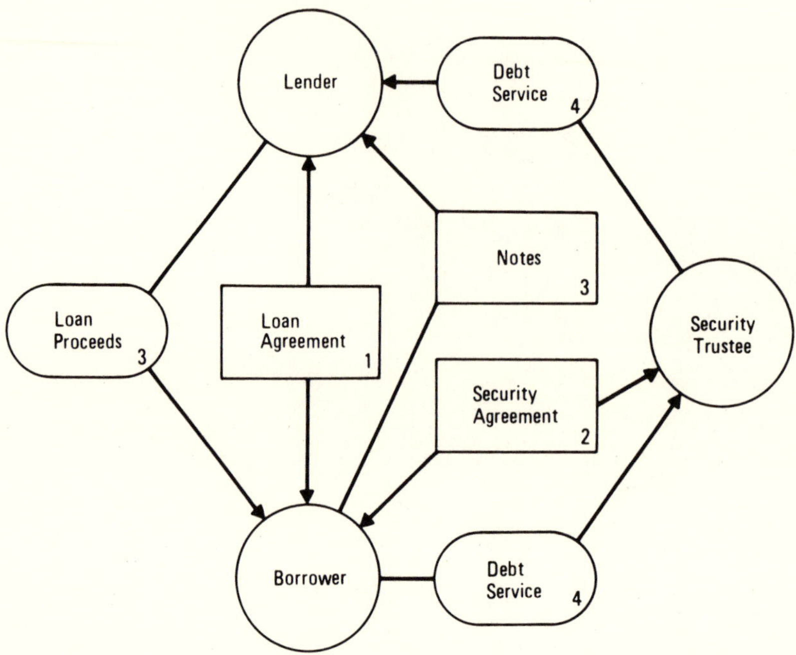

1. The project company enters into a loan agreement with the lender.
2. The project company secures the loan by pledging security under a security agreement with a security trustee. Under the security agreement, debt service is to be paid directly to the security trustee.
3. The sponsor company enters into a guarantee agreement running directly to the security trustee.
4. The notes are signed and delivered to the lender, and the loan proceeds are paid to the project company.
5. Principal and interest payments are made by the project company directly to the security trustee, which, in turn, pays principal and interest payments to the lenders.

Figure 11-5. Project financing supported by sponsor's take-or-pay contract.

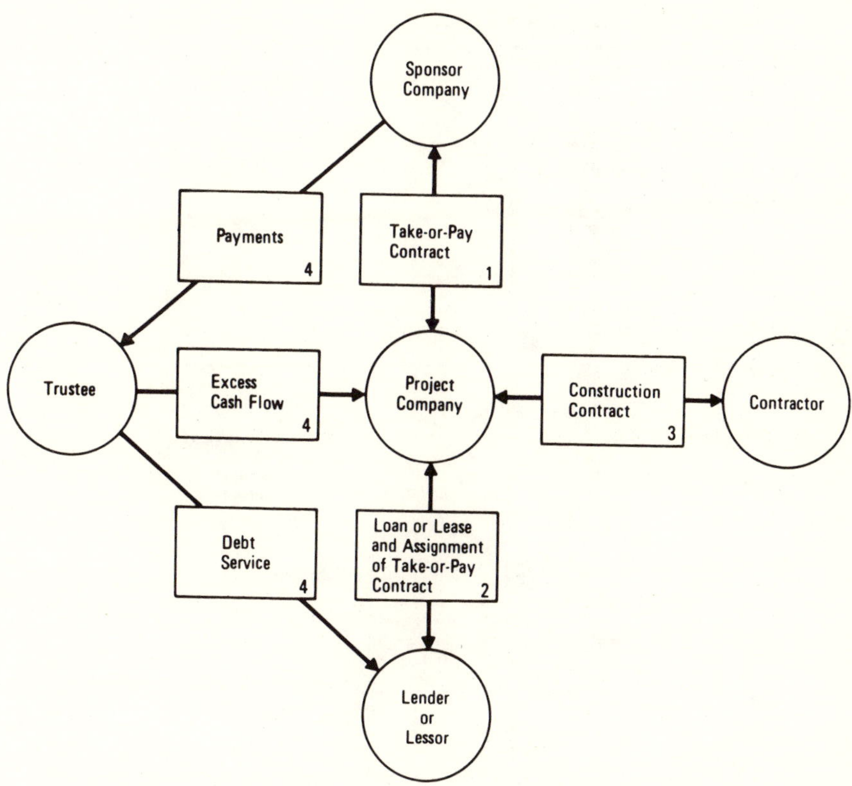

1. A sponsor company enters into a take-or-pay contract with a project.
2. A project company arranges a loan or lease with a lender or lessor and assigns the take-or-pay contract as security to the lender or lessor or to a security trustee acting for the lender or lessor.
3. Proceeds of the loan or lease are used to finance the construction of the property.
4. Take-or-pay contract payments are made to the trustee, which, in turn, pays debt service to the lender(s) or lessor(s); any excess cash flow is paid to the project company.

Figure 11-6. Project financing supported by sponsors throughput contract.

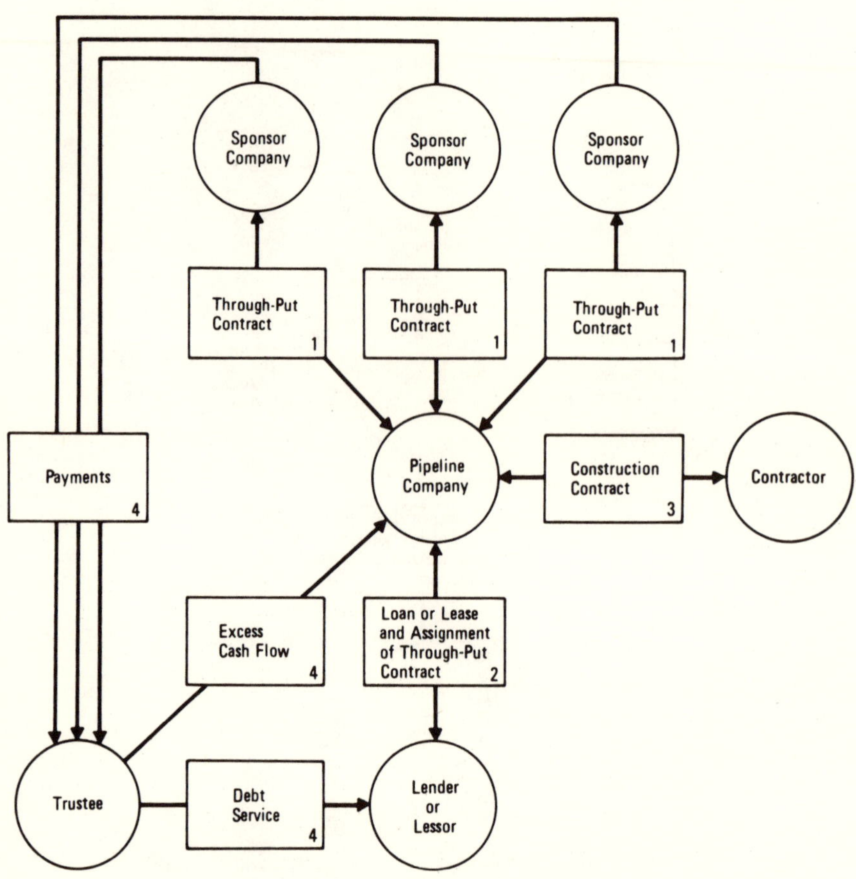

1. Three sponsor companies enter into a throughput contract with a pipeline company.
2. The pipeline company enters into a loan or lease with a lender or lessor and assigns the throughput contract as security to the lender or lessor (or to a security trustee acting for the lender or lessor).
3. Proceeds for the loan are used to build the pipeline.
4. Payments under the throughput contract are paid to the trustee; the trustee uses those payments for debt service and pays the excess cash flow to the pipeline company.

Figure 11-7. General partnership to operate a project.

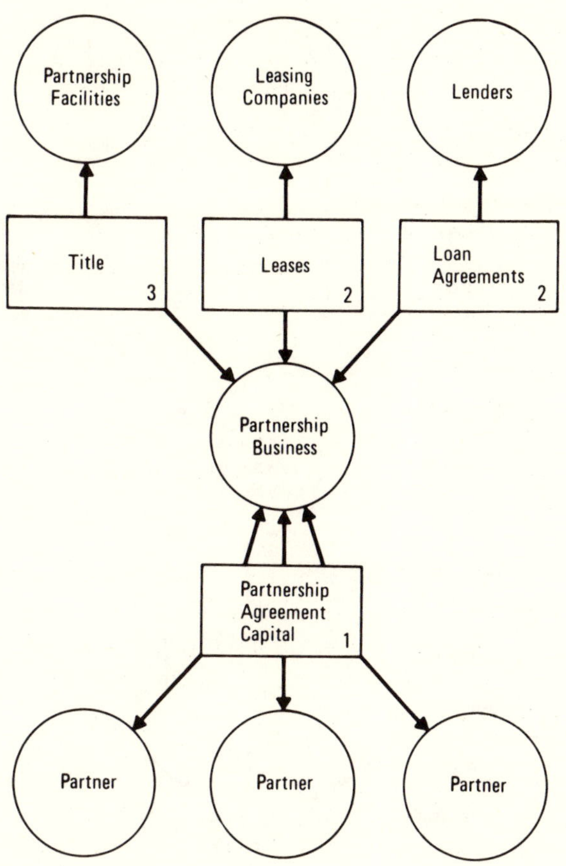

1. Three partners enter into a partnership agreement and contribute capital to a partnership to conduct and operate a certain business.
2. The partnership in its own name enters into loan agreements and enters into lease agreements.
3. The partnership holds title to property in its own name.

Figure 11-8. Corporate financing vehicle.

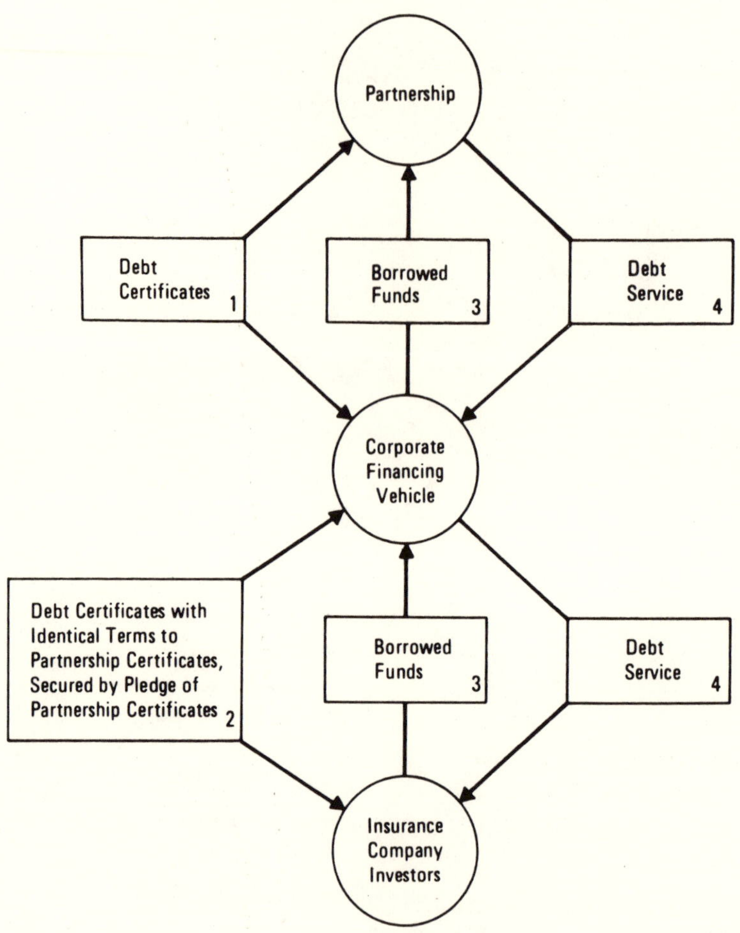

1. A partnership issues notes to a nominee corporation.
2. The nominee corporation issues notes or bonds to lenders which are identical in interest rate and maturities to the partnership securities. The partnership notes are pledged as security.
3. The lenders pay the bond or note proceeds to the nominee corporation, and the corporation pays the funds to the partnership.
4. Debt service is paid by the partnership through the nominee corporation or through a security trustee.

Figure 11-9. General partnership with limited-recourse secured debt, supported by a take-or-pay contract from the sponsor partners.

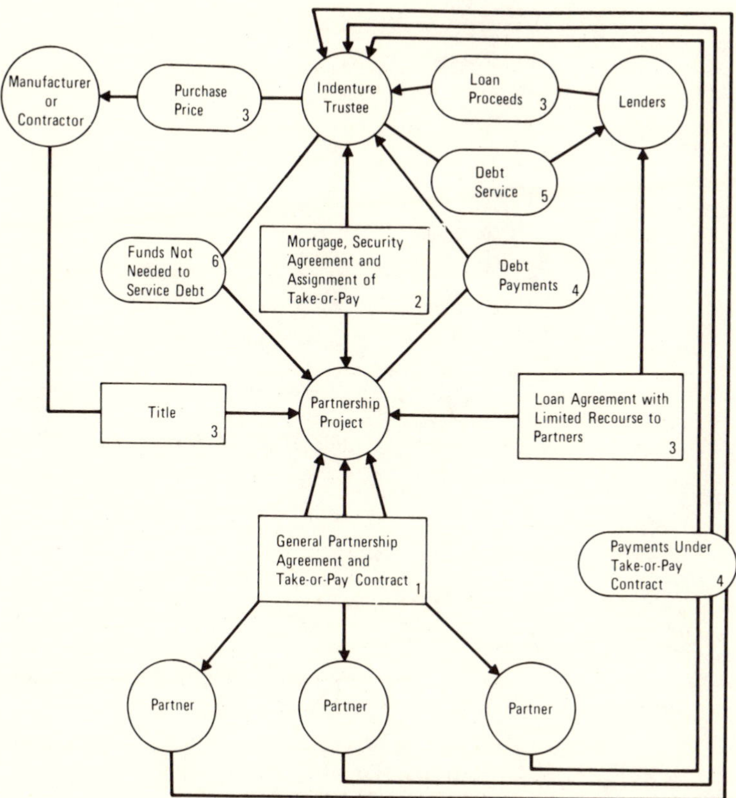

1. Three partners enter into a general partnership agreement to operate a project as a partnership. Each partner also enters into a take-or-pay contract with the project.
2. The partnership enters into a security agreement with an indenture trustee, which includes a mortgage on certain property to be acquired by the partnership and an assignment of proceeds from the take-or-pay contracts.
3. The partnership enters into a loan agreement with a group of lenders under an arrangement whereby the lenders agree to limit their recourse against the partners to the partnership assets only. Loan proceeds are paid to the indenture trustee, which, in turn, pays the manufacturer the purchase price of the property to be acquired by the project. The manufacturer then conveys title to the partnership in the partnership name, subject to the mortgage.
4. The partners make payments under the take-or-pay contract directly to the indenture trustee. The partnership makes any additional payments to the indenture trustee required to meet current debt payments.
5. The indenture trustee pays the debt service.
6. Funds not needed to service the debt are paid to the partnership.

Figure 11-10. Project facility owned through a trust.

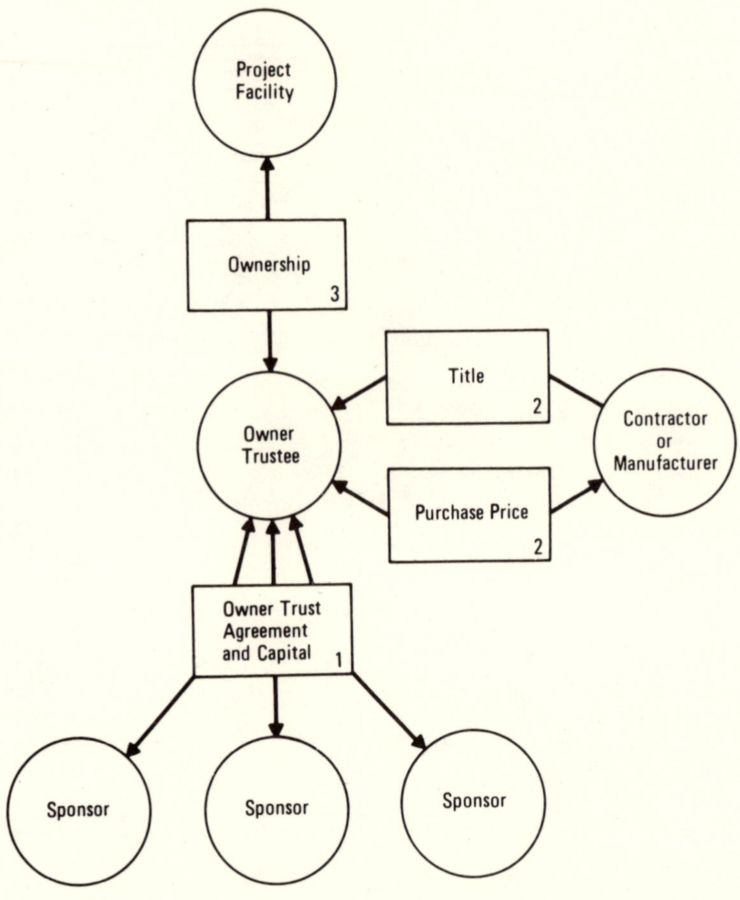

1. Three sponsors enter into an owner trust agreement establishing an owner trust to hold title to certain property to be acquired by the trust. The three sponsors contribute capital to the trust.
2. The trustee pays the purchase price for the property and takes title to the property.
3. The owner trustee owns the project facility under the trust agreement.

Figure 11-11. Joint-venture operating agreement to operate a mine.

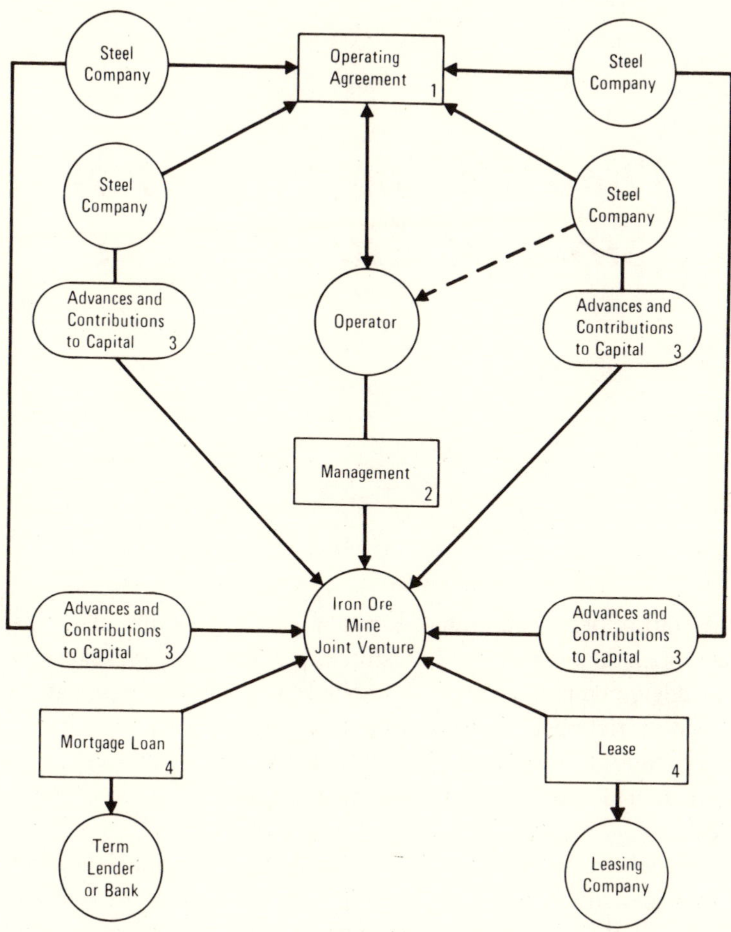

1. Four steel companies enter into an operating agreement to operate a mine as a joint venture in which each steel company owns an undivided interest in the mine properties.
2. One of the steel companies is designated the operator in charge of day-to-day management of the mine.
3. Advances and contributions to capital are made to the joint venture operation by the steel companies as needed and in accordance with the terms of the operating agreement. Each steel company arranges the financing of its contribution.
4. The parties of the joint venture may be able to secure a mortgage loan or to lease the property and facilties, depending on the security of the assets involved, the obligations of the joint venturers to support the project, and the importance of the project to the joint venturers.

CHAPTER 12

The Ongoing Process of Strategic Management

At the start of our discussion of capital budgeting we outlined the steps needed in an ongoing capital investment process. The final two steps of the strategic planning process as applied to capital budgeting are (1) to maintain a strict cost control system to measure actual costs versus estimates and (2) to periodically reassess the value of the projects in use. This chapter deals with these two final steps in the capital budgeting process.

In the foregoing chapters we described the management of the capital expenditure decision process. The primary focus was on the steps required in the evaluation process so that progress would be made toward meeting the firm's major goals as capital investment projects are selected. However, the decision-making process does not stop with the selection of the set of capital projects that the organization feels will provide maximum benefits relative to its objectives. Rather, the process is ongoing and demands that feedback be obtained throughout project implementation and operation so that control and corrective action can be taken as necessary. This final chapter provides an overview of the process that is carried out as management reviews and controls accepted capital projects. In addition, we treat the important topic of capital-project abandonment.

Review and Control of Capital Investment Projects

We have divided the review and control of capital expenditures into two major categories. First is the review and control of projects in the process of being implemented. These are termed "in-progress" projects. This review and control entails auditing the cash outflows related to the acquisition of the project. This process results in information of cost under- or overruns, which is of great importance to management.

Second is the review and control of projects as they are used in the firm's operations. This entails auditing the benefits generated by the project as well as the operating expenses incurred as the project is used. The goal is to determine the cash flows being generated over the life of the project.

Much effort is expended in evaluating capital projects in order to select those projects which *should be* most beneficial in helping the organization achieve its goals. Once a set of projects has been selected management may assume that the projects will be implemented in an optimum fashion. Of course, this is rarely the case. Witness the constantly recurring cost overruns as well as timing delays in the efforts to carry out any large-scale capital project. Thus it is necessary to strictly control in-progress projects.

There are two parts to the process of controlling in-progress capital projects. First is the establishment of internal accounting control procedures to accumulate all relevant project-related costs. Second is the use of periodic progress reports that gauge actual expenditures against estimates and provide explanations for significant variances. The timing of the reports may be on a regular calendar basis (such as monthly) and/or keyed to critical events in the acquisition process. The latter is especially useful if PERT or CPM is being employed.

The first step specified usually sees the establishment of control accounts for each in-progress capital project. These control accounts are charged with all relevant expenditures, which are further categorized into those items which will be capitalized and those which will be expensed in the current year. These accounts reflect out-of-pocket payments for materials, labor, overhead, outside purchases, and subcontracts as well as relevant allocated expenses.

The segregation of costs on a project-by-project basis facilitates the control process because appropriate attention can be given to projects as they approach various completion points and/or a cost overrun status. Further, the use of *responsibility accounting procedures* is also beneficial, since control centers which should be held accountable for any given project are notified that cost overruns are imminent and that proper control measures should be implemented.

The use of regular progress reports as projects are being implemented provides several benefits for organizations. First, such information presents advance warning of potential future difficulties, thus enabling management to take corrective action before it is too late. Second, these reports provide a basis for data inputs to the cash budgeting process. Third, these reports provide insight to management on projects that could require additional expenditures due to inflation and other unforeseen causes. Fourth, as part of the control process, these reports provide the basis for comparing cumulative actual expenditures with budgeted amounts so that variances can be computed and explanations provided for significant unfavorable variances.

In sum, these procedures should provide valuable assistance to firms in the control of in-progress capital projects.

Post-Completion Audits of Capital Projects

It is essential for firms to review and control capital projects once they are in use. This is necessary in order to compare their actual benefits with their forecasted benefits, to compare actual operating costs with forecasted operating costs, and to take timely corrective action, if necessary.

In addition to furnishing the relevant information so that timely corrective action can be taken, post-completion audits provide several additional benefits. First, the audits provide an on-the-scene verification of the profitability or savings generated by the project. The audit attempts to isolate the effects of the project under study as far as possible. The auditor, as part of his investigation, should seek out reasons why projects turned out significantly more or significantly less profitable than projected either in absolute dollars or in percentage. In making that determination, as much detail as practicable should be provided rather than arbitrarily aggregating different cost or benefit categories; the latter technique could obscure offsetting changes that would be helpful to know about.

Second, divisions and managers will act in their own (as well as the organization's) best interest relative to the implementation and operation of new capital projects if they realize that post-completion audits will be performed and that they will be held accountable for the results. The feedback provided to managers responsible for the projects should not only help them improve their future estimation of costs and benefits but also provide insight into effective operating strategies for new capital projects. Organizations should stress that post-completion audits are not designed to censure managers but rather to help them improve their forecasting and operating activities.

The post-completion audit is also beneficial in that it pinpoints the causes of difficulties in project implementation and/or operation. The focus of the audit is on variances of actual results from projected results; such variances, if discovered, raise questions that demand explanation and point to possible areas where breakdowns may have occurred. The insight provided here will often suggest corrective action that should be taken or point to alternative courses of action (including the possibility of project abandonment) that should be explored.

Finally, the results obtained from post-completion audits provide managers of divisions as well as the members of the capital budgeting review committee with information that should be helpful in evaluating similar projects in the future. Audits enable organizations to learn from past successes and difficulties so that their operations will be more effective and efficient in the future.

Given these benefits, questions arise concerning who should perform and review post-completion audits, which projects should be the subject of such audits, and how the process should be carried out.

Ideally, the post-completion audit should be performed by an independent and unbiased individual, preferably from the internal audit staff or the corporate controller's staff. This will increase the chances that an objective evaluation will be performed by an individual who does not have an axe to grind.

The post-completion audit should be reviewed by the manager of the department or division which proposed the project so that he can see the results and obtain helpful feedback for operating decisions and future proposals. The manager who recommended the project will usually be one of the major sources that the auditor uses in the performance of the post-completion audit, since the manager will be one of the more informed individuals concerning the reasons for variances of actual results from projections.

The post-completion audit should also be reviewed by everyone in the project approval process, including the group or individual that actually approved the project in question. This will facilitate the learning process among key individuals and improve the quality of future proposals.

Clearly, not all capital projects deserve the time, resources, and effort required to perform a post-completion audit. Most firms perform audits on projects requiring a very large outlay or those of special significance to management. In addition, corporate and division managers can often select projects for audit that are of interest or concern in order to gauge results and/or locate difficulties. Finally, a number of projects may be selected randomly at each division in order to provide feedback to local and corporate management.

Norman E. Pflomm[1] derived an extensive list of data frequently included on post-completion audits by the 346 manufacturing firms that participated in his Conference Board study. The following information was usually contained:

Number of the approved appropriation request.
Location that requested the appropriation.
Description of the item(s) purchased.
Purpose of the project.
Amount authorized.
Amount actually expended.
Estimated savings and/or return on investment.
Actual savings or return.
Reasons for variations.
Signatures of those who prepared and/or reviewed the post-completion audit.

In addition, Pflomm identified the following supplemental information that he often found included in the post-completion audit:[2]

Estimated versus actual project completion dates, with explanations of delays.
Explanation of project cost overruns.
Action taken to correct deficiencies.
Future prospects for projects currently failing.
Details of equipment performance.
Comments on the adequacy of local accounting records needed for making a post-completion audit.

We view the review and control of accepted projects as a vitally important link in the overall management of capital expenditures. All too often, organizations downplay or disregard entirely this essential step in obtaining feedback and taking corrective action. In order to facilitate the initiation of post-completion audits in organizations, we show as Figure 12-1 a comprehensive checklist and evaluation form developed by a food products firm to use with its standard post-completion audit form (Figure 12-2). These figures were originally published in the Conference Board report by Pflomm[3] and are reprinted with permission. Hopefully they will provide guidance for firms seeking to implement or modify their post-completion audit systems.

The Abandonment of Capital Projects

In most cases when a project is selected it is assumed that it will be kept in operation over its entire useful life. As discussed earlier, the useful life is not necessarily the same as the life used to compute depreciation for purposes of taxation or the life used for financial-reporting purposes. Rather, *the useful life is the period during which the asset is expected to have a greater productive value to the owners than abandonment value.* Recall that in selecting assets for acquisition, the decision was based on the comparison of the present value of the expected cash inflows (productive value) against the present value of the cash outflows (cost).

To put the concept of capital abandonment into perspective, consider the example of the acquisition of a new large apartment complex. We assume the owners want to maximize their wealth, which, in this example, may involve making little if any profit until the property is sold. Normally, a well-constructed apartment complex will last 30 or more years, but the useful life to the owners may be only seven. The reason is not hard to find. Using double-declining-balance depreciation over seven years for an asset with a 30-year life will exhaust about 40 percent of the depreciation tax shield. The loss of the tax shield plus expected property value appreciation and additional equity investment as the mortgage is amortized all point strongly to the sale of the complex. The owners can sell, pay the tax on the sale, and reinvest a potentially large profit. This scenario explains why many apartment complexes are regularly sold at seven-year intervals.

Figure 12.1. Audit checklist for capital projects.

CAPITAL PROJECT FINANCIAL EVALUATION AUDIT CHECKLIST

Division -

Project -

	Payback Years	Return on Funds Employed 5 Years	10 Years	Total New Funds 5-Yr. Average	10-Yr. Average
Original Request					
Latest Estimate/Actual -					

General Comments -

Audit Performed By -
Date of Audit -

Item		Points To Be Checked	Yes Sat.	No Un-sat.	Un-nec.	Remarks/Reference
Funds Employed						
1. Cash	A.	Was total computed according to formula?				
2. Receivables	A.	Compare Latest Estimate or Actual to total reported in original submission for:				
		1. Reasonableness of absolute amount.				
		2. Relationship to Net Sales.				
		3. Obtain reason for significant differences.				
	B.	Compare relationship to Net Sales for this project to the relationship for the division in total.				
	C.	Check Distribution Sales and Service allocations.				
3. Inventories	A.	Compare Latest Estimate or Actual to total reported in original submission for:				
		1. Reasonableness of absolute amount.				
		2. Inventory turnover (cost of goods sold + inventory). (a) Also compare to Divisional Turnover.				
		3. Obtain reason for significant differences.				
	B.	Is total shown incremental to this project?				
		1. Check division's allocation of inventory to this project.				
		2. Check levels of inventory for this product both before and after this project.				
4. Prepaid and Deferred Expense	A.	Compare Latest Estimate or Actual to total reported in original submission for:				
		1. Reasonableness of absolute amount.				
		2. Relationship to expense items in Profit and Loss (marketing, etc.).				
		3. Obtain reasons for significant differences.				
	B.	Check division's computations.				
	C.	Check books of account for years where actual figures are available.				
5. Current Liabilities	A.	Compare Latest Estimate or Actual to total reported in original submission for:				
		1. Reasonableness of absolute amount.				
		2. Obtain reason for significant differences.				
	B.	Check division's computation.				
		1. Has 50% of tax expense been included?				
6. Total Working Funds	A.	Verify arithmetical accuracy of total (lines 1 through 4, less line 5).				
7. Land	A.	Compare Latest Estimate or Actual to total reported in original submission for:				
		1. Reasonableness of absolute amount.				
		2. Obtain reasons for significant variation.				
	B.	Trace amount capitalized to:				
		1. Original purchase records.				
		2. Engineering reports.				
		3. Check year-end workpapers.				

Item	Points To Be Checked	Yes Sat.	No Un-sat.	Un-nec.	Remarks/Reference
8. Buildings	A. Compare Latest Estimate or Actual to total reported in original submission for:				
	1. Reasonableness of absolute amount.				
	2. Obtain reasons for significant variation.				
	B. Trace amount capitalized from Construction Work in Progress into fixed asset account.				
	1. Spot check invoices in vendor's files.				
	2. Check engineering final close-out report.				
	3. Check year-end workpapers.				
	C. Does total shown in first year plus first-year depreciation equal amount in original request?				
	D. Verify reasonableness of depreciation method:				
	1. Is method used acceptable?				
	2. Is estimated life of asset reasonable?				
9. Manufacturing and Engineering	A. Compare Latest Estimate or Actual to total reported in original submission for:				
	1. Reasonableness of absolute amount.				
	2. Obtain reasons for significant variation.				
	B. Trace amount capitalized.				
	1. Check engineering reports.				
	2. Check vendors' invoices.				
	3. Check year-end workpapers.				
	C. Does total shown in first year plus first-year depreciation equal amount in original request?				
	D. Verify reasonableness of depreciation method:				
	1. Is method used acceptable?				
	2. Is estimated life of asset reasonable?				
10. Total Engr'g.	A. Compare Latest Estimate or Actual to total reported in original submission for:				
	1. Reasonableness of absolute amount.				
	2. Obtain reasons for significant variation.				
	B. Check total to Engineering Report on Project.				
11. Other (Explain)	A. Compare Latest Estimate or Actual to total reported in original submission for:				
	1. Reasonableness of absolute amount.				
	2. Obtain reasons for significant variation.				
12. Expense (After Taxes)	A. Compare Latest Estimate or Actual to total reported in original submission for:				
	1. Reasonableness of absolute amount.				
	2. Check to total expense amount included on Appropriation Request.				
	3. Obtain reasons for significant differences.				
	B. Verify that total has been repeated for all years.				
13. Total Capital Funds	A. Verify arithmetical accuracy of total (add lines 7 through 12).				
14. Tot. New Funds	A. Verify arithmetical accuracy of total (lines 6 plus 13).				
15. Cumulative Depreciation	A. Determine that line 15 equals cumulative annual depreciation shown on line 32. (The accuracy of line 32 will be determined later.)				
16. Cum. Net Profit & Depreciation	A. Determine that this line is identical to line 34. (The accuracy of line 34 will be determined later.)				
17. New Funds to Repay	A. Determine that this line equals line 14 plus line 15 minus line 16 for each year.				
	B. Verify accuracy of payback calculation (shown on top of form).				
	1. Determine the number of years with a figure on line 17. This is the number of full years to repay that is to be listed on the first line in payback calculation above.				
	2. Determine the part year (second line above) by dividing the figure on line 17 in the last full year to repay column, by the total on line 33 in the succeeding year.				
	3. The sum of these items will determine the total years to repay.				

Item	Points To Be Checked	Yes Sat.	No Un-sat.	Un-nec.	Remarks/Reference
Profit and Loss Projection					
18. Gross Sales	A. Compare Latest Estimate or Actual to total reported in original submission for:				
	1. Reasonableness of absolute amount.				
	2. Obtain reasons for differences.				
	B. Determine whether sales were incremental to this project:				
	1. Check reasonableness and accuracy of division's calculations.				
	(a) Where appropriate, check production records and convert output to sales dollars.				
	2. If not a new product, determine capacity of previously existing facilities and subtract this from total sales for product, which should give incremental sales.				
19. Deductions	A. Compare Deductions from Gross Sales in this Profit and Loss projection to the historical and planned rate for:				
	1. The total division, and				
	2. The total product Profit and Loss, and				
	3. Obtain reasons for any significant variations.				
	4. Check divisional allocation to this project.				
20. Net Sales	A. Verify arithmetical accuracy (Line 18 less Line 19).				
21. Cost of Goods Sold & 22. Gross Profit	A. Check division computation.				
	1. Review cost records before and after capital project, thereby ascertaining savings.				
	B. Compare the Gross Profit rate in this Profit and Loss projection to the historical and planned rate for:				
	1. The original submission, and				
	2. The total division, and				
	3. The total product Profit and Loss, and				
	4. If a new product, to any similar products.				
	5. Obtain explanations of significant variations.				
23. Advertising	A. Check division's computation.				
	B. Comnare as a % of Net Sales to the historical and planned rate for:				
	1. The original submission, and				
	2. The total division, and				
	3. The total product Profit and Loss, and				
	4. If a new product, compare to similar products when possible, and				
	5. Observe trends in rate and absolute amounts,				
	6. Obtain explanations of any significant variations.				
24. Selling	A. Check division's computation.				
	B. Compare as a % of Net Sales tothe historical and planned rate for:				
	1. The original submission, and				
	2. The total division, and				
	3. The total product Profit and Loss, and				
	4. If a new product, compare to similar products when possible, and				
	5. Observe trends in rate and absolute amounts,				
	6. Obtain explanations of any significant variations.				
25. General and Administrative	A. Check division's computation.				
	B. Compare as a % of Net Sales to the historical and planned rate for:				
	1. The original submission, and				
	2. The total division, and				
	3. The total product Profit and Loss, and				
	4. If a new product, compare to similar products when possible, and				
	5. Observe trends in rate and absolute amounts,				
	6. Obtain explanations of any significant variations.				
26. Research	A. Check division's computation.				
	B. Compare as a % of Net Sales to the historical and planned rate for:				
	1. The original submission, and				
	2. The total division, and				
	3. The total product Profit and Loss, and				
	4. If a new product, compare to similar products when possible, and				
	5. Observe trends in rate and absolute amounts,				
	6. Obtain expalnations of any significant variations.				

	Item		Points To Be Checked	Yes Sat.	No Un-sat.	Un-nec.	Remarks/Reference
27.	Other	A.	Division should satisfactorily explain totals included on this line. Auditor should take steps necessary to satisfy himself of reasonableness and accuracy of these totals.				
28.	Adjustment	A.	Division should satisfactorily explain totals included on this line. Auditor should take steps necessary to satisfy himself of reasonableness and accuracy of these totals.				
29.	Profit Before Taxes	A.	Verify arithmetical accuracy.				
30.	Taxes	A.	Verify that proper tax rate has been used.				
31.	Net Profit	A.	Verify arithmetical accuracy.				
32.	Annual Depreciation	A.	Determine reasonableness of totals (see Items 8D and 9D).				
33.	Annual Net Profit & Depreciation	A.	Verify arithmetical accuracy (lines 31 plus 32).				
34.	Cumulative Net Profit and Depreciation	A.	Verify arithmetical accuracy (should equal the cumulative total of line 33).				
	5- and 10-Year Averages	A.	Verify arithmetical accuracy of all 5- and 10-year average figures shown.				
	Return on Funds	A.	Verify that correct 5- and 10-year average figures have been brought up to Return on Funds section in the upper right-hand corner of the form.				
		B.	Confirm Return on Funds calculations for both the 5- and 10-year periods.				

While some projects are kept for a short period, others are retained in service for periods well in excess of their expected useful lives. In every instance the question is, will the firm be better off abandoning the project than continuing its operations? Of course, this basic question has far-reaching implications that must focus on the organization's goals and the trade-offs that the firm is willing to accept among the goals. Furthermore, since all material as well as managerial resources are limited, organizations cannot afford to allocate such resources to projects (or even divisions) that are unlikely to help the firm achieve its goals. Nevertheless, future conditions and opportunities are often very difficult to forecast. This necessitates considering any abandonment decision most carefully.

Many organizations are rightfully very "competitor-oriented." They ask the question: If we are not involved in this operation and ready to strike when the time is right, but one of our major competitors is, what will happen to our competitive position in the short and long runs? Thus such firms also try to estimate the extent of the opportunity

FUNDS EMPLOYED AND PROFIT AND LOSS PROJECTIONS

XYZ	Chicago, Illinois	Project "A"	11	-
DIVISION	LOCATION	PROJECT TITLE	PROJECT NO.	SUPPLEMENT NO.

RETURN OF NEW FUNDS EMPLOYED	PAY BACK YEARS FROM DATE OF COMPLETION		RETURN ON NEW FUNDS EMPLOYED		FIVE-YEAR AVERAGE	TEN-YEAR AVERAGE
	NUMBER OF FULL YEARS TO PAY BACK	4.0 YEARS		A - AVERAGE FUNDS EMPLOYED - LINE 14	$ 2,902	$ 2,447
	PART YEAR CALCULATION	.5 YEARS		B - PROFIT BEFORE TAXES - LINE 32	$ 1,228	$ 1,828
	TOTAL YEARS TO PAY BACK	4.5 YEARS		C - CALCULATED RETURN - B ÷ A	42.3 %	74.7 %

FUNDS EMPLOYED	GROSS COST	1ST YEAR	2ND YEAR	3RD YEAR	4TH YEAR	5TH YEAR	5-YEAR AVG.	6TH YEAR	7TH YEAR	8TH YEAR	9TH YEAR	10TH YEAR	10-YEAR AVG.
1 CASH		290	222	209	215	221	232	233	239	251	263	276	242
2 RECEIVABLES		338	287	296	304	312	307	329	338	355	372	388	332
3 INVENTORIES		766	651	670	689	709	697	747	766	804	843	881	753
4 PREPAID AND DEFERRED EXPENSES		12	10	11	11	11	11	12	12	13	13	14	12
5 CURRENT LIABILITIES		(121)	191	502	520	543	327	581	603	643	682	721	487
6 TOTAL WORKING FUNDS (1 THRU 4-5)		1,527	979	684	699	710	920	740	752	780	809	838	852
7 LAND	100	100	100	100	100	100	100	100	100	100	100	100	100
8 BUILDINGS	1,000	976	928	881	835	790	882	747	705	664	624	586	774
9 MACHINERY AND EQUIPMENT	1,240	1,166	1,024	891	768	655	900	552	459	376	302	238	643
10 ENGINEERING	100	94	82	71	61	51	72	42	34	27	21	16	50
11 OTHER (EXPLAIN)	-	-	-	-	-	-	-	-	-	-	-	-	-
12 EXPENSE (AFTER TAXES)	60	28	28	28	28	28	28	28	28	28	28	28	28
13 TOTAL CAPITAL FUNDS (7 THRU 12)		2,364	2,162	1,971	1,792	1,624	1,982	1,469	1,326	1,195	1,075	968	1,595
14 TOTAL NEW FUNDS (6 + 13)		3,891	3,141	2,655	2,491	2,334	2,902	2,209	2,078	1,975	1,884	1,806	2,447
15 CUMULATIVE DEPRECIATION ON 8 THRU 11		104	306	497	676	844		999	1,142	1,273	1,393	1,500	
16 CUM. NET PROFIT & DEPRECIATION (LINE 37)		(108)	430	1,503	2,597	3,718		4,895	6,099	7,360	8,679	10,053	
17 NEW FUNDS TO REPAY (14 + 15-16)		4,103	3,017	1,649	570	-		-	-	-	-	-	
PROFIT AND LOSS PROJECTION													
18 UNIT VOLUME		2,000	1,700	1,750	1,800	1,850	1,820	1,950	2,000	2,100	2,200	2,300	1,965
19 GROSS SALES		7,426	6,312	6,498	6,683	6,869	6,758	7,240	7,426	7,797	8,169	8,540	7,296
20 DEDUCTIONS		670	570	586	603	620	610	653	670	704	737	771	658
21 NET SALES		6,756	5,742	5,912	6,080	6,249	6,148	6,587	6,756	7,093	7,432	7,769	6,638
22 COST OF GOODS SOLD		3,210	2,901	2,957	3,011	3,066	3,029	3,196	3,251	3,382	3,512	3,642	3,213
23 GROSS PROFIT		3,546	2,841	2,955	3,069	3,183	3,119	3,391	3,505	3,711	3,920	4,127	3,425
24 G.P. % NET SALES		52.5	49.5	50.0	50.5	50.9	50.7	51.5	51.9	52.3	52.7	53.1	51.6
25 ADVERTISING		3,358	1,725	649	661	669	1,413	719	747	799	838	887	1,105
26 SELLING		300	300	300	300	300	300	320	320	320	340	350	315
27 GENERAL AND ADMINISTRATIVE		65	65	65	75	80	70	80	80	85	85	85	77
28 RESEARCH		130	20	20	20	20	42	10	10	10	10	10	26
29 START-UP COSTS		135					27						14
30 OTHER (EXPLAIN)		2	1	1	3	1	2	1	2	1	1	2	1
31 ADJUSTMENT (EXPLAIN)		10	12	35	55	75	37	77	79	81	83	85	59
32 PROFIT BEFORE TAXES		(454)	718	1,885	1,955	2,038	1,228	2,184	2,267	2,415	2,563	2,708	1,828
33 TAXES - FEDERAL AND STATE INCOME		(242)	382	1,003	1,040	1,085	653	1,162	1,206	1,285	1,364	1,441	973
34 NET PROFIT		(212)	336	882	915	953	575	1,022	1,061	1,130	1,199	1,267	855
35 ANNUAL DEPRECIATION		104	202	191	179	168	169	155	143	131	120	107	150
36 ANNUAL NET PROFIT & DEPREC. (34 + 35)		(108)	538	1,073	1,094	1,121	744	1,177	1,204	1,261	1,319	1,374	1,005
37 CUM. NET PROFIT & DEPRECIATION		(108)	430	1,503	2,597	3,718		4,895	6,099	7,360	8,679	10,053	

Figure 12-2. Post-completion audit form for capital projects.

cost involved in not being the industry's pioneer and leader with a creative long-range planning posture. Hence the abandonment decision necessarily must consider trade-offs among the firm's multiple goals, strategies, and policies.

As an initial treatment of the abandonment option, we can incorporate abandonment values into the net present value (NPV) method that we have used throughout the book. The basic approach is to consider the possibility of abandoning the project prior to the end of its useful life. *Abandonment is preferable to continuing to use the asset whenever the abandonment value exceeds the present value of all the subsequent cash flows that would result if the asset were held until the end of its life.*

In order to determine the optimum time for abandonment, we must determine the NPV for each period in which abandonment is an option and select (as the best time to abandon) the period with the largest NPV value of the abandonment option. Naturally, the process is ongoing. On the basis of today's information it may appear that a project should be maintained in use for three more years. During that period, conditions may change, which could warrant an earlier abandonment or continuation of the project beyond the three-year period.

The evaluation of the abandonment option would proceed through the following four steps:

1. Determine the best estimates for the after-tax cash inflows and outflows for the project as usual.

2. Determine the best estimates for the after-tax abandonment value for any period during which the project can be abandoned.

3. For all periods m during which abandonment is an option, compute NPV^m, using Equation (31), which shows the project's NPV assuming that the project is abandoned at the end of period m:

$$NPV^m = \sum_{t=1}^{m} \frac{S_t}{(1 + k)^t} - A_0 + \frac{AV_m}{(1 + k)^m} \tag{31}$$

where NPV^m = net present value of the project, assuming that the project is used until the end of period m and is then abandoned

S_t = after-tax cash inflow that results from operating the asset during period t

A_0 = present value of after-tax cash outflows related to the project (for many projects this value consists entirely of the original cost of the asset unless additional expenditures for overhaul or rebuilding are required later in the project's life; if such expenditures are required, A_0 would include the present value of those expenditures)

AV_m = the after-tax abandonment value of the project at the end of period m

k = the firm's after-tax cost of capital

4. Select, as the best time to abandon, the period m that has the maximum NPV^m value as determined using Equation (31).

This four-step process is illustrated in Example 1.

EXAMPLE 1

Computation of Abandonment NPV Values

Apex Company is considering the adoption of a project that has the following estimated after-tax cash flows and after-tax abandonment values:

	Year				
	0	*1*	*2*	*3*	*4*
After-tax cash flows	−\$50,000	+\$30,000	+\$26,000	+\$21,000	+\$14,000
After-tax abandonment values		+\$42,000	+\$40,000	+\$20,000	+\$ 6,000

Apex has an after-tax cost of capital of 18 percent. Determine the optimum time to abandon this project, using Equation (31).

SOLUTION

Abandonment at the end of year 4:

$$\begin{aligned} NPV^4 &= \frac{\$30{,}000}{1.18} + \frac{\$26{,}000}{(1.18)^2} + \frac{\$21{,}000}{(1.18)^3} + \frac{\$14{,}000}{(1.18)^4} - \$50{,}000 + \frac{\$6{,}000}{(1.18)^4} \\ &= \$25{,}424 + \$18{,}673 + \$12{,}781 + \$7{,}221 - \$50{,}000 + \$3{,}094 \\ &= \$17{,}194 \end{aligned}$$

Abandonment at the end of year 3:

$$NPV^3 = \frac{\$30{,}000}{1.18} + \frac{\$26{,}000}{(1.18)^2} + \frac{\$21{,}000}{(1.18)^3} - \$50{,}000 + \frac{\$20{,}000}{(1.18)^3}$$

$$= \$25{,}424 + \$18{,}673 + \$12{,}781 - \$50{,}000 + \$12{,}173$$
$$= \$19{,}051$$

Abandonment at the end of year 2:

$$NPV^2 = \$25{,}424 + \$18{,}673 - \$50{,}000 + \frac{\$40{,}000}{(1.18)^2} = \$22{,}824$$

Abandonment at the end of year 1:

$$NPV^1 = \$25{,}424 - \$50{,}000 + \frac{\$42{,}000}{1.18} = \$11{,}017$$

As can be seen, if this project is accepted, it should be abandoned at the end of year 2. Notice that NPV^2 = \$22,824 is significantly (25 percent) greater than the NPV of the project if it were held to the end of its useful life (NPV^4 = \$17,194). □

The approach recommended here is an initial step in the evaluation of the abandonment option. Very frequently the firm faces "risky" conditions (as discussed in Chapter 8) relative to future outcomes. Thus it is likely that the firm will not know future cash flows or abandonment values precisely but rather will have to resort to "optimistic," "pessimistic," and "most likely" estimates for cash flows and abandonment values. Under such conditions, the decision trees (introduced in Chapter 8) provide guidance for management in deciding upon the best course of action given the outcomes that have occurred. As discussed in Chapter 8 also, it is logical to expect that the magnitude of cash inflows generated in later years of the life of the project will be dependent upon the magnitude of earlier cash inflows; the same holds true for abandonment values.

Decision Trees and Capital Abandonment

In making the abandonment decision, management must compare the benefits of abandoning now to those of continuing to operate the asset and abandoning later. Thus, in the decision tree for the abandonment decision, we compare (1) the expected abandonment value at the end of each period with (2) the present value of the expected cash inflows of all subsequent periods, assuming that the best decision is followed (that is, to abandon or not) at the end of each period. This process is illustrated in Example 2.

EXAMPLE 2

Using Decision Trees for the Abandonment Decision

The Green Tree Company is evaluating a project with an initial cost of \$15,000 and a useful life of two years. The project can be abandoned at the end of year 1 or held until the end of year 2, when its salvage value will be zero. Green Tree has a cost of capital of 20 percent and considers this project of average riskiness. The firm has arrived at "optimistic," "pessimistic," and "most likely" estimates for cash flows as well as their corresponding probabilities in each period. In addition, possible abandonment values at the end of year 1 have been estimated on the basis of cash inflows generated during year 1. The decision tree in Figure 12-3 shows the possible outcomes during years 1 and 2 as well as the decision facing the firm to abandon or not.

1. For each of the possible cash inflows that could occur in year 1, determine the expected value of the decision to abandon and the decision not to abandon.

2. On the basis of number 1, summarize your recommendations to management concerning the abandonment at the end of period 1.

3. Determine the expected risk-adjusted NPV for this project, assuming that the firm follows the best decision alternative at the end of period 1 for each cash inflow that may occur. Recall that cash inflows and abandonment values must be discounted back to time zero.

SOLUTION

1. (a) If the cash inflow at the end of period 1 is \$5,000:

Expected abandonment value = \$5,000 (.5) + \$7,000 (.5) = \$6,000
Expected value of not abandoning = \$3,000 (.5) + \$6,000 (.3) + \$8,000 (.2)
= \$4,900

(b) If the cash inflow at the end of period 1 is \$12,000:

Expected abandonment value = \$8,000 (.4) + \$10,000 (.6) = \$9,200
Expected value of not abandoning = \$7,500 (.2) + \$10,000 (.6) + \$15,000 (.2)
= \$10,500

(c) If the cash inflow at the end of period 1 is \$20,000:

Expected abandonment value = \$15,000 (.5) + \$20,000 (.5) = \$17,500
Expected value of not abandoning = \$18,000 (.2) + \$24,000 (.5) + \$30,000 (.3)
= \$24,600

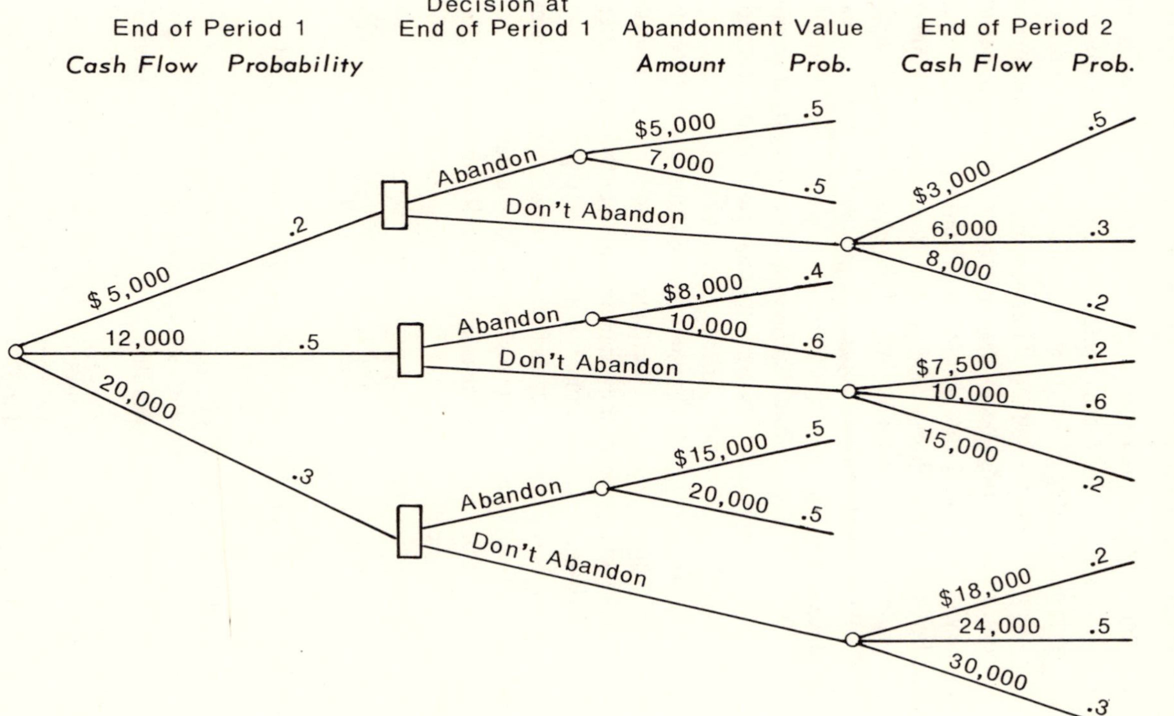

Figure 12-3. Decision tree.

2. In order to determine the preferred decision alternative at the end of period 1, we must discount the expected cash inflow at the end of period 2 (that is, the expected value of not abandoning) back one period, using the firm's cost of capital. The expected abandonment values do not require discounting, because they occur at the end of period 1. The summary in Table 12-1 compares the alternatives.

As can be seen, if the first-period cash inflow is either $5,000 or $12,000, the project should be abandoned at the end of period 1, since the expected abandonment value exceeds the present value of the expected period-2 cash inflow; on the other hand, if the cash inflow in period 1 is $20,000 the project should be continued in operation during period 2, since the present value of the expected cash inflow exceeds the expected abandonment value.

It should be noted that if the project had a useful life of three or more years, the present value of the "don't abandon" alternative would equal the present value of the expected value of the better alternative at the end of year 2, and so on. For a long-lived project the calculations become tedious but are not difficult; programs can be written to evaluate such decision trees in a straightforward manner.

3. Determining the expected risk-adjusted NPV for this project requires the following calculations:

(a) Find the sum of the period-1 cash inflow and the expected value of the optimum decision alternative at the end of period 1.
(b) Multiply the sum found in (a) by the probability that the year-1 cash inflow will occur.
(c) Find the present value of the value arrived at in (b).
(d) Repeat the process for each cash inflow that could occur in period 1 and add all these values together as well as the value arrived at in (c).
(e) Subtract the cost of the asset from the sum arrived at in (d).

Table 12-1. The abandonment decision at the end of period 1.

Cash Flow at End of Period 1	*Expected Abandonment Value*	*Present Value of Expected Value of Not Abandoning*	*Optimum Decision*
$ 5,000	$ 6,000	$ 4,900(.833) = $4,083	Abandon
12,000	9,200	10,500(.833) = $8,750	Abandon
20,000	17,500	24,600(.833) = $20,500	Don't abandon

The calculation for the project under evaluation is as follows:

$$\overline{RANPV} = .833\,(\$5{,}000 + \$6{,}000)\,.2 + .833\,(\$12{,}000 + \$9{,}200)\,.5 + .833\,(\$20{,}000 + \$20{,}500)\,.3 - \$15{,}000 = \$5{,}783$$

Therefore, this project is a candidate for acceptance, since its expected risk-adjusted net present value is positive. Furthermore, if the project is accepted, *the abandonment decisions outlined above should be followed by the firm.* □

Replacement Decisions

The decision to retain or abandon a project is also closely tied to the replacement decision. It is not uncommon for more efficient equipment to be developed, which may form the basis for replacement. Such a situation is considered in Example 3.

EXAMPLE 3
The Replacement Decision

A machine was purchased five years ago for $30,000 and had an expected life of ten years. It has been depreciated straight-line based on a ten-year life and now has a book value of $15,000 but if sold is expected to yield only $10,000 prior to any tax considerations. A new machine costing $45,000 is available. It has an estimated useful life of ten years and would result in labor saving of $6,000 per year during that period. It would be depreciated straight-line to a salvage value of $10,000. The plant engineer estimates that the old machine could be kept operating at its current level of efficiency for an additional five years beyond its original expected life with added maintenance of $1,000 per year. If the company has a 46 percent marginal tax rate and a 12 percent cost of capital, should the replacement be made?

SOLUTION

The problem is solved in three parts. First, the cash outflows to acquire the new asset are determined. Second, the incremental cash inflows resulting from the use of the new asset are determined. Last, we determine the net present value of the new machine.

Cash outflows. The new machine costs $45,000 less $4,500 for investment tax credit. The old machine could be sold for $10,000 and will result in recapture of investment tax credit of $30,000 × .10 × ⅓ = $1,000. If the old machine is sold for $10,000, it will result in a Section 1231 long-term capital loss. This will result in a tax saving of .46 ($5,000) = $2,300. Thus the net cash outflow is as tabulated below:

Purchase price of new machine	$45,000
Sale price of old machine	−10,000
Investment tax credit for new machine	−4,500
Recapture investment tax credit for old machine	+1,000
Tax savings on sale of old machine	−2,300
Net cash outflow	$29,200

The net cash outflow required to purchase the new machine is $29,200. This analysis assumes that the tax benefits will be enjoyed immediately. If this is not the case, then the value of benefits would have to be discounted back to the present.

Cash inflows. Since costs are expected to differ during the first and second five-year periods of the new asset's life, it is necessary to develop statements of changes to income and cash flow for each period. During the first five-year period, operating expenses will decrease $6,000 per year while depreciation increases $500 per year. (The new machine is depreciated at $3,500 per year while the old machine is depreciated at $3,000.) Statements reflecting these changes are shown in Table 12-2. As the table shows, during the first five years, yearly cash inflows are expected to increase by $3,470.

During the second five-year period, the old machine would be fully depreciated and also require an additional $1,000 in annual maintenance. Thus, the full $3,500 depreciation on the new machine is shown along with an annual credit of "reduced maintenance" of $1,000, since this cost is eliminated if the new machine is used. As

Table 12-2. Change to income statement and cash flows, first five years.

Expense Category	*Change to Income Statement*	*Change to Cash Flow*
Reduced labor	$6,000	$6,000
Increased depreciation	−500	
Earnings before taxes (EBT)	$5,500	
Taxes (46%)	−2,530	−2,530
Earnings after taxes (EAT)	$2,970	
	Increased cash inflow	$3,470

Table 12-3. Change to income statement and cash flows, second five-year period.

Expense Category	*Change to Income Statement*	*Change to Cash Flow*
Reduced labor	$6,000	$6,000
Reduced maintenance	+1,000	+1,000
Increased depreciation	+3,500	
Earnings before taxes	$3,500	
Taxes (46%)	−1,610	−1,610
Earnings after taxes	$1,890	
	Cash inflow	$5,390

Table 12-3 shows, during the second five-year period, the cash flows are expected to increase by $5,390.

Net present value. The computation is shown in Table 12-4. Since the NPV is negative, the old machine should be retained. The labor savings and other expected savings do not justify the $29,200 investment if the cost of capital is 12 percent. □

Summary

This chapter should be concluded with a caution to the reader. Abandonment decisions can have far-reaching effects on the entire organization. Our analysis presented here quantifies the impact of project abandonment on the basis of net present values. Of course, the impact of abandonment on the firm's other relevant goals must be carefully assessed. We therefore recommend that the quantitative NPV evaluation

Table 12-4. Calculation of NPV for Example 3.

Time	*Amount*	*Discount Factor (12%)*	*Present Value*
Present	−$29,200	1	−$29,200
1–5	+ 3,470	3.604776	+ 12,509
6–10	+ 5,390	2.045447	+ 11,025
10 (salvage)	+ 10,000	.329173	+ 3,292
		NPV =	−$ 2,374

of abandonment be supplemented with a qualitative evaluation of the impact of abandonment on the firm's goals, competitive position, strategies, and policies.

NOTES

1. *Managing Capital Expenditures,* New York: The Conference Board, 1963, pp. 83–84.
2. Ibid.
3. Ibid., pp. 90–94.

Epilogue

The increasing rate of change in all areas of our economic and business life has forced a new mode of management thinking. Under the heading of "strategic planning," the objective is to plan for contingencies such as changes in prices and availability of supplies—all within the context of maximizing wealth while reducing risk and cash outlays. In the preceding chapters we have provided the management methods and analytical tools needed to integrate the capital acquisition decision process into the firm's strategic planning system. In so doing we have presented a sound, effective capital expenditure decision process that will enable all firms to deal with the uncertainties of the 1980s—tight money, high rates of inflation, increasing costs of funds, potential government intervention, and the like.

The methods we have described to handle these uncertainties include:

- Determining relevant cash flows, including the tax impacts of all decisions.
- Discounting cash flows to incorporate the time value of money.
- Hedging against risk with the use of decision trees and risk-adjusted discount rates.
- Exploring the options of leasing as well as other project financing strategies in order to reduce the risk associated with asset owner-

ship during times of tight money, increasing costs of capital, and above-normal rates of inflation.

- Using sensitivity analysis in order to address important "what if" questions about potential changes in forecasted values as well as environmental conditions.
- Reviewing and controlling capital projects in order to obtain vital feedback information that provides timely warning of potential problem areas and identifies projects that may be candidates for replacement or abandonment.

Because of the difficulties encountered in using forecasting techniques during the late 1970s, we have proposed that managers adopt a conservative, "risk-averse" posture in their evaluation of capital expenditure and leasing alternatives. With respect to this posture, we have illustrated several hedging strategies:

- The use of NPV profiles to pinpoint changes which are likely to take place in project selection as conditions vary over time.
- The analysis of all projects under the assumption that their economic life is *limited to the longer* of either five years or 60 percent of the original estimated economic life.
- The use of a risk-adjusted DCF approach, which enables management to make probability statements about project attractiveness (for example, the firm could be 80 percent sure that the project will increase its wealth position).

All the techniques we have explored relate directly to the strategic planning process. In fact, the decision methodologies apply equally well to all long-range planning decisions. Therefore, we strongly encourage managers at every level to master the concepts, integrate them into their daily planning routines, and use them as a matter of course.

APPENDIX A

Comparative Depreciation Tables

The following tables show the annual and cumulative depreciation for various useful lives under the straight-line, 200%-declining-balance, 150%-declining-balance, 125%-declining-balance, and sum-of-the-years'-digits methods. *All amounts are expressed as percentages of the basis of the property at the time the useful life begins.*

Year	*Straight-Line*		*200%-Declining-Balance*		*150%-Declining-Balance*		*Sum-of-Digits*	
	Annual %	*Cum.* %	*Annual* %	*Cum.* %	*Annual* %	*Cum.* %	*Annual* %	*Cum.* %
				3-Year Life				
1	33.33	33.33	66.66	66.66	50.00	50.00	50.00	50.00
2	33.33	66.66	22.22	88.88	25.00	75.00	33.33	83.33
3	33.34	100.00	7.41	96.29	12.50	87.50	16.67	100.00
				4-Year Life				
1	25.00	25.00	50.00	50.00	37.50	37.50	40.00	40.00
2	25.00	50.00	25.00	75.00	23.44	60.94	30.00	70.00
3	25.00	75.00	12.50	87.50	14.65	75.59	20.00	90.00
4	25.00	100.00	6.25	93.75	9.15	84.74	10.00	100.00
				5-Year Life				
1	20.00	20.00	40.00	40.00	30.00	30.00	33.33	33.33
2	20.00	40.00	24.00	64.00	21.00	51.00	26.67	60.00
3	20.00	60.00	14.40	78.40	14.70	65.70	20.00	80.00
4	20.00	80.00	8.64	87.04	10.29	75.99	13.33	93.33
5	20.00	100.00	5.18	92.22	7.20	83.19	6.67	100.00
				6-Year Life				
1	16.67	16.67	33.34	33.34	25.00	25.00	28.57	28.57
2	16.67	33.34	22.22	55.56	18.75	43.75	23.81	52.38
3	16.66	50.00	14.81	70.37	14.06	57.81	19.05	71.43
4	16.67	66.67	9.87	80.24	10.55	68.36	14.29	85.72
5	16.67	83.34	6.58	86.82	7.91	76.27	9.52	95.24
6	16.66	100.00	4.39	91.21	5.93	82.20	4.76	100.00
				7-Year Life				
1	14.28	14.28	28.57	28.57	21.43	21.43	25.00	25.00
2	14.28	28.56	20.41	48.98	16.83	38.26	21.43	46.43
3	14.29	42.85	14.58	63.56	13.23	51.49	17.86	64.29
4	14.29	57.14	10.41	73.97	10.40	61.89	14.29	78.58
5	14.29	71.43	7.44	81.41	8.17	70.06	10.71	89.29
6	14.29	85.72	5.31	86.72	6.42	76.48	7.14	96.43
7	14.28	100.00	3.79	90.51	5.04	81.52	3.57	100.00
				8-Year Life				
1	12.50	12.50	25.00	25.00	18.75	18.75	22.22	22.22
2	12.50	25.00	18.75	43.75	15.23	33.98	19.44	41.66
3	12.50	37.50	14.06	57.81	12.38	46.36	16.67	58.33
4	12.50	50.00	10.55	68.36	10.06	56.42	13.89	72.22
5	12.50	62.50	7.91	76.27	8.17	64.59	11.11	83.33
6	12.50	75.00	5.93	82.20	6.64	71.23	8.33	91.66
7	12.50	87.50	4.45	86.65	5.39	76.62	5.56	97.22
8	12.50	100.00	3.34	89.99	4.38	81.00	2.78	100.00

Year	Straight-Line		200%-Declining-Balance		150%-Declining-Balance		125%-Declining-Balance		Sum-of-Digits	
	Annual %	Cum. %	Annual %	Cum. %	Annual %	Cum. %	Annual %	Cum. %	Annual %	Cum. %
9-Year Life										
1	11.11	11.11	22.22	22.22	16.67	16.67			20.00	20.00
2	11.11	22.22	17.28	39.50	13.89	30.56			17.78	37.78
3	11.11	33.33	13.44	52.94	11.57	42.13			15.56	53.34
4	11.11	44.44	10.45	63.39	9.65	51.78			13.33	66.67
5	11.11	55.55	8.13	71.52	8.04	59.82			11.11	77.78
6	11.11	66.66	6.32	77.84	6.70	66.52			8.89	86.67
7	11.11	77.77	4.92	82.76	5.58	72.10			6.67	93.34
8	11.11	88.88	3.83	86.59	4.65	76.75			4.44	97.78
9	11.12	100.00	2.98	89.57	3.88	80.63			2.22	100.00
10-Year Life										
1	10.00	10.00	20.00	20.00	15.00	15.00			18.18	18.18
2	10.00	20.00	16.00	36.00	12.75	27.75			16.37	34.55
3	10.00	30.00	12.80	48.80	10.84	38.59			14.56	49.09
4	10.00	40.00	10.24	59.04	9.21	47.80			12.73	61.82
5	10.00	50.00	8.19	67.23	7.83	55.63			10.91	72.73
6	10.00	60.00	6.56	73.79	6.66	62.29			9.09	81.82
7	10.00	70.00	5.24	79.03	5.66	67.95			7.27	89.09
8	10.00	80.00	4.19	83.22	4.81	72.76			5.46	94.55
9	10.00	90.00	3.36	86.58	4.09	76.85			3.63	98.18
10	10.00	100.00	2.68	89.26	3.47	80.32			1.82	100.00
15-Year Life										
1	6.67	6.67	13.33	13.33	10.00	10.00			12.50	12.50
2	6.66	13.33	11.56	24.89	9.00	19.00			11.67	24.17
3	6.67	20.00	10.01	34.90	8.10	27.10			10.83	35.00
4	6.67	26.67	8.68	43.58	7.29	34.39			10.00	45.00
5	6.66	33.33	7.53	51.11	6.56	40.95			9.17	54.17
6	6.67	40.00	6.51	57.62	5.90	46.85			8.33	62.50
7	6.67	46.67	5.65	63.27	5.32	52.17			7.50	70.00
8	6.66	53.33	4.90	68.17	4.78	56.95			6.67	76.67
9	6.67	60.00	4.25	72.42	4.30	61.25			5.83	82.50
10	6.67	66.67	3.67	76.09	3.88	65.13			5.00	87.50
11	6.66	73.33	3.19	79.28	3.49	68.62			4.17	91.67
12	6.67	80.00	2.76	82.04	3.14	71.76			3.33	95.00
13	6.67	86.67	2.40	84.44	2.82	74.58			2.50	97.50
14	6.66	93.33	2.07	86.51	2.54	77.12			1.67	99.17
15	6.67	100.00	1.80	88.31	2.29	79.41			.83	100.00
20-Year Life										
1	5.00	5.00	10.00	10.00	7.50	7.50	6.25	6.25	9.52	9.52
2	5.00	10.00	9.00	19.00	6.94	14.44	5.86	12.11	9.05	18.57
3	5.00	15.00	8.10	27.10	6.42	20.86	5.49	17.60	8.57	27.14
4	5.00	20.00	7.29	34.39	5.94	26.80	5.15	22.75	8.10	35.24
5	5.00	25.00	6.56	40.95	5.49	32.29	4.83	27.58	7.62	42.86
6	5.00	30.00	5.91	46.86	5.08	37.37	4.53	32.11	7.14	50.00
7	5.00	35.00	5.31	52.17	4.70	42.07	4.24	36.35	6.67	56.67
8	5.00	40.00	4.78	56.95	4.35	46.42	3.98	40.33	6.19	62.86
9	5.00	45.00	4.31	61.26	4.02	50.44	3.73	44.06	5.71	68.57
10	5.00	50.00	3.87	65.13	3.71	54.15	3.50	47.55	5.24	73.81
11	5.00	55.00	3.49	68.62	3.44	57.59	3.28	50.83	4.76	78.57
12	5.00	60.00	3.14	71.76	3.18	60.77	3.07	53.90	4.29	82.86
13	5.00	65.00	2.82	74.58	2.94	63.71	2.88	56.79	3.81	86.67
14	5.00	70.00	2.54	77.12	2.72	66.43	2.70	59.49	3.33	90.00
15	5.00	75.00	2.29	79.41	2.52	68.95	2.53	62.02	2.86	92.86

Year	Straight-Line		200%-Declining-Balance		150%-Declining-Balance		125%-Declining-Balance		Sum-of-Digits	
	Annual %	Cum. %	Annual %	Cum. %	Annual %	Cum. %	Annual %	Cum. %	Annual %	Cum. %
					20-Year Life *(continued)*					
16	5.00	80.00	2.06	81.47	2.33	71.28	2.37	64.39	2.38	95.24
17	5.00	85.00	1.85	83.32	2.15	73.43	2.23	66.62	1.90	97.14
18	5.00	90.00	1.67	84.99	1.99	75.42	2.09	68.70	1.43	98.57
19	5.00	95.00	1.50	86.49	1.84	77.26	1.96	70.66	.95	99.52
20	5.00	100.00	1.35	87.84	1.70	78.96	1.83	72.49	.48	100.00
					25-Year Life					
1	4.00	4.00	8.00	8.00	6.00	6.00	5.00	5.00	7.69	7.69
2	4.00	8.00	7.36	15.36	5.64	11.64	4.75	9.75	7.39	15.08
3	4.00	12.00	6.77	22.13	5.30	16.94	4.51	14.26	7.07	22.15
4	4.00	16.00	6.23	28.36	4.98	21.92	4.29	18.55	6.77	28.92
5	4.00	20.00	5.73	34.09	4.68	26.60	4.07	22.62	6.47	35.39
6	4.00	24.00	5.27	39.36	4.40	31.00	3.87	26.49	6.15	41.54
7	4.00	28.00	4.86	44.22	4.14	35.14	3.68	30.17	5.85	47.39
8	4.00	32.00	4.46	48.68	3.89	39.03	3.49	33.66	5.53	52.92
9	4.00	36.00	4.10	52.78	3.66	42.69	3.32	36.98	5.23	58.15
10	4.00	40.00	3.78	56.56	3.43	46.12	3.15	40.13	4.93	63.08
11	4.00	44.00	3.48	60.04	3.23	49.35	2.99	43.12	4.61	67.69
12	4.00	48.00	3.19	63.23	3.03	52.38	2.84	45.96	4.31	72.00
13	4.00	52.00	2.94	66.17	2.86	55.24	2.70	48.67	4.00	76.00
14	4.00	56.00	2.71	68.88	2.68	57.92	2.57	51.23	3.69	79.69
15	4.00	60.00	2.49	71.37	2.52	60.44	2.44	53.67	3.39	83.08
16	4.00	64.00	2.29	73.66	2.37	62.81	2.32	55.99	3.07	86.15
17	4.00	68.00	2.11	75.77	2.23	65.04	2.20	58.19	2.77	88.92
18	4.00	72.00	1.94	77.71	2.10	67.14	2.09	60.28	2.47	91.39
19	4.00	76.00	1.78	79.49	1.97	69.11	1.99	62.26	2.15	93.54
20	4.00	80.00	1.64	81.13	1.85	70.96	1.89	64.15	1.85	95.39
21	4.00	84.00	1.51	82.64	1.74	72.70	1.79	65.94	1.53	96.92
22	4.00	88.00	1.39	84.03	1.64	74.34	1.70	67.65	1.23	98.15
23	4.00	92.00	1.28	85.31	1.54	75.88	1.62	69.26	.93	99.08
24	4.00	96.00	1.17	86.48	1.45	77.33	1.54	70.80	.61	99.69
25	4.00	100.00	1.08	87.56	1.36	78.69	1.46	72.26	.31	100.00
					30-Year Life					
1	3.33	3.33	6.67	6.67	5.00	5.00	4.16	4.16	6.45	6.45
2	3.34	6.67	6.22	12.89	4.75	9.75	3.99	8.16	6.24	12.69
3	3.33	10.00	5.81	18.70	4.51	14.26	3.83	11.99	6.02	18.71
4	3.33	13.33	5.42	24.12	4.29	18.55	3.67	15.65	5.81	24.52
5	3.34	16.67	5.06	29.18	4.07	22.62	3.51	19.17	5.59	30.11
6	3.33	20.00	4.72	33.90	3.87	26.49	3.37	22.54	5.37	35.48
7	3.33	23.33	4.40	38.30	3.68	30.17	3.23	25.76	5.17	40.65
8	3.34	26.67	4.12	42.42	3.49	33.66	3.09	28.86	4.94	45.59
9	3.33	30.00	3.84	46.26	3.32	36.98	2.96	31.82	4.73	50.32
10	3.33	33.33	3.58	49.84	3.15	40.13	2.84	34.66	4.52	54.84
11	3.34	36.67	3.34	53.18	2.99	43.12	2.72	37.38	4.30	59.14
12	3.33	40.00	3.12	56.30	2.84	45.96	2.61	39.99	4.09	63.23
13	3.33	43.33	2.92	59.22	2.70	48.66	2.50	42.49	3.87	67.10
14	3.34	46.67	2.72	61.94	2.57	51.23	2.40	44.89	3.65	70.75
15	3.33	50.00	2.53	64.47	2.44	53.67	2.30	47.19	3.44	74.19
16	3.33	53.33	2.37	66.84	2.32	55.99	2.20	49.39	3.23	77.42
17	3.34	56.67	2.21	69.05	2.20	58.19	2.11	51.50	3.01	80.43
18	3.33	60.00	2.07	71.12	2.09	60.28	2.02	53.52	2.80	83.23
19	3.33	63.33	1.92	73.04	1.99	62.27	1.94	55.45	2.58	85.81
20	3.34	66.67	1.80	74.84	1.89	64.16	1.86	57.31	2.36	88.17

Year	Straight-Line		200%-Declining-Balance		150%-Declining-Balance		125%-Declining-Balance		Sum-of-Digits	
	Annual %	Cum. %	Annual %	Cum. %	Annual %	Cum. %	Annual %	Cum. %	Annual %	Cum. %
					30-Year Life *(continued)*					
21	3.33	70.00	1.68	76.52	1.80	65.96	1.78	59.09	2.15	90.32
22	3.33	73.33	1.56	78.08	1.70	67.66	1.70	60.79	1.94	92.26
23	3.34	76.67	1.46	79.54	1.62	69.28	1.63	62.43	1.72	93.98
24	3.33	80.00	1.37	80.91	1.54	70.82	1.57	63.99	1.61	95.49
25	3.33	83.33	1.27	82.18	1.46	72.28	1.50	65.49	1.29	96.78
26	3.34	86.67	1.19	83.37	1.39	73.67	1.44	66.93	1.07	97.85
27	3.33	90.00	1.11	84.48	1.32	74.99	1.38	68.31	.86	98.71
28	3.33	93.33	1.03	85.51	1.25	76.24	1.32	69.63	.65	99.36
29	3.34	96.67	.97	86.48	1.19	77.43	1.27	70.89	.43	99.79
30	3.33	100.00	.90	87.38	1.13	78.56	1.21	72.11	.21	100.00
					33-1/3-Year Life					
1	3.00	3.00	6.00	6.00	4.50	4.50	3.75	3.75	5.82	5.82
2	3.00	6.00	5.64	11.64	4.30	8.80	3.61	7.36	5.65	11.47
3	3.00	9.00	5.30	16.94	4.10	12.90	3.47	10.83	5.47	16.95
4	3.00	12.00	4.98	21.93	3.92	16.82	3.34	14.18	5.30	22.25
5	3.00	15.00	4.68	26.61	3.74	20.56	3.22	17.40	5.17	27.37
6	3.00	18.00	4.40	31.00	3.57	24.14	3.10	20.49	4.95	32.32
7	3.00	21.00	4.14	35.15	3.41	27.55	2.98	23.47	4.76	37.10
8	3.00	24.00	3.89	39.03	3.16	30.81	2.87	26.34	4.60	41.70
9	3.00	27.00	3.66	42.70	3.11	33.93	2.76	29.11	4.43	46.13
10	3.00	30.00	3.44	46.14	2.97	36.90	2.66	31.77	4.25	50.38
11	3.00	33.00	3.23	49.37	2.84	39.74	2.56	34.32	4.08	54.46
12	3.00	36.00	3.04	52.41	2.71	42.45	2.46	36.79	3.90	58.36
13	3.00	39.00	2.86	55.26	2.59	45.04	2.37	39.16	3.73	62.10
14	3.00	42.00	2.68	57.95	2.47	47.51	2.28	41.44	3.55	65.64
15	3.00	45.00	2.52	60.47	2.36	49.88	2.20	43.63	3.38	69.02
16	3.00	48.00	2.37	62.84	2.26	52.13	2.11	45.75	3.20	72.22
17	3.00	51.00	2.23	65.07	2.15	54.29	2.03	47.78	3.03	75.25
18	3.00	54.00	2.10	67.17	2.06	56.34	1.95	49.74	2.85	78.10
19	3.00	57.00	1.97	69.14	1.96	58.31	1.88	51.63	2.68	80.78
20	3.00	60.00	1.85	71.00	1.88	60.18	1.81	53.44	2.50	83.28
21	3.00	63.00	1.74	72.73	1.79	61.97	1.75	55.19	2.33	85.61
22	3.00	66.00	1.64	74.37	1.71	63.69	1.68	56.87	2.15	87.77
23	3.00	69.00	1.54	75.90	1.63	65.32	1.62	58.48	1.98	89.75
24	3.00	72.00	1.45	77.35	1.56	66.88	1.56	60.04	1.81	91.56
25	3.00	75.00	1.36	78.71	1.49	68.37	1.50	61.54	1.63	93.19
26	3.00	78.00	1.28	79.99	1.42	69.79	1.44	62.98	1.46	94.64
27	3.00	81.00	1.20	81.19	1.36	71.15	1.39	64.37	1.28	95.92
28	3.00	84.00	1.13	82.32	1.30	72.45	1.34	65.71	1.11	97.03
29	3.00	87.00	1.06	83.38	1.24	73.69	1.29	66.99	.93	97.96
30	3.00	90.00	1.00	84.37	1.18	74.88	1.24	68.23	.76	98.72
31	3.00	93.00	.94	85.31	1.13	76.01	1.19	69.42	.58	99.30
32	3.00	96.00	.88	86.19	1.08	77.09	1.15	70.57	.41	99.71
33	3.00	99.00	.93	87.02	1.03	78.12	1.10	71.67	.23	99.94
33⅓	1.00	100.00	.26	87.28	.33	78.45	.35	71.95	.06	100.00
					35-Year Life					
1	2.86	2.86	5.71	5.71	4.29	4.29	3.57	3.57	5.56	5.56
2	2.86	5.72	5.38	11.09	4.10	8.39	3.44	7.02	5.40	10.96
3	2.85	8.57	5.07	16.16	3.93	12.32	3.32	10.34	5.24	16.20
4	2.86	11.43	4.78	20.94	3.76	16.08	3.20	13.54	5.08	21.28
5	2.86	14.29	4.51	25.45	3.60	19.68	3.09	16.63	4.92	26.20

Year	Straight-Line		200%-Declining-Balance		150%-Declining-Balance		125%-Declining-Balance		Sum-of-Digits	
	Annual %	Cum. %	Annual %	Cum. %	Annual %	Cum. %	Annual %	Cum. %	Annual %	Cum. %
35-Year Life *(continued)*										
6	2.85	17.14	4.25	29.70	3.44	23.12	2.98	19.60	4.76	30.96
7	2.86	20.00	4.01	33.71	3.29	26.41	2.87	22.48	4.60	35.56
8	2.86	22.86	3.78	37.49	3.15	29.56	2.77	25.24	4.44	40.00
9	2.85	25.71	3.56	41.05	3.02	32.58	2.67	27.91	4.29	44.29
10	2.86	28.57	3.36	44.41	2.89	35.47	2.57	30.49	4.13	48.42
11	2.86	31.43	3.17	47.58	2.77	38.24	2.48	32.97	3.97	52.39
12	2.85	34.28	2.99	50.57	2.65	40.89	2.39	35.36	3.81	56.20
13	2.86	37.14	2.82	53.39	2.53	43.42	2.31	37.67	3.65	59.85
14	2.86	40.00	2.66	56.05	2.42	45.84	2.23	39.90	3.49	63.34
15	2.85	42.85	2.51	58.56	2.32	48.16	2.15	42.05	3.33	66.67
16	2.86	45.71	2.37	60.93	2.22	50.38	2.07	44.12	3.18	69.85
17	2.86	48.57	2.23	63.16	2.13	52.51	2.00	46.11	3.02	72.87
18	2.85	51.42	2.10	65.26	2.03	54.54	1.92	48.04	2.86	75.73
19	2.86	54.28	1.98	67.24	1.95	56.49	1.86	49.89	2.70	78.43
20	2.86	57.14	1.87	69.11	1.86	58.35	1.79	51.68	2.54	80.97
21	2.86	60.00	1.76	70.87	1.79	60.14	1.73	53.41	2.38	83.35
22	2.86	62.86	1.66	72.53	1.71	61.85	1.66	55.07	2.22	85.57
23	2.86	65.72	1.57	74.10	1.64	63.49	1.60	56.68	2.06	87.63
24	2.85	68.57	1.48	75.58	1.56	65.05	1.55	58.22	1.90	89.53
25	2.86	71.43	1.40	76.98	1.50	66.55	1.49	59.72	1.75	91.28
26	2.86	74.29	1.32	78.30	1.43	67.98	1.44	61.15	1.59	92.87
27	2.85	77.14	1.24	79.54	1.37	69.35	1.39	62.54	1.43	94.30
28	2.86	80.00	1.17	80.71	1.31	70.66	1.34	63.88	1.27	95.57
29	2.86	82.86	1.10	81.81	1.26	71.92	1.29	65.17	1.11	96.68
30	2.85	85.71	1.04	82.85	1.20	73.12	1.24	66.41	.95	97.63
31	2.86	88.57	.98	83.83	1.15	74.27	1.20	67.61	.79	98.42
32	2.86	91.43	.92	84.75	1.10	75.37	1.16	68.77	.63	99.05
33	2.85	94.28	.87	85.62	1.06	76.43	1.12	69.88	.47	99.52
34	2.86	97.14	.82	86.44	1.01	77.44	1.08	70.96	.32	99.84
35	2.86	100.00	.77	87.21	.97	78.41	1.04	72.00	.16	100.00
40-Year Life										
1	2.50	2.50	5.00	5.00	3.75	3.75	3.13	3.13	4.88	4.88
2	2.50	5.00	4.75	9.75	3.61	7.36	3.03	6.15	4.75	9.63
3	2.50	7.50	4.51	14.26	3.47	10.83	2.93	9.09	4.64	14.27
4	2.50	10.00	4.29	18.55	3.34	14.17	2.84	11.93	4.51	18.78
5	2.50	12.50	4.07	22.62	3.22	17.39	2.75	14.68	4.39	23.17
6	2.50	15.00	3.87	26.49	3.10	20.49	2.67	17.34	4.27	27.44
7	2.50	17.50	3.68	30.17	2.98	23.47	2.58	19.93	4.14	31.58
8	2.50	20.00	3.49	33.66	2.87	26.34	2.50	22.43	4.03	35.61
9	2.50	22.50	3.32	36.98	2.76	29.10	2.42	24.85	3.90	39.51
10	2.50	25.00	3.15	40.13	2.66	31.76	2.35	27.20	3.78	43.29
11	2.50	27.50	2.99	43.12	2.56	34.32	2.27	29.48	3.66	46.95
12	2.50	30.00	2.84	45.96	2.46	36.78	2.20	31.68	3.54	50.49
13	2.50	32.50	2.71	48.67	2.37	39.15	2.13	33.82	3.41	53.90
14	2.50	35.00	2.56	51.23	2.28	41.43	2.07	35.88	3.29	57.19
15	2.50	37.50	2.44	53.67	2.20	43.63	2.00	37.89	3.18	60.37
16	2.50	40.00	2.32	55.99	2.11	45.74	1.94	39.83	3.04	63.41
17	2.50	42.50	2.20	58.19	2.03	47.77	1.88	41.71	2.93	66.34
18	2.50	45.00	2.09	60.28	1.96	49.73	1.82	43.53	2.81	69.15
19	2.50	47.50	1.99	62.27	1.88	51.61	1.76	45.30	2.68	71.83
20	2.50	50.00	1.88	64.15	1.81	53.42	1.71	47.01	2.56	74.39

Year	*Straight-Line*		*200%-Declining-Balance*		*150%-Declining-Balance*		*125%-Declining-Balance*		*Sum-of-Digits*	
	Annual %	*Cum. %*	*Annual %*	*Cum. %*	*Annual %*	*Cum. %*	*Annual %*	*Cum. %*	*Annual %*	*Cum. %*
					40-Year Life *(continued)*					
21	2.50	52.50	1.79	65.94	1.75	55.17	1.66	48.66	2.44	76.83
22	2.50	55.00	1.71	67.65	1.68	56.85	1.60	50.27	2.32	79.15
23	2.50	57.50	1.62	69.27	1.62	58.47	1.55	51.82	2.19	81.34
24	2.50	60.00	1.53	70.80	1.56	60.03	1.51	53.33	2.07	83.41
25	2.50	62.50	1.46	72.26	1.50	61.53	1.46	54.78	1.94	85.37
26	2.50	65.00	1.39	73.65	1.44	62.97	1.41	56.20	1.82	87.19
27	2.50	67.50	1.32	74.97	1.39	64.36	1.37	57.57	1.71	88.90
28	2.50	70.00	1.25	76.22	1.34	65.70	1.33	58.89	1.59	90.49
29	2.50	72.50	1.19	77.41	1.29	66.99	1.28	60.18	1.46	91.95
30	2.50	75.00	1.13	78.54	1.24	68.23	1.24	61.42	1.34	93.29
31	2.50	77.50	1.07	79.61	1.19	69.42	1.21	62.63	1.22	94.51
32	2.50	80.00	1.02	80.63	1.15	70.57	1.17	63.79	1.10	95.61
33	2.50	82.50	.97	81.60	1.10	71.67	1.13	64.93	.98	96.58
34	2.50	85.00	.92	85.52	1.06	72.73	1.10	66.02	.86	97.44
35	2.50	87.50	.87	83.39	1.02	73.75	1.06	67.08	.73	98.17
36	2.50	90.00	.83	84.22	.98	74.73	1.03	68.11	.61	98.78
37	2.50	92.50	.79	85.01	.95	75.68	1.00	69.11	.49	99.27
38	2.50	95.00	.75	85.76	.91	76.59	.97	70.07	.36	99.63
39	2.50	97.50	.71	86.47	.88	77.47	.94	71.01	.25	99.88
40	2.50	100.00	.68	87.15	.85	78.32	.91	71.92	.12	100.00
					45-Year Life					
1	2.22	2.22	4.44	4.44	3.33	3.33	2.78	2.78	4.35	4.35
2	2.22	4.44	4.24	8.68	3.22	6.55	2.70	5.48	4.25	8.60
3	2.22	6.66	4.05	12.73	3.12	9.67	2.63	8.10	4.15	12.75
4	2.23	8.89	3.87	16.60	3.01	12.68	2.55	10.66	4.06	16.81
5	2.22	11.11	3.70	20.30	2.91	15.59	2.48	13.14	3.96	20.77
6	2.22	13.33	3.54	23.84	2.81	18.40	2.41	15.55	3.86	24.63
7	2.22	15.55	3.38	27.22	2.72	21.12	2.35	17.90	3.77	28.40
8	2.23	17.78	3.23	30.45	2.63	23.75	2.28	20.18	3.67	32.07
9	2.22	20.00	3.09	33.54	2.54	26.29	2.22	22.40	3.57	35.64
10	2.22	22.22	2.95	36.49	2.46	28.75	2.16	24.55	3.48	39.12
11	2.22	24.44	2.82	39.31	2.38	31.13	2.10	26.65	3.38	42.50
12	2.23	26.67	2.69	42.00	2.30	33.43	2.04	28.68	3.28	45.78
13	2.22	28.89	2.57	44.57	2.22	35.65	1.98	30.67	3.19	48.97
14	2.22	31.11	2.46	47.03	2.15	37.80	1.93	32.59	3.09	52.06
15	2.22	33.33	2.35	49.38	2.07	39.87	1.87	34.46	3.00	55.06
16	2.23	35.56	2.25	51.63	2.00	41.87	1.82	36.28	2.90	57.96
17	2.22	37.78	2.15	53.78	1.94	43.81	1.77	38.05	2.80	60.76
18	2.22	40.00	2.05	55.83	1.87	45.68	1.72	39.77	2.70	63.46
19	2.22	42.22	1.96	57.79	1.81	47.49	1.67	41.45	2.61	66.07
20	2.23	44.45	1.87	59.66	1.75	49.24	1.63	43.07	2.51	68.58
21	2.22	46.67	1.79	61.45	1.69	50.93	1.58	44.66	2.42	71.00
22	2.22	48.89	1.71	63.16	1.64	52.57	1.54	46.19	2.32	73.32
23	2.22	51.11	1.63	64.79	1.58	54.15	1.49	47.69	2.22	75.54
24	2.23	53.34	1.56	66.35	1.53	55.68	1.45	49.14	2.13	77.67
25	2.22	55.56	1.49	67.84	1.48	57.16	1.41	50.55	2.03	79.70
26	2.22	57.78	1.42	69.26	1.43	58.59	1.37	51.93	1.93	81.63
27	2.22	60.00	1.36	70.62	1.38	59.97	1.34	53.26	1.84	83.47
28	2.23	62.23	1.30	71.92	1.33	61.30	1.30	54.56	1.74	85.21
29	2.22	64.45	1.24	73.16	1.29	62.59	1.26	55.82	1.64	86.85
30	2.22	66.67	1.18	74.34	1.25	63.84	1.23	57.05	1.55	88.40

Year	Straight-Line		200%-Declining-Balance		150%-Declining-Balance		125%-Declining-Balance		Sum-of-Digits	
	Annual %	Cum. %	Annual %	Cum. %	Annual %	Cum. %	Annual %	Cum. %	Annual %	Cum. %
				45-Year Life *(continued)*						
31	2.22	68.89	1.13	75.47	1.21	65.05	1.19	58.24	1.45	89.85
32	2.23	71.12	1.08	76.55	1.17	66.22	1.16	59.40	1.35	91.20
33	2.22	73.34	1.03	77.58	1.13	67.35	1.13	60.53	1.26	92.46
34	2.22	75.56	.98	78.56	1.09	68.44	1.10	61.63	1.16	93.62
35	2.22	77.78	.94	79.50	1.05	69.49	1.07	62.69	1.06	94.68
36	2.22	80.00	.90	80.40	1.02	70.51	1.04	63.73	.97	95.65
37	2.23	82.23	.86	81.26	.98	71.49	1.01	64.74	.87	96.52
38	2.22	84.45	.82	82.08	.95	72.44	.98	65.72	.77	97.29
39	2.22	86.67	.78	82.86	.92	73.36	.95	66.67	.68	97.97
40	2.22	88.89	.75	83.61	.89	74.25	.93	67.59	.58	98.55
41	2.23	91.12	.72	84.33	.86	75.11	.90	68.49	.48	99.03
42	2.22	93.34	.69	85.02	.83	75.94	.88	69.37	.39	99.42
43	2.22	95.56	.66	85.68	.80	76.74	.85	70.22	.29	99.71
44	2.22	97.78	.63	86.31	.78	77.52	.83	71.05	.19	99.90
45	2.22	100.00	.60	86.91	.75	78.27	.80	71.85	.10	100.00
				50-Year Life						
1	2.00	2.00	4.00	4.00	3.00	3.00	2.50	2.50	3.92	3.92
2	2.00	4.00	3.84	7.84	2.91	5.91	2.44	4.94	3.85	7.77
3	2.00	6.00	3.69	11.53	2.82	8.73	2.38	7.31	3.76	11.53
4	2.00	8.00	3.54	15.07	2.74	11.47	2.32	9.63	3.69	15.22
5	2.00	10.00	3.39	18.46	2.66	14.13	2.26	11.89	3.60	18.82
6	2.00	12.00	3.26	21.72	2.58	16.71	2.20	14.09	3.53	22.35
7	2.00	14.00	3.14	24.86	2.50	19.21	2.15	16.24	3.45	25.80
8	2.00	16.00	3.00	27.86	2.42	21.63	2.09	18.33	3.38	29.18
9	2.00	18.00	2.89	30.75	2.35	23.98	2.04	20.38	3.29	32.47
10	2.00	20.00	2.77	33.52	2.28	26.26	1.99	22.37	3.22	35.69
11	2.00	22.00	2.66	36.18	2.21	28.47	1.94	24.31	3.15	38.82
12	2.00	24.00	2.55	38.73	2.15	30.62	1.89	26.20	3.06	41.88
13	2.00	26.00	2.45	41.18	2.08	32.70	1.84	28.05	2.98	44.86
14	2.00	28.00	2.35	43.53	2.02	34.72	1.80	29.84	2.91	47.77
15	2.00	30.00	2.26	45.79	1.96	36.68	1.75	31.60	2.82	50.59
16	2.00	32.00	2.17	47.96	1.90	38.58	1.71	33.31	2.74	53.33
17	2.00	34.00	2.08	50.04	1.84	40.42	1.67	34.98	2.67	56.00
18	2.00	36.00	2.00	52.04	1.79	42.21	1.63	36.60	2.59	58.59
19	2.00	38.00	1.92	53.96	1.73	43.94	1.58	38.19	2.51	61.10
20	2.00	40.00	1.84	55.80	1.68	45.62	1.55	39.73	2.43	63.53
21	2.00	42.00	1.77	57.57	1.63	47.25	1.51	41.24	2.35	65.88
22	2.00	44.00	1.70	59.27	1.58	48.83	1.47	42.71	2.28	68.16
23	2.00	46.00	1.62	60.89	1.53	50.36	1.43	44.14	2.19	70.35
24	2.00	48.00	1.57	62.46	1.49	51.85	1.40	45.54	2.12	72.47
25	2.00	50.00	1.50	63.96	1.44	53.29	1.36	46.90	2.04	74.51
26	2.00	52.00	1.44	65.40	1.40	54.69	1.33	48.23	1.96	76.47
27	2.00	54.00	1.39	66.79	1.36	56.05	1.29	49.52	1.87	78.35
28	2.00	56.00	1.33	68.12	1.32	57.37	1.26	50.78	1.81	80.16
29	2.00	58.00	1.27	69.39	1.28	58.64	1.23	52.01	1.72	81.88
30	2.00	60.00	1.22	70.61	1.24	59.89	1.20	53.21	1.65	83.53
31	2.00	62.00	1.18	71.79	1.20	61.09	1.17	54.38	1.57	85.10
32	2.00	64.00	1.13	72.92	1.17	62.26	1.14	55.52	1.49	86.59
33	2.00	66.00	1.08	74.00	1.13	63.39	1.11	56.63	1.41	88.00
34	2.00	68.00	1.04	75.04	1.10	64.49	1.08	57.72	1.33	89.33
35	2.00	70.00	1.00	76.04	1.07	65.56	1.06	58.78	1.26	90.59

Year	Straight-Line		200%-Declining-Balance		150%-Declining-Balance		125%-Declining-Balance		Sum-of-Digits	
	Annual %	Cum. %	Annual %	Cum. %	Annual %	Cum. %	Annual %	Cum. %	Annual %	Cum. %
	50-Year Life *(continued)*									
36	2.00	72.00	.96	77.00	1.03	66.59	1.03	59.81	1.18	91.77
37	2.00	74.00	.92	77.92	1.00	67.59	1.00	60.81	1.09	92.86
38	2.00	76.00	.88	78.80	.97	68.56	.98	61.79	1.02	93.88
39	2.00	78.00	.85	79.65	.94	69.50	.96	62.75	.94	94.82
40	2.00	80.00	.81	80.46	.92	70.42	.93	63.68	.87	95.69
41	2.00	82.00	.78	81.24	.89	71.31	.91	64.58	.78	96.47
42	2.00	84.00	.75	81.99	.86	72.17	.89	65.47	.71	97.18
43	2.00	86.00	.72	82.71	.84	73.01	.86	66.33	.62	97.80
44	2.00	88.00	.69	83.40	.81	73.82	.84	67.18	.55	98.35
45	2.00	90.00	.67	84.07	.79	74.61	.82	68.00	.47	98.82
46	2.00	92.00	.64	84.71	.76	75.37	.80	68.80	.40	99.22
47	2.00	94.00	.61	85.32	.74	76.11	.78	69.58	.31	99.53
48	2.00	96.00	.59	85.90	.72	76.83	.76	70.34	.24	99.77
49	2.00	98.00	.57	86.47	.70	77.53	.74	71.08	.15	99.92
50	2.00	100.00	.54	87.01	.67	78.20	.72	71.80	.08	100.00

APPENDIX B

Compound Interest and Annuity Tables

1.00 %
ANNUAL

YR	Amount Of 1	Amount Of 1 Per Period	Sinking Fund Payment	Present Worth Of 1	Present Worth Of 1 Per Period	Periodic Payment To Amortize 1	Constant Annual Percent	Total Interest	Annual Add-on Rate	YR
	What a single $1 deposit grows to in the future. The deposit is made at the beginning of the first period.	What a series of $1 deposits grow to in the future. A deposit is made at the end of each period.	The amount to be deposited at the end of each period that grows to $1 in the future.	What $1 to be paid in the future is worth today. Value today of a single payment tomorrow.	What $1 to be paid at the end of each period is worth today. Value today of a series of payments tomorrow.	The mortgage payment to amortize a loan of $1. An annuity certain, payable at the end of each period, worth $1 today.	The annual payment, including interest and principal, to amortize completely a loan of $100.	The total interest paid over the term on a loan of $1. The loan is amortized by regular periodic payments.	The average annual interest rate on a loan that is completely amortized by regular periodic payments.	
	$S=(1+i)^n$	$S_{\overline{n}}=\frac{(1+i)^n-1}{i}$	$\frac{1}{S_{\overline{n}}}=\frac{i}{(1+i)^n-1}$	$V^n=\frac{1}{(1+i)^n}$	$A_{\overline{n}}=\frac{1-V^n}{i}$	$\frac{1}{A_{\overline{n}}}=\frac{i}{1-V^n}$				
1	1.010000	1.000000	1.00000000	0.990099	0.990099	1.01000000	101.00	0.010000	1.00	1
2	1.020100	2.010000	0.49751244	0.980296	1.970395	0.50751244	50.76	0.015025	0.75	2
3	1.030301	3.030100	0.33002211	0.970590	2.940985	0.34002211	34.01	0.020066	0.67	3
4	1.040604	4.060401	0.24628109	0.960980	3.901966	0.25628109	25.63	0.025124	0.63	4
5	1.051010	5.101005	0.19603980	0.951466	4.853431	0.20603980	20.61	0.030199	0.60	5
6	1.061520	6.152015	0.16254837	0.942045	5.795476	0.17254837	17.26	0.035290	0.59	6
7	1.072135	7.213535	0.13862828	0.932718	6.728195	0.14862828	14.87	0.040398	0.58	7
8	1.082857	8.285671	0.12069029	0.923483	7.651678	0.13069029	13.07	0.045522	0.57	8
9	1.093685	9.368527	0.10674036	0.914340	8.566018	0.11674036	11.68	0.050663	0.56	9
10	1.104622	10.462213	0.09558208	0.905287	9.471305	0.10558208	10.56	0.055821	0.56	10
11	1.115668	11.566835	0.08645408	0.896324	10.367628	0.09645408	9.65	0.060995	0.55	11
12	1.126825	12.682503	0.07884879	0.887449	11.255077	0.08884879	8.89	0.066185	0.55	12
13	1.138093	13.809328	0.07241482	0.878663	12.133740	0.08241482	8.25	0.071393	0.55	13
14	1.149474	14.947421	0.06690117	0.869963	13.003703	0.07690117	7.70	0.076616	0.55	14
15	1.160969	16.096896	0.06212378	0.861349	13.865053	0.07212378	7.22	0.081857	0.55	15
16	1.172579	17.257864	0.05794460	0.852821	14.717874	0.06794460	6.80	0.087114	0.54	16
17	1.184304	18.430443	0.05425806	0.844377	15.562251	0.06425806	6.43	0.092387	0.54	17
18	1.196147	19.614748	0.05098205	0.836017	16.398269	0.06098205	6.10	0.097677	0.54	18
19	1.208109	20.810895	0.04805175	0.827740	17.226008	0.05805175	5.81	0.102983	0.54	19
20	1.220190	22.019004	0.04541531	0.819544	18.045553	0.05541531	5.55	0.108306	0.54	20
21	1.232392	23.239194	0.04303075	0.811430	18.856983	0.05303075	5.31	0.113646	0.54	21
22	1.244716	24.471586	0.04086372	0.803396	19.660379	0.05086372	5.09	0.119002	0.54	22
23	1.257163	25.716302	0.03888584	0.795442	20.455821	0.04888584	4.89	0.124374	0.54	23
24	1.269735	26.973465	0.03707347	0.787566	21.243387	0.04707347	4.71	0.129763	0.54	24
25	1.282432	28.243200	0.03540675	0.779768	22.023156	0.04540675	4.55	0.135169	0.54	25
26	1.295256	29.525631	0.03386888	0.772048	22.795204	0.04386888	4.39	0.140591	0.54	26
27	1.308209	30.820888	0.03244553	0.764404	23.559608	0.04244553	4.25	0.146029	0.54	27
28	1.321291	32.129097	0.03112444	0.756836	24.316443	0.04112444	4.12	0.151484	0.54	28
29	1.334504	33.450388	0.02989502	0.749342	25.065785	0.03989502	3.99	0.156956	0.54	29
30	1.347849	34.784892	0.02874811	0.741923	25.807708	0.03874811	3.88	0.162443	0.54	30
31	1.361327	36.132740	0.02767573	0.734577	26.542285	0.03767573	3.77	0.167948	0.54	31
32	1.374941	37.494068	0.02667089	0.727304	27.269589	0.03667089	3.67	0.173468	0.54	32
33	1.388690	38.869009	0.02572744	0.720103	27.989693	0.03572744	3.58	0.179005	0.54	33
34	1.402577	40.257699	0.02483997	0.712973	28.702666	0.03483997	3.49	0.184559	0.54	34
35	1.416603	41.660276	0.02400368	0.705914	29.408580	0.03400368	3.41	0.190129	0.54	35
36	1.430769	43.076878	0.02321431	0.698925	30.107505	0.03321431	3.33	0.195715	0.54	36
37	1.445076	44.507647	0.02246805	0.692005	30.799510	0.03246805	3.25	0.201318	0.54	37
38	1.459527	45.952724	0.02176150	0.685153	31.484663	0.03176150	3.18	0.206937	0.54	38
39	1.474123	47.412251	0.02109160	0.678370	32.163033	0.03109160	3.11	0.212572	0.55	39
40	1.488864	48.886373	0.02045560	0.671653	32.834686	0.03045560	3.05	0.218224	0.55	40
41	1.503752	50.375237	0.01985102	0.665003	33.499689	0.02985102	2.99	0.223892	0.55	41
42	1.518790	51.878989	0.01927563	0.658419	34.158108	0.02927563	2.93	0.229576	0.55	42
43	1.533978	53.397779	0.01872737	0.651900	34.810008	0.02872737	2.88	0.235277	0.55	43
44	1.549318	54.931757	0.01820441	0.645445	35.455454	0.02820441	2.83	0.240994	0.55	44
45	1.564811	56.481075	0.01770505	0.639055	36.094508	0.02770505	2.78	0.246727	0.55	45
46	1.580459	58.045885	0.01722775	0.632728	36.727236	0.02722775	2.73	0.252476	0.55	46
47	1.596263	59.626344	0.01677111	0.626463	37.353699	0.02677111	2.68	0.258242	0.55	47
48	1.612226	61.222608	0.01633384	0.620260	37.973959	0.02633384	2.64	0.264024	0.55	48
49	1.628348	62.834834	0.01591474	0.614119	38.588079	0.02591474	2.60	0.269822	0.55	49
50	1.644632	64.463182	0.01551273	0.608039	39.196118	0.02551273	2.56	0.275637	0.55	50

2.00 %
ANNUAL

YR	Amount Of 1	Amount Of 1 Per Period	Sinking Fund Payment	Present Worth Of 1	Present Worth Of 1 Per Period	Periodic Payment To Amortize 1	Constant Annual Percent	Total Interest	Annual Add-on Rate	YR
	What a single $1 deposit grows to in the future. The deposit is made at the beginning of the first period.	What a series of $1 deposits grow to in the future. A deposit is made at the end of each period.	The amount to be deposited at the end of each period that grows to $1 in the future.	What $1 to be paid in the future is worth today. Value today of a single payment tomorrow.	What $1 to be paid at the end of each period is worth today. Value today of a series of payments tomorrow.	The mortgage payment to amortize a loan of $1. An annuity certain, payable at the end of each period, worth $1 today.	The annual payment, including interest and principal, to amortize completely a loan of $100.	The total interest paid over the term on a loan of $1. The loan is amortized by regular periodic payments.	The average annual interest rate on a loan that is completely amortized by regular periodic payments.	
	$S=(1+i)^n$	$Sa=\frac{(1+i)^n-1}{i}$	$\frac{1}{Sa}=\frac{i}{(1+i)^n-1}$	$V^n=\frac{1}{(1+i)^n}$	$An=\frac{1-V^n}{i}$	$\frac{1}{An}=\frac{i}{1-V^n}$				
1	1.020000	1.000000	1.00000000	0.980392	0.980392	1.02000000	102.00	0.020000	2.00	1
2	1.040400	2.020000	0.49504950	0.961169	1.941561	0.51504950	51.51	0.030099	1.50	2
3	1.061208	3.060400	0.32675467	0.942322	2.883883	0.34675467	34.68	0.040264	1.34	3
4	1.082432	4.121608	0.24262375	0.923845	3.807729	0.26262375	26.27	0.050495	1.26	4
5	1.104081	5.204040	0.19215839	0.905731	4.713460	0.21215839	21.22	0.060792	1.22	5
6	1.126162	6.308121	0.15852581	0.887971	5.601431	0.17852581	17.86	0.071155	1.19	6
7	1.148686	7.434283	0.13451196	0.870560	6.471991	0.15451196	15.46	0.081584	1.17	7
8	1.171659	8.582969	0.11650980	0.853490	7.325481	0.13650980	13.66	0.092078	1.15	8
9	1.195093	9.754628	0.10251544	0.836755	8.162237	0.12251544	12.26	0.102639	1.14	9
10	1.218994	10.949721	0.09132653	0.820348	8.982585	0.11132653	11.14	0.113265	1.13	10
11	1.243374	12.168715	0.08217794	0.804263	9.786848	0.10217794	10.22	0.123957	1.13	11
12	1.268242	13.412090	0.07455960	0.788493	10.575341	0.09455960	9.46	0.134715	1.12	12
13	1.293607	14.680332	0.06811835	0.773033	11.348374	0.08811835	8.82	0.145539	1.12	13
14	1.319479	15.973938	0.06260197	0.757875	12.106249	0.08260197	8.27	0.156428	1.12	14
15	1.345868	17.293417	0.05782547	0.743015	12.849264	0.07782547	7.79	0.167382	1.12	15
16	1.372786	18.639285	0.05365013	0.728446	13.577709	0.07365013	7.37	0.178402	1.12	16
17	1.400241	20.012071	0.04996984	0.714163	14.291872	0.06996984	7.00	0.189487	1.11	17
18	1.428246	21.412312	0.04670210	0.700159	14.992031	0.06670210	6.68	0.200638	1.11	18
19	1.456811	22.840559	0.04378177	0.686431	15.678462	0.06378177	6.38	0.211854	1.12	19
20	1.485947	24.297370	0.04115672	0.672971	16.351433	0.06115672	6.12	0.223134	1.12	20
21	1.515666	25.783317	0.03878477	0.659776	17.011209	0.05878477	5.88	0.234480	1.12	21
22	1.545980	27.298984	0.03663140	0.646839	17.658048	0.05663140	5.67	0.245891	1.12	22
23	1.576899	28.844963	0.03466810	0.634156	18.292204	0.05466810	5.47	0.257366	1.12	23
24	1.608437	30.421862	0.03287110	0.621721	18.913926	0.05287110	5.29	0.268906	1.12	24
25	1.640606	32.030300	0.03122044	0.609531	19.523456	0.05122044	5.13	0.280511	1.12	25
26	1.673418	33.670906	0.02969923	0.597579	20.121036	0.04969923	4.97	0.292180	1.12	26
27	1.706886	35.344324	0.02829309	0.585862	20.706898	0.04829309	4.83	0.303913	1.13	27
28	1.741024	37.051210	0.02698967	0.574375	21.281272	0.04698967	4.70	0.315711	1.13	28
29	1.775845	38.792235	0.02577836	0.563112	21.844385	0.04577836	4.58	0.327572	1.13	29
30	1.811362	40.568079	0.02464992	0.552071	22.396456	0.04464992	4.47	0.339498	1.13	30
31	1.847589	42.379441	0.02359635	0.541246	22.937702	0.04359635	4.36	0.351487	1.13	31
32	1.884541	44.227030	0.02261061	0.530633	23.468335	0.04261061	4.27	0.363539	1.14	32
33	1.922231	46.111570	0.02168653	0.520229	23.988564	0.04168653	4.17	0.375656	1.14	33
34	1.960676	48.033802	0.02081867	0.510028	24.498592	0.04081867	4.09	0.387835	1.14	34
35	1.999890	49.994478	0.02000221	0.500028	24.998619	0.04000221	4.01	0.400077	1.14	35
36	2.039887	51.994367	0.01923285	0.490223	25.488842	0.03923285	3.93	0.412383	1.15	36
37	2.080685	54.034255	0.01850678	0.480611	25.969453	0.03850678	3.86	0.424751	1.15	37
38	2.122299	56.114940	0.01782057	0.471187	26.440641	0.03782057	3.79	0.437182	1.15	38
39	2.164745	58.237238	0.01717114	0.461948	26.902589	0.03717114	3.72	0.449675	1.15	39
40	2.208040	60.401983	0.01655575	0.452890	27.355479	0.03655575	3.66	0.462230	1.16	40
41	2.252200	62.610023	0.01597188	0.444010	27.799489	0.03597188	3.60	0.474847	1.16	41
42	2.297244	64.862223	0.01541729	0.435304	28.234794	0.03541729	3.55	0.487526	1.16	42
43	2.343189	67.159468	0.01488993	0.426769	28.661562	0.03488993	3.49	0.500267	1.16	43
44	2.390053	69.502657	0.01438794	0.418401	29.079963	0.03438794	3.44	0.513069	1.17	44
45	2.437854	71.892710	0.01390962	0.410197	29.490160	0.03390962	3.40	0.525933	1.17	45
46	2.486611	74.330564	0.01345342	0.402154	29.892314	0.03345342	3.35	0.538857	1.17	46
47	2.536344	76.817176	0.01301792	0.394268	30.286582	0.03301792	3.31	0.551842	1.17	47
48	2.587070	79.353519	0.01260184	0.386538	30.673120	0.03260184	3.27	0.564888	1.18	48
49	2.638812	81.940590	0.01220396	0.378958	31.052078	0.03220396	3.23	0.577994	1.18	49
50	2.691588	84.579401	0.01182321	0.371528	31.423606	0.03182321	3.19	0.591160	1.18	50

3.00 % ANNUAL

YR	Amount Of 1	Amount Of 1 Per Period	Sinking Fund Payment	Present Worth Of 1	Present Worth Of 1 Per Period	Periodic Payment To Amortize 1	Constant Annual Percent	Total Interest	Annual Add-on Rate	YR
	What a single $1 deposit grows to in the future. The deposit is made at the beginning of the first period.	What a series of $1 deposits grow to in the future. A deposit is made at the end of each period.	The amount to be deposited at the end of each period that grows to $1 in the future.	What $1 to be paid in the future is worth today. Value today of a single payment tomorrow.	What $1 to be paid at the end of each period is worth today. Value today of a series of payments tomorrow.	The mortgage payment to amortize a loan of $1. An annuity certain, payable at the end of each period, worth $1 today.	The annual payment, including interest and principal, to amortize completely a loan of $100.	The total interest paid over the term on a loan of $1. The loan is amortized by regular periodic payments.	The average annual interest rate on a loan that is completely amortized by regular periodic payments.	
	$S=(1+i)^n$	$S_{\overline{n}}=\frac{(1+i)^n-1}{i}$	$\frac{1}{S_{\overline{n}}}=\frac{i}{(1+i)^n-1}$	$V^n=\frac{1}{(1+i)^n}$	$A_{\overline{n}}=\frac{1-V^n}{i}$	$\frac{1}{A_{\overline{n}}}=\frac{i}{1-V^n}$				
1	1.030000	1.000000	1.00000000	0.970874	0.970874	1.03000000	103.00	0.030000	3.00	1
2	1.060900	2.030000	0.49261084	0.942596	1.913470	0.52261084	52.27	0.045222	2.26	2
3	1.092727	3.090900	0.32353036	0.915142	2.828611	0.35353036	35.36	0.060591	2.02	3
4	1.125509	4.183627	0.23902705	0.888487	3.717098	0.26902705	26.91	0.076108	1.90	4
5	1.159274	5.309136	0.18835457	0.862609	4.579707	0.21835457	21.84	0.091773	1.84	5
6	1.194052	6.468410	0.15459750	0.837484	5.417191	0.18459750	18.46	0.107585	1.79	6
7	1.229874	7.662462	0.13050635	0.813092	6.230283	0.16050635	16.06	0.123544	1.76	7
8	1.266770	8.892336	0.11245639	0.789409	7.019692	0.14245639	14.25	0.139651	1.75	8
9	1.304773	10.159106	0.09843386	0.766417	7.786109	0.12843386	12.85	0.155905	1.73	9
10	1.343916	11.463879	0.08723051	0.744094	8.530203	0.11723051	11.73	0.172305	1.72	10
11	1.384234	12.807796	0.07807745	0.722421	9.252624	0.10807745	10.81	0.188852	1.72	11
12	1.425761	14.192030	0.07046209	0.701380	9.954004	0.10046209	10.05	0.205545	1.71	12
13	1.468534	15.617790	0.06402954	0.680951	10.634955	0.09402954	9.41	0.222384	1.71	13
14	1.512590	17.086324	0.05852634	0.661118	11.296073	0.08852634	8.86	0.239369	1.71	14
15	1.557967	18.598914	0.05376658	0.641862	11.937935	0.08376658	8.38	0.256499	1.71	15
16	1.604706	20.156881	0.04961085	0.623167	12.561102	0.07961085	7.97	0.273774	1.71	16
17	1.652848	21.761588	0.04595253	0.605016	13.166118	0.07595253	7.60	0.291193	1.71	17
18	1.702433	23.414435	0.04270870	0.587395	13.753513	0.07270870	7.28	0.308757	1.72	18
19	1.753506	25.116868	0.03981388	0.570286	14.323799	0.06981388	6.99	0.326464	1.72	19
20	1.806111	26.870374	0.03721571	0.553676	14.877475	0.06721571	6.73	0.344314	1.72	20
21	1.860295	28.676486	0.03487178	0.537549	15.415024	0.06487178	6.49	0.362307	1.73	21
22	1.916103	30.536780	0.03274739	0.521893	15.936917	0.06274739	6.28	0.380443	1.73	22
23	1.973587	32.452884	0.03081390	0.506692	16.443608	0.06081390	6.09	0.398720	1.73	23
24	2.032794	34.426470	0.02904742	0.491934	16.935542	0.05904742	5.91	0.417138	1.74	24
25	2.093778	36.459264	0.02742787	0.477606	17.413148	0.05742787	5.75	0.435697	1.74	25
26	2.156591	38.553042	0.02593829	0.463695	17.876842	0.05593829	5.60	0.454396	1.75	26
27	2.221289	40.709634	0.02456421	0.450189	18.327031	0.05456421	5.46	0.473234	1.75	27
28	2.287928	42.930923	0.02329323	0.437077	18.764108	0.05329323	5.33	0.492211	1.76	28
29	2.356566	45.218850	0.02211467	0.424346	19.188455	0.05211467	5.22	0.511325	1.76	29
30	2.427262	47.575416	0.02101926	0.411987	19.600441	0.05101926	5.11	0.530578	1.77	30
31	2.500080	50.002678	0.01999893	0.399987	20.000428	0.04999893	5.00	0.549967	1.77	31
32	2.575083	52.502759	0.01904662	0.388337	20.388766	0.04904662	4.91	0.569492	1.78	32
33	2.652335	55.077841	0.01815612	0.377026	20.765792	0.04815612	4.82	0.589152	1.79	33
34	2.731905	57.730177	0.01732196	0.366045	21.131837	0.04732196	4.74	0.608947	1.79	34
35	2.813862	60.462082	0.01653929	0.355383	21.487220	0.04653929	4.66	0.628875	1.80	35
36	2.898278	63.275944	0.01580379	0.345032	21.832252	0.04580379	4.59	0.648937	1.80	36
37	2.985227	66.174223	0.01511162	0.334983	22.167235	0.04511162	4.52	0.669130	1.81	37
38	3.074783	69.159449	0.01445934	0.325226	22.492462	0.04445934	4.45	0.689455	1.81	38
39	3.167027	72.234233	0.01384385	0.315754	22.808215	0.04384385	4.39	0.709910	1.82	39
40	3.262038	75.401260	0.01326238	0.306557	23.114772	0.04326238	4.33	0.730495	1.83	40
41	3.359899	78.663298	0.01271241	0.297628	23.412400	0.04271241	4.28	0.751209	1.83	41
42	3.460696	82.023196	0.01219167	0.288959	23.701359	0.04219167	4.22	0.772050	1.84	42
43	3.564517	85.483892	0.01169811	0.280543	23.981902	0.04169811	4.17	0.793019	1.84	43
44	3.671452	89.048409	0.01122985	0.272372	24.254274	0.04122985	4.13	0.814113	1.85	44
45	3.781596	92.719861	0.01078518	0.264439	24.518713	0.04078518	4.08	0.835333	1.86	45
46	3.895044	96.501457	0.01036254	0.256737	24.775449	0.04036254	4.04	0.856677	1.86	46
47	4.011895	100.396501	0.00996051	0.249259	25.024708	0.03996051	4.00	0.878144	1.87	47
48	4.132252	104.408396	0.00957777	0.241999	25.266707	0.03957777	3.96	0.899733	1.87	48
49	4.256219	108.540648	0.00921314	0.234950	25.501657	0.03921314	3.93	0.921444	1.88	49
50	4.383906	112.796867	0.00886549	0.228107	25.729764	0.03886549	3.89	0.943275	1.89	50

COMPOUND INTEREST AND ANNUITY TABLE

4.00 %
ANNUAL

YR	Amount Of 1 What a single $1 deposit grows to in the future. The deposit is made at the beginning of the first period. $S=(1+i)^n$	Amount Of 1 Per Period What a series of $1 deposits grow to in the future. A deposit is made at the end of each period. $S_n=\frac{(1+i)^n-1}{i}$	Sinking Fund Payment The amount to be deposited at the end of each period that grows to $1 in the future. $\frac{1}{S_n}=\frac{i}{(1+i)^n-1}$	Present Worth Of 1 What $1 to be paid in the future is worth today. Value today of a single payment tomorrow. $V^n=\frac{1}{(1+i)^n}$	Present Worth Of 1 Per Period What $1 to be paid at the end of each period is worth today. Value today of a series of payments tomorrow. $A_n=\frac{1-V^n}{i}$	Periodic Payment To Amortize 1 The mortgage payment to amortize a loan of $1. An annuity certain, payable at the end of each period, worth $1 today. $\frac{1}{A_n}=\frac{i}{1-V^n}$	Constant Annual Percent The annual payment, including interest and principal, to amortize completely a loan of $100.	Total Interest The total interest paid over the term on a loan of $1. The loan is amortized by regular periodic payments.	Annual Add-on Rate The average annual interest rate on a loan that is completely amortized by regular periodic payments.	YR
1	1.040000	1.000000	1.00000000	0.961538	0.961538	1.04000000	104.00	0.040000	4.00	1
2	1.081600	2.040000	0.49019608	0.924556	1.886095	0.53019608	53.02	0.060392	3.02	2
3	1.124864	3.121600	0.32034854	0.888996	2.775091	0.36034854	36.04	0.081046	2.70	3
4	1.169859	4.246464	0.23549005	0.854804	3.629895	0.27549005	27.55	0.101960	2.55	4
5	1.216653	5.416323	0.18462711	0.821927	4.451822	0.22462711	22.47	0.123136	2.46	5
6	1.265319	6.632975	0.15076190	0.790315	5.242137	0.19076190	19.08	0.144571	2.41	6
7	1.315932	7.898294	0.12660961	0.759918	6.002055	0.16660961	16.67	0.166267	2.38	7
8	1.368569	9.214226	0.10852783	0.730690	6.732745	0.14852783	14.86	0.188223	2.35	8
9	1.423312	10.582795	0.09449299	0.702587	7.435332	0.13449299	13.45	0.210437	2.34	9
10	1.480244	12.006107	0.08329094	0.675564	8.110896	0.12329094	12.33	0.232909	2.33	10
11	1.539454	13.486351	0.07414904	0.649581	8.760477	0.11414904	11.42	0.255639	2.32	11
12	1.601032	15.025805	0.06655217	0.624597	9.385074	0.10655217	10.66	0.278626	2.32	12
13	1.665074	16.626838	0.06014373	0.600574	9.985648	0.10014373	10.02	0.301868	2.32	13
14	1.731676	18.291911	0.05466897	0.577475	10.563123	0.09466897	9.47	0.325366	2.32	14
15	1.800944	20.023588	0.04994110	0.555265	11.118387	0.08994110	9.00	0.349117	2.33	15
16	1.872981	21.824531	0.04582000	0.533908	11.652296	0.08582000	8.59	0.373120	2.33	16
17	1.947900	23.697512	0.04219852	0.513373	12.165669	0.08219852	8.22	0.397375	2.34	17
18	2.025817	25.645413	0.03899333	0.493628	12.659297	0.07899333	7.90	0.421880	2.34	18
19	2.106849	27.671229	0.03613862	0.474642	13.133939	0.07613862	7.62	0.446634	2.35	19
20	2.191123	29.778079	0.03358175	0.456387	13.590326	0.07358175	7.36	0.471635	2.36	20
21	2.278768	31.969202	0.03128011	0.438834	14.029160	0.07128011	7.13	0.496882	2.37	21
22	2.369919	34.247970	0.02919881	0.421955	14.451115	0.06919881	6.92	0.522374	2.37	22
23	2.464716	36.617889	0.02730906	0.405726	14.856842	0.06730906	6.74	0.548108	2.38	23
24	2.563304	39.082604	0.02558683	0.390121	15.246963	0.06558683	6.56	0.574084	2.39	24
25	2.665836	41.645908	0.02401196	0.375117	15.622080	0.06401196	6.41	0.600299	2.40	25
26	2.772470	44.311745	0.02256738	0.360689	15.982769	0.06256738	6.26	0.626752	2.41	26
27	2.883369	47.084214	0.02123854	0.346817	16.329586	0.06123854	6.13	0.653441	2.42	27
28	2.998703	49.967583	0.02001298	0.333477	16.663063	0.06001298	6.01	0.680363	2.43	28
29	3.118651	52.966286	0.01887993	0.320651	16.983715	0.05887993	5.89	0.707518	2.44	29
30	3.243398	56.084938	0.01783010	0.308319	17.292033	0.05783010	5.79	0.734903	2.45	30
31	3.373133	59.328335	0.01685535	0.296460	17.588494	0.05685535	5.69	0.762516	2.46	31
32	3.508059	62.701469	0.01594859	0.285058	17.873551	0.05594859	5.60	0.790355	2.47	32
33	3.648381	66.209527	0.01510357	0.274094	18.147646	0.05510357	5.52	0.818418	2.48	33
34	3.794316	69.857909	0.01431477	0.263552	18.411198	0.05431477	5.44	0.846702	2.49	34
35	3.946089	73.652225	0.01357732	0.253415	18.664613	0.05357732	5.36	0.875206	2.50	35
36	4.103933	77.598314	0.01288688	0.243669	18.908282	0.05288688	5.29	0.903928	2.51	36
37	4.268090	81.702246	0.01223957	0.234297	19.142579	0.05223957	5.23	0.932864	2.52	37
38	4.438813	85.970336	0.01163192	0.225285	19.367864	0.05163192	5.17	0.962013	2.53	38
39	4.616366	90.409150	0.01106083	0.216621	19.584485	0.05106083	5.11	0.991372	2.54	39
40	4.801021	95.025516	0.01052349	0.208289	19.792774	0.05052349	5.06	1.020940	2.55	40
41	4.993061	99.826536	0.01001738	0.200278	19.993052	0.05001738	5.01	1.050712	2.56	41
42	5.192784	104.819598	0.00954020	0.192575	20.185627	0.04954020	4.96	1.080688	2.57	42
43	5.400495	110.012382	0.00908989	0.185168	20.370795	0.04908989	4.91	1.110865	2.58	43
44	5.616515	115.412877	0.00866454	0.178046	20.548841	0.04866454	4.87	1.141240	2.59	44
45	5.841176	121.029392	0.00826246	0.171198	20.720040	0.04826246	4.83	1.171811	2.60	45
46	6.074823	126.870568	0.00788205	0.164614	20.884654	0.04788205	4.79	1.202574	2.61	46
47	6.317816	132.945390	0.00752189	0.158283	21.042936	0.04752189	4.76	1.233529	2.62	47
48	6.570528	139.263206	0.00718065	0.152195	21.195131	0.04718065	4.72	1.264671	2.63	48
49	6.833349	145.833734	0.00685712	0.146341	21.341472	0.04685712	4.69	1.295999	2.64	49
50	7.106683	152.667084	0.00655020	0.140713	21.482185	0.04655020	4.66	1.327510	2.66	50

COMPOUND INTEREST AND ANNUITY TABLE

5.00 % ANNUAL

YR	Amount Of 1	Amount Of 1 Per Period	Sinking Fund Payment	Present Worth Of 1	Present Worth Of 1 Per Period	Periodic Payment To Amortize 1	Constant Annual Percent	Total Interest	Annual Add-on Rate	YR
	What a single $1 deposit grows to in the future. The deposit is made at the beginning of the first period.	What a series of $1 deposits grow to in the future. A deposit is made at the end of each period.	The amount to be deposited at the end of each period that grows to $1 in the future.	What $1 to be paid in the future is worth today. Value today of a single payment tomorrow.	What $1 to be paid at the end of each period is worth today. Value today of a series of payments tomorrow.	The mortgage payment to amortize a loan of $1. An annuity certain, payable at the end of each period, worth $1 today.	The annual payment, including interest and principal, to amortize completely a loan of $100.	The total interest paid over the term on a loan of $1. The loan is amortized by regular periodic payments.	The average annual interest rate on a loan that is completely amortized by regular periodic payments.	
	$S=(1+i)^n$	$S_n=\frac{(1+i)^n-1}{i}$	$\frac{1}{S_n}=\frac{i}{(1+i)^n-1}$	$V^n=\frac{1}{(1+i)^n}$	$A_n=\frac{1-V^n}{i}$	$\frac{1}{A_n}=\frac{i}{1-V^n}$				
1	1.050000	1.000000	1.00000000	0.952381	0.952381	1.05000000	105.00	0.050000	5.00	**1**
2	1.102500	2.050000	0.48780488	0.907029	1.859410	0.53780488	53.79	0.075610	3.78	**2**
3	1.157625	3.152500	0.31720856	0.863838	2.723248	0.36720856	36.73	0.101626	3.39	**3**
4	1.215506	4.310125	0.23201183	0.822702	3.545951	0.28201183	28.21	0.128047	3.20	**4**
5	1.276282	5.525631	0.18097480	0.783526	4.329477	0.23097480	23.10	0.154874	3.10	**5**
6	1.340096	6.801913	0.14701747	0.746215	5.075692	0.19701747	19.71	0.182105	3.04	**6**
7	1.407100	8.142008	0.12281982	0.710681	5.786373	0.17281982	17.29	0.209739	3.00	**7**
8	1.477455	9.549109	0.10472181	0.676839	6.463213	0.15472181	15.48	0.237775	2.97	**8**
9	1.551328	11.026564	0.09069008	0.644609	7.107822	0.14069008	14.07	0.266211	2.96	**9**
10	1.628895	12.577893	0.07950457	0.613913	7.721735	0.12950457	12.96	0.295046	2.95	**10**
11	1.710339	14.206787	0.07038889	0.584679	8.306414	0.12038889	12.04	0.324278	2.95	**11**
12	1.795856	15.917127	0.06282541	0.556837	8.863252	0.11282541	11.29	0.353905	2.95	**12**
13	1.885649	17.712983	0.05645577	0.530321	9.393573	0.10645577	10.65	0.383925	2.95	**13**
14	1.979932	19.598632	0.05102397	0.505068	9.898641	0.10102397	10.11	0.414336	2.96	**14**
15	2.078928	21.578564	0.04634229	0.481017	10.379658	0.09634229	9.64	0.445134	2.97	**15**
16	2.182875	23.657492	0.04226991	0.458112	10.837770	0.09226991	9.23	0.476319	2.98	**16**
17	2.292018	25.840366	0.03869914	0.436297	11.274066	0.08869914	8.87	0.507885	2.99	**17**
18	2.406619	28.132385	0.03554622	0.415521	11.689587	0.08554622	8.56	0.539832	3.00	**18**
19	2.526950	30.539004	0.03274501	0.395734	12.085321	0.08274501	8.28	0.572155	3.01	**19**
20	2.653298	33.065954	0.03024259	0.376889	12.462210	0.08024259	8.03	0.604852	3.02	**20**
21	2.785963	35.719252	0.02799611	0.358942	12.821153	0.07799611	7.80	0.637918	3.04	**21**
22	2.925261	38.505214	0.02597051	0.341850	13.163003	0.07597051	7.60	0.671351	3.05	**22**
23	3.071524	41.430475	0.02413682	0.325571	13.488574	0.07413682	7.42	0.705147	3.07	**23**
24	3.225100	44.501999	0.02247090	0.310068	13.798642	0.07247090	7.25	0.739302	3.08	**24**
25	3.386355	47.727099	0.02095246	0.295303	14.093945	0.07095246	7.10	0.773811	3.10	**25**
26	3.555673	51.113454	0.01956432	0.281241	14.375185	0.06956432	6.96	0.808672	3.11	**26**
27	3.733456	54.669126	0.01829186	0.267848	14.643034	0.06829186	6.83	0.843880	3.13	**27**
28	3.920129	58.402583	0.01712253	0.255094	14.898127	0.06712253	6.72	0.879431	3.14	**28**
29	4.116136	62.322712	0.01604551	0.242946	15.141074	0.06604551	6.61	0.915320	3.16	**29**
30	4.321942	66.438848	0.01505144	0.231377	15.372451	0.06505144	6.51	0.951543	3.17	**30**
31	4.538039	70.760790	0.01413212	0.220359	15.592811	0.06413212	6.42	0.988096	3.19	**31**
32	4.764941	75.298829	0.01328042	0.209866	15.802677	0.06328042	6.33	1.024973	3.20	**32**
33	5.003189	80.063771	0.01249004	0.199873	16.002549	0.06249004	6.25	1.062171	3.22	**33**
34	5.253348	85.066959	0.01175545	0.190355	16.192904	0.06175545	6.18	1.099685	3.23	**34**
35	5.516015	90.320307	0.01107171	0.181290	16.374194	0.06107171	6.11	1.137510	3.25	**35**
36	5.791816	95.836323	0.01043446	0.172657	16.546852	0.06043446	6.05	1.175640	3.27	**36**
37	6.081407	101.628139	0.00983979	0.164436	16.711287	0.05983979	5.99	1.214072	3.28	**37**
38	6.385477	107.709546	0.00928423	0.156605	16.867893	0.05928423	5.93	1.252801	3.30	**38**
39	6.704751	114.095023	0.00876462	0.149148	17.017041	0.05876462	5.88	1.291820	3.31	**39**
40	7.039989	120.799774	0.00827816	0.142046	17.159086	0.05827816	5.83	1.331126	3.33	**40**
41	7.391988	127.839763	0.00782229	0.135282	17.294368	0.05782229	5.79	1.370714	3.34	**41**
42	7.761588	135.231751	0.00739471	0.128840	17.423208	0.05739471	5.74	1.410578	3.36	**42**
43	8.149667	142.993339	0.00699333	0.122704	17.545912	0.05699333	5.70	1.450713	3.37	**43**
44	8.557150	151.143006	0.00661625	0.116861	17.662773	0.05661625	5.67	1.491115	3.39	**44**
45	8.985008	159.700156	0.00626173	0.111297	17.774070	0.05626173	5.63	1.531778	3.40	**45**
46	9.434258	168.685164	0.00592820	0.105997	17.880066	0.05592820	5.60	1.572697	3.42	**46**
47	9.905971	178.119422	0.00561421	0.100949	17.981016	0.05561421	5.57	1.613868	3.43	**47**
48	10.401270	188.025393	0.00531843	0.096142	18.077158	0.05531843	5.54	1.655285	3.45	**48**
49	10.921333	198.426663	0.00503965	0.091564	18.168722	0.05503965	5.51	1.696943	3.46	**49**
50	11.467400	209.347996	0.00477674	0.087204	18.255925	0.05477674	5.48	1.738837	3.48	**50**

COMPOUND INTEREST AND ANNUITY TABLE — 6.00 % ANNUAL

YR	Amount Of 1 What a single $1 deposit grows to in the future. The deposit is made at the beginning of the first period. $S=(1+i)^n$	Amount Of 1 Per Period What a series of $1 deposits grow to in the future. A deposit is made at the end of each period. $S_{\overline{n}}=\frac{(1+i)^n-1}{i}$	Sinking Fund Payment The amount to be deposited at the end of each period that grows to $1 in the future. $\frac{1}{S_{\overline{n}}}=\frac{i}{(1+i)^n-1}$	Present Worth Of 1 What $1 to be paid in the future is worth today. Value today of a single payment tomorrow. $V^n=\frac{1}{(1+i)^n}$	Present Worth Of 1 Per Period What $1 to be paid at the end of each period is worth today. Value today of a series of payments tomorrow. $A_{\overline{n}}=\frac{1-V^n}{i}$	Periodic Payment To Amortize 1 The mortgage payment to amortize a loan of $1. An annuity certain, payable at the end of each period, worth $1 today. $\frac{1}{A_{\overline{n}}}=\frac{i}{1-V^n}$	Constant Annual Percent The annual payment, including interest and principal, to amortize completely a loan of $100.	Total Interest The total interest paid over the term on a loan of $1. The loan is amortized by regular periodic payments.	Annual Add-on Rate The average annual interest rate on a loan that is completely amortized by regular periodic payments.	YR
1	1.060000	1.000000	1.00000000	0.943396	0.943396	1.06000000	106.00	0.060000	6.00	1
2	1.123600	2.060000	0.48543689	0.889996	1.833393	0.54543689	54.55	0.090874	4.54	2
3	1.191016	3.183600	0.31410981	0.839619	2.673012	0.37410981	37.42	0.122329	4.08	3
4	1.262477	4.374616	0.22859149	0.792094	3.465106	0.28859149	28.86	0.154366	3.86	4
5	1.338226	5.637093	0.17739640	0.747258	4.212364	0.23739640	23.74	0.186982	3.74	5
6	1.418519	6.975319	0.14336263	0.704961	4.917324	0.20336263	20.34	0.220176	3.67	6
7	1.503630	8.393838	0.11913502	0.665057	5.582381	0.17913502	17.92	0.253945	3.63	7
8	1.593848	9.897468	0.10103594	0.627412	6.209794	0.16103594	16.11	0.288288	3.60	8
9	1.689479	11.491316	0.08702224	0.591898	6.801692	0.14702224	14.71	0.323200	3.59	9
10	1.790848	13.180795	0.07586796	0.558395	7.360087	0.13586796	13.59	0.358680	3.59	10
11	1.898299	14.971643	0.06679294	0.526788	7.886875	0.12679294	12.68	0.394722	3.59	11
12	2.012196	16.869941	0.05927703	0.496969	8.383844	0.11927703	11.93	0.431324	3.59	12
13	2.132928	18.882138	0.05296011	0.468839	8.852683	0.11296011	11.30	0.468481	3.60	13
14	2.260904	21.015066	0.04758491	0.442301	9.294984	0.10758491	10.76	0.506189	3.62	14
15	2.396558	23.275970	0.04296276	0.417265	9.712249	0.10296276	10.30	0.544441	3.63	15
16	2.540352	25.672528	0.03895214	0.393646	10.105895	0.09895214	9.90	0.583234	3.65	16
17	2.692773	28.212880	0.03544480	0.371364	10.477260	0.09544480	9.55	0.622562	3.66	17
18	2.854339	30.905653	0.03235654	0.350344	10.827603	0.09235654	9.24	0.662418	3.68	18
19	3.025600	33.759992	0.02962086	0.330513	11.158116	0.08962086	8.97	0.702796	3.70	19
20	3.207135	36.785591	0.02718456	0.311805	11.469921	0.08718456	8.72	0.743691	3.72	20
21	3.399564	39.992727	0.02500455	0.294155	11.764077	0.08500455	8.51	0.785095	3.74	21
22	3.603537	43.392290	0.02304557	0.277505	12.041582	0.08304557	8.31	0.827003	3.76	22
23	3.819750	46.995828	0.02127848	0.261797	12.303379	0.08127848	8.13	0.869405	3.78	23
24	4.048935	50.815577	0.01967900	0.246979	12.550358	0.07967900	7.97	0.912296	3.80	24
25	4.291871	54.864512	0.01822672	0.232999	12.783356	0.07822672	7.83	0.955668	3.82	25
26	4.549383	59.156383	0.01690435	0.219810	13.003166	0.07690435	7.70	0.999513	3.84	26
27	4.822346	63.705766	0.01569717	0.207368	13.210534	0.07569717	7.57	1.043823	3.87	27
28	5.111687	68.528112	0.01459255	0.195630	13.406164	0.07459255	7.46	1.088591	3.89	28
29	5.418388	73.639798	0.01357961	0.184557	13.590721	0.07357961	7.36	1.133809	3.91	29
30	5.743491	79.058186	0.01264891	0.174110	13.764831	0.07264891	7.27	1.179467	3.93	30
31	6.088101	84.801677	0.01179222	0.164255	13.929086	0.07179222	7.18	1.225559	3.95	31
32	6.453387	90.889778	0.01100234	0.154957	14.084043	0.07100234	7.11	1.272075	3.98	32
33	6.840590	97.343165	0.01027293	0.146186	14.230230	0.07027293	7.03	1.319007	4.00	33
34	7.251025	104.183755	0.00959843	0.137912	14.368141	0.06959843	6.96	1.366346	4.02	34
35	7.686087	111.434780	0.00897386	0.130105	14.498246	0.06897386	6.90	1.414085	4.04	35
36	8.147252	119.120867	0.00839483	0.122741	14.620987	0.06839483	6.84	1.462214	4.06	36
37	8.636087	127.268119	0.00785743	0.115793	14.736780	0.06785743	6.79	1.510725	4.08	37
38	9.154252	135.904206	0.00735812	0.109239	14.846019	0.06735812	6.74	1.559609	4.10	38
39	9.703507	145.058458	0.00689377	0.103056	14.949075	0.06689377	6.69	1.608857	4.13	39
40	10.285718	154.761966	0.00646154	0.097222	15.046297	0.06646154	6.65	1.658461	4.15	40
41	10.902861	165.047684	0.00605886	0.091719	15.138016	0.06605886	6.61	1.708413	4.17	41
42	11.557033	175.950545	0.00568342	0.086527	15.224543	0.06568342	6.57	1.758703	4.19	42
43	12.250455	187.507577	0.00533312	0.081630	15.306173	0.06533312	6.54	1.809324	4.21	43
44	12.985482	199.758032	0.00500606	0.077009	15.383182	0.06500606	6.51	1.860266	4.23	44
45	13.764611	212.743514	0.00470050	0.072650	15.455832	0.06470050	6.48	1.911522	4.25	45
46	14.590487	226.508125	0.00441485	0.068538	15.524370	0.06441485	6.45	1.963083	4.27	46
47	15.465917	241.098612	0.00414768	0.064658	15.589028	0.06414768	6.42	2.014941	4.29	47
48	16.393872	256.564529	0.00389765	0.060998	15.650027	0.06389765	6.39	2.067087	4.31	48
49	17.377504	272.958401	0.00366356	0.057546	15.707572	0.06366356	6.37	2.119515	4.33	49
50	18.420154	290.335905	0.00344429	0.054288	15.761861	0.06344429	6.35	2.172214	4.34	50

COMPOUND INTEREST AND ANNUITY TABLE

7.00 %
ANNUAL

YR	Amount Of 1	Amount Of 1 Per Period	Sinking Fund Payment	Present Worth Of 1	Present Worth Of 1 Per Period	Periodic Payment To Amortize 1	Constant Annual Percent	Total Interest	Annual Add-on Rate	YR
	What a single $1 deposit grows to in the future. The deposit is made at the beginning of the first period.	What a series of $1 deposits grow to in the future. A deposit is made at the end of each period.	The amount to be deposited at the end of each period that grows to $1 in the future.	What $1 to be paid in the future is worth today. Value today of a single payment tomorrow.	What $1 to be paid at the end of each period is worth today. Value today of a series of payments tomorrow.	The mortgage payment to amortize a loan of $1. An annuity certain, payable at the end of each period, worth $1 today.	The annual payment, including interest and principal, to amortize completely a loan of $100	The total interest paid over the term on a loan of $1. The loan is amortized by regular periodic payments.	The average annual interest rate on a loan that is completely amortized by regular periodic payments.	
	$S=(1+i)^n$	$S_{\overline{n}}=\frac{(1+i)^n-1}{i}$	$\frac{1}{S_{\overline{n}}}=\frac{i}{(1+i)^n-1}$	$V^n=\frac{1}{(1+i)^n}$	$A_{\overline{n}}=\frac{1-V^n}{i}$	$\frac{1}{A_{\overline{n}}}=\frac{i}{1-V^n}$				
1	1.070000	1.000000	1.00000000	0.934579	0.934579	1.07000000	107.00	0.070000	7.00	1
2	1.144900	2.070000	0.48309179	0.873439	1.808018	0.55309179	55.31	0.106184	5.31	2
3	1.225043	3.214900	0.31105167	0.816298	2.624316	0.38105167	38.11	0.143155	4.77	3
4	1.310796	4.439943	0.22522812	0.762895	3.387211	0.29522812	29.53	0.180912	4.52	4
5	1.402552	5.750739	0.17389069	0.712986	4.100197	0.24389069	24.39	0.219453	4.39	5
6	1.500730	7.153291	0.13979580	0.666342	4.766540	0.20979580	20.98	0.258775	4.31	6
7	1.605781	8.654021	0.11555322	0.622750	5.389289	0.18555322	18.56	0.298873	4.27	7
8	1.718186	10.259803	0.09746776	0.582009	5.971299	0.16746776	16.75	0.339742	4.25	8
9	1.838459	11.977989	0.08348647	0.543934	6.515232	0.15348647	15.35	0.381378	4.24	9
10	1.967151	13.816448	0.07237750	0.508349	7.023582	0.14237750	14.24	0.423775	4.24	10
11	2.104852	15.783599	0.06335690	0.475093	7.498674	0.13335690	13.34	0.466926	4.24	11
12	2.252192	17.888451	0.05590199	0.444012	7.942686	0.12590199	12.60	0.510824	4.26	12
13	2.409845	20.140643	0.04965085	0.414964	8.357651	0.11965085	11.97	0.555461	4.27	13
14	2.578534	22.550488	0.04434494	0.387817	8.745468	0.11434494	11.44	0.600829	4.29	14
15	2.759032	25.129022	0.03979462	0.362446	9.107914	0.10979462	10.98	0.646919	4.31	15
16	2.952164	27.888054	0.03585765	0.338735	9.446649	0.10585765	10.59	0.693722	4.34	16
17	3.158815	30.840217	0.03242519	0.316574	9.763223	0.10242519	10.25	0.741228	4.36	17
18	3.379932	33.999033	0.02941260	0.295864	10.059087	0.09941260	9.95	0.789427	4.39	18
19	3.616528	37.378965	0.02675301	0.276508	10.335595	0.09675301	9.68	0.838307	4.41	19
20	3.869684	40.995492	0.02439293	0.258419	10.594014	0.09439293	9.44	0.887859	4.44	20
21	4.140562	44.865177	0.02228900	0.241513	10.835527	0.09228900	9.23	0.938069	4.47	21
22	4.430402	49.005739	0.02040577	0.225713	11.061240	0.09040577	9.05	0.988927	4.50	22
23	4.740530	53.436141	0.01871393	0.210947	11.272187	0.08871393	8.88	1.040420	4.52	23
24	5.072367	58.176671	0.01718902	0.197147	11.469334	0.08718902	8.72	1.092536	4.55	24
25	5.427433	63.249038	0.01581052	0.184249	11.653583	0.08581052	8.59	1.145263	4.58	25
26	5.807353	68.676470	0.01456103	0.172195	11.825779	0.08456103	8.46	1.198587	4.61	26
27	6.213868	74.483823	0.01342573	0.160930	11.986709	0.08342573	8.35	1.252495	4.64	27
28	6.648838	80.697691	0.01239193	0.150402	12.137111	0.08239193	8.24	1.306974	4.67	28
29	7.114257	87.346529	0.01144865	0.140563	12.277674	0.08144865	8.15	1.362011	4.70	29
30	7.612255	94.460786	0.01058640	0.131367	12.409041	0.08058640	8.06	1.417592	4.73	30
31	8.145113	102.073041	0.00979691	0.122773	12.531814	0.07979691	7.98	1.473704	4.75	31
32	8.715271	110.218154	0.00907292	0.114741	12.646555	0.07907292	7.91	1.530333	4.78	32
33	9.325340	118.933425	0.00840807	0.107235	12.753790	0.07840807	7.85	1.587466	4.81	33
34	9.978114	128.258765	0.00779674	0.100219	12.854009	0.07779674	7.78	1.645089	4.84	34
35	10.676581	138.236878	0.00723396	0.093663	12.947672	0.07723396	7.73	1.703189	4.87	35
36	11.423942	148.913460	0.00671531	0.087535	13.035208	0.07671531	7.68	1.761751	4.89	36
37	12.223618	160.337402	0.00623685	0.081809	13.117017	0.07623685	7.63	1.820763	4.92	37
38	13.079271	172.561020	0.00579505	0.076457	13.193473	0.07579505	7.58	1.880212	4.95	38
39	13.994820	185.640292	0.00538676	0.071455	13.264928	0.07538676	7.54	1.940084	4.97	39
40	14.974458	199.635112	0.00500914	0.066780	13.331709	0.07500914	7.51	2.000366	5.00	40
41	16.022670	214.609570	0.00465962	0.062412	13.394120	0.07465962	7.47	2.061045	5.03	41
42	17.144257	230.632240	0.00433591	0.058329	13.452449	0.07433591	7.44	2.122108	5.05	42
43	18.344355	247.776496	0.00403590	0.054513	13.506962	0.07403590	7.41	2.183543	5.08	43
44	19.628460	266.120851	0.00375769	0.050946	13.557908	0.07375769	7.38	2.245338	5.10	44
45	21.002452	285.749311	0.00349957	0.047613	13.605522	0.07349957	7.35	2.307481	5.13	45
46	22.472623	306.751763	0.00325996	0.044499	13.650020	0.07325996	7.33	2.369958	5.15	46
47	24.045707	329.224386	0.00303744	0.041587	13.691608	0.07303744	7.31	2.432760	5.18	47
48	25.728907	353.270093	0.00283070	0.038867	13.730474	0.07283070	7.29	2.495873	5.20	48
49	27.529930	378.999000	0.00263853	0.036324	13.766799	0.07263853	7.27	2.559288	5.22	49
50	29.457025	406.528929	0.00245985	0.033948	13.800746	0.07245985	7.25	2.622992	5.25	50

COMPOUND INTEREST AND ANNUITY TABLE

8.00 %
ANNUAL

YR	Amount Of 1	Amount Of 1 Per Period	Sinking Fund Payment	Present Worth Of 1	Present Worth Of 1 Per Period	Periodic Payment To Amortize 1	Constant Annual Percent	Total Interest	Annual Add-on Rate	YR
	What a single $1 deposit grows to in the future. The deposit is made at the beginning of the first period.	What a series of $1 deposits grow to in the future. A deposit is made at the end of each period.	The amount to be deposited at the end of each period that grows to $1 in the future.	What $1 to be paid in the future is worth today. Value today of a single payment tomorrow.	What $1 to be paid at the end of each period is worth today. Value today of a series of payments tomorrow.	The mortgage payment to amortize a loan of $1. An annuity certain, payable at the end of each period, worth $1 today.	The annual payment, including interest and principal, to amortize completely a loan of $100.	The total interest paid over the term on a loan of $1. The loan is amortized by regular periodic payments.	The average annual interest rate on a loan that is completely amortized by regular periodic payments.	
	$S=(1+i)^n$	$S_n=\frac{(1+i)^n-1}{i}$	$\frac{1}{S_n}=\frac{i}{(1+i)^n-1}$	$V^n=\frac{1}{(1+i)^n}$	$A_n=\frac{1-V^n}{i}$	$\frac{1}{A_n}=\frac{i}{1-V^n}$				
1	1.080000	1.000000	1.00000000	0.925926	0.925926	1.08000000	108.00	0.080000	8.00	1
2	1.166400	2.080000	0.48076923	0.857339	1.783265	0.56076923	56.08	0.121538	6.08	2
3	1.259712	3.246400	0.30803351	0.793832	2.577097	0.38803351	38.81	0.164101	5.47	3
4	1.360489	4.506112	0.22192080	0.735030	3.312127	0.30192080	30.20	0.207683	5.19	4
5	1.469328	5.866601	0.17045645	0.680583	3.992710	0.25045645	25.05	0.252282	5.05	5
6	1.586874	7.335929	0.13631539	0.630170	4.622880	0.21631539	21.64	0.297892	4.96	6
7	1.713824	8.922803	0.11207240	0.583490	5.206370	0.19207240	19.21	0.344507	4.92	7
8	1.850930	10.636628	0.09401476	0.540269	5.746639	0.17401476	17.41	0.392118	4.90	8
9	1.999005	12.487558	0.08007971	0.500249	6.246888	0.16007971	16.01	0.440717	4.90	9
10	2.158925	14.486562	0.06902949	0.463193	6.710081	0.14902949	14.91	0.490295	4.90	10
11	2.331639	16.645487	0.06007634	0.428883	7.138964	0.14007634	14.01	0.540840	4.92	11
12	2.518170	18.977126	0.05269502	0.397114	7.536078	0.13269502	13.27	0.592340	4.94	12
13	2.719624	21.495297	0.04652181	0.367698	7.903776	0.12652181	12.66	0.644783	4.96	13
14	2.937194	24.214920	0.04129685	0.340461	8.244237	0.12129685	12.13	0.698156	4.99	14
15	3.172169	27.152114	0.03682954	0.315242	8.559479	0.11682954	11.69	0.752443	5.02	15
16	3.425943	30.324283	0.03297687	0.291890	8.851369	0.11297687	11.30	0.807630	5.05	16
17	3.700018	33.750226	0.02962943	0.270269	9.121638	0.10962943	10.97	0.863700	5.08	17
18	3.996019	37.450244	0.02670210	0.250249	9.371887	0.10670210	10.68	0.920638	5.11	18
19	4.315701	41.446263	0.02412763	0.231712	9.603599	0.10412763	10.42	0.978425	5.15	19
20	4.660957	45.761964	0.02185221	0.214548	9.818147	0.10185221	10.19	1.037044	5.19	20
21	5.033834	50.422921	0.01983225	0.198656	10.016803	0.09983225	9.99	1.096477	5.22	21
22	5.436540	55.456755	0.01803207	0.183941	10.200744	0.09803207	9.81	1.156706	5.26	22
23	5.871464	60.893296	0.01642217	0.170315	10.371059	0.09642217	9.65	1.217710	5.29	23
24	6.341181	66.764759	0.01497796	0.157699	10.528758	0.09497796	9.50	1.279471	5.33	24
25	6.848475	73.105940	0.01367878	0.146018	10.674776	0.09367878	9.37	1.341969	5.37	25
26	7.396353	79.954415	0.01250713	0.135202	10.809978	0.09250713	9.26	1.405185	5.40	26
27	7.988061	87.350768	0.01144810	0.125187	10.935165	0.09144810	9.15	1.469099	5.44	27
28	8.627106	95.338830	0.01048891	0.115914	11.051078	0.09048891	9.05	1.533689	5.48	28
29	9.317275	103.965936	0.00961854	0.107328	11.158406	0.08961854	8.97	1.598938	5.51	29
30	10.062657	113.283211	0.00882743	0.099377	11.257783	0.08882743	8.89	1.664823	5.55	30
31	10.867669	123.345868	0.00810728	0.092016	11.349799	0.08810728	8.82	1.731326	5.58	31
32	11.737083	134.213537	0.00745081	0.085200	11.434999	0.08745081	8.75	1.798426	5.62	32
33	12.676050	145.950620	0.00685163	0.078889	11.513888	0.08685163	8.69	1.866104	5.65	33
34	13.690134	158.626670	0.00630411	0.073045	11.586934	0.08630411	8.64	1.934340	5.69	34
35	14.785344	172.316804	0.00580326	0.067635	11.654568	0.08580326	8.59	2.003114	5.72	35
36	15.968172	187.102148	0.00534467	0.062625	11.717193	0.08534467	8.54	2.072408	5.76	36
37	17.245626	203.070320	0.00492440	0.057986	11.775179	0.08492440	8.50	2.142203	5.79	37
38	18.625276	220.315945	0.00453894	0.053690	11.828869	0.08453894	8.46	2.212480	5.82	38
39	20.115298	238.941221	0.00418513	0.049713	11.878582	0.08418513	8.42	2.283220	5.85	39
40	21.724521	259.056519	0.00386016	0.046031	11.924613	0.08386016	8.39	2.354406	5.89	40
41	23.462483	280.781040	0.00356149	0.042621	11.967235	0.08356149	8.36	2.426021	5.92	41
42	25.339482	304.243523	0.00328684	0.039464	12.006699	0.08328684	8.33	2.498047	5.95	42
43	27.366640	329.583005	0.00303414	0.036541	12.043240	0.08303414	8.31	2.570468	5.98	43
44	29.555972	356.949646	0.00280152	0.033834	12.077074	0.08280152	8.29	2.643267	6.01	44
45	31.920449	386.505617	0.00258728	0.031328	12.108402	0.08258728	8.26	2.716428	6.04	45
46	34.474085	418.426067	0.00238991	0.029007	12.137409	0.08238991	8.24	2.789936	6.07	46
47	37.232012	452.900152	0.00220799	0.026859	12.164267	0.08220799	8.23	2.863776	6.09	47
48	40.210573	490.132164	0.00204027	0.024869	12.189136	0.08204027	8.21	2.937933	6.12	48
49	43.427419	530.342737	0.00188557	0.023027	12.212163	0.08188557	8.19	3.012393	6.15	49
50	46.901613	573.770156	0.00174286	0.021321	12.233485	0.08174286	8.18	3.087143	6.17	50

COMPOUND INTEREST AND ANNUITY TABLE

9.00 %
ANNUAL

YR	Amount Of 1	Amount Of 1 Per Period	Sinking Fund Payment	Present Worth Of 1	Present Worth Of 1 Per Period	Periodic Payment To Amortize 1	Constant Annual Percent	Total Interest	Annual Add-on Rate	YR
	What a single $1 deposit grows to in the future. The deposit is made at the beginning of the first period.	What a series of $1 deposits grow to in the future. A deposit is made at the end of each period.	The amount to be deposited at the end of each period that grows to $1 in the future.	What $1 to be paid in the future is worth today. Value today of a single payment tomorrow.	What $1 to be paid at the end of each period is worth today. Value today of a series of payments tomorrow.	The mortgage payment to amortize a loan of $1. An annuity certain, payable at the end of each period, worth $1 today.	The annual payment, including interest and principal, to amortize completely a loan of $100.	The total interest paid over the term on a loan of $1. The loan is amortized by regular periodic payments.	The average annual interest rate on a loan that is completely amortized by regular periodic payments.	
	$S=(1+i)^n$	$S_n=\frac{(1+i)^n-1}{i}$	$\frac{1}{S_n}=\frac{i}{(1+i)^n-1}$	$V^n=\frac{1}{(1+i)^n}$	$A_n=\frac{1-V^n}{i}$	$\frac{1}{A_n}=\frac{i}{1-V^n}$				
1	1.090000	1.000000	1.00000000	0.917431	0.917431	1.09000000	109.00	0.090000	9.00	1
2	1.188100	2.090000	0.47846890	0.841680	1.759111	0.56846890	56.85	0.136938	6.85	2
3	1.295029	3.278100	0.30505476	0.772183	2.531295	0.39505476	39.51	0.185164	6.17	3
4	1.411582	4.573129	0.21866866	0.708425	3.239720	0.30866866	30.87	0.234675	5.87	4
5	1.538624	5.984711	0.16709246	0.649931	3.889651	0.25709246	25.71	0.285462	5.71	5
6	1.677100	7.523335	0.13291978	0.596267	4.485919	0.22291978	22.30	0.337519	5.63	6
7	1.828039	9.200435	0.10869052	0.547034	5.032953	0.19869052	19.87	0.390834	5.58	7
8	1.992563	11.028474	0.09067438	0.501866	5.534819	0.18067438	18.07	0.445395	5.57	8
9	2.171893	13.021036	0.07679880	0.460428	5.995247	0.16679880	16.68	0.501189	5.57	9
10	2.367364	15.192930	0.06582009	0.422411	6.417658	0.15582009	15.59	0.558201	5.58	10
11	2.580426	17.560293	0.05694666	0.387533	6.805191	0.14694666	14.70	0.616413	5.60	11
12	2.812665	20.140720	0.04965066	0.355535	7.160725	0.13965066	13.97	0.675808	5.63	12
13	3.065805	22.953385	0.04356656	0.326179	7.486904	0.13356656	13.36	0.736365	5.66	13
14	3.341727	26.019189	0.03843317	0.299246	7.786150	0.12843317	12.85	0.798064	5.70	14
15	3.642482	29.360916	0.03405888	0.274538	8.060688	0.12405888	12.41	0.860883	5.74	15
16	3.970306	33.003399	0.03029991	0.251870	8.312558	0.12029991	12.03	0.924799	5.78	16
17	4.327633	36.973705	0.02704625	0.231073	8.543631	0.11704625	11.71	0.989786	5.82	17
18	4.717120	41.301338	0.02421229	0.211994	8.755625	0.11421229	11.43	1.055821	5.87	18
19	5.141661	46.018458	0.02173041	0.194490	8.950115	0.11173041	11.18	1.122878	5.91	19
20	5.604411	51.160120	0.01954648	0.178431	9.128546	0.10954648	10.96	1.190930	5.95	20
21	6.108808	56.764530	0.01761663	0.163698	9.292244	0.10761663	10.77	1.259949	6.00	21
22	6.658600	62.873338	0.01590499	0.150182	9.442425	0.10590499	10.60	1.329910	6.05	22
23	7.257874	69.531939	0.01438188	0.137781	9.580207	0.10438188	10.44	1.400783	6.09	23
24	7.911083	76.789813	0.01302256	0.126405	9.706612	0.10302256	10.31	1.472541	6.14	24
25	8.623081	84.700896	0.01180625	0.115968	9.822580	0.10180625	10.19	1.545156	6.18	25
26	9.399158	93.323977	0.01071536	0.106393	9.928972	0.10071536	10.08	1.618599	6.23	26
27	10.245082	102.723135	0.00973491	0.097608	10.026580	0.09973491	9.98	1.692842	6.27	27
28	11.167140	112.968217	0.00885205	0.089548	10.116128	0.09885205	9.89	1.767857	6.31	28
29	12.172182	124.135356	0.00805572	0.082155	10.198283	0.09805572	9.81	1.843616	6.36	29
30	13.267678	136.307539	0.00733635	0.075371	10.273654	0.09733635	9.74	1.920091	6.40	30
31	14.461770	149.575217	0.00668560	0.069148	10.342802	0.09668560	9.67	1.997254	6.44	31
32	15.763329	164.036987	0.00609619	0.063438	10.406240	0.09609619	9.61	2.075078	6.48	32
33	17.182028	179.800315	0.00556173	0.058200	10.464441	0.09556173	9.56	2.153537	6.53	33
34	18.728411	196.982344	0.00507660	0.053395	10.517835	0.09507660	9.51	2.232604	6.57	34
35	20.413968	215.710755	0.00463584	0.048986	10.566821	0.09463584	9.47	2.312254	6.61	35
36	22.251225	236.124723	0.00423505	0.044941	10.611763	0.09423505	9.43	2.392462	6.65	36
37	24.253835	258.375948	0.00387033	0.041231	10.652993	0.09387033	9.39	2.473202	6.68	37
38	26.436680	282.629783	0.00353820	0.037826	10.690820	0.09353820	9.36	2.554452	6.72	38
39	28.815982	309.066463	0.00323555	0.034703	10.725523	0.09323555	9.33	2.636186	6.76	39
40	31.409420	337.882445	0.00295961	0.031838	10.757360	0.09295961	9.30	2.718384	6.80	40
41	34.236268	369.291865	0.00270789	0.029209	10.786569	0.09270789	9.28	2.801023	6.83	41
42	37.317532	403.528133	0.00247814	0.026797	10.813366	0.09247814	9.25	2.884082	6.87	42
43	40.676110	440.845665	0.00226837	0.024584	10.837950	0.09226837	9.23	2.967540	6.90	43
44	44.336960	481.521775	0.00207675	0.022555	10.860505	0.09207675	9.21	3.051377	6.93	44
45	48.327286	525.858734	0.00190165	0.020692	10.881197	0.09190165	9.20	3.135574	6.97	45
46	52.676742	574.186021	0.00174160	0.018984	10.900181	0.09174160	9.18	3.220113	7.00	46
47	57.417649	626.862762	0.00159525	0.017416	10.917597	0.09159525	9.16	3.304977	7.03	47
48	62.585237	684.280411	0.00146139	0.015978	10.933575	0.09146139	9.15	3.390147	7.06	48
49	68.217908	746.865648	0.00133893	0.014659	10.948234	0.09133893	9.14	3.475608	7.09	49
50	74.357520	815.083556	0.00122687	0.013449	10.961683	0.09122687	9.13	3.561343	7.12	50

COMPOUND INTEREST AND ANNUITY TABLE

10.00 % ANNUAL

YR	Amount Of 1	Amount Of 1 Per Period	Sinking Fund Payment	Present Worth Of 1	Present Worth Of 1 Per Period	Periodic Payment To Amortize 1	Constant Annual Percent	Total Interest	Annual Add-on Rate	YR
	What a single $1 deposit grows to in the future. The deposit is made at the beginning of the first period.	What a series of $1 deposits grow to in the future. A deposit is made at the end of each period.	The amount to be deposited at the end of each period that grows to $1 in the future.	What $1 to be paid in the future is worth today. Value today of a single payment tomorrow.	What $1 to be paid at the end of each period is worth today. Value today of a series of payments tomorrow.	The mortgage payment to amortize a loan of $1. An annuity certain, payable at the end of each period, worth $1 today.	The annual payment, including interest and principal, to amortize completely a loan of $100.	The total interest paid over the term on a loan of $1. The loan is amortized by regular periodic payments.	The average annual interest rate on a loan that is completely amortized by regular periodic payments.	
	$S=(1+i)^n$	$S_n=\frac{(1+i)^n-1}{i}$	$\frac{1}{S_n}=\frac{i}{(1+i)^n-1}$	$V^n=\frac{1}{(1+i)^n}$	$A_n=\frac{1-V^n}{i}$	$\frac{1}{A_n}=\frac{i}{1-V^n}$				
1	1.100000	1.000000	1.00000000	0.909091	0.909091	1.10000000	110.00	0.100000	10.00	1
2	1.210000	2.100000	0.47619048	0.826446	1.735537	0.57619048	57.62	0.152381	7.62	2
3	1.331000	3.310000	0.30211480	0.751315	2.486852	0.40211480	40.22	0.206344	6.88	3
4	1.464100	4.641000	0.21547080	0.683013	3.169865	0.31547080	31.55	0.261883	6.55	4
5	1.610510	6.105100	0.16379748	0.620921	3.790787	0.26379748	26.38	0.318987	6.38	5
6	1.771561	7.715610	0.12960738	0.564474	4.355261	0.22960738	22.97	0.377644	6.29	6
7	1.948717	9.487171	0.10540550	0.513158	4.868419	0.20540550	20.55	0.437838	6.25	7
8	2.143589	11.435888	0.08744402	0.466507	5.334926	0.18744402	18.75	0.499552	6.24	8
9	2.357948	13.579477	0.07364054	0.424098	5.759024	0.17364054	17.37	0.562765	6.25	9
10	2.593742	15.937425	0.06274539	0.385543	6.144567	0.16274539	16.28	0.627454	6.27	10
11	2.853117	18.531167	0.05396314	0.350494	6.495061	0.15396314	15.40	0.693595	6.31	11
12	3.138428	21.384284	0.04676332	0.318631	6.813692	0.14676332	14.68	0.761160	6.34	12
13	3.452271	24.522712	0.04077852	0.289664	7.103356	0.14077852	14.08	0.830121	6.39	13
14	3.797498	27.974983	0.03574622	0.263331	7.366687	0.13574622	13.58	0.900447	6.43	14
15	4.177248	31.772482	0.03147378	0.239392	7.606080	0.13147378	13.15	0.972107	6.48	15
16	4.594973	35.949730	0.02781662	0.217629	7.823709	0.12781662	12.79	1.045066	6.53	16
17	5.054470	40.544703	0.02466413	0.197845	8.021553	0.12466413	12.47	1.119290	6.58	17
18	5.559917	45.599173	0.02193022	0.179859	8.201412	0.12193022	12.20	1.194744	6.64	18
19	6.115909	51.159090	0.01954687	0.163508	8.364920	0.11954687	11.96	1.271390	6.69	19
20	6.727500	57.274999	0.01745962	0.148644	8.513564	0.11745962	11.75	1.349192	6.75	20
21	7.400250	64.002499	0.01562439	0.135131	8.648694	0.11562439	11.57	1.428112	6.80	21
22	8.140275	71.402749	0.01400506	0.122846	8.771540	0.11400506	11.41	1.508111	6.86	22
23	8.954302	79.543024	0.01257181	0.111678	8.883218	0.11257181	11.26	1.589152	6.91	23
24	9.849733	88.497327	0.01129978	0.101526	8.984744	0.11129978	11.13	1.671195	6.96	24
25	10.834706	98.347059	0.01016807	0.092296	9.077040	0.11016807	11.02	1.754202	7.02	25
26	11.918177	109.181765	0.00915904	0.083905	9.160945	0.10915904	10.92	1.838135	7.07	26
27	13.109994	121.099942	0.00825764	0.076278	9.237223	0.10825764	10.83	1.922956	7.12	27
28	14.420994	134.209936	0.00745101	0.069343	9.306567	0.10745101	10.75	2.008628	7.17	28
29	15.863093	148.630930	0.00672807	0.063039	9.369606	0.10672807	10.68	2.095114	7.22	29
30	17.449402	164.494023	0.00607925	0.057309	9.426914	0.10607925	10.61	2.182377	7.27	30
31	19.194342	181.943425	0.00549621	0.052099	9.479013	0.10549621	10.55	2.270383	7.32	31
32	21.113777	201.137767	0.00497172	0.047362	9.526376	0.10497172	10.50	2.359095	7.37	32
33	23.225154	222.251544	0.00449941	0.043057	9.569432	0.10449941	10.45	2.448480	7.42	33
34	25.547670	245.476699	0.00407371	0.039143	9.608575	0.10407371	10.41	2.538506	7.47	34
35	28.102437	271.024368	0.00368971	0.035584	9.644159	0.10368971	10.37	2.629140	7.51	35
36	30.912681	299.126805	0.00334306	0.032349	9.676508	0.10334306	10.34	2.720350	7.56	36
37	34.003949	330.039486	0.00302994	0.029408	9.705917	0.10302994	10.31	2.812108	7.60	37
38	37.404343	364.043434	0.00274692	0.026735	9.732651	0.10274692	10.28	2.904383	7.64	38
39	41.144778	401.447778	0.00249098	0.024304	9.756956	0.10249098	10.25	2.997148	7.68	39
40	45.259256	442.592556	0.00225941	0.022095	9.779051	0.10225941	10.23	3.090377	7.73	40
41	49.785181	487.851811	0.00204980	0.020086	9.799137	0.10204980	10.21	3.184042	7.77	41
42	54.763699	537.636992	0.00185999	0.018260	9.817397	0.10185999	10.19	3.278120	7.81	42
43	60.240069	592.400692	0.00168805	0.016600	9.833998	0.10168805	10.17	3.372586	7.84	43
44	66.264076	652.640761	0.00153224	0.015091	9.849089	0.10153224	10.16	3.467418	7.88	44
45	72.890484	718.904837	0.00139100	0.013719	9.862808	0.10139100	10.14	3.562595	7.92	45
46	80.179532	791.795321	0.00126295	0.012472	9.875280	0.10126295	10.13	3.658096	7.95	46
47	88.197485	871.974853	0.00114682	0.011338	9.886618	0.10114682	10.12	3.753901	7.99	47
48	97.017234	960.172338	0.00104148	0.010307	9.896926	0.10104148	10.11	3.849991	8.02	48
49	106.718957	1057.189572	0.00094590	0.009370	9.906296	0.10094590	10.10	3.946349	8.05	49
50	117.390853	1163.908529	0.00085917	0.008519	9.914814	0.10085917	10.09	4.042959	8.09	50

COMPOUND INTEREST AND ANNUITY TABLE

11.00 % ANNUAL

YR	Amount Of 1	Amount Of 1 Per Period	Sinking Fund Payment	Present Worth Of 1	Present Worth Of 1 Per Period	Periodic Payment To Amortize 1	Constant Annual Percent	Total Interest	Annual Add-on Rate	YR
	What a single $1 deposit grows to in the future. The deposit is made at the beginning of the first period.	What a series of $1 deposits grow to in the future. A deposit is made at the end of each period.	The amount to be deposited at the end of each period that grows to $1 in the future.	What $1 to be paid in the future is worth today. Value today of a single payment tomorrow.	What $1 to be paid at the end of each period is worth today. Value today of a series of payments tomorrow.	The mortgage payment to amortize a loan of $1. An annuity certain, payable at the end of each period, worth $1 today.	The annual payment, including interest and principal, to amortize completely a loan of $100.	The total interest paid over the term on a loan of $1. The loan is amortized by regular periodic payments.	The average annual interest rate on a loan that is completely amortized by regular periodic payments.	
	$S=(1+i)^n$	$S_{\overline{n}}=\frac{(1+i)^n-1}{i}$	$\frac{1}{S_{\overline{n}}}=\frac{i}{(1+i)^n-1}$	$V^n=\frac{1}{(1+i)^n}$	$A_{\overline{n}}=\frac{1-V^n}{i}$	$\frac{1}{A_{\overline{n}}}=\frac{i}{1-V^n}$				
1	1.110000	1.000000	1.00000000	0.900901	0.900901	1.11000000	111.00	0.110000	11.00	1
2	1.232100	2.110000	0.47393365	0.811622	1.712523	0.58393365	58.40	0.167867	8.39	2
3	1.367631	3.342100	0.29921307	0.731191	2.443715	0.40921307	40.93	0.227639	7.59	3
4	1.518070	4.709731	0.21232635	0.658731	3.102446	0.32232635	32.24	0.289305	7.23	4
5	1.685058	6.227801	0.16057031	0.593451	3.695897	0.27057031	27.06	0.352852	7.06	5
6	1.870415	7.912860	0.12637656	0.534641	4.230538	0.23637656	23.64	0.418259	6.97	6
7	2.076160	9.783274	0.10221527	0.481658	4.712196	0.21221527	21.23	0.485507	6.94	7
8	2.304538	11.859434	0.08432105	0.433926	5.146123	0.19432105	19.44	0.554568	6.93	8
9	2.558037	14.163972	0.07060166	0.390925	5.537048	0.18060166	18.07	0.625415	6.95	9
10	2.839421	16.722009	0.05980143	0.352184	5.889232	0.16980143	16.99	0.698014	6.98	10
11	3.151757	19.561430	0.05112101	0.317283	6.206515	0.16112101	16.12	0.772331	7.02	11
12	3.498451	22.713187	0.04402729	0.285841	6.492356	0.15402729	15.41	0.848327	7.07	12
13	3.883280	26.211638	0.03815099	0.257514	6.749870	0.14815099	14.82	0.925963	7.12	13
14	4.310441	30.094918	0.03322820	0.231995	6.981865	0.14322820	14.33	1.005195	7.18	14
15	4.784589	34.405359	0.02906524	0.209004	7.190870	0.13906524	13.91	1.085979	7.24	15
16	5.310894	39.189948	0.02551675	0.188292	7.379162	0.13551675	13.56	1.168268	7.30	16
17	5.895093	44.500843	0.02247148	0.169633	7.548794	0.13247148	13.25	1.252015	7.36	17
18	6.543553	50.395936	0.01984287	0.152822	7.701617	0.12984287	12.99	1.337172	7.43	18
19	7.263344	56.939488	0.01756250	0.137678	7.839294	0.12756250	12.76	1.423688	7.49	19
20	8.062312	64.202832	0.01557564	0.124034	7.963328	0.12557564	12.56	1.511513	7.56	20
21	8.949166	72.265144	0.01383793	0.111742	8.075070	0.12383793	12.39	1.600597	7.62	21
22	9.933574	81.214309	0.01231310	0.100669	8.175739	0.12231310	12.24	1.690888	7.69	22
23	11.026267	91.147884	0.01097118	0.090693	8.266432	0.12097118	12.10	1.782337	7.75	23
24	12.239157	102.174151	0.00978721	0.081705	8.348137	0.11978721	11.98	1.874893	7.81	24
25	13.585464	114.413307	0.00874024	0.073608	8.421745	0.11874024	11.88	1.968506	7.87	25
26	15.079865	127.998771	0.00781258	0.066314	8.488058	0.11781258	11.79	2.063127	7.94	26
27	16.738650	143.078636	0.00698916	0.059742	8.547800	0.11698916	11.70	2.158707	8.00	27
28	18.579901	159.817286	0.00625715	0.053822	8.601622	0.11625715	11.63	2.255200	8.05	28
29	20.623691	178.397187	0.00560547	0.048488	8.650110	0.11560547	11.57	2.352559	8.11	29
30	22.892297	199.020878	0.00502460	0.043683	8.693793	0.11502460	11.51	2.450738	8.17	30
31	25.410449	221.913174	0.00450627	0.039354	8.733146	0.11450627	11.46	2.549694	8.22	31
32	28.205599	247.323624	0.00404329	0.035454	8.768600	0.11404329	11.41	2.649385	8.28	32
33	31.308214	275.529222	0.00362938	0.031940	8.800541	0.11362938	11.37	2.749770	8.33	33
34	34.752118	306.837437	0.00325905	0.028775	8.829316	0.11325905	11.33	2.850808	8.38	34
35	38.574851	341.589555	0.00292749	0.025924	8.855240	0.11292749	11.30	2.952462	8.44	35
36	42.818085	380.164406	0.00263044	0.023355	8.878594	0.11263044	11.27	3.054696	8.49	36
37	47.528074	422.982490	0.00236416	0.021040	8.899635	0.11236416	11.24	3.157474	8.53	37
38	52.756162	470.510564	0.00212535	0.018955	8.918590	0.11212535	11.22	3.260763	8.58	38
39	58.559340	523.266726	0.00191107	0.017077	8.935666	0.11191107	11.20	3.364532	8.63	39
40	65.000867	581.826066	0.00171873	0.015384	8.951051	0.11171873	11.18	3.468749	8.67	40
41	72.150963	646.826934	0.00154601	0.013860	8.964911	0.11154601	11.16	3.573386	8.72	41
42	80.087569	718.977896	0.00139086	0.012486	8.977397	0.11139086	11.14	3.678416	8.76	42
43	88.897201	799.065465	0.00125146	0.011249	8.988646	0.11125146	11.13	3.783813	8.80	43
44	98.675893	887.962666	0.00112617	0.010134	8.998780	0.11112617	11.12	3.889552	8.84	44
45	109.530242	986.638559	0.00101354	0.009130	9.007910	0.11101354	11.11	3.995609	8.88	45
46	121.578568	1096.168801	0.00091227	0.008225	9.016135	0.11091227	11.10	4.101964	8.92	46
47	134.952211	1217.747369	0.00082119	0.007410	9.023545	0.11082119	11.09	4.208596	8.95	47
48	149.796954	1352.699580	0.00073926	0.006676	9.030221	0.11073926	11.08	4.315485	8.99	48
49	166.274619	1502.496533	0.00066556	0.006014	9.036235	0.11066556	11.07	4.422612	9.03	49
50	184.564827	1668.771152	0.00059924	0.005418	9.041653	0.11059924	11.06	4.529962	9.06	50

COMPOUND INTEREST AND ANNUITY TABLE

12.00 %
ANNUAL

YR	Amount Of 1	Amount Of 1 Per Period	Sinking Fund Payment	Present Worth Of 1	Present Worth Of 1 Per Period	Periodic Payment To Amortize 1	Constant Annual Percent	Total Interest	Annual Add-on Rate	YR
	What a single $1 deposit grows to in the future. The deposit is made at the beginning of the first period.	What a series of $1 deposits grow to in the future. A deposit is made at the end of each period.	The amount to be deposited at the end of each period that grows to $1 in the future.	What $1 to be paid in the future is worth today. Value today of a single payment tomorrow.	What $1 to be paid at the end of each period is worth today. Value today of a series of payments tomorrow.	The mortgage payment to amortize a loan of $1. An annuity certain, payable at the end of each period, worth $1 today.	The annual payment, including interest and principal, to amortize completely a loan of $100.	The total interest paid over the term on a loan of $1. The loan is amortized by regular periodic payments.	The average annual interest rate on a loan that is completely amortized by regular periodic payments.	
	$S=(1+i)^n$	$S_n=\frac{(1+i)^n-1}{i}$	$\frac{1}{S_n}=\frac{i}{(1+i)^n-1}$	$V^n=\frac{1}{(1+i)^n}$	$A_n=\frac{1-V^n}{i}$	$\frac{1}{A_n}=\frac{i}{1-V^n}$				
1	1.120000	1.000000	1.00000000	0.892857	0.892857	1.12000000	112.00	0.120000	12.00	1
2	1.254400	2.120000	0.47169811	0.797194	1.690051	0.59169811	59.17	0.183396	9.17	2
3	1.404928	3.374400	0.29634898	0.711780	2.401831	0.41634898	41.64	0.249047	8.30	3
4	1.573519	4.779328	0.20923444	0.635518	3.037349	0.32923444	32.93	0.316938	7.92	4
5	1.762342	6.352847	0.15740973	0.567427	3.604776	0.27740973	27.75	0.387049	7.74	5
6	1.973823	8.115189	0.12322572	0.506631	4.111407	0.24322572	24.33	0.459354	7.66	6
7	2.210681	10.089012	0.09911774	0.452349	4.563757	0.21911774	21.92	0.533824	7.63	7
8	2.475963	12.299693	0.08130284	0.403883	4.967640	0.20130284	20.14	0.610423	7.63	8
9	2.773079	14.775656	0.06767889	0.360610	5.328250	0.18767889	18.77	0.689110	7.66	9
10	3.105848	17.548735	0.05698416	0.321973	5.650223	0.17698416	17.70	0.769842	7.70	10
11	3.478550	20.654583	0.04841540	0.287476	5.937699	0.16841540	16.85	0.852569	7.75	11
12	3.895976	24.133133	0.04143681	0.256675	6.194374	0.16143681	16.15	0.937242	7.81	12
13	4.363493	28.029109	0.03567720	0.229174	6.423548	0.15567720	15.57	1.023804	7.88	13
14	4.887112	32.392602	0.03087125	0.204620	6.628168	0.15087125	15.09	1.112197	7.94	14
15	5.473566	37.279715	0.02682424	0.182696	6.810864	0.14682424	14.69	1.202364	8.02	15
16	6.130394	42.753280	0.02339002	0.163122	6.973986	0.14339002	14.34	1.294240	8.09	16
17	6.866041	48.883674	0.02045673	0.145644	7.119630	0.14045673	14.05	1.387764	8.16	17
18	7.689966	55.749715	0.01793731	0.130040	7.249670	0.13793731	13.80	1.482872	8.24	18
19	8.612762	63.439681	0.01576300	0.116107	7.365777	0.13576300	13.58	1.579497	8.31	19
20	9.646293	72.052442	0.01387878	0.103667	7.469444	0.13387878	13.39	1.677576	8.39	20
21	10.803848	81.698736	0.01224009	0.092560	7.562003	0.13224009	13.23	1.777042	8.46	21
22	12.100310	92.502584	0.01081051	0.082643	7.644646	0.13081051	13.09	1.877831	8.54	22
23	13.552347	104.602894	0.00955996	0.073788	7.718434	0.12955996	12.96	1.979879	8.61	23
24	15.178629	118.155241	0.00846344	0.065882	7.784316	0.12846344	12.85	2.083123	8.68	24
25	17.000064	133.333870	0.00749997	0.058823	7.843139	0.12749997	12.75	2.187499	8.75	25
26	19.040072	150.333934	0.00665186	0.052521	7.895660	0.12665186	12.67	2.292948	8.82	26
27	21.324881	169.374007	0.00590409	0.046894	7.942554	0.12590409	12.60	2.399411	8.89	27
28	23.883866	190.698887	0.00524387	0.041869	7.984423	0.12524387	12.53	2.506828	8.95	28
29	26.749930	214.582754	0.00466021	0.037383	8.021806	0.12466021	12.47	2.615146	9.02	29
30	29.959922	241.332684	0.00414366	0.033378	8.055184	0.12414366	12.42	2.724310	9.08	30
31	33.555113	271.292606	0.00368606	0.029802	8.084986	0.12368606	12.37	2.834268	9.14	31
32	37.581726	304.847719	0.00328033	0.026609	8.111594	0.12328033	12.33	2.944970	9.20	32
33	42.091533	342.429446	0.00292031	0.023758	8.135352	0.12292031	12.30	3.056370	9.26	33
34	47.142517	384.520979	0.00260064	0.021212	8.156564	0.12260064	12.27	3.168422	9.32	34
35	52.799620	431.663496	0.00231662	0.018940	8.175504	0.12231662	12.24	3.281082	9.37	35
36	59.135574	484.463116	0.00206414	0.016910	8.192414	0.12206414	12.21	3.394309	9.43	36
37	66.231843	543.598690	0.00183959	0.015098	8.207513	0.12183959	12.19	3.508065	9.48	37
38	74.179664	609.830533	0.00163980	0.013481	8.220993	0.12163980	12.17	3.622312	9.53	38
39	83.081224	684.010197	0.00146197	0.012036	8.233030	0.12146197	12.15	3.737017	9.58	39
40	93.050970	767.091420	0.00130363	0.010747	8.243777	0.12130363	12.14	3.852145	9.63	40
41	104.217087	860.142391	0.00116260	0.009595	8.253372	0.12116260	12.12	3.967667	9.68	41
42	116.723137	964.359478	0.00103696	0.008567	8.261939	0.12103696	12.11	4.083552	9.72	42
43	130.729914	1081.082615	0.00092500	0.007649	8.269589	0.12092500	12.10	4.199775	9.77	43
44	146.417503	1211.812529	0.00082521	0.006830	8.276418	0.12082521	12.09	4.316309	9.81	44
45	163.987604	1358.230032	0.00073625	0.006098	8.282516	0.12073625	12.08	4.433131	9.85	45
46	183.666116	1522.217636	0.00065694	0.005445	8.287961	0.12065694	12.07	4.550219	9.89	46
47	205.706050	1705.883752	0.00058621	0.004861	8.292822	0.12058621	12.06	4.667552	9.93	47
48	230.390776	1911.589803	0.00052312	0.004340	8.297163	0.12052312	12.06	4.785110	9.97	48
49	258.037669	2141.980579	0.00046686	0.003875	8.301038	0.12046686	12.05	4.902876	10.01	49
50	289.002190	2400.018249	0.00041666	0.003460	8.304498	0.12041666	12.05	5.020833	10.04	50

COMPOUND INTEREST AND ANNUITY TABLE

13.00 % ANNUAL

YR	Amount Of 1	Amount Of 1 Per Period	Sinking Fund Payment	Present Worth Of 1	Present Worth Of 1 Per Period	Periodic Payment To Amortize 1	Constant Annual Percent	Total Interest	Annual Add-on Rate	YR
	What a single $1 deposit grows to in the future. The deposit is made at the beginning of the first period.	What a series of $1 deposits grow to in the future. A deposit is made at the end of each period.	The amount to be deposited at the end of each period that grows to $1 in the future.	What $1 to be paid in the future is worth today. Value today of a single payment tomorrow.	What $1 to be paid at the end of each period is worth today. Value today of a series of payments tomorrow.	The mortgage payment to amortize a loan of $1. An annuity certain, payable at the end of each period, worth $1 today.	The annual payment, including interest and principal, to amortize completely a loan of $100.	The total interest paid over the term on a loan of $1. The loan is amortized by regular periodic payments.	The average annual interest rate on a loan that is completely amortized by regular periodic payments.	
	$S=(1+i)^n$	$S_n=\frac{(1+i)^n-1}{i}$	$\frac{1}{S_n}=\frac{i}{(1+i)^n-1}$	$V^n=\frac{1}{(1+i)^n}$	$A_n=\frac{1-V^n}{i}$	$\frac{1}{A_n}=\frac{i}{1-V^n}$				
1	1.130000	1.000000	1.00000000	0.884956	0.884956	1.13000000	113.00	0.130000	13.00	1
2	1.276900	2.130000	0.46948357	0.783147	1.668102	0.59948357	59.95	0.198967	9.95	2
3	1.442897	3.406900	0.29352197	0.693050	2.361153	0.42352197	42.36	0.270566	9.02	3
4	1.630474	4.849797	0.20619420	0.613319	2.974471	0.33619420	33.62	0.344777	8.62	4
5	1.842435	6.480271	0.15431454	0.542760	3.517231	0.28431454	28.44	0.421573	8.43	5
6	2.081952	8.322706	0.12015323	0.480319	3.997550	0.25015323	25.02	0.500919	8.35	6
7	2.352605	10.404658	0.09611080	0.425061	4.422610	0.22611080	22.62	0.582776	8.33	7
8	2.658444	12.757263	0.07838672	0.376160	4.798770	0.20838672	20.84	0.667094	8.34	8
9	3.004042	15.415707	0.06486890	0.332885	5.131655	0.19486890	19.49	0.753820	8.38	9
10	3.394567	18.419749	0.05428956	0.294588	5.426243	0.18428956	18.43	0.842896	8.43	10
11	3.835861	21.814317	0.04584145	0.260698	5.686941	0.17584145	17.59	0.934256	8.49	11
12	4.334523	25.650178	0.03898608	0.230706	5.917647	0.16898608	16.90	1.027833	8.57	12
13	4.898011	29.984701	0.03335034	0.204165	6.121812	0.16335034	16.34	1.123554	8.64	13
14	5.534753	34.882712	0.02866750	0.180677	6.302488	0.15866750	15.87	1.221345	8.72	14
15	6.254270	40.417464	0.02474178	0.159891	6.462379	0.15474178	15.48	1.321127	8.81	15
16	7.067326	46.671735	0.02142624	0.141496	6.603875	0.15142624	15.15	1.422820	8.89	16
17	7.986078	53.739060	0.01860844	0.125218	6.729093	0.14860844	14.87	1.526343	8.98	17
18	9.024268	61.725138	0.01620085	0.110812	6.839905	0.14620085	14.63	1.631615	9.06	18
19	10.197423	70.749406	0.01413439	0.098064	6.937969	0.14413439	14.42	1.738553	9.15	19
20	11.523088	80.946829	0.01235379	0.086782	7.024752	0.14235379	14.24	1.847076	9.24	20
21	13.021089	92.469917	0.01081433	0.076798	7.101550	0.14081433	14.09	1.957101	9.32	21
22	14.713831	105.491006	0.00947948	0.067963	7.169513	0.13947948	13.95	2.068549	9.40	22
23	16.626629	120.204837	0.00831913	0.060144	7.229658	0.13831913	13.84	2.181340	9.46	23
24	18.788091	136.831465	0.00730826	0.053225	7.282883	0.13730826	13.74	2.295398	9.56	24
25	21.230542	155.619556	0.00642593	0.047102	7.329985	0.13642593	13.65	2.410648	9.64	25
26	23.990513	176.850098	0.00565451	0.041683	7.371668	0.13565451	13.57	2.527017	9.72	26
27	27.109279	200.840611	0.00497907	0.036888	7.408556	0.13497907	13.50	2.644435	9.79	27
28	30.633486	227.949890	0.00438693	0.032644	7.441200	0.13438693	13.44	2.762834	9.87	28
29	34.615839	258.583376	0.00386722	0.028889	7.470088	0.13386722	13.39	2.882150	9.94	29
30	39.115898	293.199215	0.00341065	0.025565	7.495653	0.13341065	13.35	3.002320	10.01	30
31	44.200965	332.315113	0.00300919	0.022624	7.518277	0.13300919	13.31	3.123285	10.08	31
32	49.947090	376.516078	0.00265593	0.020021	7.538299	0.13265593	13.27	3.244990	10.14	32
33	56.440212	426.463168	0.00234487	0.017718	7.556016	0.13234487	13.24	3.367381	10.20	33
34	63.777439	482.903380	0.00207081	0.015680	7.571696	0.13207081	13.21	3.490407	10.27	34
35	72.068506	546.680819	0.00182922	0.013876	7.585572	0.13182922	13.19	3.614023	10.33	35
36	81.437412	618.749325	0.00161616	0.012279	7.597851	0.13161616	13.17	3.738182	10.38	36
37	92.024276	700.186738	0.00142819	0.010867	7.608718	0.13142819	13.15	3.862843	10.44	37
38	103.987432	792.211014	0.00126229	0.009617	7.618334	0.13126229	13.13	3.987967	10.49	38
39	117.505798	896.198445	0.00111582	0.008510	7.626844	0.13111582	13.12	4.113517	10.55	39
40	132.781552	1013.704243	0.00098648	0.007531	7.634376	0.13098648	13.10	4.239459	10.60	40
41	150.043153	1146.485795	0.00087223	0.006665	7.641040	0.13087223	13.09	4.365761	10.65	41
42	169.548763	1296.528948	0.00077129	0.005898	7.646938	0.13077129	13.08	4.492394	10.70	42
43	191.590103	1466.077712	0.00068209	0.005219	7.652158	0.13068209	13.07	4.619330	10.74	43
44	216.496816	1657.667814	0.00060326	0.004619	7.656777	0.13060326	13.07	4.746543	10.79	44
45	244.641402	1874.164630	0.00053357	0.004088	7.660864	0.13053357	13.06	4.874011	10.83	45
46	276.444784	2118.806032	0.00047196	0.003617	7.664482	0.13047196	13.05	5.001710	10.87	46
47	312.382606	2395.250816	0.00041749	0.003201	7.667683	0.13041749	13.05	5.129622	10.91	47
48	352.992345	2707.633422	0.00036933	0.002833	7.670516	0.13036933	13.04	5.257728	10.95	48
49	398.881350	3060.625767	0.00032673	0.002507	7.673023	0.13032673	13.04	5.386010	10.99	49
50	450.735925	3459.507117	0.00028906	0.002219	7.675242	0.13028906	13.03	5.514453	11.03	50

COMPOUND INTEREST AND ANNUITY TABLE

14.00 %
ANNUAL

YR	Amount Of 1 What a single $1 deposit grows to in the future. The deposit is made at the beginning of the first period. $S=(1+i)^n$	Amount Of 1 Per Period What a series of $1 deposits grow to in the future. A deposit is made at the end of each period. $S_{\overline{n}}=\frac{(1+i)^n-1}{i}$	Sinking Fund Payment The amount to be deposited at the end of each period that grows to $1 in the future. $\frac{1}{S_{\overline{n}}}=\frac{i}{(1+i)^n-1}$	Present Worth Of 1 What $1 to be paid in the future is worth today. Value today of a single payment tomorrow. $V^n=\frac{1}{(1+i)^n}$	Present Worth Of 1 Per Period What $1 to be paid at the end of each period is worth today. Value today of a series of payments tomorrow. $A_{\overline{n}}=\frac{1-V^n}{i}$	Periodic Payment To Amortize 1 The mortgage payment to amortize a loan of $1. An annuity certain, payable at the end of each period, worth $1 today. $\frac{1}{A_{\overline{n}}}=\frac{i}{1-V^n}$	Constant Annual Percent The annual payment, including interest and principal, to amortize completely a loan of $100.	Total Interest The total interest paid over the term on a loan of $1. The loan is amortized by regular periodic payments	Annual Add-on Rate The average annual interest rate on a loan that is completely amortized by regular periodic payments.	YR
1	1.140000	1.000000	1.00000000	0.877193	0.877193	1.14000000	114.00	0.140000	14.00	1
2	1.299600	2.140000	0.46728972	0.769468	1.646661	0.60728972	60.73	0.214579	10.73	2
3	1.481544	3.439600	0.29073148	0.674972	2.321632	0.43073148	43.08	0.292194	9.74	3
4	1.688960	4.921144	0.20320478	0.592080	2.913712	0.34320478	34.33	0.372819	9.32	4
5	1.925415	6.610104	0.15128355	0.519369	3.433081	0.29128355	29.13	0.456418	9.13	5
6	2.194973	8.535519	0.11715750	0.455587	3.888668	0.25715750	25.72	0.542945	9.05	6
7	2.502269	10.730491	0.09319238	0.399637	4.288305	0.23319238	23.32	0.632347	9.03	7
8	2.852586	13.232760	0.07557002	0.350559	4.638864	0.21557002	21.56	0.724560	9.06	8
9	3.251949	16.085347	0.06216838	0.307508	4.946372	0.20216838	20.22	0.819515	9.11	9
10	3.707221	19.337295	0.05171354	0.269744	5.216116	0.19171354	19.18	0.917135	9.17	10
11	4.226232	23.044516	0.04339427	0.236617	5.452733	0.18339427	18.34	1.017337	9.25	11
12	4.817905	27.270749	0.03666933	0.207559	5.660292	0.17666933	17.67	1.120032	9.33	12
13	5.492411	32.088654	0.03116366	0.182069	5.842362	0.17116366	17.12	1.225128	9.42	13
14	6.261349	37.581065	0.02660914	0.159710	6.002072	0.16660914	16.67	1.332528	9.52	14
15	7.137938	43.842414	0.02280896	0.140096	6.142168	0.16280896	16.29	1.442134	9.61	15
16	8.137249	50.980352	0.01961540	0.122892	6.265060	0.15961540	15.97	1.553846	9.71	16
17	9.276464	59.117601	0.01691544	0.107800	6.372859	0.15691544	15.70	1.667562	9.81	17
18	10.575169	68.394066	0.01462115	0.094561	6.467420	0.15462115	15.47	1.783181	9.91	18
19	12.055693	78.969235	0.01266316	0.082948	6.550369	0.15266316	15.27	1.900600	10.00	19
20	13.743490	91.024928	0.01098600	0.072762	6.623131	0.15098600	15.10	2.019720	10.10	20
21	15.667578	104.768418	0.00954486	0.063826	6.686957	0.14954486	14.96	2.140442	10.19	21
22	17.861039	120.435996	0.00830317	0.055988	6.742944	0.14830317	14.84	2.262670	10.28	22
23	20.361585	138.297035	0.00723081	0.049112	6.792056	0.14723081	14.73	2.386309	10.38	23
24	23.212207	158.658620	0.00630284	0.043081	6.835137	0.14630284	14.64	2.511268	10.46	24
25	26.461916	181.870827	0.00549841	0.037790	6.872927	0.14549841	14.55	2.637460	10.55	25
26	30.166584	208.332743	0.00480001	0.033149	6.906077	0.14480001	14.49	2.764800	10.63	26
27	34.389906	238.499327	0.00419288	0.029078	6.935155	0.14419288	14.42	2.893208	10.72	27
28	39.204493	272.889233	0.00366449	0.025507	6.960662	0.14366449	14.37	3.022606	10.80	28
29	44.693122	312.093725	0.00320417	0.022375	6.983037	0.14320417	14.33	3.152921	10.87	29
30	50.950159	356.786847	0.00280279	0.019627	7.002664	0.14280279	14.29	3.284084	10.95	30
31	58.083181	407.737006	0.00245256	0.017217	7.019881	0.14245256	14.25	3.416029	11.02	31
32	66.214826	465.820186	0.00214675	0.015102	7.034983	0.14214675	14.22	3.548696	11.09	32
33	75.484902	532.035012	0.00187958	0.013248	7.048231	0.14187958	14.19	3.682026	11.16	33
34	86.052788	607.519914	0.00164604	0.011621	7.059852	0.14164604	14.17	3.815965	11.22	34
35	98.100178	693.572702	0.00144181	0.010194	7.070045	0.14144181	14.15	3.950463	11.29	35
36	111.834203	791.672881	0.00126315	0.008942	7.078987	0.14126315	14.13	4.085473	11.35	36
37	127.490992	903.507084	0.00110680	0.007844	7.086831	0.14110680	14.12	4.220952	11.41	37
38	145.339731	1030.998076	0.00096993	0.006880	7.093711	0.14096993	14.10	4.356857	11.47	38
39	165.687293	1176.337806	0.00085010	0.006035	7.099747	0.14085010	14.09	4.493154	11.52	39
40	188.883514	1342.025099	0.00074514	0.005294	7.105041	0.14074514	14.08	4.629806	11.57	40
41	215.327206	1530.908613	0.00065321	0.004644	7.109685	0.14065321	14.07	4.766781	11.63	41
42	245.473015	1746.235819	0.00057266	0.004074	7.113759	0.14057266	14.06	4.904052	11.68	42
43	279.839237	1991.708833	0.00050208	0.003573	7.117332	0.14050208	14.06	5.041590	11.72	43
44	319.016730	2271.548070	0.00044023	0.003135	7.120467	0.14044023	14.05	5.179370	11.77	44
45	363.679072	2590.564800	0.00038602	0.002750	7.123217	0.14038602	14.04	5.317371	11.82	45
46	414.594142	2954.243872	0.00033850	0.002412	7.125629	0.14033850	14.04	5.455571	11.86	46
47	472.637322	3368.838014	0.00029684	0.002116	7.127744	0.14029684	14.03	5.593951	11.90	47
48	538.806547	3841.475336	0.00026032	0.001856	7.129600	0.14026032	14.03	5.732495	11.94	48
49	614.239464	4380.281883	0.00022830	0.001628	7.131228	0.14022830	14.03	5.871186	11.98	49
50	700.232988	4994.521346	0.00020022	0.001428	7.132656	0.14020022	14.03	6.010011	12.02	50

COMPOUND INTEREST AND ANNUITY TABLE

15.00 % ANNUAL

YR	Amount Of 1	Amount Of 1 Per Period	Sinking Fund Payment	Present Worth Of 1	Present Worth Of 1 Per Period	Periodic Payment To Amortize 1	Constant Annual Percent	Total Interest	Annual Add-on Rate	YR
	What a single $1 deposit grows to in the future. The deposit is made at the beginning of the first period.	What a series of $1 deposits grow to in the future. A deposit is made at the end of each period.	The amount to be deposited at the end of each period that grows to $1 in the future.	What $1 to be paid in the future is worth today. Value today of a single payment tomorrow.	What $1 to be paid at the end of each period is worth today. Value today of a series of payments tomorrow.	The mortgage payment to amortize a loan of $1. An annuity certain, payable at the end of each period, worth $1 today.	The annual payment, including interest and principal, to amortize completely a loan of $100.	The total interest paid over the term on a loan of $1. The loan is amortized by regular periodic payments.	The average annual interest rate on a loan that is completely amortized by regular periodic payments.	
	$S=(1+i)^n$	$S_{\overline{n}}=\frac{(1+i)^n-1}{i}$	$\frac{1}{S_{\overline{n}}}=\frac{i}{(1+i)^n-1}$	$V^n=\frac{1}{(1+i)^n}$	$A_{\overline{n}}=\frac{1-V^n}{i}$	$\frac{1}{A_{\overline{n}}}=\frac{i}{1-V^n}$				
1	1.150000	1.000000	1.00000000	0.869565	0.869565	1.15000000	115.00	0.150000	15.00	1
2	1.322500	2.150000	0.46511628	0.756144	1.625709	0.61511628	61.52	0.230233	11.51	2
3	1.520875	3.472500	0.28797696	0.657516	2.283225	0.43797696	43.80	0.313931	10.46	3
4	1.749006	4.993375	0.20026535	0.571753	2.854978	0.35026535	35.03	0.401061	10.03	4
5	2.011357	6.742381	0.14831555	0.497177	3.352155	0.29831555	29.84	0.491578	9.83	5
6	2.313061	8.753738	0.11423691	0.432328	3.784483	0.26423691	26.43	0.585421	9.76	6
7	2.660020	11.066799	0.09036036	0.375937	4.160420	0.24036036	24.04	0.682523	9.75	7
8	3.059023	13.726819	0.07285009	0.326902	4.487322	0.22285009	22.29	0.782801	9.79	8
9	3.517876	16.785842	0.05957402	0.284262	4.771584	0.20957402	20.96	0.886166	9.85	9
10	4.045558	20.303718	0.04925206	0.247185	5.018769	0.19925206	19.93	0.992521	9.93	10
11	4.652391	24.349276	0.04106898	0.214943	5.233712	0.19106898	19.11	1.101759	10.02	11
12	5.350250	29.001667	0.03448078	0.186907	5.420619	0.18448078	18.45	1.213769	10.11	12
13	6.152788	34.351917	0.02911046	0.162528	5.583147	0.17911046	17.92	1.328436	10.22	13
14	7.075706	40.504705	0.02468849	0.141329	5.724476	0.17468849	17.47	1.445639	10.33	14
15	8.137062	47.580411	0.02101705	0.122894	5.847370	0.17101705	17.11	1.565256	10.44	15
16	9.357621	55.717472	0.01794769	0.106865	5.954235	0.16794769	16.80	1.687163	10.54	16
17	10.761264	65.075093	0.01536686	0.092926	6.047161	0.16536686	16.54	1.811237	10.65	17
18	12.375454	75.836357	0.01318629	0.080805	6.127966	0.16318629	16.32	1.937353	10.76	18
19	14.231772	88.211811	0.01133635	0.070265	6.198231	0.16133635	16.14	2.065391	10.87	19
20	16.366537	102.443583	0.00976147	0.061100	6.259331	0.15976147	15.98	2.195229	10.98	20
21	18.821518	118.810120	0.00841679	0.053131	6.312462	0.15841679	15.85	2.326753	11.08	21
22	21.644746	137.631638	0.00726577	0.046201	6.358663	0.15726577	15.73	2.459847	11.18	22
23	24.891458	159.276384	0.00627839	0.040174	6.398837	0.15627839	15.63	2.594403	11.28	23
24	28.625176	184.167841	0.00542983	0.034934	6.433771	0.15542983	15.55	2.730316	11.38	24
25	32.918953	212.793017	0.00469940	0.030378	6.464149	0.15469940	15.47	2.867485	11.47	25
26	37.856796	245.711970	0.00406981	0.026415	6.490564	0.15406981	15.41	3.005815	11.56	26
27	43.535315	283.568766	0.00352648	0.022970	6.513534	0.15352648	15.36	3.145215	11.65	27
28	50.065612	327.104080	0.00305713	0.019974	6.533508	0.15305713	15.31	3.285600	11.73	28
29	57.575454	377.169693	0.00265133	0.017369	6.550877	0.15265133	15.27	3.426888	11.82	29
30	66.211772	434.745146	0.00230020	0.015103	6.565980	0.15230020	15.24	3.569006	11.90	30
31	76.143538	500.956918	0.00199618	0.013133	6.579113	0.15199618	15.20	3.711882	11.97	31
32	87.565068	577.100456	0.00173280	0.011420	6.590533	0.15173280	15.18	3.855450	12.05	32
33	100.699829	664.665524	0.00150452	0.009931	6.600463	0.15150452	15.16	3.999649	12.12	33
34	115.804803	765.365353	0.00130657	0.008635	6.609099	0.15130657	15.14	4.144423	12.19	34
35	133.175523	881.170156	0.00113485	0.007509	6.616607	0.15113485	15.12	4.289720	12.26	35
36	153.151852	1014.345680	0.00098586	0.006529	6.623137	0.15098586	15.10	4.435491	12.32	36
37	176.124630	1167.497532	0.00085653	0.005678	6.628815	0.15085653	15.09	4.581692	12.38	37
38	202.543324	1343.622161	0.00074426	0.004937	6.633752	0.15074426	15.08	4.728282	12.44	38
39	232.924823	1546.165485	0.00064676	0.004293	6.638045	0.15064676	15.07	4.875224	12.50	39
40	267.863546	1779.090308	0.00056209	0.003733	6.641778	0.15056209	15.06	5.022483	12.56	40
41	308.043078	2046.953854	0.00048853	0.003246	6.645025	0.15048853	15.05	5.170030	12.61	41
42	354.249540	2354.996933	0.00042463	0.002823	6.647848	0.15042463	15.05	5.317834	12.66	42
43	407.386971	2709.246473	0.00036911	0.002455	6.650302	0.15036911	15.04	5.465872	12.71	43
44	468.495017	3116.633443	0.00032086	0.002134	6.652437	0.15032086	15.04	5.614118	12.76	44
45	538.769269	3585.128460	0.00027893	0.001856	6.654293	0.15027893	15.03	5.762552	12.81	45
46	619.584659	4123.897729	0.00024249	0.001614	6.655907	0.15024249	15.03	5.911154	12.85	46
47	712.522358	4743.482388	0.00021082	0.001403	6.657310	0.15021082	15.03	6.059908	12.89	47
48	819.400712	5456.004746	0.00018328	0.001220	6.658531	0.15018328	15.02	6.208798	12.93	48
49	942.310819	6275.405458	0.00015935	0.001061	6.659592	0.15015935	15.02	6.357808	12.98	49
50	1083.657442	7217.716277	0.00013855	0.000923	6.660515	0.15013855	15.02	6.506927	13.01	50

COMPOUND INTEREST AND ANNUITY TABLE

16.00 % ANNUAL

YR	Amount Of 1	Amount Of 1 Per Period	Sinking Fund Payment	Present Worth Of 1	Present Worth Of 1 Per Period	Periodic Payment To Amortize 1	Constant Annual Percent	Total Interest	Annual Add-on Rate	YR
	What a single $1 deposit grows to in the future. The deposit is made at the beginning of the first period.	What a series of $1 deposits grow to in the future. A deposit is made at the end of each period.	The amount to be deposited at the end of each period that grows to $1 in the future.	What $1 to be paid in the future is worth today. Value today of a single payment tomorrow.	What $1 to be paid at the end of each period is worth today. Value today of a series of payments tomorrow.	The mortgage payment to amortize a loan of $1. An annuity certain, payable at the end of each period, worth $1 today.	The annual payment, including interest and principal, to amortize completely a loan of $100.	The total interest paid over the term on a loan of $1. The loan is amortized by regular periodic payments.	The average annual interest rate on a loan that is completely amortized by regular periodic payments.	
	$S=(1+i)^n$	$S_{\overline{n}}=\frac{(1+i)^n-1}{i}$	$\frac{1}{S_{\overline{n}}}=\frac{i}{(1+i)^n-1}$	$V^n=\frac{1}{(1+i)^n}$	$A_{\overline{n}}=\frac{1-V^n}{i}$	$\frac{1}{A_{\overline{n}}}=\frac{i}{1-V^n}$				
1	1.160000	1.000000	1.00000000	0.862069	0.862069	1.16000000	116.00	0.160000	16.00	1
2	1.345600	2.160000	0.46296296	0.743163	1.605232	0.62296296	62.30	0.245926	12.30	2
3	1.560896	3.505600	0.28525787	0.640658	2.245890	0.44525787	44.53	0.335774	11.19	3
4	1.810639	5.066496	0.19737507	0.552291	2.798181	0.35737507	35.74	0.429500	10.74	4
5	2.100342	6.877135	0.14540938	0.476113	3.274294	0.30540938	30.55	0.527047	10.54	5
6	2.436396	8.977477	0.11138987	0.410442	3.684736	0.27138987	27.14	0.628339	10.47	6
7	2.826220	11.413873	0.08761268	0.353830	4.038565	0.24761268	24.77	0.733289	10.48	7
8	3.278415	14.240093	0.07022426	0.305025	4.343591	0.23022426	23.03	0.841794	10.52	8
9	3.802961	17.518508	0.05708249	0.262953	4.606544	0.21708249	21.71	0.953742	10.60	9
10	4.411435	21.321469	0.04690108	0.226684	4.833227	0.20690108	20.70	1.069011	10.69	10
11	5.117265	25.732904	0.03886075	0.195417	5.028644	0.19886075	19.89	1.187468	10.80	11
12	5.936027	30.850169	0.03241473	0.168463	5.197107	0.19241473	19.25	1.308977	10.91	12
13	6.885791	36.786196	0.02718411	0.145227	5.342334	0.18718411	18.72	1.433393	11.03	13
14	7.987518	43.671987	0.02289797	0.125195	5.467529	0.18289797	18.29	1.560572	11.15	14
15	9.265521	51.659505	0.01935752	0.107927	5.575456	0.17935752	17.94	1.690363	11.27	15

17.00 % ANNUAL

YR										YR
1	1.170000	1.000000	1.00000000	0.854701	0.854701	1.17000000	117.00	0.170000	17.00	1
2	1.368900	2.170000	0.46082949	0.730514	1.585214	0.63082949	63.09	0.261659	13.08	2
3	1.601613	3.538900	0.28257368	0.624371	2.209585	0.45257368	45.26	0.357721	11.92	3
4	1.873887	5.140513	0.19453311	0.533650	2.743235	0.36453311	36.46	0.458132	11.45	4
5	2.192448	7.014400	0.14256386	0.456111	3.199346	0.31256386	31.26	0.562819	11.26	5
6	2.565164	9.206848	0.10861480	0.389839	3.589185	0.27861480	27.87	0.671689	11.19	6
7	3.001242	11.772012	0.08494724	0.333195	3.922380	0.25494724	25.50	0.784631	11.21	7
8	3.511453	14.773255	0.06768989	0.284782	4.207163	0.23768989	23.77	0.901519	11.27	8
9	4.108400	18.284708	0.05469051	0.243404	4.450566	0.22469051	22.47	1.022215	11.36	9
10	4.806828	22.393108	0.04465660	0.208037	4.658604	0.21465660	21.47	1.146566	11.47	10
11	5.623989	27.199937	0.03676479	0.177810	4.836413	0.20676479	20.68	1.274413	11.59	11
12	6.580067	32.823926	0.03046558	0.151974	4.988387	0.20046558	20.05	1.405587	11.71	12
13	7.698679	39.403993	0.02537814	0.129892	5.118280	0.19537814	19.54	1.539916	11.85	13
14	9.007454	47.102672	0.02123022	0.111019	5.229299	0.19123022	19.13	1.677223	11.98	14
15	10.538721	56.110126	0.01782209	0.094888	5.324187	0.18782209	18.79	1.817331	12.12	15

COMPOUND INTEREST AND ANNUITY TABLE

18.00 % ANNUAL

YR	Amount Of 1 — What a single \$1 deposit grows to in the future. The deposit is made at the beginning of the first period. $S=(1+i)^n$	Amount Of 1 Per Period — What a series of \$1 deposits grow to in the future. A deposit is made at the end of each period. $S_n=\frac{(1+i)^n-1}{i}$	Sinking Fund Payment — The amount to be deposited at the end of each period that grows to \$1 in the future. $\frac{1}{S_n}=\frac{i}{(1+i)^n-1}$	Present Worth Of 1 — What \$1 to be paid in the future is worth today. Value today of a single payment tomorrow. $V^n=\frac{1}{(1+i)^n}$	Present Worth Of 1 Per Period — What \$1 to be paid at the end of each period is worth today. Value today of a series of payments tomorrow. $A_n=\frac{1-V^n}{i}$	Periodic Payment To Amortize 1 — The mortgage payment to amortize a loan of \$1. An annuity certain, payable at the end of each period, worth \$1 today. $\frac{1}{A_n}=\frac{i}{1-V^n}$	Constant Annual Percent — The annual payment, including interest and principal, to amortize completely a loan of \$100.	Total Interest — The total interest paid over the term on a loan of \$1. The loan is amortized by regular periodic payments.	Annual Add-on Rate — The average annual interest rate on a loan that is completely amortized by regular periodic payments.	YR
1	1.180000	1.000000	1.00000000	0.847458	0.847458	1.18000000	118.00	0.180000	18.00	1
2	1.392400	2.180000	0.45871560	0.718184	1.565642	0.63871560	63.88	0.277431	13.87	2
3	1.643032	3.572400	0.27992386	0.608631	2.174273	0.45992386	46.00	0.379772	12.66	3
4	1.938778	5.215432	0.19173867	0.515789	2.690062	0.37173867	37.18	0.486955	12.17	4
5	2.287758	7.154210	0.13977784	0.437109	3.127171	0.31977784	31.98	0.598889	11.98	5
6	2.699554	9.441968	0.10591013	0.370432	3.497603	0.28591013	28.60	0.715461	11.92	6
7	3.185474	12.141522	0.08236200	0.313925	3.811528	0.26236200	26.24	0.836534	11.95	7
8	3.758859	15.326996	0.06524436	0.266038	4.077566	0.24524436	24.53	0.961955	12.02	8
9	4.435454	19.085855	0.05239482	0.225456	4.303022	0.23239482	23.24	1.091553	12.13	9
10	5.233836	23.521309	0.04251464	0.191064	4.494086	0.22251464	22.26	1.225146	12.25	10
11	6.175926	28.755144	0.03477639	0.161919	4.656005	0.21477639	21.48	1.362540	12.39	11
12	7.287593	34.931070	0.02862781	0.137220	4.793225	0.20862781	20.87	1.503534	12.53	12
13	8.599359	42.218663	0.02368621	0.116288	4.909513	0.20368621	20.37	1.647921	12.68	13
14	10.147244	50.818022	0.01967806	0.098549	5.008062	0.19967806	19.97	1.795493	12.82	14
15	11.973748	60.965266	0.01640278	0.083516	5.091578	0.19640278	19.65	1.946042	12.97	15

19.00 % ANNUAL

YR	Amount Of 1	Amount Of 1 Per Period	Sinking Fund Payment	Present Worth Of 1	Present Worth Of 1 Per Period	Periodic Payment To Amortize 1	Constant Annual Percent	Total Interest	Annual Add-on Rate	YR
1	1.190000	1.000000	1.00000000	0.840336	0.840336	1.19000000	119.00	0.190000	19.00	1
2	1.416100	2.190000	0.45662100	0.706165	1.546501	0.64662100	64.67	0.293242	14.66	2
3	1.685159	3.606100	0.27730789	0.593416	2.139917	0.46730789	46.74	0.401924	13.40	3
4	2.005339	5.291259	0.18899094	0.498669	2.638586	0.37899094	37.90	0.515964	12.90	4
5	2.386354	7.296598	0.13705017	0.419049	3.057635	0.32705017	32.71	0.635251	12.71	5
6	2.839761	9.682952	0.10327429	0.352142	3.409777	0.29327429	29.33	0.759646	12.66	6
7	3.379315	12.522713	0.07985490	0.295918	3.705695	0.26985490	26.99	0.888984	12.70	7
8	4.021385	15.902028	0.06288506	0.248671	3.954366	0.25288506	25.29	1.023080	12.79	8
9	4.785449	19.923413	0.05019220	0.208967	4.163332	0.24019220	24.02	1.161730	12.91	9
10	5.694684	24.708862	0.04047131	0.175602	4.338935	0.23047131	23.05	1.304713	13.05	10
11	6.776674	30.403546	0.03289090	0.147565	4.486500	0.22289090	22.29	1.451800	13.20	11
12	8.064242	37.180220	0.02689602	0.124004	4.610504	0.21689602	21.69	1.602752	13.36	12
13	9.596448	45.244461	0.02210215	0.104205	4.714709	0.21210215	21.22	1.757328	13.52	13
14	11.419773	54.840909	0.01823456	0.087567	4.802277	0.20823456	20.83	1.915284	13.68	14
15	13.589530	66.260682	0.01509191	0.073586	4.875863	0.20509191	20.51	2.076379	13.84	15

COMPOUND INTEREST AND ANNUITY TABLE

20.00 %
ANNUAL

YR	Amount Of 1	Amount Of 1 Per Period	Sinking Fund Payment	Present Worth Of 1	Present Worth Of 1 Per Period	Periodic Payment To Amortize 1	Constant Annual Percent	Total Interest	Annual Add-on Rate	YR
	What a single $1 deposit grows to in the future. The deposit is made at the beginning of the first period.	What a series of $1 deposits grow to in the future. A deposit is made at the end of each period.	The amount to be deposited at the end of each period that grows to $1 in the future.	What $1 to be paid in the future is worth today. Value today of a single payment tomorrow.	What $1 to be paid at the end of each period is worth today. Value today of a series of payments tomorrow.	The mortgage payment to amortize a loan of $1. An annuity certain, payable at the end of each period, worth $1 today.	The annual payment, including interest and principal, to amortize completely a loan of $100.	The total interest paid over the term on a loan of $1. The loan is amortized by regular periodic payments.	The average annual interest rate on a loan that is completely amortized by regular periodic payments.	
	$S=(1+i)^n$	$S_{\overline{n}}=\frac{(1+i)^n-1}{i}$	$\frac{1}{S_{\overline{n}}}=\frac{i}{(1+i)^n-1}$	$V^n=\frac{1}{(1+i)^n}$	$A_{\overline{n}}=\frac{1-V^n}{i}$	$\frac{1}{A_{\overline{n}}}=\frac{i}{1-V^n}$				
1	1.200000	1.000000	1.00000000	0.833333	0.833333	1.20000000	120.00	0.200000	20.00	1
2	1.440000	2.200000	0.45454545	0.694444	1.527778	0.65454545	65.46	0.309091	15.45	2
3	1.728000	3.640000	0.27472527	0.578704	2.106481	0.47472527	47.48	0.424176	14.14	3
4	2.073600	5.368000	0.18628912	0.482253	2.588735	0.38628912	38.63	0.545156	13.63	4
5	2.488320	7.441600	0.13437970	0.401878	2.990612	0.33437970	33.44	0.671899	13.44	5
6	2.985984	9.929920	0.10070575	0.334898	3.325510	0.30070575	30.08	0.804234	13.40	6
7	3.583181	12.915904	0.07742393	0.279082	3.604592	0.27742393	27.75	0.941967	13.46	7
8	4.299817	16.499085	0.06060942	0.232568	3.837160	0.26060942	26.07	1.084875	13.56	8
9	5.159780	20.798902	0.04807946	0.193807	4.030967	0.24807946	24.81	1.232715	13.70	9
10	6.191736	25.958682	0.03852276	0.161506	4.192472	0.23852276	23.86	1.385228	13.85	10
11	7.430084	32.150419	0.03110379	0.134588	4.327060	0.23110379	23.12	1.542142	14.02	11
12	8.916100	39.580502	0.02526496	0.112157	4.439217	0.22526496	22.53	1.703180	14.19	12
13	10.699321	48.496603	0.02062000	0.093464	4.532681	0.22062000	22.07	1.868060	14.37	13
14	12.839185	59.195923	0.01689306	0.077887	4.610567	0.21689306	21.69	2.036503	14.55	14
15	15.407022	72.035108	0.01388212	0.064905	4.675473	0.21388212	21.39	2.208232	14.72	15

21.00 %
ANNUAL

YR										YR
1	1.210000	1.000000	1.00000000	0.826446	0.826446	1.21000000	121.00	0.210000	21.00	1
2	1.464100	2.210000	0.45248869	0.683013	1.509460	0.66248869	66.25	0.324977	16.25	2
3	1.771561	3.674100	0.27217550	0.564474	2.073934	0.48217550	48.22	0.446526	14.88	3
4	2.143589	5.445661	0.18363244	0.466507	2.540441	0.39363244	39.37	0.574530	14.36	4
5	2.593742	7.589250	0.13176533	0.385543	2.925984	0.34176533	34.18	0.708827	14.18	5
6	3.138428	10.182992	0.09820296	0.318631	3.244615	0.30820296	30.83	0.849218	14.15	6
7	3.797498	13.321421	0.07506707	0.263331	3.507946	0.28506707	28.51	0.995469	14.22	7
8	4.594973	17.118919	0.05841490	0.217629	3.725576	0.26841490	26.85	1.147319	14.34	8
9	5.559917	21.713892	0.04605347	0.179859	3.905434	0.25605347	25.61	1.304481	14.49	9
10	6.727500	27.273809	0.03666521	0.148644	4.054078	0.24666521	24.67	1.466652	14.67	10
11	8.140275	34.001309	0.02941063	0.122846	4.176924	0.23941063	23.95	1.633517	14.85	11
12	9.849733	42.141584	0.02372953	0.101526	4.278450	0.23372953	23.38	1.804754	15.04	12
13	11.918177	51.991317	0.01923398	0.083905	4.362355	0.22923398	22.93	1.980042	15.23	13
14	14.420994	63.909493	0.01564713	0.069343	4.431698	0.22564713	22.57	2.159060	15.42	14
15	17.449402	78.330487	0.01276642	0.057309	4.489007	0.22276642	22.28	2.341496	15.61	15

COMPOUND INTEREST AND ANNUITY TABLE

**22.00 %
ANNUAL**

YR	Amount Of 1	Amount Of 1 Per Period	Sinking Fund Payment	Present Worth Of 1	Present Worth Of 1 Per Period	Periodic Payment To Amortize 1	Constant Annual Percent	Total Interest	Annual Add-on Rate	YR
	What a single $1 deposit grows to in the future. The deposit is made at the beginning of the first period.	What a series of $1 deposits grow to in the future. A deposit is made at the end of each period.	The amount to be deposited at the end of each period that grows to $1 in the future.	What $1 to be paid in the future is worth today. Value today of a single payment tomorrow.	What $1 to be paid at the end of each period is worth today. Value today of a series of payments tomorrow.	The mortgage payment to amortize a loan of $1. An annuity certain, payable at the end of each period, worth $1 today.	The annual payment, including interest and principal, to amortize completely a loan of $100.	The total interest paid over the term on a loan of $1. The loan is amortized by regular periodic payments.	The average annual interest rate on a loan that is completely amortized by regular periodic payments.	
	$S=(1+i)^n$	$S_{\overline{n}}=\frac{(1+i)^n-1}{i}$	$\frac{1}{S_{\overline{n}}}=\frac{i}{(1+i)^n-1}$	$V^n=\frac{1}{(1+i)^n}$	$A_{\overline{n}}=\frac{1-V^n}{i}$	$\frac{1}{A_{\overline{n}}}=\frac{i}{1-V^n}$				
1	1.220000	1.000000	1.00000000	0.819672	0.819672	1.22000000	122.00	0.220000	22.00	1
2	1.488400	2.220000	0.45045045	0.671862	1.491535	0.67045045	67.05	0.340901	17.05	2
3	1.815848	3.708400	0.26965807	0.550707	2.042241	0.48965807	48.97	0.468974	15.63	3
4	2.215335	5.524248	0.18102011	0.451399	2.493641	0.40102011	40.11	0.604080	15.10	4
5	2.702708	7.739583	0.12920593	0.369999	2.863640	0.34920593	34.93	0.746030	14.92	5
6	3.297304	10.442291	0.09576443	0.303278	3.166918	0.31576443	31.58	0.894587	14.91	6
7	4.022711	13.739595	0.07278235	0.248589	3.415506	0.29278235	29.28	1.049476	14.99	7
8	4.907707	17.762306	0.05629900	0.203761	3.619268	0.27629900	27.63	1.210392	15.13	8
9	5.987403	22.670013	0.04411114	0.167017	3.786285	0.26411114	26.42	1.377000	15.30	9
10	7.304631	28.657416	0.03489498	0.136899	3.923184	0.25489498	25.49	1.548950	15.49	10
11	8.911650	35.962047	0.02780709	0.112213	4.035397	0.24780709	24.79	1.725878	15.69	11
12	10.872213	44.873697	0.02228477	0.091978	4.127375	0.24228477	24.23	1.907417	15.90	12
13	13.264100	55.745911	0.01793854	0.075391	4.202766	0.23793854	23.80	2.093201	16.10	13
14	16.182202	69.010011	0.01449065	0.061796	4.264562	0.23449065	23.45	2.282869	16.31	14
15	19.742287	85.192213	0.01173816	0.050653	4.315215	0.23173816	23.18	2.476072	16.51	15

**23.00 %
ANNUAL**

YR										YR
1	1.230000	1.000000	1.00000000	0.813008	0.813008	1.23000000	123.00	0.230000	23.00	1
2	1.512900	2.230000	0.44843049	0.660982	1.473990	0.67843049	67.85	0.356861	17.84	2
3	1.860867	3.742900	0.26717251	0.537384	2.011374	0.49717251	49.72	0.491518	16.38	3
4	2.288866	5.603767	0.17845139	0.436897	2.448272	0.40845139	40.85	0.633806	15.85	4
5	2.815306	7.892633	0.12670042	0.355201	2.803473	0.35670042	35.68	0.783502	15.67	5
6	3.462826	10.707939	0.09338865	0.288781	3.092254	0.32338865	32.34	0.940332	15.67	6
7	4.259276	14.170765	0.07056782	0.234782	3.327036	0.30056782	30.06	1.103975	15.77	7
8	5.238909	18.430041	0.05425924	0.190879	3.517916	0.28425924	28.43	1.274074	15.93	8
9	6.443859	23.668950	0.04224944	0.155187	3.673102	0.27224944	27.23	1.450245	16.11	9
10	7.925946	30.112809	0.03320846	0.126168	3.799270	0.26320846	26.33	1.632085	16.32	10
11	9.748914	38.038755	0.02628898	0.102576	3.901846	0.25628898	25.63	1.819179	16.54	11
12	11.991164	47.787669	0.02092590	0.083395	3.985240	0.25092590	25.10	2.011111	16.76	12
13	14.749132	59.778833	0.01672833	0.067801	4.053041	0.24672833	24.68	2.207468	16.98	13
14	18.141432	74.527964	0.01341778	0.055122	4.108163	0.24341778	24.35	2.407849	17.20	14
15	22.313961	92.669396	0.01079105	0.044815	4.152978	0.24079105	24.08	2.611866	17.41	15

COMPOUND INTEREST AND ANNUITY TABLE

24.00 % ANNUAL

YR	Amount Of 1	Amount Of 1 Per Period	Sinking Fund Payment	Present Worth Of 1	Present Worth Of 1 Per Period	Periodic Payment To Amortize 1	Constant Annual Percent	Total Interest	Annual Add-on Rate	YR
	What a single $1 deposit grows to in the future. The deposit is made at the beginning of the first period.	What a series of $1 deposits grow to in the future. A deposit is made at the end of each period.	The amount to be deposited at the end of each period that grows to $1 in the future.	What $1 to be paid in the future is worth today. Value today of a single payment tomorrow.	What $1 to be paid at the end of each period is worth today. Value today of a series of payments tomorrow.	The mortgage payment to amortize a loan of $1. An annuity certain, payable at the end of each period, worth $1 today.	The annual payment, including interest and principal, to amortize completely a loan of $100.	The total interest paid over the term on a loan of $1. The loan is amortized by regular periodic payments.	The average annual interest rate on a loan that is completely amortized by regular periodic payments.	
	$S=(1+i)^n$	$S_{\overline{n}}=\frac{(1+i)^n-1}{i}$	$\frac{1}{S_{\overline{n}}}=\frac{i}{(1+i)^n-1}$	$V^n=\frac{1}{(1+i)^n}$	$A_{\overline{n}}=\frac{1-V^n}{i}$	$\frac{1}{A_{\overline{n}}}=\frac{i}{1-V^n}$				
1	1.240000	1.000000	1.00000000	0.806452	0.806452	1.24000000	124.00	0.240000	24.00	1
2	1.537600	2.240000	0.44642857	0.650364	1.456816	0.68642857	68.65	0.372857	18.64	2
3	1.906624	3.777600	0.26471834	0.524487	1.981303	0.50471834	50.48	0.514155	17.14	3
4	2.364214	5.684224	0.17592551	0.422974	2.404277	0.41592551	41.60	0.663702	16.59	4
5	2.931625	8.048438	0.12424771	0.341108	2.745384	0.36424771	36.43	0.821239	16.42	5
6	3.635215	10.980063	0.09107416	0.275087	3.020471	0.33107416	33.11	0.986445	16.44	6
7	4.507667	14.615278	0.06842155	0.221844	3.242316	0.30842155	30.85	1.158951	16.56	7
8	5.589507	19.122945	0.05229320	0.178907	3.421222	0.29229320	29.23	1.338346	16.73	8
9	6.930988	24.712451	0.04046543	0.144280	3.565502	0.28046543	28.05	1.524189	16.94	9
10	8.594426	31.643440	0.03160213	0.116354	3.681856	0.27160213	27.17	1.716021	17.16	10
11	10.657088	40.237865	0.02485221	0.093834	3.775691	0.26485221	26.49	1.913374	17.39	11
12	13.214789	50.894953	0.01964831	0.075673	3.851363	0.25964831	25.97	2.115780	17.63	12
13	16.386338	64.109741	0.01559825	0.061026	3.912390	0.25559825	25.56	2.322777	17.87	13
14	20.319059	80.496079	0.01242297	0.049215	3.961605	0.25242297	25.25	2.533922	18.10	14
15	25.195633	100.815138	0.00991915	0.039689	4.001294	0.24991915	25.00	2.748787	18.33	15

25.00 % ANNUAL

YR	Amount Of 1	Amount Of 1 Per Period	Sinking Fund Payment	Present Worth Of 1	Present Worth Of 1 Per Period	Periodic Payment To Amortize 1	Constant Annual Percent	Total Interest	Annual Add-on Rate	YR
1	1.250000	1.000000	1.00000000	0.800000	0.800000	1.25000000	125.00	0.250000	25.00	1
2	1.562500	2.250000	0.44444444	0.640000	1.440000	0.69444444	69.45	0.388889	19.44	2
3	1.953125	3.812500	0.26229508	0.512000	1.952000	0.51229508	51.23	0.536885	17.90	3
4	2.441406	5.765625	0.17344173	0.409600	2.361600	0.42344173	42.35	0.693767	17.34	4
5	3.051758	8.207031	0.12184674	0.327680	2.689280	0.37184674	37.19	0.859234	17.18	5
6	3.814697	11.258789	0.08881950	0.262144	2.951424	0.33881950	33.89	1.032917	17.22	6
7	4.768372	15.073486	0.06634165	0.209715	3.161139	0.31634165	31.64	1.214392	17.35	7
8	5.960464	19.841858	0.05039851	0.167772	3.328911	0.30039851	30.04	1.403188	17.54	8
9	7.450581	25.802322	0.03875620	0.134218	3.463129	0.28875620	28.88	1.598806	17.76	9
10	9.313226	33.252903	0.03007256	0.107374	3.570503	0.28007256	28.01	1.800726	18.01	10
11	11.641532	42.566129	0.02349286	0.085899	3.656403	0.27349286	27.35	2.008421	18.26	11
12	14.551915	54.207661	0.01844758	0.068719	3.725122	0.26844758	26.85	2.221371	18.51	12
13	18.189894	68.759576	0.01454343	0.054976	3.780098	0.26454343	26.46	2.439065	18.76	13
14	22.737368	86.949470	0.01150093	0.043980	3.824078	0.26150093	26.16	2.661013	19.01	14
15	28.421709	109.686838	0.00911686	0.035184	3.859263	0.25911686	25.92	2.886753	19.25	15

COMPOUND INTEREST AND ANNUITY TABLE

30.00 % ANNUAL

YR	Amount Of 1	Amount Of 1 Per Period	Sinking Fund Payment	Present Worth Of 1	Present Worth Of 1 Per Period	Periodic Payment To Amortize 1	Constant Annual Percent	Total Interest	Annual Add-on Rate	YR
	What a single $1 deposit grows to in the future. The deposit is made at the beginning of the first period.	What a series of $1 deposits grow to in the future. A deposit is made at the end of each period.	The amount to be deposited at the end of each period that grows to $1 in the future.	What $1 to be paid in the future is worth today. Value today of a single payment tomorrow.	What $1 to be paid at the end of each period is worth today. Value today of a series of payments tomorrow.	The mortgage payment to amortize a loan of $1. An annuity certain, payable at the end of each period, worth $1 today.	The annual payment, including interest and principal, to amortize completely a loan of $100.	The total interest paid over the term on a loan of $1. The loan is amortized by regular periodic payments.	The average annual interest rate on a loan that is completely amortized by regular periodic payments.	
	$S=(1+i)^n$	$S_{\overline{n}}=\frac{(1+i)^n-1}{i}$	$\frac{1}{S_{\overline{n}}}=\frac{i}{(1+i)^n-1}$	$V^n=\frac{1}{(1+i)^n}$	$A_{\overline{n}}=\frac{1-V^n}{i}$	$\frac{1}{A_{\overline{n}}}=\frac{i}{1-V^n}$				
1	1.300000	1.000000	1.00000000	0.769231	0.769231	1.30000000	130.00	0.300000	30.00	1
2	1.690000	2.300000	0.43478261	0.591716	1.360947	0.73478261	73.48	0.469565	23.48	2
3	2.197000	3.990000	0.25062657	0.455166	1.816113	0.55062657	55.07	0.651880	21.73	3
4	2.856100	6.187000	0.16162922	0.350128	2.166241	0.46162922	46.17	0.846517	21.16	4
5	3.712930	9.043100	0.11058155	0.269329	2.435570	0.41058155	41.06	1.052908	21.06	5
6	4.826809	12.756030	0.07839430	0.207176	2.642746	0.37839430	37.84	1.270366	21.17	6
7	6.274852	17.582839	0.05687364	0.159366	2.802112	0.35687364	35.69	1.498115	21.40	7
8	8.157307	23.857691	0.04191521	0.122589	2.924702	0.34191521	34.20	1.735322	21.69	8
9	10.604499	32.014998	0.03123536	0.094300	3.019001	0.33123536	33.13	1.981118	22.01	9
10	13.785849	42.619497	0.02346344	0.072538	3.091539	0.32346344	32.35	2.234634	22.35	10
11	17.921604	56.405346	0.01772882	0.055799	3.147338	0.31772882	31.78	2.495017	22.68	11
12	23.298085	74.326950	0.01345407	0.042922	3.190260	0.31345407	31.35	2.761449	23.01	12
13	30.287511	97.625036	0.01024327	0.033017	3.223277	0.31024327	31.03	3.033163	23.33	13
14	39.373764	127.912546	0.00781784	0.025398	3.248675	0.30781784	30.79	3.309450	23.64	14
15	51.185893	167.286310	0.00597778	0.019537	3.268211	0.30597778	30.60	3.589667	23.93	15

35.00 % ANNUAL

YR										YR
1	1.350000	1.000000	1.00000000	0.740741	0.740741	1.35000000	135.00	0.350000	35.00	1
2	1.822500	2.350000	0.42553191	0.548697	1.289438	0.77553191	77.56	0.551064	27.55	2
3	2.460375	4.172500	0.23966447	0.406442	1.695880	0.58966447	58.97	0.768993	25.63	3
4	3.321506	6.632875	0.15076419	0.301068	1.996948	0.50076419	50.08	1.003057	25.08	4
5	4.484033	9.954381	0.10045828	0.223014	2.219961	0.45045828	45.05	1.252291	25.05	5
6	6.053445	14.438415	0.06925968	0.165195	2.385157	0.41925968	41.93	1.515558	25.26	6
7	8.172151	20.491860	0.04879987	0.122367	2.507523	0.39879987	39.88	1.791599	25.59	7
8	11.032404	28.664011	0.03488695	0.090642	2.598165	0.38488695	38.49	2.079096	25.99	8
9	14.893745	39.696415	0.02519119	0.067142	2.665308	0.37519119	37.52	2.376721	26.41	9
10	20.106556	54.590160	0.01831832	0.049735	2.715043	0.36831832	36.84	2.683183	26.83	10
11	27.143850	74.696715	0.01338747	0.036841	2.751884	0.36338747	36.34	2.997262	27.25	11
12	36.644198	101.840566	0.00981927	0.027289	2.779173	0.35981927	35.99	3.317831	27.65	12
13	49.469667	138.484764	0.00722101	0.020214	2.799387	0.35722101	35.73	3.643873	28.03	13
14	66.784051	187.954431	0.00532044	0.014974	2.814361	0.35532044	35.54	3.974486	28.39	14
15	90.158469	254.738482	0.00392559	0.011092	2.825453	0.35392559	35.40	4.308884	28.73	15

COMPOUND INTEREST AND ANNUITY TABLE

40.00 %
ANNUAL

YR	Amount Of 1	Amount Of 1 Per Period	Sinking Fund Payment	Present Worth Of 1	Present Worth Of 1 Per Period	Periodic Payment To Amortize 1	Constant Annual Percent	Total Interest	Annual Add-on Rate	YR
	What a single $1 deposit grows to in the future. The deposit is made at the beginning of the first period.	What a series of $1 deposits grow to in the future. A deposit is made at the end of each period.	The amount to be deposited at the end of each period that grows to $1 in the future.	What $1 to be paid in the future is worth today. Value today of a single payment tomorrow.	What $1 to be paid at the end of each period is worth today. Value today of a series of payments tomorrow.	The mortgage payment to amortize a loan of $1. An annuity certain, payable at the end of each period, worth $1 today.	The annual payment, including interest and principal, to amortize completely a loan of $100.	The total interest paid over the term on a loan of $1. The loan is amortized by regular periodic payments.	The average annual interest rate on a loan that is completely amortized by regular periodic payments.	
	$S=(1+i)^n$	$S_n=\frac{(1+i)^n-1}{i}$	$\frac{1}{S_n}=\frac{i}{(1+i)^n-1}$	$V^n=\frac{1}{(1+i)^n}$	$A_n=\frac{1-V^n}{i}$	$\frac{1}{A_n}=\frac{i}{1-V^n}$				
1	1.400000	1.000000	1.00000000	0.714286	0.714286	1.40000000	140.00	0.400000	40.00	1
2	1.960000	2.400000	0.41666667	0.510204	1.224490	0.81666667	81.67	0.633333	31.67	2
3	2.744000	4.360000	0.22935780	0.364431	1.588921	0.62935780	62.94	0.888073	29.60	3
4	3.841600	7.104000	0.14076577	0.260308	1.849229	0.54076577	54.08	1.163063	29.08	4
5	5.378240	10.945600	0.09136091	0.185934	2.035164	0.49136091	49.14	1.456805	29.14	5
6	7.529536	16.323840	0.06126010	0.132810	2.167974	0.46126010	46.13	1.767561	29.46	6
7	10.541350	23.853376	0.04192279	0.094865	2.262839	0.44192279	44.20	2.093460	29.91	7
8	14.757891	34.394726	0.02907422	0.067760	2.330599	0.42907422	42.91	2.432594	30.41	8
9	20.661047	49.152617	0.02034480	0.048400	2.378999	0.42034480	42.04	2.783103	30.92	9
10	28.925465	69.813664	0.01432384	0.034572	2.413571	0.41432384	41.44	3.143238	31.43	10
11	40.495652	98.739129	0.01012770	0.024694	2.438265	0.41012770	41.02	3.511405	31.92	11
12	56.693912	139.234781	0.00718211	0.017639	2.455904	0.40718211	40.72	3.886185	32.38	12
13	79.371477	195.928693	0.00510390	0.012599	2.468503	0.40510390	40.52	4.266351	32.82	13
14	111.120068	275.300171	0.00363240	0.008999	2.477502	0.40363240	40.37	4.650854	33.22	14
15	155.568096	386.420239	0.00258786	0.006428	2.483930	0.40258786	40.26	5.038818	33.59	15

APPENDIX C

Sources of Economic and Financial Information from The Conference Board

This annotated bibliography of well-known sources of economic data is limited to basic references. It should not be construed as a comprehensive listing of available material on economic information.

For the convenience of the user, the bibliography has been divided into several broad categories. All, except one devoted to international economic statistics, relate to the U.S. economy. Entries in the bibliography are listed by title, publisher, and frequency of issue.

Because economists generally depend to a great extent on official statistics, most of these entries are government publications. The bibliography includes, however, a selected sample of sources published by The Conference Board and other organizations.

Publications of the federal government, unless otherwise noted, can be obtained from The Superintendent of Documents, U.S. Government Printing Office, Washington, D.C. 20402. Entries published by The Conference Board are denoted by an asterisk (*). To order them, or to inquire about further details of their contents, please contact Information Service Division, The Conference Board, 845 Third Avenue, New York, N.Y. 10022.

The Conference Board, Inc., founded in 1916, is an independent, nonprofit institution for business and economic research. Its purpose is to promote broader understanding of business and the economy for the enlightenment both of those who manage business enterprises and of the society which shapes the business system. It pursues this by encouraging exchange of experience and opinion, by objective analyses of significant business and economic developments, and by widespread distribution of facts developed through these activities. The board is a fact-finding agency; it takes no positions on public policy issues nor does it act as a consulting organization. Its work is supported by more than 4,000 associates (members).

GENERAL REFERENCES

Survey of Current Business *Monthly*

U.S. Department of Commerce, Bureau of Economic Analysis

Each issue contains over 2,000 statistical series relating to Gross National Product (GNP), prices and employment, plus a wide variety of industrial data and other business indicators. July issue contains annual revisions of national income and product accounts.

Business Statistics *Biennial*

U.S. Department of Commerce, Office of Business Economics

A supplement to the *Survey of Current Business*. Presents historical data for the statistical series covered in that publication; also gives explanatory notes to their sources of data.

Business Conditions Digest *Monthly*

U.S. Department of Commerce, Bureau of Economic Analysis

A compilation of numerous economic statistical series, including charts, arranged for convenient analysis of business cycles.

Federal Reserve Bulletin *Monthly*

Board of Governors of the Federal Reserve System
Ordering address: Division of Administrative Services
Board of Governors of the Federal Reserve System
Washington, D.C. 20551

A compendium of financial, industrial and commercial statistics for the United States. Also includes data on the U.S. balance of payments and international exchange rates.

The Economic Report of the President and the Council of Economic Advisers *Annual*

Executive Office of the President

The President's economic program and an elaboration of the goals of the U.S. economy by the Council of Economic Advisers. The analysis is supplemented by statistics on GNP, industrial production, personal income, employment, prices, profits and other aspects of the economy.

Statistical Abstract of the United States *Annual*

U.S. Department of Commerce

A basic reference source summarizing statistics on industrial, social, political and economic organizations of the United States; includes statistics obtained from both government and private sources.

Economic Indicators *Monthly*

U.S. Congress, Joint Economic Committee

Basic series on prices, wages, industrial production, consumer purchasing power, money supply, and receipts and expenditures of the Federal Government

The Conference Board Statistical Bulletin (*) *Monthly*

Gives GNP forecasts and information on various statistical series, including leading business indicators, help-wanted advertising indexes, diffusion indexes, capital appropriations, profit margins, discretionary spending and automobile sales.

Current Economic Trends (*) *Quarterly*
Presents current and historical statistics on major economic indicators in chart analysis form.

AGGREGATE MEASURES OF INCOME, DEMAND, AND PRODUCTION

Gross National Product and Income

Survey of Current Business *Monthly*
U.S. Department of Commerce, Bureau of Economic Analysis
See annotation under General References.

Consumer Spending

The Conference Board RECORD (*) *Monthly*
Each issue includes a section on "Consumer Markets," which reports on various facets of consumer spending.

Consumer Attitudes and Buying Plans (*) *Bimonthly*
Statistics measuring consumer attitudes toward current and future economic conditions; also interprets consumers' intentions to purchase durable goods.

Consumer Market Indicators (*) *Monthly*
Statistics on consumption expenditures, consumer price index, consumer confidence index, and other market indicators.

Current Retail Trade Reports *Weekly and Monthly*
U.S. Department of Commerce, Bureau of the Census
Data on estimated weekly and monthly retail sales, by lines of business, for the United States and for selected metropolitan statistical areas (SMSA's).

A Guide to Consumer Markets (*) *Annual*
A statistical handbook. Contains data on employment, consumer income and expenditures, and the production and distribution of purchased goods and services.

Survey of Buying Power *Annual*
Sales Management
630 Third Avenue
New York, New York 10017
Each edition includes data related to total retail sales and consumer buying indexes for the 50 states, their counties, and SMSA's.

Surveys of Consumers *Annual*
Institute of Social Research
University of Michigan
Ann Arbor, Michigan 48106

National survey data on family incomes, household assets and liabilities, and consumer expenditures for durable goods. Also includes an outlook on consumer demand.

Survey of Consumer Expenditures *Irregular*
U.S. Department of Labor, Bureau of Labor Statistics
Data show expenditure patterns according to various family characteristics.

BUSINESS SPENDING

Survey of Current Business *Monthly*
U.S. Department of Commerce, Bureau of Economic Analysis
See annotation under General References.

Annual McGraw-Hill Survey of Business Plans for New Plants and Equipment *Annual*
McGraw-Hill Publications Co.
Economics Department,
1221 Avenue of the Americas
New York, New York 10020
Statistical data on planned capital investment, broken down by industry groups and regional areas.

Census of Manufacturers *Every five years, in years ending in 2 and 7*
U.S. Department of Commerce, Bureau of the Census
Statistical data on size of establishments, employment and expenditures by industry, and inventories by industry for regions of the United States.

Annual Survey of Manufacturers *Annual*
U.S. Department of Commerce, Bureau of the Census
Survey of manufacturing industries published in the years between the five-year Census of Manufactures.

Quarterly Survey of Capital Appropriations (*) *Quarterly*
Statistics on business investment in plant and equipment based on a survey of the nation's 1,000 largest manufacturers.

Capital Investment Conditions (*) *Semiannually*
Data on capacity utilization and factors affecting financing of capital spending based on a survey of the nation's 1,000 largest manufacturers.

CONSTRUCTION

Construction Reports *See entries below*
U.S. Department of Commerce, Bureau of the Census
Housing and construction statistics under the following categories:

C20. Housing Starts *Monthly*
Statistics on new housing starts by ownership, location and type of structure.

C22. Housing Completions *Monthly*
Data on number of new units completed and currently under construction.

C25. New One-Family Sold and For Sale *Monthly and Annually*
Corresponding data on sales and number of unsold new one-family dwellings.

C30. Value of New Construction Put in Place *Monthly*
Current estimates of private and public construction, by aggregate value of these classifications.

C40. Housing Authorized by Building Permits and Public Contracts *Monthly and Annually*
Statistics on the number of new housing units authorized in the United States under private building permits and public contracts.

C50. Residential Alterations and Repairs *Quarterly and Annually*
Figures on quarterly and annual expenditures, according to type of work and size of property, for geographical regions of the United States.

Construction Review *Monthly*
U.S. Department of Commerce, Bureau of Domestic Commerce
Contains timely, in-depth articles, as well as current data on expenditures, building starts, and employment levels in the construction industry.

Dodge Construction Potentials *Monthly*
McGraw-Hill Information Systems Co.
F. W. Dodge Division
1221 Avenue of the Americas
New York, New York 10020
Statistical summary of construction contracts for new and major alteration projects; data are broken down by types of projects and by regions of the United States.

Government Spending

1. Federal Government

The Budget of the U.S. Government *Annual*
U.S. Office of Management and Budget
Contains the official text of the President's budget message, a description of the budget system, data on budget receipts and expenditures, and line-item details of the budget as a whole.

The Budget of the U.S. Government: Appendix *Annual*
U.S. Office of Management and Budget
Detailed information on the legislative authority for the budget; also data on programs in the budget, requests for supplemental appropriations and new program proposals.

The U.S. Budget in Brief *Annual*
U.S. Office of Management and Budget
The President's budget message and a condensed overview of the budget. Includes major summary tables.

The Federal Budget: Its Impact on the Economy (*) *Annual*
Analysis of the federal budget as a whole, special analysis of some of its programs, and background information on major expenditure patterns in relation to the national economy.

Treasury Bulletin *Monthly*
U.S. Department of the Treasury, Office of the Secretary
A monthly summary of the Treasury's activities as related to federal fiscal operations. Includes international financial statistics and data on capital transfers between the United States and foreign countries.

Monthly Statement of Receipts and Outlays of the U.S. Government *Monthly*
U.S. Department of the Treasury, Bureau of Accounts
Details on receipts and expenditures for the U.S. budget and trust accounts.

Annual Report of the Secretary of the Treasury with Statistical Appendix *Annual*
U.S. Department of the Treasury, Bureau of Accounts
Statistical tables include summary of the Treasury's receipts and expenditures; also data on federal aid to states and other activities of the Treasury Department.

Facts and Figures on Government Finance *Biennial*
Tax Foundation, Inc.
50 Rockefeller Plaza
New York, New York 10020
Information about taxes, expenditures and debts for federal, state and local governments.

2. State and Local Governments

Governmental Finances *Annual*
U.S. Department of Commerce, Bureau of the Census
A series of reports that give fiscal data for the Federal Government, the 50 states, numerous cities, and selected SMSA's.

Census of Governments *Every five years, in years ending in 2 and 7*
U.S. Department of Commerce, Bureau of the Census
Various series of fiscal data for state and local governments of the United States.

EXPORTS

U.S. Commodity Exports and Imports as Related to Output *Annual*
U.S. Department of Commerce, Bureau of the Census
Statistical data on relationship between domestic output and foreign trade in commodities.

Commodity Yearbook *Annual*
Commodity Research Bureau
140 Broadway
New York, New York 10005
Latest trends in the supply and demand of numerous commodities. Price data are illustrated by charts.

LABOR AND PRODUCTIVITY

General Sources

Handbook of Labor Statistics *Annual*
U.S. Department of Labor, Bureau of Labor Statistics
A statistical compendium of all phases of labor economics.

Manpower Report of the President *Annual*
Executive Office of the President
Documents current and historical trends in population, labor force, employment and unemployment, productivity and occupational data.

Employment

Employment and Earnings *Monthly*
U.S. Department of Labor, Bureau of Labor Statistics
Statistics on employment, work hours, earnings, and labor turnover.

Labor Turnover *Monthly*
U.S. Department of Labor, Bureau of Labor Statistics
Summarizes factory labor-turnover rates for major industry groups.

Monthly Labor Review *Monthly*
U.S. Department of Labor, Bureau of Labor Statistics
Articles on employment, wages, prices, productivity and labor developments abroad. Also includes current statistics for most of these areas.

Productivity

Indexes of Output per Man-Hour for Selected Industries *Annual*
U.S. Department of Labor, Bureau of Labor Statistics
Updates indexes of output per man-hour and output per employee for industries currently included in the Federal Government's productivity measurement program.

DEMOGRAPHIC DATA

General Sources

Manpower Report of the President *Annual*
Executive Office of the President
See annotation under Labor and Productivity (General Sources).

A Guide to Consumer Markets (*) *Annual*
See annotation under Aggregate Measures of Income, Demand and Production (Consumer Spending).

POPULATION

Census of Population *Every 10 years, when the last digit is 0*
U.S. Department of Commerce, Bureau of the Census
A compendium of statistics related to the population of the United States and the social and economic living patterns of the American people. Gives statistics for U.S. territories, the 50 states and their counties, the District of Columbia, and the country's major SMSA's.

Current Population Reports *Irregular*
U.S. Department of Commerce, Bureau of the Census
Up-to-date statistics on population, economic and social characteristics, and other demographic trends of the American people. Statistics are published in eight separate series of reports:

P-20 Population Characteristics *Irregular*
Current national data on school enrollment, mobility and household characteristics.

P-23 Special Studies *Irregular*
Infrequent reports containing specialized demographic data.

P-25 Population Estimates and Projections *Irregular*
Monthly estimates of the total population of the United States, broken down by geographic area and other classifications. Includes projections on the future population of the entire United States—the 50 states, the District of Columbia, and the territories.

P-26 Federal-State Cooperative Program for Population Estimates *Irregular*
Population estimates for counties in selected states where figures are prepared by state agencies as part of the Federal-State Cooperative Program for Local Population Estimates.

P-27 Farm Population *Irregular*
Data on size and other selected characteristics of the U.S. farm population. Issued jointly with the Economic Research Service, U.S. Department of Agriculture.

P-28 Special Censuses *Irregular*
Results of population censuses requested and funded by city or county governments. Reports show population changes in each locality since the last general census.

P-60 Consumer Income *Irregular*
Information on the number of families and employed individuals at various income levels.

P-65 Consumer Buying Indicators *Annual*
Information on home ownership and purchases of automobiles and major household appliances. Statistics are broken down by income, age of family head, residence, and other characteristics.

Vital Statistics of the United States *Annual*
U.S. Department of Health, Education and Welfare, National Center for Health Statistics
A source of data on births, deaths, marriages and divorces. Regional information is classified by cities, counties and SMSA's.

EDUCATION

Digest of Educational Statistics *Annual*
U.S. Department of Health, Education and Welfare, Office of Education
An abstract of statistical information on American education. Contains data compiled from both government and private sources on number of schools, enrollments and graduates.

Fall Enrollment in Higher Education *Annual*
U.S. Department of Health, Education and Welfare, Office of Education
Enrollment data broken down by state, regional area, and individual institution.

Projections of Educational Statistics *Annual*
U.S. Department of Health, Education and Welfare, Office of Education
Ten-year projections for enrollments, number of graduates and teachers, institutional budgets, and related matters.

WAGES AND PRICES

GENERAL SOURCES

Business Conditions Digest *Monthly*
U.S. Department of Commerce, Bureau of Economic Analysis
See annotation under General References.

Economic Indicators *Monthly*
U.S. Congress, Joint Economic Committee
See annotation under General References.

WAGE RATES

Employment and Earnings *Monthly*
U.S. Department of Labor, Bureau of Labor Statistics
See annotation under Labor and Productivity (Employment).

Handbook of Labor Statistics *Annual*
U.S. Department of Labor, Bureau of Labor Statistics
See annotation under Labor and Productivity (General Sources).

Manpower Report of the President *Annual*
Executive Office of the President
See annotation under Labor and Productivity (General Sources).

CONSUMER PRICES

The Consumer Price Index *Monthly*
U.S. Department of Labor, Bureau of Labor Statistics
Statistical measures of the average changes in prices of goods and services (about 400 items) purchased by urban wage earners and clerical workers living in 56 urban areas across the country.

A Guide to Consumer Markets (*) *Annual*
See annotation under Aggregate Measures of Income, Demand and Production (Consumer Spending).

WHOLESALE PRICES

Wholesale Prices and Price Indexes *Monthly*
U.S. Department of Labor, Bureau of Labor Statistics
A basic reference on wholesale price movements; includes statistical tables and technical notes.

INDUSTRY STATISTICS

GENERAL SOURCES

Survey of Current Business *Monthly*
U.S. Department of Commerce, Bureau of Economic Analysis
See annotation under General References.

Federal Reserve Bulletin *Monthly*
Board of Governors of the Federal Reserve System
See annotation under General References.

Industrial Production *Monthly*
Board of Governors of the Federal Reserve System
Ordering address: Division of Administrative Services
Board of Governors of the Federal Reserve System
Washington, D.C. 20551
Preliminary statistics for the total FRB Index; also carries revisions of the previous month's figures.

Moody's Industrial Manual *Biweekly and Annual*
Moody's Investors Service, Inc.
99 Church Street
New York, New York 10007
Various statistics on U.S. industrial corporations; includes separate section on classification of companies by industries and products.

Predicasts *Quarterly*
Predicasts, Inc.
11001 Cedar Avenue
Cleveland, Ohio 44106
Abstracts published forecasts for general economic indicators, industries, products and services.

Standard & Poor's Industry Survey *Quarterly and Annual*
Standard & Poor's Corporation
345 Hudson Street
New York, New York 10014
More than 40 basic surveys, each devoted to a major industry group; provides both financial statistics and detailed industry data.

Industry Profiles *Annual*
U.S. Department of Commerce, Bureau of the Census
Published as part of *Annual Survey of Manufacturers;* gives basic data series for past decade for selected major industry groups.

U.S. Industrial Outlook *Annual*
U.S. Department of Commerce, Domestic and International Business Administration
Detailed analysis and projections for more than 200 individual manufacturing and nonmanufacturing industries.

SECTORS

1. Manufacturing

Current Industrial Reports *Monthly, Quarterly and Annual*
U.S. Department of Commerce, Bureau of the Census
Information on production, shipments and inventories for 5,000 manufactured items.

Annual Survey of Manufacturers *Annual*
U.S. Department of Commerce, Bureau of the Census
See annotation under Aggregate Measures of Income, Demand and Production (Business Spending).

Census of Manufactures *Every five years in years ending in 2 and 7*
U.S. Department of Commerce, Bureau of the Census
See annotation under Aggregate Measures of Income, Demand and Production (Business Spending).

2. Mining and Energy

Mineral Industry Surveys *Weekly, Monthly and Quarterly*
U.S. Department of the Interior, Bureau of Mines
Periodic reports update information published in the *Mineral Yearbook* (see below).

Mineral Yearbook *Annual*
U.S. Department of the Interior, Bureau of Mines
A statistical handbook on U.S. production of all metallic, nonmetallic and mineral fuel commodities; also gives similar statistics for more than 100 countries.

Census of Mineral Industries *Every five years, in years ending in 2 and 7*
U.S. Department of Commerce, Bureau of the Census
Statistical data for each of 42 extractive industries on quantity and value of products shipped, quantity and cost of fuels, and electrical energy produced.

3. Utilities

Electric Power Statistics *Monthly*
U.S. Federal Power Commission
Summaries of statistics on production of electric power, capacities of power plants, and sales of electricity.

Statistics of Communications Common Carriers *Annual*
U.S. Federal Power Commission
Financial and operating data for 42 major telephone and telegraph companies operating in the United States.

Statistics of Publicly Owned Electric Utilities in the U.S. *Annual*
U.S. Federal Power Commission
Financial and operating data for publicly owned utilities operating in the United States.

Statistics of Privately Owned Electric Utilities in the U.S. *Annual*
U.S. Federal Power Commission
Financial and operating data for privately owned utilities operating in the United States.

4. Financial

See section below on Financial Markets.

5. Trade and Services

Current Retail Trade Reports *Weekly and Monthly*
U.S. Department of Commerce, Bureau of the Census
See annotation under Aggregate Measures of Income, Demand and Production (Consumer Spending).

Monthly Selected Service Receipts *Monthly*
U.S. Department of Commerce, Bureau of the Census
Estimated monthly revenues for a number of service fields—including the hotel and motel trades, various personnel and office services, automobile and appliance repairs, and leisure-time industries.

Monthly Wholesale Trade: Sales and Inventories *Monthly*
U.S. Department of Commerce, Bureau of the Census
Data on sales and inventory trends of merchant wholesalers in over 70 lines of business.

Census of Business *Every five years in years ending in 2 and 7*
U.S. Department of Commerce, Bureau of the Census
National and regional statistics on retail and wholesale industries, as well as on selected service trades.

6. Agriculture

Agricultural Prices *Monthly*
U.S. Department of Agriculture, Crop Reporting Board
Prices received and paid by farmers compared to parity prices for all groups of agricultural products; data include state and regional analyses.

Agricultural Statistics *Annual*
U.S. Department of Agriculture
Compendium of principal statistical series on agricultural production and consumption; includes historical data for the most recent ten years.

Commodity Yearbook *Annual*
Commodity Research Bureau
140 Broadway
New York, New York 10005
See annotation under Aggregate Measures of Income, Demand and Production (Exports).

7. Transportation

Transport Economics *Monthly*
U.S. Interstate Commerce Commission
Ordering address: Bureau of Economics, Interstate Commerce Commission
Washington, D.C. 20423
Current statistics on the operating income and working capital of Class I railroads and Class A freight forwarders.

Transport Statistics in the United States *Annual*
U.S. Interstate Commerce Commission
Statistics on rail, motor and water carriers; also includes statistics on oil pipelines.

Handbook of Airline Statistics *Annual*
Civil Aeronautics Board
Data on finances and traffic of major U.S. trunk carriers; also similar data on local service and helicopter carriers. Includes glossary of air-transport terms.

Census of Transportation *Every five years, in years ending in 2 and 7*
U.S. Department of Commerce, Bureau of the Census
Data on uses and modes of transportation in the United States.

FINANCIAL MARKETS

General Sources

Federal Reserve Bulletin *Monthly*
Board of Governors of the Federal Reserve System
See annotation under General References.

The Federal Reserve System and Monetary Policy

Annual Report of the Board of Governors of the Federal Reserve System *Annual*
Board of Governors of the Federal Reserve System
Information about the operations and conditions of the Federal Reserve Banks for the most recent calendar year.

Deposits, Reserves and Borrowings of Member Banks *Weekly*
Board of Governors of the Federal Reserve System
Deposits, reserves and borrowings of reserve city banks and other member banks, by district.

Factors Affecting Bank Reserves and Conditions Statement of Federal Reserve Banks *Weekly*
Board of Governors of the Federal Reserve System
Weekly averages of daily figures on factors affecting bank reserves, along with changes from week-ago and year-ago figures.

Commercial Banks

Annual Report of the Federal Deposit Insurance Corporation *Annual*
Federal Deposit Insurance Corporation
550 17th Street
Washington, D.C. 20429
Data on both insured and noninsured banks in the United States; also discusses the structure of the nation's banking system and gives aggregate statistics on its assets and liabilities.

Assets and Liabilities—Commercial and Mutual Savings Banks *Semiannual*
Federal Deposit Insurance Corporation
Assets and liabilities of both insured banks and all operating banks by class of bank and by state.

Assets and Liabilities of all Commercial Banks in the United States *Weekly*
Board of Governors of the Federal Reserve System
Weekly statistics on the principal assets and liabilities of all U.S. commercial banks.

Summary of Accounts and Deposits in All Commercial Banks *Annual*
Federal Deposit Insurance Corporation
Summarizes accounts and deposits for all commercial banks by FDIC region, state and SMSA's.

Weekly Condition Report of Large Commercial Banks and Domestic Subsidiaries *Weekly*
Board of Governors of the Federal Reserve System
Weekly breakdowns of assets and liabilities of reporting member banks in New York, Chicago and other leading cities, with separate figures by Federal Reserve district.

FINANCIAL INTERMEDIARIES

Annual Report of the Federal Deposit Insurance Corporation *Annual*
Federal Deposit Insurance Corporation
See annotation under Commercial Banks.

Assets and Liabilities—Commercial and Mutual Savings Banks *Semiannual*
Federal Deposit Insurance Corporation
See annotation under Commercial banks.

Federal Home Loan Bank Board Journal *Monthly*
Federal Home Loan Bank Board
Statistical series on housing industry; includes articles on thrift institutions.

Life Insurance Fact Book *Annual*
Institute of Life Insurance
277 Park Avenue
New York, New York 10017
Statistical tables and charts for all U.S. life insurance companies; also includes interpretive text.

National Fact Book of Mutual Savings Banking *Annual*
National Association of Mutual Savings Banks
200 Park Avenue
New York, New York 10017
Basic data on all aspects of savings banking.

Savings and Home Financing Source Book *Annual*
Federal Home Loan Bank Board
Statistics on Federal Home Loan Banks, including selected balance-sheet data, flow of savings, and mortgage-lending activity.

Savings and Loan Fact Book *Annual*
United States Savings and Loan League
221 North La Salle Street
Chicago, Illinois 60601
A comprehensive reference source on savings and loan associations, giving statistics on savings, home ownership, and financing of residential construction.

Statistical Bulletin *Monthly*
U.S. Securities and Exchange Commission
Data on new securities, securities sales, common stock prices and transactions; periodically shows the asset composition of all private noninsured pension funds.

Summary of Accounts and Deposits in All Mutual Savings Banks *Annual*
Federal Deposit Insurance Corporation
Summarizes accounts and deposits for all mutual savings banks by state, county and SMSA's.

MONEY MARKETS

Monthly Chart Book *Monthly*
Board of Governors of the Federal Reserve System
A variety of leading financial and economic statistical series in chart from: updated monthly.

Moody's Bank and Finance Manual *Biweekly and Annual*
Moody's Investors Service, Inc.
99 Church Street
New York, New York 10007
A source of comprehensive financial information on banks, insurance companies, investment companies, and miscellaneous financial enterprises.

Open Market Money Rates and Bond Prices *Monthly*
Board of Governors of the Federal Reserve System
Weekly data on yields of U.S. Treasury issues, Federal Funds, and commercial paper.

Reserve Positions of Major Reserve City Banks *Weekly*
Board of Governors of the Federal Reserve System
Weekly reports on the Federal Funds market and related transactions of major reserve city banks.

Weekly Condition Report of Large Commercial Banks and Domestic Subsidiaries *Weekly*
Board of Governors of the Federal Reserve System
See annotation under Commercial Banks.

CAPITAL MARKETS

Bond Outlook *Weekly*
Standard & Poor's Corporation
345 Hudson Street
New York, New York 10014
Analyzes all phases of current bond markets.

Census of Shareowners *Irregular*
The New York Stock Exchange
11 Wall Street
New York, New York 10005

Data on the number of shareowners of public corporations by state, region, and personal income.

Fact Book *Annual*
The New York Stock Exchange
11 Wall Street
New York, New York 10005
Summarizes various statistical series issued by the Exchange.

FHA Homes: Data for States and Selected Areas *Annual*
U.S. Department of Housing and Urban Development, Federal Housing Administration
Data on mortgages, represented property values, and other FHA classifications for states and selected housing areas.

FHA Trends of Home Mortgage Characteristics *Quarterly*
U.S. Department of Housing and Urban Development, Federal Housing Administration
Data on insured FHA mortgages for existing and proposed family homes.

The Money Manager *Weekly*
The Bond Buyer
77 Water Street
New York, New York 10005
Daily quotations for U.S. Treasury issues and federal agency securities; also includes a weekly index of municipal and corporate bond yields.

Moody's Bank and Finance Manual *Biweekly & Annual*
Moody's Investors Service, Inc.
99 Church Street
New York, New York 10007
See annotation under Money Markets

Moody's Municipal and Government Manual *Biweekly & Annual*
Moody's Investors Service, Inc.
99 Church Street
New York, New York 10007
Financial statistics on state governments and municipalities; also rates municipal and corporate bonds for quality.

Standard Corporation Records *Daily & Bimonthly*
Standard & Poor's Corporation
345 Hudson Street
New York, New York 10014
Factual information on corporations and their securities—for example, description and history of the company, abstracts of financial statements, and related data. Updated by daily news bulletins.

Statistical Bulletin *Monthly*
U.S. Securities and Exchange Commission
See annotation under Financial Intermediaries.

Value Line Investment Survey *Weekly*
Arnold Bernhard & Co.
5 East 44th Street
New York, New York 10017
Continuous review and analysis of 1,000 leading corporate stocks.

INTERNATIONAL ECONOMIC STATISTICS

General Sources

Federal Reserve Bulletin *Monthly*
See annotation under General References.

General Statistics *Monthly*
Statistical Office of the European Communities
P.O. Box 1003
Luxembourg
Gives key economic statistics for the European Community.

International Economic Report of the President *Annual*
Executive Office of the President
Discusses international economic goals of the United States and related issues. Statistical appendix on U.S. foreign trade, balance of payments, overseas investment, and economic aid.

International Financial Statistics *Monthly*
International Monetary Fund
19th and H Streets, N.W.
Washington, D.C. 20431
Statistics, by country, on exports and imports, exchange rates, and monetary reserves.

Main Economic Indicators *Monthly*
Organization for Economic Cooperation and Development, Paris, France
Ordering address: OECD Publications Center
1750 Pennsylvania Avenue, N.W.
Washington, D.C. 20006
A basic source of international statistics; particularly useful for data on foreign trade.

Monthly Bulletin of Statistics *Monthly*
United Nations, Sales Section
United Nations Plaza
New York, New York 10017
Statistics on trade, national accounts, and financial markets of over 100 countries.

Statistical Yearbook *Annual*
United Nations, Sales Section
United Nations Plaza
New York, New York 10017

A comprehensive compilation of data on balance of payments, wages and prices, and national accounts of member countries.

FOREIGN ECONOMICS

Foreign Economic Trends and Their Implications for the United States *Irregular*
U.S. Department of Commerce, Bureau of International Commerce
Each issue is devoted to a particular trading partner of the United States, and summarizes that country's key economic indicators and their trends.

OECD Financial Statistics *Semiannual with bi-monthly supplements*
Organization for Economic Cooperation and Development, Paris, France
Ordering address: OECD Publications Center
1750 Pennsylvania Avenue, N.W.
Washington, D.C. 20006
Detailed financial statistics and descriptions of OECD countries' exchange-control regulations. Reports also discuss the institutional aspects and functioning of each country's financial system.

Overseas Business Reports *Irregular*
U.S. Department of Commerce, Bureau of International Commerce
Individual reports give basic market and investment information on various foreign countries; include statistics related to trade, regulations governing trade, and foreign market indicators.

Yearbook of National Accounts Statistics *Annual*
United Nations, Sales Section
United Nations Plaza
New York, New York 10017
Data on national income, disposable income, and per capita gross domestic product for over 100 countries.

FOREIGN TRADE

Direction of Trade *Annual and monthly*
International Monetary Fund
19th and H Streets, N.W.
Washington, D.C. 20431
Data on foreign trade, by country, for over 100 countries.

Foreign Trade Reports *Monthly*
U.S. Department of Commerce, Bureau of the Census
U.S. foreign trade as listed below:

FT135. U.S. Imports for Consumption and General Imports, Commodity by Country.
U.S. imports by commodities.

FT410. U.S. Exports of Domestic and Foreign Merchandise, Commodity by Country of Destination.

Quantity and value of exports of individual commodities, plus various consolidations of these items according to destination.

FT800. U.S. Trade with Puerto Rico and with U.S. Possessions
Quantity, value and tonnage of individual commodities shipped between the United States and its territories and possessions.

FT990. Highlights of U.S. Export and Import Trade
Interrelated statistical tables summarizing significant trade movements by commodity, country, U.S. Customs District, and shipping method.

Yearbook of International Trade Statistics *Annual*
United Nations, Sales Section
United Nations Plaza
New York, New York 10017
Detailed data for individual countries, with summary tables on trade in principal commodities, and their value in foreign currencies and U.S. dollars.

Balance of Payments

Balance of Payments Yearbook *Monthly*
International Monetary Fund
19th and H Streets, N.W.
Washington, D.C. 20431
Balance-of-payments data for about 100 countries, presented in various formats.

Exchange Rates

Foreign Exchange Rates *Weekly*
Board of Governors of the Federal Reserve System
Ordering address: Division of Administrative Services
Board of Governors of the Federal Reserve System
Washington, D.C. 20551
Statistical release gives current exchange rates for various countries.

APPENDIX D

Table of Normal Distribution

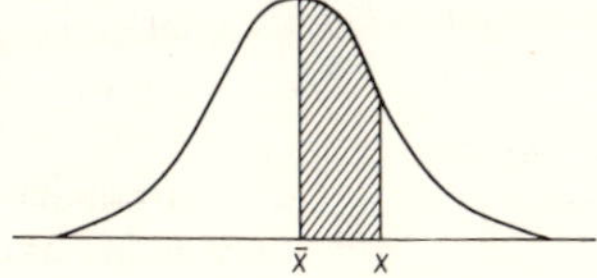

The table of areas of the normal curve between $\overline{X}$ and X for Z values is computed as follows:

$$Z = \frac{X - \overline{X}}{\sigma}$$

Normal Curve

Z	*.00*	*.01*	*.02*	*.03*	*.04*	*.05*	*.06*	*.07*	*.08*	*.09*
0.0	.0000	.0041	.0080	.0120	.0160	.0199	.0239	.0279	.0319	.0359
0.1	.0398	.0438	.0478	.0517	.0557	.0596	.0636	.0675	.0714	.0753
0.2	.0793	.0832	.0871	.0910	.0948	.0987	.1026	.1064	.1103	.1141
0.3	.1179	.1217	.1255	.1293	.1331	.1368	.1406	.1443	.1480	.1517
0.4	.1554	.1591	.1628	.1664	.1700	.1736	.1772	.1808	.1844	.1879
0.5	.1915	.1950	.1985	.2019	.2054	.2088	.2123	.2157	.2190	.2224
0.6	.2257	.2291	.2324	.2357	.2389	.2422	.2454	.2486	.2517	.2549
0.7	.2580	.2611	.2642	.2673	.2704	.2734	.2764	.2794	.2823	.2852
0.8	.2881	.2910	.2939	.2967	.2995	.3023	.3051	.3078	.3106	.3133
0.9	.3159	.3186	.3212	.3238	.3264	.3289	.3315	.3340	.3365	.3389
1.0	.3413	.3438	.3461	.3485	.3508	.3531	.3554	.3577	.3599	.3621
1.1	.3643	.3665	.3686	.3708	.3729	.3749	.3770	.3790	.3810	.3830
1.2	.3849	.3869	.3888	.3907	.3925	.3944	.3962	.3980	.3997	.4015
1.3	.4032	.4049	.4066	.4082	.4099	.4115	.4131	.4147	.4162	.4177
1.4	.4192	.4207	.4222	.4236	.4251	.4265	.4279	.4292	.4306	.4319
1.5	.4332	.4345	.4357	.4370	.4382	.4391	.4406	.4418	.4429	.4441
1.6	.4452	.4463	.4474	.4484	.4495	.4505	.4515	.4525	.4535	.4545
1.7	.4554	.4564	.4573	.4582	.4591	.4599	.4608	.4616	.4625	.4633
1.8	.4641	.4649	.4656	.4664	.4671	.4678	.4686	.4693	.4699	.4706
1.9	.4713	.4719	.4726	.4732	.4738	.4744	.4750	.4756	.4761	.4767
2.0	.4772	.4778	.4783	.4788	.4793	.4798	.4803	.4808	.4812	4817
2.1	.4821	.4826	.4830	.4834	.4838	.4842	.4846	.4850	.4854	.4857

Normal Curve (*continued*)

Z	*.00*	*.01*	*.02*	*.03*	*.04*	*.05*	*.06*	*.07*	*.08*	*.09*
2.2	.4861	.4864	.4868	.4871	.4875	.4878	.4881	.4884	.4887	.4890
2.3	.4893	.4896	.4898	.4901	.4904	.4906	.4909	.4911	.4913	.4916
2.4	.4918	.4920	.4922	.4925	.4927	.4929	.4931	.4932	.4934	.4936
2.5	.4938	.4940	.4941	.4943	.4945	.4946	.4948	.4949	.4951	.4952
2.6	.4953	.4955	.4956	.4957	.4959	.4960	.4961	.4962	.4963	.4964
2.7	.4965	.4966	.4967	.4968	.4969	.4970	.4971	.4972	.4973	.4974
2.8	.4974	.4975	.4976	.4977	.4977	.4978	.4979	.4979	.4980	.4981
2.9	.4981	.4982	.4982	.4983	.4984	.4984	.4985	.4985	.4986	.4986
3.0	.4987	.4987	.4987	.4988	.4988	.4989	.4989	.4989	.4990	.4990

APPENDIX E

Detailed Business Plan Outline

1. Current Situation and Description of the Business
   - A. Name
   - B. Location
   - C. Description of physical plant
   - D. Distinctive characteristics
   - E. Business goals and objectives
   - F. National economic outlook
   - G. Industry economic outlook
   - H. Is the business recession resistant?
   - I. Stage in product life cycle
   - J. Projected earnings for three years/return on investment
2. Objectives
   - A. Personal goals of owners/managers
   - B. Role of the business in the community
   - C. Business objectives
     - (1). Growth and expansion plans
     - (2). Salaries desired for owners/managers
     - (3). Profit (return on/of investment)
     - (4). Other goals
   - D. Quality of product or service to be marketed
   - E. Plans for new product or service development
3. Market Analysis
   - A. Description of the total market (national, regional, local)
   - B. Primary area of influence
   - C. Population of the market (growing, static, declining)

- D. Average size of business customers
- E. Demographics of individual customers
- F. Industry trends (growing, static, declining; new products or services coming)
- G. Target markets/market segmentation
- H. Competition (number, kind, character, location)
- I. Map of primary market and location of competitors
- J. Boundaries of trading area
- K. Zoning
- L. Tax structure
- M. Age, type of building, adequacy
- N. Parking facilities

4. Product/Service Mix (Product Positioning)
   - A. What product lines are made or sold
   - B. Proprietary interest (patents, logos, trademarks)
   - C. Product position (high-end style—low-end discount)
   - D. Proprietary brand names
   - E. Comparison with competitors' products or services
5. Pricing Objectives/Methods
   - A. Pricing objectives/desired image
   - B. Pricing methods/formulas/timing of price reviews
   - C. Competitive pricing
   - D. High, low, midrange, discount
   - E. Traditional techniques
   - F. Pricing for volume versus profit
   - G. Seasonality in pricing
   - H. Negotiated pricing
   - I. Rate per size/time of job
   - J. Price lining
   - K. Suggested list/list less discount
6. Marketing Strategy
   - A. The marketing thrust
   - B. Controllable variables
     - (1). Product
     - (2). Price
     - (3). Place (location)
     - (4). Promotion
     - (5). Postsale service
   - C. Plant/store atmosphere
   - D. Plant/store layout
   - E. Traffic/product flow
   - F. Numbers and kinds of customers
7. Marketing Tactics
   - A. Distinctive business proposition
   - B. Deciding what to promote
   - C. Selection of theme or slogan

- D. Securing total support for theme
- E. Special services
- F. Exchange/refund policies
- G. Determining the advertising-promotion budget
- H. Determining the marketing mix

8. Advertising/Promotion/Public Relations
   - A. Determining the media
     - (1). Television
     - (2). Newspaper
     - (3). Radio
     - (4). Direct advertising
     - (5). Magazines
     - (6). Trade publications
     - (7). Handbills
     - (8). Outdoor
     - (9). Industrial directories
     - (10). Transit advertising
   - B. Allocating the advertising/promotion budget
     - (1). Competition
     - (2). Industry practice
     - (3). Influence of business proposition
   - C. Advertising services
   - D. Reach, frequency, and continuity
   - E. Seasonality and timing
   - F. Sales promotion
     - (1). Displays/point-of-purchase
     - (2). Windows
     - (3). Coupons
     - (4). Premiums
     - (5). Incentives
     - (6). Advertising specialties
     - (7). Discounts/markdowns/closeouts
     - (8). Signs
     - (9). Joint promotions
   - G. Public relations
     - (1). Publicity
     - (2). Public appearances
     - (3). Trade shows/exhibits
     - (4). Movies/slide films
9. Personnel
   - A. Job classifications
   - B. Number of people needed
   - C. Full-time versus part-time
   - D. Position descriptions
   - E. Expected turnover
   - F. Experience needed

   G. Sources of personnel
   H. Salary structure
   I. Budget items/cost of fringes
   J. Need for management by objectives

10. Personnel Policies
   A. Promotion
   B. Salary increases
   C. Salary advances
   D. Retirement
   E. Workers' compensation
   F. Hospitalization
   G. Vacation
   H. Sick leave
   I. Days off
   J. Tardiness
   K. Overtime
   L. Employee discounts

11. Purchasing
   A. Present suppliers/potential suppliers
   B. The supplier relationship
   C. Trade credit financing
   D. Supplier information
   E. Negotiated purchasing
   F. Buying right

12. Location Analysis
   A. Importance of location
   B. Importance of traffic
   C. Lease versus purchase
   D. Neighborhood changes
   E. Needed space
   F. Expansion possibilities
   G. Traffic analysis/car and foot

13. Legal Structure
   A. Corporation
   B. Proprietorship
   C. Partnership
   D. Joint Venture
   E. Subchapter "S" corporation

14. Insurance
   A. Product liability
   B. Personal/business liability
   C. Plate glass
   D. Fire
   E. Theft/burglary
   F. Life
   G. Business interruption

H. Auto/truck
I. Disability
J. Unemployment
K. Workers' compensation

15. Credit Policy
    A. Customer credit (benefits)
        (1). Credit brings more business
        (2). Credit gets it on the record
        (3). Charge accounts
        (4). Installments
        (5). Budget accounts
        (6). Revolving charge
        (7). Bank credit cards
    B. Customer credit (drawbacks)
        (1). Credit costs money
        (2). Credit reduces cash flow
        (3). Bad debts a possibility
        (4). Competition may not offer it
        (5). Could actually decrease sales
16. Budget/Forecast
    A. Budget: a plan for spending
    B. Short-range plan
    C. Sources of income
        (1). By type of product or service
        (2). By class of customer
        (3). By month or season
    D. Purchasing plan (borrowing/discounts)
    E. Inventory levels/seasonality
    F. Long-range forecasting
    G. Sources of macro-forecast data
        (1). Business publications
        (2). Trade publications
        (3). Trade associations
        (4). Business letters
    H. Detailing forecast assumptions
    I. Developing a sales forecast
        (1). Monthly
        (2). Quarterly
        (3). Annually
        (4). Long term
    J. Reviews/updates by exception
17. Accounting Methods
    A. Cash versus accrual
    B. Straight-line versus accelerated-depreciation
    C. Banking relationship
    D. Accounting relationship

18. Cash Budget/Break-Even Analysis
    A. Using forecasts to develop a cash budget
    B. Estimating expenditures as a function of sales
    C. Preparing the cash budget
    D. Fixed and variable costs
    E. Break-even analysis
19. Valuation of the Business
    A. Establish current valuation
    B. Annual valuation
20. Financial Reporting
    A. Audited versus unaudited statements (review or compilation)
    B. Capital requirements
    C. CPA functions/timing of audits
21. Management by Objectives
    A. Use of management by objectives technique (MBO)
    B. Determining marketing MBO
    C. Determining financial MBO
    D. Implementing an MBO system
    E. Management by exception
    F. Improving the management process
22. Strategic Evaluation of Capital Expenditures
    A. Basic assumptions
        (1). Increase value of business
        (2). Current versus future income—time value of money
        (3). Owner risk preferences
        (4). Evaluate incremental cash flows
        (5). Forecasting is essential
        (6). Asset acquisition exhibits management risk posture
        (7). Liquidity preference
        (8). Fixed assets require working capital
        (9). Resources are limited
    B. Developing the capital budget
        (1). Determine owners' objectives
        (2). Establish basic financial goals
        (3). Establish basic nonfinancial goals
        (4). Evaluate position in market—develop business plans
        (5). Develop managerial policies for data collection
        (6). Develop managerial policies for assessing worth of proposed projects (discounted cash flow)
        (7). Determine the cost of capital
        (8). Develop policies for assessing projects of differing risk
        (9). Develop cash budget for planning period
        (10). Evaluate historical spending pattern for nonbudgeted items
        (11). Evaluate proposed projects and develop capital budget
        (12). Develop managerial policies to authorize expenditures
        (13). Implement those projects which best meet firm's needs within budget constraint

(14). Maintain strict cost controls
(15). Periodically reassess value of projects in use

23. Leasing
   A. Reasons to lease
      (1). Less expensive (lessor's accelerated depreciation, investment tax credits, low risk posture)
      (2). Alternative source of capital
      (3). Constant-cost financing
      (4). Extended-length financing (lease term approximates asset life; avoids balloon repayments)
      (5). Conserves existing credit
      (6). Provides total financing
      (7). Hedge against inflation
      (8). Fast, flexible financing
      (9). Simplifies bookkeeping
      (10). Provides for tax "write-off" of land
      (11). Reduces risk of obsolescence
      (12). Provides trial use periods
      (13). May reduce maintenance costs
   B. Reasons not to lease
      (1). Leasing usually costs more
      (2). Lessors are owners—no residual value at lease termination
      (3). Inflated value of assets enjoyed by lessor
   C. Types of lessors
      (1). Third-party
      (2). Vendor
      (3). Commercial banks
      (4). Investment bankers and insurance companies
   D. Types of leases
      (1). "True" lease for IRS
      (2). Conditional sales contract
      (3). Capital lease
      (4). Operating (maintenance) lease
      (5). Financial (full-payout and non-full-payout) lease
      (6). Direct lease
      (7). Middle-market lease
      (8). Master lease
      (9). Sale-and-leaseback contract
      (10). Net and net-net lease
      (11). Leveraged lease

BIBLIOGRAPHY

Books

Clark, John J., Thomas J. Hindelang, and Robert E. Pritchard. *Capital Budgeting: Planning and Control of Capital Expenditures.* Englewood Cliffs, N.J.: Prentice-Hall, 1979.

Davey, P. J. *Capital Investments: Appraisals and Hints.* New York: The Conference Board, 1974.

Dean, J. *Capital Budgeting.* New York: Columbia University Press, 1951.

Edwards, James W. *Effects of Federal Income Taxes on Capital Budgeting.* New York: National Association of Accountants, 1969.

Grant, Eugene I., and W. Grant Ireson. *Principles of Engineering Economy.* New York: The Ronald Press, 1976.

Hirshleifer, Jack. *Investment, Interest, and Capital.* Englewood Cliffs, N.J.: Prentice-Hall, 1970.

Lewellen, Wilbur G. *The Cost of Capital.* Belmont, Calif.: Wadsworth Publishing Co., 1969.

Pflomm, Norman E. *Managing Capital Expenditures.* New York: The Conference Board, 1963.

Porterfield, James T. S. *Investment Decisions and Capital Costs.* Englewood Cliffs, N.J.: Prentice-Hall, 1965.

Pritchard, Robert E. *Operational Financial Management.* Englewood Cliffs, N.J.: Prentice-Hall, 1977.

———, and Thomas J. Hindelang. *The Lease/Buy Decision.* New York: AMACOM, 1980.

Robicheck, Alexander A., and Stewart C. Myers. *Optimal Financing Decisions.* Englewood Cliffs, N.J.: Prentice-Hall, 1965.

Solomon, Ezra. *The Theory of Financial Management.* New York: Columbia University Press, 1963.

Van Horne, James C. *Financial Management and Policy,* 5th Edition. Englewood Cliffs, N.J.: Prentice-Hall, 1980.

Weston, J. Fred, and Eugene F. Brigham. *Managerial Finance,* 7th Edition. Hinsdale, Ill.: The Dryden Press, 1981.

Articles

Arditti, Fred D. "Risk and the Required Return on Equity." *Journal of Finance,* March 1967, pp. 19–36.

———, and Stephen A. Tysseland. "Three Ways to Present the Marginal Cost of Capital." *Financial Management,* Summer 1973, pp. 63–67.

Bierman, Harold, Jr. "Analysis of the Lease-or-Buy Decision: Comment." *Journal of Finance,* September 1973, pp. 1019–1021.

Bower, Richard S. "Issues in Lease Financing." *Financial Management,* Winter 1973, pp. 25–34.

———, Frank C. Herringer, and J. Peter Williamson. "Lease Evaluation." *Accounting Review,* April 1966, pp. 257–265.

Bower, Richard S., and Donald R. Lessard. "An Operational Approach to Risk-Screening." *Journal of Finance,* May 1973, pp. 321–337.

Brigham, Eugene F. "Equipment Lease Financing: A Bank Management Imperative." *The Banker's Magazine,* Winter 1966, pp. 65–75.

———. "The Impact of Bank Entry on Market Conditions in the Equipment Leasing Industry." *National Banking Review,* September 1964, pp. 11–26.

———. "Hurdle Rates for Screening Capital Expenditure Proposals." *Financial Management,* Autumn 1975, pp. 17–26.

Cooper, Kerry, and Robert H. Strawser. "Evaluation of Capital Investment Projects Involving Asset Leases." *Financial Management,* Spring 1976, pp. 44–49.

Davidson, Sidney, and Roman L. Weil. "Lease Capitalization and Inflation Accounting." *Financial Analysts Journal,* November–December 1975, pp. 22–29, 57.

Defliese, Philip L. "Accounting for Leases: A Broader Perspective." *Financial Executive,* July 1974, pp. 14–23.

Doenges, E. C. "The Cost of Leasing." *Engineering Economist,* Winter 1971, pp. 31–44.

Edelman, Franz, and Joel S. Greenberg. "Venture Analysis: The Assessment of Uncertainty and Risk." *Financial Executive,* August 1969, pp. 56–62.

Evans, Jack, and Stephen H. Archer. "Diversification and the Reduction of Dispersion: An Empirical Analysis." *Journal of Finance,* December 1968, pp. 761–767.

Ferrara, William L. "Lease vs. Purchase: A Quasi-Financing Approach." *Management Accounting,* May 1974, pp. 37–41.

Fremgen, James M. "Capital Budgeting Practices: A Survey." *Management Accounting,* May 1973, pp. 19–25.

Hall, Thomas W. "Post-Completion Audit Procedure." *Management Accounting,* September 1975, pp. 33–37.

Hastie, K. Larry. "One Businessman's View of Capital Budgeting." *Financial Management,* Winter 1974, pp. 36–44.

Hicks, Carl F., Jr., and L. Lee Schmidt, Jr. "Post-Auditing the Capital Budgeting Decision." *Management Accounting,* August 1971, pp. 24–32.

Hillier, Frederick S. "A Basic Model for Capital Budgeting of Risky Interrelated Projects." *Engineering Economist,* October–November 1971, pp. 1–20.

———. "The Derivation of Probabilistic Information for the Evaluation of Risky Investments." *Management Science,* April 1963, pp. 443–457.

Jarrett, Jeffrey E. "An Abandonment Decision Model." *Engineering Economist,* Fall 1973, pp. 35–46.

Johnson, Robert W., and W. G. Lewellen. "Analysis of the Lease or Buy Decision." *Journal of Finance,* September 1972, pp. 815–823.

———. "Reply." *Journal of Finance,* September 1973, pp. 1024–1028.

Joy, O. Maurice. "Abandonment Values and Abandonment Decisions: A Clarification." *Journal of Finance,* September 1976, pp. 1225–1228.

———, and Jerry O. Bradley. "A Note on Sensitivity Analysis of Rates of Return." *Journal of Finance,* December 1973, pp. 1255–1261.

Kemp, Patrick S. "Post-Completion Audits of Capital Investment Projects." *Management Accounting,* August 1966, pp. 49–54.

Lerner, E. M., and A. Rappaport. "Limit DCF in Capital Budgeting." *Harvard Business Review,* September–October 1968, pp. 133–138.

Lewellen, Wilbur G., Howard P. Ianser, and John J. McConnell. "Payback Substitutes for Discounted Cash Flow." *Financial Management,* Summer 1973, pp. 17–23.

Mao, James C. T. "Survey of Capital Budgeting: Theory and Practice." *Journal of Finance,* May 1970, pp. 349–360.

Montgomery, John L. "Appraising Capital Expenditures." *Management Accounting,* September 1965, pp. 3–10.

Myers, Stewart C., David A. Dill, and Albert J. Bautista. "Valuation of Financial Lease Contracts." *Journal of Finance,* June 1976, pp. 799–819.

Nantell, Timothy J. "Equivalence of Lease versus Buy Analyses." *Financial Management,* Autumn 1973, pp. 61–65.

Nelson, A. Thomas. "Capitalized Leases—The Effect on Financial Ratios." *Journal of Accountancy,* July 1963, pp. 49–58.

Ofer, Aharon R. "The Evaluation of the Lease Versus Purchase Alternatives." *Financial Management,* Summer 1976, pp. 67–72.

Petry, Glenn H. "Effective Use of Capital Budgeting Tools." *Business Horizons,* October 1975, pp. 57–65.

Petty, J. William, David F. Scott, Jr., and Monroe M. Bird. "The Capital Expenditure Decision-Making Process of Large Corporations." *Engineering Economist,* Spring 1975, pp. 159–172.

Pogue, Gerald A., and Kishore Lall. "Corporate Finance: An Overview." *Sloan Management Review,* 15 (Spring 1974), pp. 19–33.

Robichek, Alexander A., and James C. Van Horne. "Abandonment Value and Capital Budgeting." *Journal of Finance,* December 1967, pp. 577–589.

———. "Reply." *Journal of Finance,* March 1969, pp. 96–97.

Schnell, James S., and Roy S. Nicolost. "Capital Expenditure Feedback: Project Reappraisal." *Engineering Economist,* July–August 1974, pp. 253–261.

Schwab, B., and P. Lusztig. "A Note on Abandonment Value and Capital Budgeting." *Journal of Financial and Quantitative Analysis,* September 1970, pp. 377–379.

Shillinglaw, Gordon. "Profit Analysis for Abandonment Decisions." In Ezra Solomon, ed. *The Management of Corporate Capital.* New York: The Free Press of Glencoe, 1959, pp. 269–281.

Spies, Richard R. "The Dynamics of Corporate Capital Budgeting." *Journal of Finance,* June 1974, pp. 829–845.

Tuttle, Donald L., and Robert H. Litzenberger. "Leverage, Diversification, and Capital Market Effects on a Risk-Adjusted Capital Budgeting Framework." *Journal of Finance,* June 1968, pp. 427–443.

Vandell, Robert F., and Paul J. Stonich. "Capital Budgeting: Theory or Results?" *Financial Executive,* August 1973, pp. 46–56.

Van Horne, James C. "The Analysis of Uncertainty Resolution in Capital Budgeting for New Products." *Management Science,* April 1969, pp. 376–386.

———. "Capital-Budgeting Decisions Involving Combinations of Risky Investments." *Management Science,* October 1966, pp. 84–92.

Vernon, Thomas H. "Capital Budgeting and the Evaluation Process." *Management Accounting,* October 1972, pp. 19–24.

Weaver, James B. "Organizing and Maintaining a Capital Expenditure Program." *Engineering Economist,* Fall 1974, pp. 1–35.

Weinwurm, Ernest H. "Utilization of Sophisticated Capital Budgeting Techniques in Industry." *Engineering Economist,* Summer 1974, pp. 271–272.

INDEX